DEMOCRACIES AGAINST HITLER

Democracies Against Hitler

Myth, Reality and Prologue

ALEXANDER J. GROTH
Professor Emeritus
University of California, Davis

Ashgate

Aldershot • Brookfield USA • Singapore • Sydney

Published by
Ashgate Publishing Limited
Gower House
Croft Road
Aldershot
Hants GU11 3HR
England

Ashgate Publishing Company
Old Post Road
Brookfield
Vermont 05036
USA

British Library Cataloguing in Publication Data
Groth, Alexander J. (Alexander Jacob), 1932-
    Democracies against Hitler : myth, reality and prologue
    1.Hitler, Adolf, 1889-1945 2.Democracy 3.Democracy -
    History - 20th century
    I.Title
    321.8

Library of Congress Cataloging-in-Publication Data
Groth, Alexander J., 1932-
    Democracies against Hitler : myth, reality, and prologue /
    Alexander J. Groth.
        p.   cm.
    Includes bibliographical references and index.
    ISBN 1-84014-465-3 (hb)
    1. World politics–1900-1945. 2. Hitler, Adolf, 1889-1945.
    3. Democracy–History–20th century. 4. Germany–Politics and
    government–1918-1933. I. Title.
    D437.G76   1998
    943.087–dc21   98-19213
                                                                  CIP

ISBN 1 84014 465 3

Printed and bound in Great Britain by MPG Books Ltd, Bodmin, Cornwall

TABLE OF CONTENTS

PREFACE

For a long time, and especially since the Second World War, a substantial literature in the social sciences has attributed all manner of problem-solving efficacy to democracies. This study analyzes the relationship between political democracy and the Hitler phenomenon in its various aspects: from Hitler's rise to power and his ascendancy in Europe to his ultimate downfall in 1945.

This is not a diplomatic nor a military history, although it has many references to both diplomatic and military events. Sympathetic to the values historically associated with political democracy, the author nevertheless believes that the reality of the confrontation between democracies and Hitlerism was not nearly as flattering to the capacities of democracy as myth would have it. Posterity has turned some fortuitous war outcomes into imaginary achievements and unwarranted certainties.

The perennial attempts to identify human self-interest with the common good, and the widely expected benefits of free discussion were not validated by the world's Hitler experience. The assumptions about the rational and benign character of people were put in grave doubt.

Are there any lessons in these events of the 1920s, 1930s, and 1940s for the future? The study concludes with an extrapolation looking beyond the Pax Americana of the last 50 years toward the 21st century.

1 HITLER AND THE DEMOCRATIC MYTH

Great events in history illuminate the human condition. Usually, "the moral of the story" is applicable to earlier as well as subsequent occurrences, and to many things by analogy and extension. One such event was the career of a monstrously evil political leader, Adolf Hitler.

In the aftermath of the Second World War, and in the midst of the prosperous Pax Americana of the post-war era, a considerable literature extolling the virtues of political democracy has developed, especially in the United States. To those who, like the present author, respect the ideals of human liberty, individual dignity, and the rule of law, the moral claims of democracy are both understandable and admirable. But in human affairs, success, or what seems like success, often leads to excessive and misplaced confidence. In the post-Second World War period the idea has taken root that democracy, apart from any moral virtues it may possess, is a "fix-it" scheme. In effect, it is the notion that letting people do, and be, whatever they like, is also the best way of solving any and all social problems. It is a claim not about "right" but about "efficacy". There is much about the career of Adolf Hitler from the days of his political struggle in the 1920s to his ascendancy and fall in the 1940s which suggests that the claims of democratic "efficacy" are spurious. Myth has obscured reality. It has clouded the memory of the past and the perspective on the present and the future.

The many triumphs of Adolf Hitler from the 1920s to the 1940s undermined the "democratic myth" in two important respects. They demonstrated the relative ineffectiveness of democracies in a variety of crisis situations. They also, from the collective experience of all those millions of people who supported and cooperated with Hitler, and also all those millions who passively watched him conduct his international crime spree, undermined the liberal assumptions about human beings. The terms "rational" and "benign" do not fit those situations well; perhaps no better than a corset fits an octopus. In fact, it was political democracy that nourished Adolf Hitler to power. It was the medium which the future Fuehrer successfully cultivated. Democratic public opinion of the 1930s, in Germany and out, demonstrated

1

much more irrationality in many different ways than it did that wonderful, and largely mythical, attachment to "reason" so fondly postulated by various democratic ideologues.[1]

Through the vices of myopic self-indulgence and domestic discord, the democracies of the world allowed Adolf Hitler to achieve enormous power in Germany and in Europe by the end of the 1930s. Between 1939 and 1941 they came much closer to losing the war than is now generally admitted, and ultimately won it largely, if not entirely, because of fortuitous circumstances. One of these was that the Fuehrer's "genius" let him down; another was some critical assistance from a very undemocratic source, i.e., Stalin's Russia.

In this period of political history (from the 1920s to the 1940s) there is especially one theme important not only for what occurred *then* but for what occurs now, and for what may occur in the future. That theme is the critical relationship among information, freedom of discussion, and social action.

If ever there was reason to doubt liberal assumptions about the reliability of public opinion responding to "truth" and "facts" with sensible and prudent actions, Hitler's challenge to the rest of the world strongly affirmed it. Moreover, what makes this tragic episode in history so significant for our knowledge of "democracy" is that it involved not the failure of one, or two, or three democratic systems.   In the 1930s, in the sense of collectively understanding the threat which Hitler posed for the world at large; responding to this threat both by individual states and by collective, international action; opposing Hitler by force of arms when the war broke out in 1939; in all these respects, the failures of world democracy were multiple, prolonged, and general.

There are no heroic tales to tell about world democracies between 1933 and 1939.   There are not even encouraging ones during that period. Between 1939 and 1941 what sometimes passes for great Allied victories was largely self-serving exaggeration.   That was the true democratic legacy from that time to the present and the future.

Naturally, what has obscured the story of Hitler's confrontation with the democracies was his ultimate downfall in 1945.   The blunders and transgressions of the winners tended to be forgotten.   The great successes of the losers tended to be overwhelmed by the ultimate result, however fortuitous that might have been.[2]

As American General Omar Bradley once put it:

> There are those who are quick to say how misguided our leadership was, that other plans and decisions would have achieved better results. Perhaps. But the fact remains, we did win the war.[3]

Obviously, the interpretation of Hitler's career in world politics offered in this book is very much at odds with several types of "mythical" literature: much, though certainly not all, of the Western interpretation of the Second World War, some of which has just been mentioned; post-war studies about democracy and political development; and, ultimately, the early "classics" of liberalism which picture a world very much controverted by what may be termed "the Hitler experience".

With an apology to the reader for the turgid style of some of the scholarly discourse, a few examples of "mythology" are worth citing.

Consider, for example, the highly influential point of view of the liberal political scholar, Gabriel Almond:

> The dominant and legitimate culture of totalitarian systems is ideological in its intellectual characteristics. There are limits on rational calculation and analysis. ... Decision making, thus, tends to be relatively rigid in comparison with the more open process of balancing and combining ends and means characteristic of the political process in fully differentiated and secularized democracies. ... The profile of capability of the most developed democracies is more versatile and adaptive. What this means is that *all* types of capability are developed in both the input and output phases of the political process.[4] The political system can respond to or adapt to the demands that are being made upon it from its own social environment or from the international environment, and at the same time it can cope with and manipulate its social and international environments.[5]

In the perspective of the democratic experience during the 20s, 30s, and 40s, this point of view is nothing short of spectacular illusion and misrepresentation. But, of course, it has had many Western advocates and imitators.

In the context of a discussion about American foreign policy, Professor Kenneth Waltz has observed:

It was long believed that America's democratic institutions would prevent her from behaving effectively and responsibly in the world. The judgment should be reversed. American institutions facilitate rather than discourage the quick identification of problems, the pragmatic quest for solutions, the ready confrontation of dangers, the willing expenditure of energies and the open criticism of policies.[6]

... Disagreement about events openly expressed in democratic states may cause some opportunities for gaining national advantage to be missed. But the running of risks foolishly is then also impeded. Democracies less often enjoy the brilliant success that bold acts secretly prepared and ruthlessly executed may bring. With the ground of action more thoroughly prepared and the context of policy more widely debated, they may, however, suffer fewer resounding failures. Coherent policy, executed with a nice combination of caution and verve, is difficult to achieve in any political system, but no more so for democratic states than for others.[7]

In still another recent example:

Broadly speaking, people are more productive when there is a free flow of information, the state is unoppressive and predictable, and commercial values outweigh political; these conditions are seldom to be maintained except in a democratic order. The advantages of central control of flow of resources in an authoritarian state are undone by the inability of the central planners [always? generally?] to make rational choices in countless complicated situations. The potential advantages of the strong state are also offset by the prevalence of corruption, which wastes resources and frustrates orderly government. The only reliable means of coping with corruption is freedom to criticize and to hold officeholders responsible, that is, democracy.[8]

And also:

... democratic states fight less than authoritarian ones but when they do, they win; and when they have won, democracy increases in the world (owing both to changes in regime and to their 'effect on the environment').[9]

And in this rather fulsome version:

1. Democracy is a form and process of government consistent with human behavioural tendencies, needs, and desires. Democracy requires a set of civic values that animate and reinforce the attitudes and behaviour of those who live according to its precepts.

2. The basic structure of enduring democratic institutions is observable and generally replicable.

3. Democratic structures, methods, and procedures are transferable, and their institutional forms are adaptable to varying historical, cultural, and other indigenous conditions.

4. As a consequence of centuries of theorization (?) and practical democratic development, there exists enough systematic knowledge about democracy and democratic institutions to provide a strong basis for the production of further well-confirmed knowledge about this system of human self-governance.[10]

What makes all these formulations particularly unrealistic and misleading is their unspoken assumption about the character of human beings, who, naturally, must operate the democratic political system to make it work. To appreciate the problem, one needs to partake of some traditional democratic axioms about "humanity". The most fundamental of these is, no doubt, the rational character of the human being, or, as eighteenth and nineteenth century literature would have it, the "nature of man". In this view, people's behaviour is ultimately governed by thoughtful calculation.

To be sure, the meaning of "rationality" is not always specified by those who use the term. A great deal of talk about "reason" often does not get into any specifics and seems to take the form of a pretty, or perhaps prestigious adjective. Rationality is to all appearances a diffuse term, one with several, somewhat different meanings. In common usage, prudence and foresight are elements of rationality. When we hike across the desert, we take a canister of water. Another meaning is capacity for accurate comprehension of the empirical world -- natural and social -- in which human beings live. (Some would call it "reality testing". Those who hallucinate are not rational.) In this sense of rationality, one would expect that most people would appreciate the fact that palm trees and pine trees look different and thrive under different conditions; that the aroma of roses is different, and to most people, more pleasant, and easier to bear, than that of, say sulfuric acid; and that it is easier to breathe at the seashore than in the high Himalayas. "Rationality" also reflects the general appreciation of physical, spatial relationships, recognizing, for example, that the shortest distance between two points is a straight line; and that a fall of, say, 20 feet, is usually dangerous to human well-being and survival. This comes under the rubric of "common sense", another traditional ingredient of rationality.

"Rationality" sometimes also refers to logical thinking which may be illustrated by the human appreciation of syllogisms or transitivity. If all things marked "A" are bad, and item X is marked "A", we can presumably all appreciate (or at least most of us can appreciate) that X is something "bad".

Rationality, in another of its meanings, may indicate an ability to learn from more complex experiences, from careful and accurate observation of many cases, past and present, including, of course, systematically collected information which one might identify as "science" in the category of "biology", "chemistry", "physics", "medicine", etc.

Human beings are represented by democratic ideologues as not only generally "rational" but also as "benign". Each member of society is considered to be well disposed toward other members of society, and also toward the society as a whole, all other things being equal. Liberal democracy tends to shun or minimize all the negative human propensities -- such as a delight in perpetuating gratuitous wrong, sadism, or in cheating, lying, stealing, and killing. Such phenomena are seen as marginal or ephemeral, induced by unusual circumstances, and capable of being overcome by the distribution or supply, of adequate knowledge or information.

Simply put, people who are somehow innately and generally predisposed to be "good", will certainly be so if they can be furnished with accurate knowledge about all the relevant circumstances of their situations. Liberal democracy greatly prizes education, communication, and information as keys to the good life for individuals and societies alike -- especially the kinds of education, communication and information which are free or unconstrained by any punitive, monopolistic, social agencies and, above all, by the juridical entity of the state, or its practical representative, government.

The conjunction of the rational human being with benign propensities and an open-ended supply of information produces (in the liberal democratic scenario) all manner of social good -- whether one thinks of public health, world peace, social cooperation, or economic well-being. The implication of this conjunction in the liberal perspective is an enormous faith in human spontaneity. In economics, this faith was initially represented by the great liberal spokesman and author of *Wealth of Nations*, Adam Smith (with many followers in our time, too) who believed that the greatest economic successes for both individuals and whole societies would be simultaneously achieved if people were allowed to do whatever they wished to do -- under conditions of unrestrained free exchange of products and services among them, and given open access to information by all participants in the "market".

In Adam Smith's classic formulation of the coincidence of private and public interests in society:

> Every individual is continually exerting himself to find out the most advantageous employment for whatever capital he can command. It is his own advantage, indeed, and not that of the society, which he has in view. But the study of his own advantage, naturally, or rather necessarily, leads him to prefer that employment which is most advantageous to the society.[11]

It is indeed remarkable how easily maxims such as this one are accepted by those who either find the formulation personally advantageous, or who believe it because "everyone else" does. Conceding the points that free markets may at times promote wonders of economic efficiency and human satisfaction, would a free market be the best possible economic mechanism in a society suffering from famine? Would it be reasonable to allow most people to die of starvation because, conceivably, one person could afford to buy up all the available grain or milk and sell it abroad, or set it ablaze for the sheer enjoyment of the spectacle?

Somehow, Adam Smith never thought of the wonderful free market possibilities of family enrichment through paedophilia, prostitution, murder-for-hire, strong narcotics, and the intriguing prospects of selling public services to the highest bidder in an open market, especially fire, police, and emergency medical assistance, with perhaps even some sensitive state military secrets up for grabs at openly set market prices.

In the purely political sphere, liberal democracy's most representative original figure was probably John Stuart Mill, whose argument in the famous essay *On Liberty* is the basis of the modern democratic creed. "Truth" in Mill's version is the prize of an open exchange of information and ideas. All opinions need to be subjected to the rigours of an untrammelled, public dialogue in order for people to be able, somehow, eventually, if not always immediately, to figure out just what is true and what is false, what makes sense and what doesn't. "Truth" in this view is tested by the open combat of ideas.

As John Stuart Mill himself put the matter in *On Liberty*, when he concluded his famous exposition of the merits of free discussion:

> We have now recognized the necessity to the mental well-being of mankind (on which all their other well-being depends) of freedom of opinion, on four distinct grounds ... First, if any opinion is compelled to silence, that opinion may ... be true. To deny this is to assume our own infallibility.   Second ... since the general or prevailing opinion on any subject is rarely or never the whole truth, it is only by the collision of adverse opinions that the remainder of the truth has any chance of being supplied. Thirdly, even if [wholly' true] ... unless it is ... rigorously and earnestly contested ... [it will be held] in the manner of prejudice with little comprehension or feeling for its rational grounds, with fourthly ... the danger of ... preventing the growth of any real and heartfelt conviction, from reason or personal experience.[12]

Thus, all possible perspectives need to be given a hearing. The logical implication of this view is that one can always get better results in the analysis of any problem in a situation (or society) where that analysis is a "free-for-all" as opposed to a situation (or society) where the analysis or the discussion is controlled or restrained by some dominant actor, such as a government or an autocratic ruler.

To be sure, Mill never precisely explained what he meant by "truth" in arguments or opinions, and never really differentiated between such propositions as "fire requires the presence of oxygen", on the one hand, and something like "justice demands a progressive system of public taxation", on the other. While one might be able to actually test the empirical correctness of the first proposition, it is not clear what one might do with the second, no matter the nature of the analysis or discussion, other than perhaps discover that different people would prefer different systems of taxation based on self-serving interests rather than the kind of inescapable empirical conclusion that one would reach by looking into the linkage between "oxygen" and "fire".

Or one might find, as often occurs with public opinion polls, and with advertising, that people's opinions of things are more closely linked to the relative attractiveness and the volume of arguments that are aimed at them, rather than any objectively ascertainable correctness of the information. After all, how are beer sales, or cigarette sales, in all their huge volume, promoted in the most free of the free societies? Isn't it likely that if people paid attention to what scientists working in their laboratories might have to say about beer, and cigarettes, the consumption of these products would be a good deal less than it is, and has been for a very long time? Beer commercials on television and radio, in magazines and newspapers, promote the alcoholic beverage with all sorts of entertaining and appealing irrelevancies. Scantily dressed maidens and muscular young men play about in the snow or frolic on the beach. The arguments about obesity, cirrhosis of the liver, drunkenness, effects on blood pressure and the cardiovascular system, etc., though available, are not widely disseminated even in the freest of societies, partly because the people who could make these arguments don't have the resources and sufficient motive to incessantly bombard the public with such messages, and partly because people, (including many of the experts themselves) by and large, are so fond of beer, and its immediate short-term effects on their bodies, that they are not terribly anxious to have such arguments loudly proclaimed.[13] Contrary to what Mill may have thought, there are many things which, however "true" they might be, people would simply rather not hear about ... This involves an important human propensity for denial of what is seen as unpleasant, or unpalatable, or perhaps dangerous.

As a practical matter, we know that not all economic liberals are also political liberals and vice versa. Some people who accept the "free market" idea also support authoritarian political systems. Some people who value freedom of speech and idiosyncratic life styles are openly hostile to a "free-for-all" in the economic arena. Nevertheless, the modern understanding of what constitutes a liberal democracy, especially as developed in Europe and in America, partakes of both of these notions to a considerable degree. There is enormous faith in dialogue, or discussion, as a means of solving conflicts among people. With the implicit premises of rationality and benignness, the liberal faith sees an open and full discussion as the best possible way of overcoming strife and trouble. The idea is to get people, everyone with a "stake" in an issue, to see each other's circumstances, to get all the facts "on the table", to discuss everyone's needs and options, and with the usual requirements of patience and persistence (not to mention "good will") no problem is too overwhelming to be thus overcome. One just needs to work at it. Two of the most familiar terms of liberal democracy are "negotiation" and "compromise". Reasonable people can always find a way to accommodate one another. Why shouldn't they? Don't people know, for example, that the costs of war are ultimately too high for everyone? Is it not always better to get *something*, if not "everything", rather than risk*all* in a deadly confrontation?

At the heart of the liberal democratic value system is the participatory myth: it is the desirability of the involvement of the largest possible number of human beings in the largest possible number of social decisions. "Nothing about me without me" is the motto of the creed. Here we find the ideology's most important prescription for action, "the more the merrier", or, in fact, wiser, better, more efficient, and, above all, more legitimate. Part of the reasoning behind the participatory imperative stems from the previous assumption of human rationality and benignness, modified by the assumption of equality.

If all of us are indeed, somehow, in some way at least, equally sensible and well disposed toward each other, and toward the community as a whole, then clearly, the matter of choice in all social decisions should, logically enough, go to the greatest number. If we assign equal value to all chess pieces, 50 per cent plus one beats all possibly remaining combinations, clearly, simply, and unequivocally. Of course, in chess not all pieces are equal. Providing a simple decision-rule, liberal democracy endows popular participation in social decisions with a mythical aura of competence and rectitude.[14]

Among the more amusing examples of putting a "good spin" on the qualities of the democratic electorate, we find this view:

> While information levels are indeed low and information about public issues unevenly distributed, citizens are generally found to employ sensible decision rules, or heuristics, in acquiring and storing information about politics. These decision rules do, in fact, entail remaining ignorant on most issues most of the time, making inferences about the likely behaviour of officeholders from very little information, and basing one's vote or other political actions on a relatively sparse set of signals about governmental activity. Even if individuals, taken alone, are remarkable for their ignorance and even if most individuals make poor inferences a lot of the time, as Condorcet noted long ago, electorates like juries *can exhibit a high level of aggregate sophistication*. And, insofar as politicians are motivated to compete for public office, they have strong incentives to make appropriate inferences about these aggregated public wishes and base their actions on them. If they don't, they risk losing their offices to opponents who will. The result is that even in situations of incomplete information, there are powerful

equilibrating forces pushing public policy in the direction of the representation of public sentiment.[15]

"Can exhibit"? Here we have an open door to the unknown. Liberal ideologues have never been quite able to face up to the old maxim about "too many cooks spoiling the broth".

People, in the liberal-democratic perspective, are actually alleged to be made better off by the effects of the process itself, i.e., if they share in those decisions that influence the course of their lives. Participation is seen as a cure for alienation and indifference. People are said to be more concerned about things if they are empowered to decide what to do about them. Voluntary participation is seen as more effective than passive or coerced participation because it presumably engages people more directly in critical roles and inspires them with a sense of responsibility, dignity, and self-esteem. Voluntary participation respects individual freedom.

One of the most familiar themes of American politics and civic education is the plea for greater popular participation in elections, with recurrent reproaches to those who shirk their civic duty to participate, and with recurrent complaints about the deplorable apathy of much of the potential electorate. "If you want to make things better, get involved" is the democratic slogan-of-slogans. The good citizen is an involved citizen. Only by maximizing participation can we hope to make better decisions with better consequences for the whole community. Whatever the issues, the wisdom of the many is always to be preferred to the wisdom of a few.

People called "elites", that is, those who in various circumstances may be the rich or the learned, the old and the experienced, the professionals or the experts, are to be viewed with suspicion since their judgments are likely to be clouded by narrow, self-serving interests. In contrast, the broad masses of the people, especially if fully engaged, are likely to demonstrate wisdom and rectitude.[16] The notions of mass participation, and voluntary participation, are augmented by the myth of spontaneity; allowing people to adapt freely their individual actions and behaviours to any common purpose makes the end-product of their efforts all the more effective.[17] This is assumed to be the case because giving people autonomy is likely to unleash their ingenuity in situations where the grass-root performer may be facing constantly changing circumstances without the opportunity of frequently consulting "leaders".

These positive liberal views of mass participation are combined with condemnations of authoritarianism in any number of possible guises. Without regard to autocratic sub-types among Left, Right, Totalitarian, Traditionalist and the like, dictatorial systems are seen as stifling human initiative preventing effective access to information for those who formulate and implement policies on behalf of the "state"; as lacking true political strength because of the substitution of coercion and fear for agreement and consensus as the bases of state power; and consequently, having little ability to adapt to rapidly changing circumstances and new demands emanating from within the political environment. These flaws may be described as allegedly "empirical" and "objective" as opposed to the additional, moral, normative flaws of authoritarian regimes which regardless of power or success -- violate people's rights to freedom, individual security, dignity, and self-determination.

One of the more provocative liberal formulae of recent years has been the notion that the "capacity" of nation states derives from their long-term "legitimacy". "Capacity" in ordinary usage means being able to solve relevant problems (e.g., what is the capacity of a vacuum cleaner or the capacity of a surgical team?). Thus presumably doing "more", "better" and "faster" shows greater capacity than providing "fewer", "worse" and "slower". (Naturally, given such complex notions as "capacity" applied to "politics", how would one know if "more" and "slower" is a higher capacity than "fewer" and "faster"?) At any rate, "legitimacy" in the liberal view is always linked with voluntarily given consent. Thus, a legitimate regime is one whose population, by and large, obeys its leaders or its institutions because it wants to do so, because it is convinced that what they ask or command is "rightful" or "proper". Obedience not only is, but must be, voluntary in the "strong" state. The very idea of "strength" or "high capacity" is linked here with voluntarism.

Thus, we find one liberal writer asserting the view that:

> ... political life centers on the exercise of power, and that, unlike physical force, power is intrinsically relational (!?).

> Although all states have the capability to inflict physical sanctions, their ability to exercise power is the key element of their political capacity. In this context, the prolonged use of force reflects a loss of power and is fundamentally apolitical (?!) because it indicates a deterioration in the relationship between rulers and ruled.[18]

The great dynamism of Nazi Germany in the 1930s and 1940s confronted by a stodgy timidity of Britain and France could hardly be recognized and appreciated by anyone taken in by this sort of ideological wishful thinking.[19] In fact, any relatively objective analysis of the interactions of nations during the Second World War and in the decade preceding it, would readily discredit these sorts of views, numerous as they may be, for the sheer puffery and political posturing which they represent.

Presumably, whatever it was that Hitler and Stalin exercised, it was not *political power*. And presumably, whatever it was that Neville Chamberlain and Edouard Daladier exercised (if they exercised anything) was genuine political power -- with more "capacity", following the outline of this scheme!

While our author here -- characteristically -- stays generally as far away from the subject of war as he possibly can, he makes one reference to General George C. Marshall during the Second World War, a reference which illustrates the vacuity of the case. He says: "... in 1942, Army Chief of Staff George C. Marshall wrote all commanding generals that the growing use of courts martial in the citizen army was unsatisfactory and prima facie evidence of poor discipline: 'Reliance on courts-martial to enforce discipline indicates lack of leadership and faulty command.'" (p. 31, en. 6).

The reference to a "citizen army" suggests normative criteria which, depending on one's outlook may be, or may not be, appealing. But it should be noted that the Nazi Wehrmacht, estimated to have carried out perhaps between 25 and 30,000 disciplinary executions of its troops, compared with only one execution for desertion in the American army during the Second World War, could hardly, for that reason, or for any other reason, be considered a less effective fighting force, unit for unit, than was any other army in Second World War. Intellectual honesty requires the recognition of the fact that "good guys" are not always stronger and more successful than "bad guys". Sometimes quite the opposite. Nor is it the case, as Plato implied in *The Republic*, that in the world as it really exists, good always triumphs over evil, and "positive" incentives excel "negative" incentives, many liberal social scientists notwithstanding.[20]

Hitler's rise to power in the 1930s, and his subsequent challenge to the peace of Europe and the world, provided a formidable test of most of these liberal conceptions. Apart from the normative issues, and given a genuinely factual accounting, this test was, and must forever remain, a severe reproof of the basic hopes and claims of liberal democracy. Rarely, if ever, have the ideas of evil, violence, and demonstrable falsehood been put forward more openly, unabashedly, and, above all, frequently, than they were by Adolf Hitler.[21] Yet, under the circumstances of admirable personal freedoms, in a nation whose information capabilities exceeded the great majority of its neighbours in the world community of nations, these very ideas and their purveyor succeeded in repeatedly capturing a plurality following of public opinion, and ultimately, in consequence of it, political power. Having accomplished this -- one might think -- improbable task, Adolf Hitler then proceeded to deceive, divide, and confuse the public opinion of all the remaining democracies sufficiently to allow his Nazi Germany a short but successful career of conquest in the 1930s and 1940s, a career brought to an end not primarily by the actions of those democracies still left alive in the 1940s, but largely by his own impulsive mistakes and by the counteractions of his fellow dictator, Joseph Stalin.

In the course of this conflict, the democracies exhibited lack of foresight, strategic timidity, mismanagement, lethargy, and an appalling moral indifference to the most systematic and brutal crimes of extermination in recorded history; all this despite their access to prodigious amounts of information; despite their seemingly significant capability to process the information; and to intervene on behalf of the millions of victims of Nazi persecution. Is it possible that democratic failures of three decades were actually endemic, not coincidental? If the answer to this question is affirmative, then the episode of Nazism-ascendant was not merely a nightmare. It was a warning of repeatable tragedy.

NOTES

[1] On occasion, these are referred to here as "liberal" or "liberal-democratic".

[2] Naturally, here one encounters massive denial. See, e.g., Alan J. Levine, "Was World War II a Near-run Thing?", *The Journal of Strategic Studies*, Vol. 8, No. 1, March 1985, pp. 38-63, for an extremely unimpressive case that the victory over Hitler was, implicitly, "in the bag" from the first day of the war. "One of the more remarkable ... misconceptions is the notion that the Nazis came very close to winning the war", p. 38. Mr. Levine is a far more fortunate man than he realizes. See also Marc Milner, "The Battle of the Atlantic", *The Journal of Strategic Studies*, Vol. 13, No. 1, March 1990, pp. 45-66; "... the war at sea was not within [Nazi] capacity to win, although the Allies -- like Jellicoe at Jutland -- might have lost it (?!) through utter incompetence", pp. 63-64.

In the category of myth, few have excelled Bruce M. Russett, *No Clear and Present Danger, A Skeptical View of the United States Entry Into World War II* (New York: Harper and Row, 1972). Says Russett: "By the end of 1941 Hitler had already lost his gamble to control Europe. In large part this was due to British skill, courage and good luck in the summer of 1940", p. 25. Note also "... by the end of 1941 Britain's survival was essentially assured", p. 26. "The attack [on Russia] was an admission [by Hitler] that the war against Britain had gone badly", p. 27.

[3] See Omar N. Bradley, "Foreward to D-Day", in Theodore A. Wilson (ed.), *D-Day 1944* (Abilene, KS: University Press of Kansas, 1994), p. xxviii.

[4] In Almond's scheme, "inputs" refer to demands made upon the "system" and to the supports furnished to it. "Capabilities" include the power to regulate, distribute and extract "resources", and also the power to respond to demands and satisfy symbolic (psychological) needs of people composing the "system".

[5] See Gabriel A. Almond and G. Bingham Powell, Jr., *Comparative Politics: A Developmental Approach* (Boston: Little, Brown & Company, 1966), pp. 312-313. Italics in the original.

[6] Kenneth N. Waltz, *Foreign Policy and Democratic Politics: The American and British Experience* (Boston: Little, Brown & Company, 1966), pp. 307-308.

[7] *Ibid.*, p. 311.

[8] See Robert Wesson (ed.), *Democracy, A Worldwide Survey* (New York: Praeger, 1987). Introduction, pp. 4-7, especially. Quotation on p. 7.

[9] See Luigi Bonante in Daniele Archibugi and David Held (eds.), *Cosmopolitan Democracy, An Agenda for a New World Order* (Bodmin, UK: Polity Press, 1994), p. 62.

[10] See Ralph M. Goldman and William A. Douglas (eds.), *Promoting Democracy, Opportunities and Issues* (New York: Praeger, 1988), p. 257. Also see pp. 261-262 for a list of operational characteristics of democracy.

[11] Adam Smith, *An Inquiry Into The Nature and Causes of the Wealth of Nations* with notes by J. R. McCulloch (London: Ward, Lock, Bowden & Company, n.d.) p. 352.

[12] See John Stuart Mill, *On Liberty* (New York: W. W. Norton, 1975), pp. 50-51.

[13] Ilustratively, the American Medical Association's *Encyclopedia of Medicine*, edited by Dr. Charles B. Clayman (New York: Random House, 1989), provides the following list of the major pathological consequences of alcoholism:

> 1. Increase in the incidence of cancer of the mouth, tongue, pharynx (back of the throat), larynx (voice box) and esophagus as well as liver cancer; 2. liver damage and disease including alcoholic hepatitis and cirrhosis; 3. nervous system disorders, including confusion and disturbances of speech and gait; 4. heart and circulatory disorders, including heart failure, edema, hypertension and stroke; 5. other physical disorders, including fetal damage during pregnancy, and also gastritis, pancreatitis, and peptic ulcer; 6. psychiatric illness, including anxiety, depression, and dementia. "The incidence of suicide attempts and actual suicides is also higher among alcoholics", p. 85.

[14] See the interesting essay by Peter Loewenberg, "Arno Mayer's 'Internal Causes and Purposes of War in Europe, 1870-1956' -- The Inadequate Model of Human Behavior, National Conflict, and Historical Change", *The Journal of Modern History*, Vol. 42, No. 4, December 1970, pp. 628-636. Loewenberg stresses the importance of violent and irrational, or perhaps unrational, impulses governing human action in war, and, of course, by fairly natural extension, in other fields of political activity.

[15] See John A. Ferejohn, "Information and the Electoral Process" in J. A. Ferejohn and J. H. Kuklinski, *Information and Democratic Processes* (Chicago: University of Illinois Press, 1990), p. 7. Italics added.

[16] For a fuller discussion of the proposition that people's perceptions of "information" tend to be seriously distorted by their psychological dispositions and subjectively perceived "interests", whether they are many or few, see Alexander J. Groth and John Drew Froeliger, "Unheeded Warnings: Some Intelligence Lessons of the 1930s and 1940s", *Comparative Strategy*, Vol. 10, No. 4, Winter 1991, pp. 331-346.

[17] See Thomas A. Bailey, *A Diplomatic History of the American People*, Second Edition (New York: F. S. Crofts, 1945), p. VI, for this remarkable quotation by former U.S. Secretary of State, Elihu Root, originally published in 1922. It illustrates nicely most of the optimistic illusions of liberalism with respect to the nexus between knowledge and conduct on the part of "the people".

> "When foreign affairs were ruled by autocracies or oligarchies the danger of war was in sinister purpose. When foreign affairs are ruled by democracies the danger of war will be in mistaken beliefs. The world will be the gainer by the change, for, while there is no human way to prevent a king from having a bad heart, there is a human way to prevent a people from having an erroneous opinion. That way is to furnish the whole people, as a part of their ordinary education, with correct information about their relations to other peoples, about the limitations upon their own rights, about their duties to respect the rights of others, about what has happened and is happening in international affairs, and about the effects upon national life of the things that are done or refused as between nations; so that the people themselves will have the means to test misinformation and appeals to prejudice and passion based upon error."

[18] Some writers on this subject don't even define "political capacity" beyond vaguely suggesting "something": e.g., Jackman, "political capacity involves the creation of institutions that are surrounded with some aura of legitimacy", p. 38. But to what purpose? With capacity to accomplish what? Jackman's distinction between "power"

and "force" suggests that politics and violence are separate worlds, a trick every bit as good as separating rainfall from water. Robert W. Jackman, *Power Without Force: The Political Capacity of Nation-States* (Ann Arbor: The University of Michigan Press, 1993), p. 30. See also pp. 156-157.

[19] This is not to say that "legitimacy" in the sense discussed here may not be, in all sorts of circumstances, a useful component of "power". It is merely to say that if power is completely and generally equated with "legitimacy", the proposition is analogous to saying that only honestly earned money can buy goods and services in the market place.

[20] Considering the techniques of Stalinist industrial management in the Second World War, it is interesting to, however briefly, glimpse the thrust of democratic literature about work. Note, e.g., H. B. Wilson, *Democracy and the Work Place* (Montreal: Black Rose Books, 1974) for this rather typically liberal and also socialist idea about work: "Coercion and the threat of starvation are no longer effective managerial weapons ...". "... All [management] texts I am aware of dealing with personnel, stress the importance of motivation", pp. 77-78. "Manipulative techniques ... are even more destructive." Once again, we find the illusional "ought" displacing an unpleasant "is".

[21] Some of the theoretical issues involved here were first examined in Alexander J. Groth and Larry L. Wade, "Prolegomenon to Democracy, Dictatorship and Rational Choice", *The Journal of East Asian Affairs*, Vol. IV, No. 2, Summer/Fall 1990, pp. 435-474.

2 HITLER AGAINST WEIMAR DEMOCRACY: THE CONQUEST OF POWER

That a man of Hitler's character, background, and outlook, within a few short years, could have risen to the mastery of a great nation, and to the domination of Europe, is an unwelcome tribute to the demagogic possibilities of political democracy. One can only wonder if with the help of colour television Hitler would not have achieved this goal even sooner.

· In his translator's note to a 1943 edition of *Mein Kampf*, Ralph Manheim makes two interesting observations that go to the very heart of Hitler's challenge to the assumptions of democracy. The first of these is that "[Hitler] makes the most extraordinary allegations without so much as an attempt to prove them. Often there is no visible connection between one paragraph and the next".[1] On the other hand, Manheim observes that "Germany was a land of high general culture, with the largest reading public of any country in the world".[2]

Therein, of course, lies a formidable paradox and also a grave charge against the axioms of liberal democracy. A few testimonies may be in order.

Writing about German education in the late nineteenth century, Professor V. R. Berghan noted that "Germany was one of the first countries to develop a system of compulsory education from the ages of six to fourteen ... Illiteracy rates were, so far as is known, lower than in Britain and France, although the state of official statistics and regional variations makes it difficult to provide absolutely reliable figures ... beyond the elementary level, barriers were in operation and it required more than an above-average intelligence to overcome them. Money was indispensable".[3]

Historian Koppel Pinson observed in his acclaimed account of modern Germany:

> In keeping with the general nineteenth century trend toward mass education, Germany, in perhaps higher degree than any other country in the world, witnessed the spread of *Bildung*, of education and knowledge. Nowhere else did the prestige of a university education for even the average merchant or industrialist attain such

18

a high degree of acceptance as in the Germany of the Second Reich, and nowhere else did such a profusion of Ph.D.'s blossom forth as from the German universities.[4]

He also noted that the "German newspaper, unlike the American, was conceived to be an educational agency" and in the number, variety, and circulation of newspapers and books, Germany was also one of the world's leaders.[5]

The Weimar period, for all its problems and difficulties, was "one of the most dynamic in German history" and one in which as Professor Pinson observed, "there was a release of a vast amount of cultural and spiritual energy that manifested itself in practically every phase of literature, art, philosophy, and academic scholarship. Germany now recovered its position of intellectual eminence even more rapidly than it achieved economic recovery. During the first year following the end of the war Germany fairly seethed with new and experimental movements".[6]

Another author, David Childs, has observed that:

Between 1901 and 1919 Germans were awarded 18 Nobel Prizes in science -- more than those awarded to the scientists of any other nation. This was no accident nor was it the result of native German brilliance. It was the outcome of Germany's investment in education over a long period ... there can be no doubt that most Germans were receiving some kind of meaningful instruction long before the bulk of the population in England, Wales and Ireland.

... Germany's system of technical education came to be admired even more than its elementary schools and its long-established universities ....

... German education faced a variety of critics, both at home and abroad. Some criticized the patriotic indoctrination, others claimed there was too much learning by rote. But such criticisms could have been made about all educational systems at the time.[7]

Candor requires the acknowledgement that in Weimar Germany the combination of high levels of literacy and education, on the one hand, and great political freedom, on the other, did not produce the kind of political consequences which liberal ideology generally postulates.

Admittedly, in the 1930s, the great achievements of German education, especially its expansion and the opening of opportunities under Weimar to more middle and working class elements, had its drawback in the seemingly inevitable prospects of unemployment for the academically educated.   As Oswald Garrison Villard wrote in 1933 "... doctors of philosophy ... are happy to be salesmen in department stores ..." [and] some are even glad to collect fares on Berlin buses ..."[8]

Once again, however, the issue is what do the rationally trained and proficient do when faced with a difficult social and economic situation? Surely, banging heads against walls or blowing up buildings would not have been sensible, even if, for the very desperate, that, too, might have been seen as somehow "understandable".[9]

Democratic ideologues have always attempted to "explain away" this apparent failure of human reason in Germany so central to their cosmology.[10] Before discussing the "explanations," however, let us more fully explore the Hitler mind set.

Konrad Heiden, in his Introduction to *Mein Kampf* says that what gives *Mein Kampf* its terrific impact is not the aims but the methods ... "Whether [Hitler] speaks of art, of education, of economics, he always sees blood ... The lightheartedness with which he threatens murder at the slightest provocation is perhaps even more frightful than the threats themselves. That such a man could go so far toward realizing his ambitions, and -- above all -- could find millions of willing tools and helpers; that is a phenomenon the world will ponder for centuries to come"[11]

At the core of Hitler's ideology, elucidated in *Mein Kampf*, stood what may be termed his Jewish syllogism. The first proposition of this syllogism was that violent conflict, struggle to the death, and extermination of weaker adversaries by stronger adversaries was the rule of life, and hence also of all politics and international relations. We may call it proposition A.

The second proposition was that Jews were the most dangerous and important adversaries Hitler knew. Let us call this proposition B. Quite appropriately, therefore, the implication of this syllogism, its third line, was proposition C, that -- subject to Hitler's ability to achieve what he wanted -- Jews must be exterminated. Both parts of the syllogism A-B, demanding in its logical conclusion the extermination of the Jews were stated, not once or twice, but many times throughout the pages of Mein Kampf. Hitler *hinted* at the content of proposition A with the following language:

... Only when an epoch ceases to be haunted by the shadow of its own consciousness of guilt will it achieve the inner calm and outward strength brutally and ruthlessly to prune off the wild shoots and tear out the weeds.

And also ... Terror at the place of employment, in the factory, in the meeting hall, and on the occasion of mass demonstrations will always be successful unless opposed by equal terror.[12]

And, more clearly "... in a universe where planets revolve around suns, and moons turn about planets ... force alone forever masters weakness, compelling it to be an obedient slave or else crushing it ..."[13] "Just as our ancestors did not receive the soil on which we live today as a gift from Heaven, but had to fight for it at the risk of their lives, in the future no folkish grace will win soil for us and hence life for our people, but only the might of a victorious sword".[14] But at times Hitler even exhibited proposition C, the conclusion of his syllogism, as for example, in his discussion about the role of the Jews in undermining the wartime morale of the German people after 1914. Hitler wrote:

... the time had come to take steps against the whole treacherous brotherhood of these Jewish poisoners of the people. Now was the time to deal with them summarily without the slightest consideration for any screams or complaints that might arise ... exterminate mercilessly the agitators who were misleading the nation ... If the best men were dying at the front, the least we could do was to wipe out the vermin.[15]

[The Jew] is and remains the typical parasite, a sponger who like a noxious bacillus keeps spreading as soon as a favourable medium invites him. And ... wherever he appears, the host people dies out after a shorter or longer period.[16]

[The Jew] is [an] adversary of all humanity ...[17]

[The Jew] is the eternal blood-sucker.[18]

... keenest (Jewish) minds see the dream of world domination tangibly approaching.[19]

The Jew, despite all his love of sacrifice, naturally never becomes personally impoverished.[20] Freemasonry is joined by a second weapon in the service of the Jews: the press.[21] [The Jew] ... talks ... of the equality of all men without regard to race and color. The fools begin to believe him.[22] [The Jew] advocates parliamentary democracy because it puts political power in the hands of a majority characterized by stupidity, incompetence, and last but not least, cowardice.[23] [The Jew] establishes the Marxist doctrine -- to promote class hatred and divide the nation.[24] [The Jew] is planning the enslavement and with it the destruction of all non-Jewish peoples.[25] [The Jew] desires not the preservation of an independent national economy but its destruction.[26] [The Jew] is restrained by no moral scruple.[27] [The Jew] stops at nothing, and in his vileness he becomes so gigantic that no one need be surprised if among our people the personification of the devil as the symbol of all evil answers the living shape of the Jew.[28] With satanic joy in his face, the black-haired Jewish youth lurks in wait for the unsuspecting girl whom he defiles with his blood, thus stealing her from her people.[29] [The Jew] tries systematically to lower the racial level by a continuous poisoning of individuals.[30] ... And in politics he begins to replace the idea of democracy by the dictatorship of the proletariat.[31]

Hitler's discussion of the alleged persistence of the Jewish parasite, the parasite's endurance and determination no matter the obstacles and setbacks, implied that the *best* solution of the "Jewish problem" would be, and must be, extermination. Anything short of this, would allow the Jews to resume their presumably customary resurgence and malevolent influence. Logically, "confinement" and "enslavement" would clearly not suffice given Hitler's view of Jewish history.

> ... In gaining political power the Jew casts off the few cloaks that he still wears. The democratic people's Jew becomes the blood-Jew and tyrant over peoples. In a few years he tries to exterminate the national intelligentsia and by robbing the peoples of their natural intellectual leadership makes them ripe for the slave's lot of permanent subjugation.

The most frightful example of this kind is offered by Russia, where he killed or starved about thirty million people with positively fanatical savagery, in part amid inhuman tortures, in order to give a gang of Jewish journalists and stock-exchange bandits domination over a great people.

The end is not only the end of the freedom of the peoples oppressed by the Jew, but also the end of this parasite upon the nations. After the death of his victim, the vampire sooner or later dies too.

If we pass all the causes of the German collapse in review, the ultimate and most decisive remains the failure to recognize the racial problem and especially the Jewish menace.

The defeats on the battlefield in August 1918 would have been child's play to bear. They stood in no proportion to the victories of our people. It was not they that caused our downfall; no, it was brought about by that power which prepared these defeats by systematically over many decades robbing our people of the political and moral instincts and forces which alone make nations capable and hence worthy of existence.

In heedlessly ignoring the question of the preservation of the racial foundations of our nation, the old Reich disregarded the sole right which gives life in this world. Peoples which bastardize themselves, or let themselves be bastardized, sin against the will of eternal Providence, and when their ruin is encompassed by a stronger enemy it is not an injustice done to them, but only the restoration of justice. If a people no longer wants to respect the Nature-given qualities of its being which root in its blood, it has no further right to complain over the loss of its earthly existence.[32]

These considerations, not unexpectedly, led Hitler to the following explicit conclusion:

Today it is not princes and princes' mistresses who haggle and bargain over state borders; it is the inexorable Jew who struggles for his domination over the nations. No nation can remove this hand from its throat except by the sword. Only the assembled and concentrated might of a national passion rearing up in its strength can defy the international enslavement of peoples. Such a process is and remains a bloody one.[33] The Jew is "intensifying the struggle to the point of bloodily exterminating his hated foes.   In Russian Bolshevism we must see the attempt undertaken by the Jews in the twentieth century to achieve world domination".[34]

And finally, and chillingly, Hitler declared:

If at the beginning of the War (1914-1918) and during the War twelve or fifteen thousand of these Hebrew corrupters of the people had been held under poison gas, as happened to hundreds of thousands of our very best German workers in the field, the sacrifice of millions at the front would not have been in vain.   On the contrary: twelve thousand scoundrels eliminated in time might have saved the lives of a million real Germans, valuable for the future.[35]

Some of these arguments Hitler was to repeat in the early 1940s whenever he engaged in private discussion of his Final Solution.   On 14 February 1942, Nazi Propaganda Minister, Dr. Joseph Goebbels, reported in his Diaries the following observations by Hitler:[36]

World Jewry will suffer a great catastrophe at the same time as Bolshevism.   The Fuhrer once more expressed his determination to clean up the Jews in Europe pitilessly.   There must be no squeamish sentimentalism about it.   The Jews have deserved the catastrophe that has now overtaken them.   Their destruction will go hand in hand with the destruction of our enemies.   We must hasten this process with cold ruthlessness.   We shall thereby render an inestimable service to a humanity tormented for thousands of years by the Jews.   This uncompromising antisemitic attitude must prevail among our own people despite all objectors.   The Fuhrer expressed this idea vigorously and repeated it afterward to a group of officers who can put that in their pipes and smoke it.

The Fuhrer realizes the full implications of the great opportunities offered by this war. He is conscious of the fact that he is fighting a battle of gigantic dimensions and that the fate of the entire civilized world depends upon its issue.

An entry of 27 March 27 1942 added these comments reflecting, and possibly even paraphrasing, the Fuehrer's words:

A judgment is being visited upon the Jews that, while barbaric, is fully deserved by them. The prophesy which the Fuhrer made about them for having brought on a new world war is beginning to come true in a most terrible manner. One must not be sentimental in these matters. If we did not fight the Jews, they would destroy us. It's a life-and-death struggle between the Aryan race and the Jewish bacillus. No other government and no other regime would have the strength for such a global solution of this question. Here, too, the Fuhrer is the undismayed champion of a radical solution necessitated by conditions and therefore inexorable. Fortunately a whole series of possibilities presents itself for us in wartime that would be denied us in peacetime. We shall have to profit by this.

The ghettos that will be emptied in the cities of the General Government will now be refilled with Jews thrown out of the Reich. This process is to be repeated from time to time. There is nothing funny in it for the Jews, and the fact that Jewry's representatives in England and America are today organizing and sponsoring the war against Germany must be paid for dearly by its representatives in Europe -- and that's only right.

How could a man such as Hitler achieve the support of a sizeable plurality of a well-educated German electorate of the 1930s? Here was a mind filled with well-nigh unbelievable hatred and madness, advancing propositions so bizarre in their multitudinous, audacious, and undifferentiated nonsense as to suggest a condition of delirium. It is suggested here, even on the basis of the few passages cited above, that Hitler demonstrated an extraordinary unfitness for any serious position of public responsibility.

Consider for a moment the alternative of removing the word "Jew" from all the passages assembled here, and substituting some other entity -- any other, in fact. Apart from the specific issues of anti-Semitism, what kind of thinking does Hitler demonstrate in *Mein Kampf*? Here we see a mind which operates in the grossest of stereotypes, unable to distinguish between such concepts as, let us say, "Many Arabs", "Some Arabs", "A few Arabs", "An occasional Arab". Moreover the promiscuous use of terms laden with hate and violence in all references to the stereotype suggests an individual who is so obsessed with his singular hatred that he can barely, if at all, control himself. It suggests someone who can hardly resist an urge to leap out of his seat to strangle or butcher the stereotyped foe.

Hitler's mind developed a most far reaching, world-wide, across-the-centuries, conspiracy without any factual foundation. One of Hitler's wilder charges against the Jews in *Mein Kampf* was lack of intellectual creativity. Illustratively -- and such illustrations could be multiplied virtually to infinity -- Werner Maser in his book, *Hitler's Mein Kampf: An Analysis* (London: Faber & Faber, 1970) listed 12 Nobel prize winners of German or Austrian nationality who were "Jews or had Jewish ancestors" between the years 1905 and the publication of the second volume of*Mein Kampf*in 1926 (p. 159).

The real problem, however, is that the relationship of "facts" -- any facts -- to public opinion is not nearly as clear as liberal ideologues like to believe, or perhaps pretend. With Hitler, the characterizations of the "Jewish foe", as well as the alleged sequence and nature of his activities, not only suggested someone who had very little formal education, but also someone who could be described as simultaneously maniacal and ignorant -- as well as lacking in such attributes as common sense, balance, and, with all certainty, intellectual honesty. Hitler's "histories" were absurd caricatures. His description of the activities of Jews would strain the credulity of any but the most obsessed fellow-haters. Even more disturbingly, Hitler's view of violence as an inevitable method of resolving political conflicts among people and nations showed him to be a disastrous prospect as a potential overseer of Germany's international destinies.

A representative sample of Hitler's publicly stated opinions on what may be termed the "methods of politics" in the years between the publication of *Mein Kampf* and his elevation to the Chancellorship of Germany is presented in the collection assembled by Gordon Prange. Among these, one finds such "highlights" as the following:[37]

> We Germans have no reason to wish, even in the slightest degree, that through events, no matter of what nature they be, a so-called 'World Peace' should be preserved which makes possible, indeed confirms ... the most terrible plundering and extortion as the only possible fate for our people ... Germany can have only one ardent wish, namely, that the spirit of misfortune should hover over every conference, that discord should arise therefrom, and that finally a world peace which would otherwise ruin our nation should dissolve in blood and fire ...
>
> The goal of foreign policy is the preservation of a people's means of subsistence; it is nothing else than the preservation of the life of a

nation. The path to this goal will, in the final analysis, always be war ...

If men wish to live, then they are forced to kill others ... one is either the hammer or the anvil. We confess that it is our purpose to prepare the German people again for the role of the hammer ... There is only power, which creates justice.

... Insofar as we deliver the people from the atmosphere of pitiable belief in possibilities which lie outside the bounds of one's own strength -- such as the belief in reconciliation, understanding, world peace, the League of Nations, and international solidarity -- we destroy these ideas. There is only one right in this world and this right is one's own strength.

Given the nature of Hitler's public utterances, it is not surprising that people with an interest and expertise in psychiatry have long suspected the balance of Hitler's mind. Although most of the studies on this subject appeared after the Second World War, much of their supporting data were drawn from the 1920s and 1930s.

The pioneering work, done during the War, was by Walter C. Langer and a team of American psychiatrists and submitted to the OSS in 1943. The picture that the Langer team put together indicated a personality driven by profoundly destructive impulses, given to delusions and uncontrollable fits of rage, one lacking in conscience and empathy for the feelings and needs of others, and unable to maintain close and intimate relationships with other human beings. It was a personality in which the sense of self was grossly warped and distorted, and most of the feelings projected onto the external world consisted of hatred, fear, and contempt.

With laudable accuracy, Langer predicted suicide as the most likely end of Hitler's life and career ("... from what we know of his psychology it is the most likely possibility"). The predictions of the study that Hitler would become more reclusive, more given to rages, and more reliant on brutal measures to stem the tide of defeat, all proved accurate, too.

In the words of the author: "The course he will follow will almost certainly be the one that seems to him to be the surest road to immortality and that at the same time wreaks the greatest vengeance on a world he despises".[38]

Among those who had private access to the person of the Leader, there were also some who seriously wondered and worried about his psyche. Probably the most prominent of these was Hermann Rauschning, one-time

Party chief in Danzig (Gdansk), who had broken with Hitler before the War and wound up in the United States.

In his well-nigh prophetic work, *The Voice of Destruction* (New York: G. P. Putnam's Sons, 1940), Hermann Rauschning described the Adolf Hitler whom he knew before the outbreak of the Second World War in two striking sentences:

> ... Self-surrender to the uncontrollable impulse to wreak destruction seems to be the essence of the spirit that guides this insane adventurer (254) ... Hatred is like wine to him, it intoxicates him. (262)

In describing the Hitler personality, Rauschning posed a basic question which he still felt unable to resolve:

> Is Hitler mad? I think everyone who has met the Fuhrer two or three times must have asked himself this question. Anyone who has seen this man face to face, has met his uncertain glance, without depth or warmth, from eyes that seem hard and remote, and has then seen that gaze grow rigid, will certainly have experienced the uncanny feeling: 'that man is not normal'. (255)

To the extent that one is known by one's deeds as much, or even more than, by one's words, Hitler's political activity was substantially political thuggery. His SA first and SS later were engaged in a deliberate, long-term, policy of physical attacks -- beating and killing of political opponents, principally the Communists but also Socialists, and, on occasion, most anybody who seemed in the way. Communists, and to a lesser degree the SPD, responded with violence of their own. Weimar police forces were generally not very effective in controlling the street clashes; occasionally the level of violence gave Germany the atmosphere of an incipient civil war, not to minimize, of course, the more usual, mundane attributes of such violence, namely public intimidation and sense of chaos. During the single worst month of Nazi, Nazi-Communist, and Nazi-other party violence in July of 1932, over 1,200 people were killed or injured in all of Germany.[39]

An important insight into the mind and character of Adolf Hitler was provided in August 1932 in connection with the so-called Potempa murder. On 10 August in the Upper Silesian village of Potempa, nine uniformed SA members broke into a house where one Konrad Pietrzuch, a young coal miner, lived with his brother and mother. Pietrzuch was a Communist. The SA men, in the presence of Pietrzuch's mother, proceeded to beat and stomp upon the young man for half an hour until he died. There were no extenuating circumstances in this crime; the victim had no personal connection to the perpetrators. Within less than two weeks of the event, five of the nine Nazi storm troopers were sentenced to death by a court of law. The very next day, the amoral and immoral Adolf Hitler sent a telegram to the convicted killers which read:

> In the face of this monstrous verdict I feel myself bound to you in limitless devotion. From this moment on your freedom is a question of our honour. The battle against a regime under which this was possible, our duty.[40]

In Hitler's view, there was no possible "wrong", no conceivable sin, in service to "Germany". Even many National Socialists were shocked by the senseless bestiality of the Potempa crime. But Hitler had no problem at all.

In addition to his pathological state of mind, Hitler brought with him other doubtful credentials. He was no more than a recycled drifter and felon. The Fuehrer not only could lay no claim to a completed education, academic or vocational. He had never held a steady job to support himself. He drifted out of hostels and doss houses before the Great War. He never found or pursued steady work after the war either -- except, of course, as a paid agitator of the Freikorps and later the Nazi Party. His interest in art could only be described as desultory. Hitler never earned a month's wages or salary from anybody. And, of course, in 1923, he had organized and participated in the failed but violent and illegal attempt to overthrow the government of Bavaria for which he was duly sentenced to jail by a German court to a five year term of imprisonment, and he served eight and half months of his sentence.[41]

Nor did the "Leader" ever really exercise any leadership -- apart from his "movement". Hitler simply had had no experience in running or managing any organization, business, or collective-social entity of any kind like, say, even an amateur theatre group. Neither in the private nor in the public sector. He was a socially-estranged loner whose only organizational link in life was with the Party. He could give a speech to an audience of 10,000, but he was unable to converse with small groups of people, especially if they were not his admirers and supporters, and in no way at all if they were opponents. Did all this amount to solid public credibility?

Before even considering the content and manner of Hitler's campaign techniques, one must first recognize the element of coercion attached to it. The original function of Hitler's storm troopers was to maintain "security" at the Leader's meetings, i.e., terrorizing any possible vocal objectors to Hitler's speeches. If there is any truth in the idea that sometimes the medium is the message, Hitler communicated, or should have communicated, a great many cautionary signals to his German audiences.[42]

To be sure, Hitler developed a tremendous reputation as a public speaker. Some have regarded him as the greatest demagogue of all time. There is no doubt that Hitler was very effective in addressing mass audiences. Hundreds of thousands were spellbound. Hitler frequently aroused feelings of devotion, adulation, and frenzy in his audiences. Many sobbed and trembled in response to his words.

But how did he do it? Hitler's speeches were not known for their factual accuracy, superb logic, intricately woven arguments, or even specific suggestions for the solution of current public problems. Hitler spoke in vague symbols and generalities. What Hitler projected to his audiences were powerful emotions, especially anger and resentment, emotions in which Hitler appeared to be so completely personally caught up that he seemed totally sincere in whatever he was saying. He expressed passions, and with his style of total immersion in the message that he was delivering, Hitler evoked analogous emotions in his audiences. It was time to put an end to Jewish machinations in Germany. The November criminals should never be allowed to do to Germany what they did in 1918. Bolshevism must be rooted out of German life once and for all. The French have always been plotting Germany's demise. The party politics and parliamentary regime were ruining Germany through chaos, fraud and cowardice. The Jews were behind the rot afflicting the German people. The German people needed to awake to their plight.

By design, because Hitler justified this approach in *Mein Kampf,* Hitler's oratorical appeal was the very antithesis of rational speech. He was interested in emotions and in hearts, not in minds. Hitler mocked the rationality of the masses and simultaneously advocated the notion that only mass following and mass acceptance could bring his movement political power.

As Rudolf Olden put it:

... [Hitler] did not want to persuade and still less to convince; his one aim was to hypnotize. Nothing proves this more clearly than his principle that an agitator should speak only in the evening, when his audience is tired and its power of resistance lowered.[43]

And further:

In Hitler's speeches, argument and production of proof are of little importance. Instead we have concentration on a few points, persistent repetition, self-confident and self-assured interpretation of the main theme ... and perseverance in waiting for the effect to make itself felt.[44] According to the Leader, one must "take account equally of people's weaknesses and bestiality".[45]

In Alan Bullock's view, Hitler's great gift of oratory had very little to do with what might be termed rational persuasion. It was not in the logic or the facts. It was all in the emotion.[46]

Hitler showed a marked preference for the spoken over the written word. 'The force which ever set in motion the great historical avalanches of religious and political movements is the magic power of the spoken word. The broad masses of a population are more amenable to the appeal of rhetoric than to any other force.' The employment of verbal violence, the repetition of such words as 'smash,' 'force,' 'ruthless,' 'hatred' was deliberate. Hitler's gestures and the emotional character of his speaking, lashing himself up to a pitch of near-hysteria in which he would scream and spit out his resentment, had the same effect on an audience. Many descriptions have been given of the way in which he succeeded in communicating passion to his listeners, so that men groaned or hissed and women sobbed involuntarily, if only to relieve the tension, caught up in the spell of powerful emotions of hatred and exaltation, from which all restraint had been removed.

William Shirer, who had attended all of Hitler's major speeches from the 1930s until the early 1940s, left us this reminiscence:

At Nuremberg I grasped for the first time that it was Hitler's eloquence, his astonishing ability to move a German audience by speech, that more than anything else had swept him from oblivion to power as dictator and seemed likely to keep him there. The words he uttered, the thoughts he expressed, often seemed to me ridiculous, but that week in Nuremberg I began to comprehend that it did not matter so much what he said but how he said it. Hitler's communication with his audiences was uncanny. He established a rapport almost immediately and deepened and intensified it as he went on speaking, holding them completely in his spell. In such a state, it seemed to me, they easily believed anything he said, even the most foolish nonsense. Over the years as I listened to scores of Hitler's major speeches I would pause in my own mind to exclaim: 'What utter rubbish! What brazen lies!'. Then I would look around at the audience. His German listeners were lapping up every word as the utter truth.[47]

As he worked toward the inevitable climax of his discourse, [he] would become shrill and he would begin to shriek hysterically and reach, as one Irish correspondent irreverently put it, an orgasm of sound and fury, followed by an ecstasy such as I had never seen in a speaker, and which the awed listeners seemed to fully share.[48]

Hitler could always manage to appear sincere, even possessed. He could project passion to his audiences. He was totally unscrupulous in the substance of what he said. And he never made the mistake of overestimating "the people".[49]

Joachim Fest observed that Hitler's *Mein Kampf* contained some deep insights "born directly of Hitler's profound irrationality", in a work he otherwise described as tedious, verbose, neurotic, disorganized, and amoral, among others. He also observed that the "paucity of the actual Nazi programme as against the energy and noise level of its agitation, caused many people to underestimate the NSDAP".[50]

In Fest's view, Hitler's was "fundamentally ... a theatrical person, trusting dramatic effects more than ideological persuasion and trusting himself only in those sham worlds that he opposed to reality".[51]

William Carr noted that what distinguished the Nazis from other right-wing parties in Weimar Germany was the "ruthless will to victory and the fanatical sense of commitment emanating from the Fuehrer and his followers".[52] As for Hitler's style of persuasion, he found that his audiences could, in his presence, "suspend all rational judgments and wallow in the ecstasy of complete dependence on a messianic figure". ... they were not greatly interested in the details of the new Jerusalem ...".[53]

A former follower, Kurt Ludecke, implied much the same state of things when he remarked that

> ... thousands trembled when he spoke ...[54] he was always the centre of a spellbound audience ... his success sprang largely from the way he hammered time after time on the same few points. Audiences never tired of this repetition, any more than a Sunday-school class tires of the Holy Gospel.[55] ... He had a matchless instinct for taking advantage of every breeze to raise a political whirlwind.[56]

American correspondent Louis Lochner recalled how Hitler's "young adherents" were hypnotized by him. "I came away from [one of Hitler's speeches] wondering how a man whose diction was by no means faultless, who ranted and fumed and stomped, could so impress young intellectuals. Of all people, I thought, they should have detected the palpable flaws in his logic".[57] Albert Speer, one of those intellectuals, later observed that Hitler's speaking style "swept away any scepticism, any reservations".[58]

In addition to the public record of Hitler's so-called fundamental beliefs, his persona, and his campaign speeches of more than a decade, there was also another record: the record of the day-to-day activities of the Nazi movement. It may be granted that for some individuals, lost in the midst of Germany's great depression and what they perceived as the cultural anarchy of Weimar, the Nazi Party provided a kind of supplement, if not substitute for "home" and "family".

Here they could find comradeship, a sense of mission, faith in the Leader, a shared certainty about the external world, the fun and respectability of a quasi-military uniform, and thus all manner of psychological gratifications. But much of the Party *activity* was, and had to be, profoundly disturbing for any thoughtful person because of the violence, intolerance, and contempt for law which it exhibited. Nazi tactics were notorious, and well into the 1930s it was not really clear whether Hitler meant to achieve power legally and peacefully, or violently and illegally.

Obviously, many people in Germany in the 1930s concluded that Nazi tactics were highly effective, and promising, in thwarting the "Communist menace".[59] Simultaneously, they thought that the democratic republic was not capable of keeping order in the streets and "stopping the Reds". In this perspective, a vote for Hitler might actually *seem* rational. Candor requires us to acknowledge that people everywhere often make political choices on no better grounds. Taken as a whole, however, voting for Hitler was as rational as buying insurance from a snake-oil salesman, or a clinically insane individual, just because he advertised more complete coverage and lower premiums than any then available on the market. A vote for Hitler was a blank cheque for a would-be-dictator of dubious credentials.

After all, any literate person either knew, or should have known, that Hitler had absolute contempt for parliamentary democracy. Anyone might have known that the organization of the Nazi Party, with the Fuehrer at its apex, had obvious implications for the management of the State should Hitler succeed in his quest for power. Analogously, the truly *rational* voter would have had to ask himself: "What would my choice (i.e., Hitler) bring to the position of leadership, not in terms of *my* preferences, but in terms of *his* preferences? And how likely is it that the private wants and aspirations which *I* project onto the Leader will be as important, or more important, than his own repeatedly articulated preferences?". These questions, once asked, would oblige the "rational voter" to confront the risks of Hitler's real, personal programme: violence against opponents at home, and violence against opponents abroad; war not peace; conquest not reconciliation or mutual understanding.

Political scientist John A. Ferejohn makes a good case for paying attention to the qualities of the candidate, apart from programme, by reference to the agency-model of political representation:

> In agency models, the principal can know exactly what he or she wants the agent to do in each conceivable situation. In political life the principal cannot know exactly what he or she wants to do in each conceivable situation. In political life the principal is not a single individual at all: rather it is a collectivity, an electorate, and it is not likely to have well-defined preferences in all circumstances. Rather, the normal case is one in which there is substantial disagreement within the electorate. In this circumstance it is not clear how one might even define the notion of control.[60]

Even if the electorate were unanimous on a programme of some sort, constantly changing circumstances and new problems would, naturally, bring the issue back to the critical query: "Can we trust the character and judgment of this official whom we have elected?".

It is true, to be sure, that Nazi storm troopers, the SA and SS, carried on violent demonstrations and attacks on Hitler's political opponents, and promoted all manner of disturbance, but, in fact, this did not keep over 80 per cent of the eligible German electorate from turning out at the polls: a far better figure than that of any US election in a century.

The honesty of the vote count was not in any way compromised by the antics of the Nazi (and Communist) street thugs. The choice on the Reichstag ballot confronting German voters was about as delightfully pluralistic as could be imagined. The openness and variety of media outlets, enabling the German electorate to inform itself of the great variety of viewpoints and political options available to it in these elections, were well-nigh exemplary. These were the conditions of the two 1932 parliamentary elections, and although there was much more intimidation in 1933, the choice at the ballot was still quite pluralistic and open. The distribution of the popular vote in the three elections is shown in Table 1.

TABLE 1

THE VOTE OF THE 4 MAJOR PARTIES IN 3 WEIMAR
PARLIAMENTARY ELECTIONS, 1932-1933

First Parliamentary Election of 1932		Second Parliamentary Election of 1932		Parliamentary Election of 1933	
NSDAP	37.3	NSDAP	33.1	NSDAP	43.9
SPD	21.6	SPD	20.4	SPD	18.3
CENTRE	16.7	CENTRE	16.2	CENTRE	15.0
KPD	14.3	KPD	16.85	KDP	12.3

See Seymour Martin Lipset, *Political Man: The Social Bases of Politics* (Garden City: Doubleday & Company, 1963) p. 139.

While there has been a lively debate in the scholarly literature on the sources of Hitler's electoral following, there is clearly no question that in the 1930s it was more substantial than that of any other political party in Germany; and what is especially interesting from the standpoint of the various theories and intellectual defences of liberal democracy, much of that support came from the best educated elements of the German society, its university trained elite.[61]

The question remains, how could so many highly literate, educated, and informed people cast their votes for Adolf Hitler, a man whose political ideas constituted, literally, an open book for many years prior to the period in which he had harvested all this intelligent and learned following? Is not the very fact of such support a reproach to the democratic faith in the rationality, good will, and common sense of humanity?

For those who would observe that Hitler never received *majority* support of the German electorate, it should be noted that in Britain and the United States, two very old and highly regarded democracies, *all* governments emerging out of elections in the twentieth century have been plurality governments, representing less than 50 per cent of the eligible voters. In 1860, Abraham Lincoln was chosen President of the United States with the support of just under 40 per cent of those voting. In 1974, the Labour Party in Britain formed a Government with roughly 37 per cent of the popular vote.

There have been many explanations for Hitler's electoral appeal in the 1930s; some better than others. There was the Great Depression, with its massive unemployment, business failures, despondency about the future, and considerable consequent social and political unrest. There were haunting memories of earlier economic and social instability, especially inflation, in the early years of the Weimar Republic. There were lingering resentments over Germany's treatment by the victors of the First World War. There was chagrin over the inability of the German political parties, indeed the electorate itself, to come together in a meaningful way so as to offer the nation leadership and hope in the midst of its travails. There was the alienation, mass rootlessness idea, suggesting that a great many German voters became detached from their institutional, associational, and social moorings, and thus especially prone to be swept into the vortex of the Nazi movement. There was the alleged anxiety of the nation's lower middle class, fearful of losing its social and economic status in consequence of the Depression and sinking into the ranks of the proletariat. There was also the "trump card", as it were, of German national character, the allegedly particular, unique legacy of German history and culture which predisposed the Germans to follow and to accept a leader like Hitler.

According to Richard Hamilton, a very careful sociologist and one not willing to take all the previous claims on the sources of Hitler's support at face value, the people who were apparently most vulnerable to Hitler's demagogic appeals were the upper and upper middle class elements of German society.[62] It was they who "within the urban context, actually supplied Hitler with his greatest percentage support".[63] According to Hamilton, Hitler was also receiving heavy support -- clearly preponderant support -- from university students, especially if they were Protestant, and especially if they were from middle or upper middle class backgrounds.[64] Other authors, including especially Seymour Martin Lipset, ascribe Hitler's following more to lower middle class strata than does Hamilton.[65] There is no disagreement, in aggregate terms, on the Nazis' university support, nor is there any question that Hitler drew his votes in huge numbers from literate, and well-educated elements of German society, even if some of them could be classified as "lower middle class".

As Thomas Childers notes in a subsequent analysis:

> By 1932 the [Nazis] had won considerable support among the upper middle-class student bodies of the universities, among civil servants, even in the middle and upper grades, and in affluent electoral districts of Berlin, Hamburg, and other cities. Motivations were myriad, including fear of the Marxist left, frustrated career ambitions, and resentment at the erosion of social prestige and professional security. Yet, while sizable elements of these groups undoubtedly felt their positions or prospects challenged during the Weimar era, they cannot be described as uneducated, economically devastated, or socially marginal. They belonged, in fact, to the established elites of German society.[66]

Theodore Abel, in his pioneering work based on the life histories of 600 persons who had joined the Nazi movement, prior to 1933, discovered that only 8 per cent were unemployed when they became Nazis, and only 6 per cent described themselves to have been in "economic difficulties". Abel actually classified 80 per cent of his respondents (478 out of 600) as "economically secure".[67]

Thirty-four per cent of Abel's 600 had high school, university, or professional school education. Only 11 per cent either did not complete a public school curriculum or did not report their educational attainments. It should be noted that Abel's respondents most likely somewhat overrepresented the lower end of the German class spectrum in the Nazi Party. Among his 600 Nazis, skilled and unskilled workers accounted for 35 per cent of the total, and lower middle class persons for 51 per cent; peasants constituted another 7 per cent, while the upper middle class and the aristocracy accounted for the final 7 per cent. (One possible reason for the distortion is that Abel offered relatively very small prizes to his respondents; the reward for the best essay submitted was only 125 marks; second prize was 50 marks, and the remaining prizes ranged from 25 to 10 marks each.)[68]

Remarkably, it would seem, 60 per cent of Abel's respondents made "no reference whatsoever to indicate that they harbored anti-Semitic feelings", while an additional 4 per cent expressed various degrees of disapproval of anti-Semitism. Thus, only 36 per cent of Abel's Nazi Party respondents outwardly shared, to some degree at least, Hitler's hatred of the Jews;[69] even among these, many apparently did not match the extreme, lethally hostile nature of Hitler's anti-Semitism. But they all willingly followed the Leader, and of that they could not be absolved.

In 1928, only 2.6 per cent of the German electorate supported Hitler, but with the Great Depression, in just two years' time, Hitler's vote rose to 18 per cent. In two more years, it reached a peak of 37 per cent-plus. And how precisely was Hitler, the "ultimate leader" of the Nazi movement, courting the German electorate? He was still offering out the same simplified generalities that he had offered ten years earlier.[70] "... he still said the same things and made the same promises. Nothing had changed in his style either. The hoarse voice, the bathetic poses, the mannerisms that seemed so absurd to outsiders, the flow of oratory -- all were the same, except that in the early days he was talking to himself and his nondescript disciples, and now he was talking to one-third of the German people. The man who looked to jaundiced eyes like a 'marriage swindler', 'a stigmatized headwaiter', or a beach photographer at a seedy resort came to appear as a knight in splendid armor, the true Fuhrer ...".[71] "... His fury and his hatreds, repeated as leit-motive -- what much later the world would call his oratorical charisma -- were aimed at people very much like himself, "the sensible simplifiers", who exchanged with one another easy answers to hard questions. It was a politically, culturally, and socially unsophisticated audience ... they subsisted on half-truths, shreds of learning, and an unshakable belief in a world conspiracy against them and against the Fatherland made in their image".[72] But, unlike many others, Hitler's "brought his hearers to their feet with his overwhelming, hysterical passion, shouting the same message they had heard over and over again, that they had been done in by traitors, by conspirators against the German Volk, by Communists, plutocrats, and Jews".[73]

Amazingly, the Hitler message and method are still unacknowledged or dismissed out of hand in some of the scholarly literature long after the fact. Thus, for example, we find one recent author, William Brustein, concluding as follows:

It is highly unlikely that the millions of self-interested German citizens voting for or joining the Nazi Party in 1932 could have realized at the time that their decision would culminate in first dictatorship, then a world war, and finally the murder of millions of innocent people between 1939 and 1945.[74]

Unlikely? All they had to do was read *Mein Kampf* carefully, and, admittedly, reflect on what they read. (They might have reflected also on what they saw and heard of Nazi conduct.) Professor Brustein tells us that he has found the literature's emphasis on "the naiveté, gullibility and bigotry of the Nazi constituency" unsatisfying. The clue to his own strangely unsatisfying answer ("they did it precisely because they were rational") is to be found in his Preface: "I had been taught that human beings are not essentially evil. How could then so many Germans", etc., etc.[75]

What much of the literature *about* Nazism suggests -- quite properly -- is that Hitler did an excellent job of fooling the German electorate, and no less many of the Nazi Party members, too. Of course, many of them -- probably most -- did not know and did not think that Hitler would seek to kill all the Jews he could possibly get his hands on or embroil Germany in another world war. They did not know this and did not think this because they chose to disregard all the available, obvious evidence pointing in that direction. With a certain short-sighted, lazy, self-absorbed, and narrowly focused foolishness -- characteristic of many people everywhere, not just in Germany -- they found all the evidence they needed to misinterpret the Nazi movement.

Clearly, one can agree that Nazi propaganda did not *always* replay the themes of *Mein Kampf*, or *all* of them. In particular electoral campaigns, in 1928, 1930, 1932, etc., the Nazis, including Hitler, made various, more immediately practical appeals to all sorts of constituencies: whether subsidies to farmers, higher wages to workers, better pensions to civil servants, assistance to university students, and so forth. Sometimes they mentioned anti-Semitism more, sometimes they mentioned it less, occasionally even not at all. When they did mention it, it was often linked to specific problems like industrial strife in Germany, or the burden of reparations, giving the impression that phrases establishing the "Jewish connection" to such problems may have been only ritualistic. Nothing to take seriously.

But, of course, none of the above could deny the reality of *Mein Kampf* which -- quite apart from the Party literature handed out to people at election times -- the Nazis continued to promote, not repudiate or abandon. None of it could deny the dictatorial role of Adolf Hitler within the Nazi movement.[76] None of it could deny that Hitler's public utterances of a whole decade, especially if taken together, reinforced rather than washed away the basic *Mein Kampf* positions.   None of it could change the fact that the behaviour of the Nazi Party in its struggle for power was so fundamentally linked to violence and suppression of dissent -- in faithful accord with the master's teachings -- that to expect anything but dictatorship from a Hitler-in-power was distinctly naive. And none of this could deny the reality of Hitler's person -- a crude, vicious, and morally flawed human being.

The reality of the situation was described well-nigh perfectly by Gerhard Weinberg when he wrote:

> Certainly one should not overlook the belief of many [Germans] that the National Socialists did not necessarily mean precisely what they said; that Hitler's more extreme ideas should not be taken seriously; that once in power, the movement would find itself forced into a more reasonable course by the impact of responsibility and reality. Many of those who deluded themselves in this opinion were to argue after World War II that Hitler had deluded them. But he had not lied to them; they had misled themselves.[77]

The reasons generally offered why the Germans voted for Hitler may constitute *explanations*, but they are hardly *justifications*. A vote for Hitler was not a genuinely "rational" vote. It may have been a vote of despair, frustration, or anger, but it was not a vote of informed, sensible, and also humane calculation.   The explanations suggested by many scholars are somewhat analogous to those given by people who crash their cars into buildings or into pedestrians because they have had bad experiences at home or at work; because they lost their fortunes; or have had major disappointments in their lives; such explanations cannot justify murder, mayhem, or any other grave crimes against human beings. Granted that many of those who voted for Hitler in 1932 or 1933 hoped, and believed, that he would be able to lift Germany out of the Depression and solve a variety of problems facing them at the time, it is noteworthy that Hitler himself had said very little in his campaign speeches *specifically* about what he would do if successful in his quest for power.

It is probably fair to say that the clearest implication of his own message to Germany was that he would establish or restore order in the country, raise Germany to a new greatness, somehow, and that he would rein in, if not downright suppress, the Communists. But that raises questions. How might Hitler go about doing all this? Abolish public liberties in Germany? Establish a dictatorship? Provoke a war? Any speculation along these lines needed to take into account the person and background of the Leader. Political leadership involves a fiduciary role -- something more than saying "yes" on one issue and "no" on another. Was Hitler a sufficiently honest, mature, capable, responsible, and even ultimately sane person, to do what the public interest of Germany might have reasonably required?

Given so much evidence of Hitler's persona, as a leader and a politician, and simply as a human being, how could anyone voting so heedlessly of the available facts be viewed as "rational"? The answer is affirmative only if the word "rational" leaves mankind precious little to celebrate. In fact, most Nazi supporters probably voted for Hitler and his Party on the basis of vague impressions and feelings, of wishful thinking having little to do with anybody's "facts", and also, in fact, on the basis of interests so narrowly and selfishly drawn that they could hardly provide a standard or safeguard for anyone anywhere, including, of course, Germany of the 1930s.

A plurality of the Weimar electorate passed a heedless death sentence upon the peace of the world and the liberties and lives of millions, including in many cases, their own. In free elections, with all sorts of information available to it, an intelligent and educated plurality committed a political crime. Nazi voters either knew or should have known better. But they chose not to know or care. They thought Hitler could somehow serve their own particular purposes. Their perceptions were selfishly selective. And while the Nazi voters of 1932-1933 were not the only contributors to the tragedy of Hitler's rule and influence in the world, their culpability was undeniable and critically important.

All of these considerations are not only relevant to the question of *voting* for Hitler's, i.e., up to 1933. They are equally important for various forms of political behaviour in the period that followed. In order to consolidate his power and transform himself from a mere Chancellor to the omnipotent Fuehrer of the German Reich, Hitler needed to secure support of various interest groups, especially the German armed forces. The purge of the SA and of his friend and colleague, Ernst Roehm, in the so-called Night of the Long Knives of 30 June 1934, was part of Hitler's "deal" with the armed forces. In return for their support, Hitler was willing to kill Roehm and analogously murder hundreds, perhaps even thousands of his hitherto faithful followers, with not even a pretence of judicial process, in order to assure the Army that the SA would not supplant the Wehrmacht as Germany's legitimate military establishment.

The German Army of the 1930s was led by very intelligent and highly educated, even cultured, men. Hitler could, admittedly, make them an attractive offer, apart from the liquidation of Roehm. He would expand the armed services and he would throw lots more professional opportunities to the Officer Corps -- more money, more promotions, more missions, more status, and a much more important role in the German society of the future. But at what cost and at what risks? The murder of General Kurt von Schleicher, coincident with the Roehm Purge, foreshadowed the costs and the risks quite accurately, if only in part. Germany's military bureaucrats were willing to take an enormous chance on a man who could be accurately described in the language of American slang as a bona fide "criminal whacko" with world-wide appetites. The risk they took strained and burst the bounds of rationality.

On 1 February 1933, General Erich Ludendorff (himself an early Hitler collaborator) had written a letter to President Paul von Hindenburg prophetically denouncing the appointment of Hitler:

> By naming Hitler as Reichschancellor, you have delivered up our holy Fatherland to one of the greatest demagogues of all time. I solemnly prophesy to you that this accursed man will plunge our Reich into the abyss and bring our nation into inconceivable misery. Because of what you have done, coming generations will curse you in your grave.[78]

There were, of course, still other ways in which German democracy failed. The leaders, and followers, of the roughly two-thirds of the Weimar electorate which remained outside the Nazi fold until 1933 never managed to act co-operatively and responsibly so as to deny Hitler power. The German party system under Weimar was a cacophony of discord and failure. The Communists denounced the Social Democrats as no better than "fascists"; the Catholic Centre would not co-operate with the Social Democrats.

German political parties were unable -- within the framework of Weimar Democracy with all the advantages of liberal rules and free communications -- to co-operate for the purpose of saving the Republic. Above all, they shared the sin of underestimating Hitler and Nazism, and of misunderstanding the irrational dynamism of Hitler's movement. Illustratively, Donna Harsch in her recent book recalls the judgment of Otto Wels, SPD leader in 1933, that "a ruler such as Hitler could not last long, even after the Nazis smashed the trade unions, the SPD and the KPD and banned other political parties".[79] She also remarks that "as a rule, Social Democrats denied the importance of non-economic issues in political life and only reluctantly catered to non-rational sensibilities".[80] Above all, perhaps, the divisions within the Party itself, quite logically, bred paralysis in terms of action and policy.[81]

In an earlier study, Richard Breitman concluded that "it would be hard to find a political party less responsible for the many failures of the Weimar Republic than the SPD".[82] But he, too, found the Socialist Party inclined to a fateful passivity based on false assumptions, especially the belief that "parliamentary democracy provided a secure pathway to socialism".[83] By and large, the Party's leaders and followers tended to believe "that the rational process of economic development would eventually bring about socialism".[84] The leaders, especially, in his view, "underestimated the difficulties that they faced".[85] As Breitman puts it, "from their stance of passive political opposition ... the SPD leaders could gain neither the enthusiasm of the voters nor leverage within the upper levels of government. At least one, and perhaps both, would have been required to prevent the Nazi triumph"[86].

Writing about the two major, middle class, liberal parties of Germany, the DDP (German Democratic Party) and the DVP (German People's Party) Larry Jones deplores the fragmentation of interest groups which affected these two liberal entities as well as German politics more generally on the eve of Hitler's seizure of power.[87]

He presents this discouraging vista of German liberal politics in practice:

> By the end of the 1920s the penetration of organized economic interests into the political sphere and the fragmentation of the Weimar party system along lines of economic self-interest had reached such a point that the leaders of the German liberal movement had begun to despair about the fate of the system of government in whose establishment they had played such a prominent role.[88]

It should be duly noted that, in its essentials, the problem discussed by Jones was Liberalism's old and recurrent dilemma, universal in its framework. Granted that particular individuals and particular groups are, or can be, very clever about pursuing what they see as their individual interests, economic or otherwise, the sum total of contradictory and/or different aspirations may be no more than a cacophony, lacking any overall direction or design, and quite conceivably, frustrating to all involved.

Moving along the partisan spectrum, one finds the Catholic Centre Party of the 1930s unwilling, even in the face of all of Hitler's great electoral inroads, to make itself into a more substantial, non-denominational Christian Party, i.e., seek the participation of Protestants in its organization, while simultaneously it seemed to have lost all sense of principle by negotiating for a parliamentary coalition with the Nazis.[89]

These negotiations were occurring in late 1932, as Noel Cary notes, "despite two years of Centrist claims that the Nazis were not only irresponsible and uncommitted to the path of legality but also violently anticlerical, heathenistic, and pagan in their Weltanschauung".[90]   In fact, he observes the "the Centre was spared the historical ignominy of a coalition with the Nazis only because Hitler, holding out for the power of decree that went with presidential government, refused the offer".[91]   On 23 March 1933, the Catholic Centre Party of Germany, notwithstanding all its past pronouncements, voted, en masse, in favour of Hitler's Enabling Bill, the legitimization of his dictatorship, ostensibly at least in return for certain "concessions".

These concessions, however, were, characteristically, embodied by Hitler in his speech to the Reichstag, not in the Enabling Bill. They were harmlessly meaningless and Hitler violated every one of them in his subsequent conduct. One of them was Hitler's promise not to disturb the rights of the President, for example.   Another was to preserve the institutions of parliament, and still another was the promise not to purge the bureaucracy or the judiciary.[92]   There was no end to self-deception and rationalized promotion of what was seen (how incorrectly, ultimately!) as self-interest.

And, finally, what about the seemingly most militant opponents of Nazism, the Communist Party of Germany? Here, too, illusions and narrow self-interest carried the day.   For one thing, the Communists, like others, greatly underestimated the appeals and strengths of Hitler's movement.   There was the familiar hope that Hitler's Nazis were so preposterously reactionary in their outlook and programme that they could not possibly last as a government of Germany, that, in fact, their success would lead to their undoing, "unmasking" in a favourite Marxist term, and hence to a highly desired revolution from below against the "real" enemy -- capitalism.

In the Communist perspective, Hitlerism was but a facet of capitalism in one of its more repulsive forms.   As Conan Fischer observes: "The KPD leaders believed that National Socialism's ideological and social heterogeneity would, ultimately, prove to be its Achilles' heel. In the event, however, this very diversity, while not without its problems, was a vital factor in permitting the emergence of National Socialism as a mass movement sufficiently powerful first to undermine the Weimar Republic and then to set the Third Reich in its stead".[93]

The Party had greatly underestimated the possibilities of illegal operations under a Nazi regime.[94] It was also seemingly more interested in combating the appeals of its moderate Marxist rival, the SPD, than in seeking political alliances to thwart and contain the march of Hitlerism in Germany. Simultaneously, however, the Communists sought to present themselves to the "working class" as the true enemies of Nazism (unlike Social Democrats, presumably) by a policy of physical confrontations and street fights with Nazi militants.[95]

The people of Germany under the rules of Weimar democracy were free to form and support whatever political parties they wished, but they proved unequal to the task.[96]

The most frequent Western explanation of this failure was the alleged peculiarity and inadequacy of German political culture. Under Weimar, the Germans had formal political rights but they did not have the traditions and the habits of democratic self-government such as those of Britain and the United States. Germans, the heirs of Prussia and the Bismarckian Reich, it has been said, had a tradition of authoritarianism and militarism which did not properly prepare them for effective participation in a political democracy. Given the economic hardships, and the unfavourable international circumstances surrounding the rise of Weimar -- out of ruinous war and the "shackles of Versailles" -- it was no wonder that the experiment in democracy failed.

There may be some validity in this explanation of what happened in Germany in the 1930s. But it does not fit well into a universal democratic theory of the rational human being. Habits may be helpful to political practice but habit is not "reason". It is, in fact, the opposite of reason. Habit connotes practice so well accepted that it is no longer the subject of conscious, critical choice. Habit represents the force of subconscious inertia. We behave as we do because we have been conditioned to do it over long periods of time in many successive situations. We rely upon customs, habits, and traditions, as if by reflex, not by deliberation or calculation. The ultimate logic of this "peculiar-culture" argument is that the German people of 1919 should have declared to themselves: "we are culturally unfit to practice democracy among ourselves. We should not try having it because our minds are clouded by our past experiences." After all, how could they undo their own collective social and political history? There was no escaping it. The past could be reinterpreted and reevaluated, but, whatever it was, it could not be lived over again. New habits could be started, but previous habits could not be unlived.

This criticism at its fullest implies that the democratic idea is not universal but particularistic. Above all, however, it is one more explanation of human failure pretending to be a justification.

NOTES

[1] See Adolf Hitler, *Mein Kampf*, translated by Ralph Manheim, Sentry Edition (Boston: Houghton Mifflin, 1943), pp. XI-XII.

[2] *Ibid.*, p. XII.

[3] V. R. Berghan, *Modern Germany, Society, Economy and Politics in the Twentieth Century* (Cambridge: University Press, 1987), pp. 13-14.

[4] Koppel S. Pinson, *Modern Germany, Its History and Civilization*, Second Edition (London: Macmillan, 1996) p. 252.

[5] *Ibid.*, p. 253.

[6] *Ibid.*, p. 454.

[7] David Childs, *Germany In the Twentieth Century* (London: B. T. Batsford, 1991), p. 4.

[8] See Oswald G. Villard, *The German Phoenix, The Story of the Republic* (New York: Harrison Smith and Robert Haas, 1933), pp. 231-232. Villard reports 80,200 students in German universities at the beginning of the First World War and 132,090 in 1930, p. 232.

[9] See also Calvin B. Hoover, *Germany Enters The Third Reich* (New York: Macmillan, 1933), pp. 24-26. "The overcrowding of the professions was ... greatly accentuated by the economic crisis", p. 26. "It was [university] students and unemployed graduates who furnished members, leaders, enthusiasts, and fanaticism to the National Socialist fighting organizations", p. 26. See also Warren B. Morris, Jr., *The Weimar Republic and Nazi Germany* (Chicago: Nelson Hall, 1982) who observed that "the schools and the universities became centers of the [Nazi] movement", p. 152.

[10] See Martin Travers, "The Parameters of Commitment: the German Literary Intelligentsia On the Eve of the Third Reich", *Journal of European Studies*, Vol. XXI, No. 1, Spring 1991, pp. 19-41, on the many German intellectuals who, somehow, "beset by hesitations, equivocations and confusions" did not oppose, and in many cases, accepted Hitler, p. 38. See also Jeremy Noakes, "The Ivory Tower Under Siege: German Universities in the Third Reich", *Journal of European Studies*, Vol.

XXII, No. 4, Winter 1993, pp. 371-407, on the same theme: "... the history of German academics' involvement in some of the worst crimes of the Third Reich demonstrates how scholars can be vulnerable to ... temptation of allowing themselves to be used by politicians [and] ignore the moral dimension of their work" (p. 399).

[11] *Mein Kampf, op. cit.*, pp. XX-XXI.

[12] *Ibid.*, p. 44.

[13] *Ibid.*, p. 245.

[14] *Ibid.*, p. 653.

[15] *Ibid.*, p. 169.

[16] *Ibid.*, p. 305.

[17] *Ibid.*, p. 307.

[18] *Ibid.*, p. 310.

[19] *Ibid.*, p. 313.

[20] *Ibid.*, p. 314.

[21] *Ibid.*, p. 315.

[22] *Ibid.*, p. 316.

[23] *Ibid.*

[24] *Ibid.*, p. 319.

[25] *Ibid.*, p. 320.

[26] *Ibid.*, p. 322.

[27] *Ibid.*

[28] *Ibid.*, p. 324.

[29] *Ibid.*, p. 329.

[30] *Ibid.*

[31] *Ibid.*

[32] *Ibid.*, p. 651.

[33] *Ibid.*, p. 651.

[34] *Ibid.*, p. 661.

[35] *Ibid.*, p. 679.

[36] Louis P. Lochner, (ed.) *The Goebbels Diaries, 1942-1943* (Garden City, NY: Doubleday, 1948), pp. 86 and 148, respectively. See also Fritz Nova, *Alfred Rosenberg, Nazi Theorist of the Holocaust* (New York: Hippocrene Books, 1986): Rosenberg's *Myth of the Twentieth Century* in 1931 elaborated the same premises of destruction with respect to Jews as did Hitler's *Mein Kampf*. Rosenberg's work never became as "official" in status as *Mein Kampf*, but in Nazi literature it ranked second to it in circulation. Although explicitly rejecting Zionism and a Jewish homeland in

Palestine as solutions to the Jewish question, Rosenberg at times spoke of the forced emigration of Jews to some isolated area of the world, Guyana and Madagascar, for example, in 1939. In March of 1941, Rosenberg wrote a memo which indicated that he viewed the war as a means to a still more radical final solution of the Jewish question (pp. 119-120). He indicated that the war would serve to "exterminate directly all those racially inferior genes of Jewry". p. 121.

[37]   See Gordon W. Prange, *Hitler's Words: Two Decades of National Socialism 1923-1943* (Washington, DC: American Council on Public Affairs, 1944), pp. 41, 9, 10-11, 29, 40. Note Gerhard L. Weinberg, "National Socialist Organization and Foreign Policy Aims in 1927", *The Journal of Modern History*, Vol. XXXVI, No. 4, December 1964, pp. 428-433. Weinberg concludes that even in the 1920's Hitler held "ideas [of world domination] and that they must form a major part of any effort to understand him and his politics ... against those of writers like A. J. P. Taylor who, in the face of all the evidence, still attempt to transmute the ruthless dictator with world-wide ambitions into a statesman with limited aims" p. 429.

[38]   Walter C. Langer, *The Mind of Adolf Hitler* (New York: Basic Books, 1972), note pp. 211-212, 212-213. See also Norbert Bromberg and Verna V. Small, *Hitler's Psychopathology* (New York International Universities Press, Inc., 1983), 306-15, 316-17, for an excellent discussion of the fit between the pathological and functional qualities in the Hitler personality, and also R. G. L. Waite, *The Psychopathic God: Adolf Hitler* (New York Basic Books, 1977) and his "Adolf Hitler's Anti-Semitism" in B. B. Wolman, ed., *The Psychoanalytic Interpretation of History* (New York: Basic Books, 1971) and especially Norbert Bromberg and Verna V. Small, *op. cit.* Note also the useful definitions of "psychosis" and "psychopathy", with considerable relevance to the biographical details of Hitler's life in William Harris and Judith S. Level, eds., *The New Columbia Encyclopedia* (New York: Columbia University Press, 1975), p. 2236 and William Carr, *Hitler: A Study in Personality and Politics* (New York: St. Martin's Press, 1979). Also note the recent, excellent Edleff H. Schwaab, *Hitler's Mind: A Plunge Into Madness* (New York: Praeger, 1992).

[39]   Eugene Davidson, *The Making of Adolf Hitler* (New York: Macmillan, 1977), p. 331.

[40]   *Ibid.*, p. 333; see also Alan Bullock, *Hitler, A Study in Tyranny* (New York: Harper & Brothers, 1952), p. 202.

[41]   Konrad Heiden, *Der Fuehrer, Hitler's Rise to Power* (Boston: Houghton Mifflin, 1944), p. 206.

[42]   See Henri Lichtenberg, *The Third Reich* (New York: The Greystone Press, 1937), p. 24: "During the first phase of his activity [early 1920's] Hitler's chief concern was to recruit a solid, robust, disciplined, trained, and fanatical militia, which would permit him to hold meetings without the danger of obstruction by his better organized and more determined opponents".

[43] Rudolf Olden, *Hitler* (New York: Covici Friede, 1936), p. 85.

[44] *Ibid.*, p. 90.

[45] *Ibid.*, p. 91.

[46] Alan Bullock, *Hitler, A Study in Tyranny* (New York: Harper and Brothers, 1952), p. 64.

[47] William L. Shirer, *20th Century Journey, The Nightmare Years 1930-1940*, Volume II (Toronto: Bantam Books, 1984), pp. 127-128.

[48] *Ibid.*, p. 128.

[49] One of Hitler's biographers, Konrad Heiden, reports him as saying to an aide, sometime in the 1920's, "You can tell people anything", *Der Fuehrer, Hitler's Rise to Power* (Boston: Houghton Mifflin, 1944), p. 376. Eugene Davidson, *The Making of Adolf Hitler* (New York: Macmillan, 1977), p. 129: "Hitler's themes were few and uncomplicated ... What he gave his audiences was their own diverse collection of incitements to self-pity, brought together with a passion that overwhelmed any criticism". Charles B. Flood, *Hitler's, The Path to Power* (Boston: Houghton Mifflin, 1989), p. 171.

[50] Joachim C. Fest, *Hitler* (New York: Harcourt Brace Jovanovich, 1973), p. 203 and pp. 203-209.

[51] *Ibid.*, p. 277.

[52] William Carr, *Hitler: A Study in Personality and Politics* (New York: St. Martin's Press, 1979), pp. 8-9.

[53] *Ibid.*, p. 9.

[54] Kurt G. W. Ludecke, *I Knew Hitler* (London: Jarrolds, 1938), p. 94.

[55] *Ibid.*, p. 98.

[56] *Ibid.*, p. 99. A very valuable insight is offered by Carl Schorske in his essay, "A New Look at the Nazi Movement" in *World Politics*, Vol. 9, No. 1, October 1956, pp. 88-97. Note p. 94 especially: "The function of the [Hitler] mass meeting ... was not the presentation of programs for the solution of problems or even the formulation of a party line, but the creation of a fanatical solidarity and loyalty. The speaker was not a debater but a 'drummer'. His function was to arouse unlimited aggressiveness toward the world outside the party. It was therefore a maxim of Hitler to address only multi-group audiences. 'Never try to speak to the intelligentsia or to trade associations. Whatever you may be able to teach them by reasoned enlightenment will be eradicated the next day by opposite information'. A large and socially mixed crowd was the proper audience. 'Whatever you tell a crowd when it is in that receptive state of fanatical abandonment ... will remain like an order given under hypnosis; it is ineradicable and will withstand any reasoned argument.' Hitler accordingly did not try

to reconcile group interests; he sought to avoid mentioning them, in order the better to sever the individual from his social group."

[57] John Toland, *Adolf Hitler* (New York: Doubleday, 1976), p. 234.

[58] *Ibid.*, p. 235.

[59] On Hitler's use of violence and street gangs and the emergence of his SA units from the Freikorps ranks and its traditions, see Nigel H. Jones, *Hitler's Heralds, The Story of the Freikorps, 1918-1923* (London: John Murray, 1987). The author reports that between 1919 and 1922, some 400 political murders were committed in Germany. Of these, 354 were the work of the Right and 22 of the Left. German justice meted out 10 death sentences to Leftist assassins but "of the 354 right-wing murders, 326 went entirely unpunished". The average jail sentence for the rest was 4 months, p. 209.

[60] *Op. cit.*, p. 7.

[61] See Geoffrey J. Giles, *Students and National Socialism in Germany* (Princeton, NJ: Princeton University Press, 1985) on the take-over of the German University Students' Union by the Nazis in 1931, pp. 62-72. "You have no idea how much this means to me" Hitler told Baldur von Schirach, "now that I am able to say in the coming negotiations [that] the majority of the young intelligentsia stands behind me", p. 71.

[62] Richard F. Hamilton, *Who Voted For Hitler?* (Princeton: Princeton University Press, 1982), p. 435. Also p. 630.

[63] *Ibid.*, p. 436. See also p. 592.

[64] *Ibid.*, pp. 592-593. See also Geoffrey Pridham, *Hitler's Rise to Power: The Nazi Movement in Bavaria, 1923-1933* (New York: Harper & Row, 1973), p. 134.

[65] See Seymour Martin Lipset, *Political Man: The Social Bases of Politics* (Garden City, NJ: Anchor Books, 1963), pp. 138-139. Note also Brustein, *Logic of Evil*, p. 78, "... NSDAP [was] particularly [popular] among farmers, shopkeepers and artisans...".

[66] Thomas Childers, *The Nazi Voter, The Social Foundations of Fascism in Germany, 1919-1933* (Chapel Hill: The University of North Carolina Press, 1983), pp. 264-265. Note also Michael H. Kater, *The Nazi Party: A Social Profile of Members and Leaders, 1919-1945* (Cambridge: Harvard University Press, 1983), p. 235: "... men predominated over women ... ... the working class was under-represented while the lower middle class and the elite were over-represented".

[67] Theodore Abel, *The Nazi Movement: Why Hitler Came to Power* (New York: Atherton Press, 1966), p. 315.

[68] *Ibid.*, p. 3.

[69] *Ibid.*, p. 164.

[70] See Peter Fritzsche, "Did Weimar Fail?", *Journal of Modern History*, Vol. 68, No, 3, September 1996, pp. 629-656. Fritzsche points in the right direction when he says: "The sweep of Nazi gains among even Social Democratic workers challenges the value of a class-based interpretation of German Fascism. Conventional social categories such as worker, shopkeeper, or employee, and the political markers of Left and Right or socialist and bourgeois they encompass, simply did not make sense of the dynamic of German politics after the First World War. To understand the primacy of politics that seems manifest here, historians have little choice but to venture onto the flimsy superstructure of collective identities, cultural practices, and nationalist sentiments" (p. 641). See Rudy Koshar, "From Stammtisch to Party: Nazi Joiners and the Contradictions of Grass Roots Fascism in Weimar Germany", *Journal of Modern History*, Vol. 59, No. 1, March 1987, pp. 1-24. "Nazi joiners constituted a cross-class movement" (p. 23). See also Donna Harsch, *Social Democracy and the Rise of Nazism* (Chapel Hill: The University of North Carolina Press, 1993), pp. 105-106: "From the 1930s to the 1970s the dominant paradigm in the electoral sociology of the NSDAP assumed it to be a movement that disproportionally attracted the lower middle class. Over the last decade this interpretation has been effectively challenged. By subjecting electoral data to sophisticated statistical techniques, researchers have shown, first, that the lower middle class did not vote as a block. ... researchers disagree about which other groups contributed most to the Nazi rise, and how much. Richard Hamilton, in particular, has found that the upper middle class (higher civil servants and professionals) voted disproportionatcly for the NSDAP. More controversial is the claim of Jurgen Falter and Dirk Hanisch that the employed working class, although not the unemployed, contributed significantly to the NSDAP's growth. Against them, Thomas Childers has maintained that workers voted at a relatively low rate for the NSDAP, while admitting that the absolute number was large. Falter and Hanisch and Conan Fischer have argued that especially *after* September 1930 the SPD lost many votes to the NSDAP".

[71] Eugene Davidson, *The Making of Adolf Hitler* (New York: Macmillan, 1977), p. 364.

[72] *Ibid.*, p. 183.

[73] *Ibid.*

[74] William Brustein, *The Logic of Evil, The Social Origins of the Nazi Party 1925-1933* (New Haven: Yale University Press, 1996), p. 184.

[75] *Ibid.*, p. XI. See also the earlier article by William Brustein and Barry Markovsky, "The Rational Fascist: Interwar Fascist Party Membership in Italy and Germany", *Journal of Political and Military Sociology*, Vol. 17, No. 1, Spring 1989, pp. 177-202. As the authors themselves concede "our evidence is somewhat fragmentary at present" p. 196. But the attempt to rationalize, no matter the objections, must somehow continue!

[76] Note Sarah Gordon's discussion in *Hitler, Germans and the "Jewish Question'* (Princeton, NJ: Princeton University Press, 1984), especially pp. 65-71. The treatment of anti-Semitism among early Nazi Party members by Peter Merkl, *Political Violence Under the Swastika: 581 Early Nazis* (Princeton, NJ: Princeton University Press, 1975) implicitly suggests that the "credit" for the Final Solution must go to Hitler, not to some sort of "natural group pressure" from within the Nazi rank-and-file, or even less likely "German society".

[77] See Gerhard L. Weinberg, *Germany, Hitler, and World War II Essays in Modern German and World History* (Cambridge: Cambridge University Press, 1995), p. 52.

[78] Davidson, *op. cit.*, p. 363.

[79] Donna Harsch, *op. cit.*, p. 240.

[80] *Ibid.*, p. 241, p. 245.

[81] *Ibid.*, pp. 241-244. "Immediately after Hitler's accession to power, the KPD central committee instructed its functionaries that the struggle against Social Democracy would continue", p. 227.

[82] Richard Breitman, *German Socialism and Weimar Democracy* (Chapel Hill: The University of North Carolina Press, 1981), p. 194.

[83] *Ibid.*

[84] *Ibid.*, p. 191.

[85] *Ibid.*, p. 190.

[86] *Ibid.*, p. 188.

[87] Larry Eugene Jones, *German Liberalism and the Dissolution of the Weimar Party System, 1918-1933* (Chapel Hill: The University of North Carolina Press, 1988), p. 480.

[88] Noel D. Cary, *The Path to Christian Democracy, German Catholics and the Party System from Windthorst to Adenauer* (Cambridge: Harvard University Press, 1996), p. 135.

[89] *Ibid.*, p. 480.

[90] *Ibid.*, pp. 135-136.

[91] *Ibid.*, p. 136.

[92] *Ibid.*, pp. 138-139.

[93] Conan Fischer, *The German Communists and the Rise of Nazism* (London: Macmillan, 1991), p. 196.

[94] *Ibid.*, p. 189.

[95] See Eve Rosenhaft, *Beating the Fascists? The German Communists and Political Violence 1929-199* (Cambridge: Cambridge University Press, 1983). Fischer notes that "The SPD, was clearly outpointed by the Communists when it came to instigating

violence in northern Germany, and taking Germany as a whole, it is telling that of 356 injuries inflicted on the SA between June and October of 1932, 228 were attributed to he KPD". *Op. cit.*, p. 149. In all likelihood, *this* form of anti-Nazi activity by the Communists probably helped Hitler by strengthening the appeal of the "real Menace" ultimately useful to Nazi propaganda. See W. L. Guttsman, *The German Social Democratic Party, 1875-1933* (London: George Allen & Unwin, 1981) on the KPD attitude to the SPD as "social fascists", p. 322. The author sees the SPD as expecting that "circumstances" would, through a parliamentary political process, create the revolution that they ultimately desired to see. *Ibid.* Note also the "social fascist" concept applied to the Socialists by the KPD in Rosa Levine-Meyer, *Inside German Communism, Memoirs of Party Life in the Weimar Republic* (London: Pluto Press, 1977), pp. 172-175. See Otis C. Mitchell, *Hitler Over Germany: The Establishment of the Nazi Dictatorship, 1918-1934* (Philadelphia: Institute for the Study of Human Issues, 1983), p. 200: "The Communists were consistently short sighted. They argued, rather stupidly, that the Weimar government policies and methods of governing were exactly the same as those of Fascism". They believed that a "short-lived Nazi dictatorship would lead directly to a mass uprising ... and ... a Soviet-style state".

[96] See Lewis J. Edinger, "German Social Democracy and Hitler's National Revolution of 1933: A Study in Democratic Leadership", *World Politics*, Vol. V, No. 3, April 1953, pp. 330-367. "None of the German parties was either mentally or physically prepared for the ruthless Nazi drive for total power in 1933", p. 362. Edinger ruefully observes that the Nazi experience "should induce the student of world politics to ponder the validity and relevance of ... non-intervention in contemporary international relations", p. 367. Note David Abraham, "Constituting Hegemony: The Bourgeois Crisis of Weimar Germany", *The Journal of Modern History*, Vol. 51, No. 3, September 1979, pp. 417-433. As the author says: "that no stable voting bloc could be organized under a democratic form of state did not, of itself, indicate that a fascist solution would follow or what the nature of the fascist system would be. But neither does recognition of the contingent nature of the Nazi victory mean that the problem of organizing support for the various dominant classes of Weimar society could be resolved within the existing framework of democrative politics", pp. 432-433. For sources concerning disorder in the Weimar Republic see Richard Breitman, *German Socialism and Weimar Democracy* (Chapel Hill: University of North Carolina Press, 1981); Alex De Jonge, *The Weimar Chronicle: Prelude to Hitler* (New York: Paddington Press, 1978); Erick Eyck, *A History of the Weimar Republic* (Cambridge: Harvard University Press, 1962), see especially pp. 408-409. In one month, May-June 1932, 99 persons were killed and 1,125 wounded in the streets of Germany; also pp. 418-421. Warren B. Morris, *The Weimar Republic and Nazi Germany* (Chicago: Nelson Hall, 1982), on economic crisis, see pp. 159-161. John Willett, *The Weimar Years* (London: Thames & Hudson, 1984), pp. 144-147. S. William Halperin,

Germany Tried Democracy (London: Archon Books, 1963), pp. 438-446, especially on widespread disorders and government impotence between July and September 1930. See also pp. 478-481, "the wave of unbridled gangsterism [was] everywhere undermining respect for law and order", p. 479.

HITLER AGAINST WORLD DEMOCRACIES: PREPARING FOR THE KILL

Between 1919 and 1933, democracy in Weimar Germany failed its crucial Hitler test. The forces of public opinion and democratic institutions proved inadequate to the task of stopping Nazism. Between 1933 and 1939, the failure of Weimar was replicated and greatly magnified on an international scale when the democracies of the world failed to act, individually and collectively, to stop Hitler's aggression.

Unlike the "local", Weimar situation, however, some old excuses were now lacking. After all, in the case of Weimar Germany, it had been contended that the "injustices" of the Treaty of Versailles, compounded by the Prussian legacy of the Bismarckian Reich, made it very difficult for Germans to be, and to remain, democratic.

But the same argument could not be made about Britain, France, the United States, Canada, Australia, Sweden, Switzerland, Holland, Belgium, and Norway, to name some. There was no Prussian legacy here, and no one was being hurt by the Treaty of Versailles. On the other hand, these were all political systems and societies well known for their freedom of the press, for the rights of free speech, assembly, petition, and association, and despite some differences in judicial systems, for due process and respect for law. No one could doubt the basic integrity of their electoral systems, and the broadly representative nature of their political institutions. Here, public opinion was king. Moreover, these were countries with highly developed educational, cultural, and economic infrastructures.

But, notwithstanding these "high credentials", the public opinion and the political leadership of every one of these countries never quite caught up to the challenge of Hitler's Germany. Between 1933 and 1939 the democracies all but lost the Second World War through their individual and collective failures.

The first failure was diagnostic. None of the democracies was able to achieve, not merely consensual, but even "prevalent," early determination about the seriousness of the threat that Hitler posed for the safety, welfare, and stability of the world. Granted differences of perception and outlook within the democracies, those who did see the Nazi threat more or less realistically were unable to mobilize the intensity of will, purpose, and, if necessary sacrifice, to meet the challenge of Hitler's aggression. These conditions led to all the derivative failures, all of them of immense significance for the task of dealing with Hitler.

The larger democracies proved unable and unwilling to step up the volume and tempo of their armament programmes to match, let alone exceed, what Hitler was doing in Germany. Even though they had collectively, and in some cases individually (France) started well ahead of Germany in 1933, soon they were all behind. More importantly perhaps than "volume" and "tempo", and more embarrassingly, given liberalism's claims about the alleged effects of freedom and democracy, these nations failed to innovate and modernize their armed forces for the warfare of the mid-twentieth century. They were hopelessly outdated and backward in their understandings, methods, and general preparedness for the war of movement that Hitler would soon unleash upon Europe and the world.[1] The democracies simply did not adapt to the changes around them.[2]

Both large and small, the democracies were also very deficient in measures of collective action designed to inhibit, thwart, and punish Hitler's aggression, and, of course, ultimately to provide for co-ordinated, collective defence in case of containment proving ineffective. Such measures would have been -- and needed to be -- diplomatic, economic, cultural, as well as military. But while the democracies produced a lot of conferencing, dialoguing, and discussing, they showed very little policy cohesion in response to the challenges posed by Hitler's conduct in Germany and in Europe.

It may be recalled that the popular Nazi slogan, "Today Germany, Tomorrow the World!" was well founded in the very last words of the first volume of *Mein Kampf*, where Hitler wrote:

> A state which in this age of racial poisoning dedicates itself to the care of its best racial elements must some day become lord of the earth.

Sensible responses by the world democracies -- assuming that there were such things as intelligent, attentive, and informed publics -- would have involved individual and co-operative acts of preparation and intervention against the menace of Nazi aggression. For the larger states, it certainly would have entailed significant military preparedness. For the smaller democracies, countries like Denmark, Holland, or Norway, it would not have been realistic to "arm-to-the-teeth" in order to unilaterally thwart the German tiger. What France alone could have done against Nazi Germany even as late as 1936 (when Hitler in violation of treaty obligations marched his troops into the demilitarized left bank of the Rhine on 7 March 1936, for example) could not have been done by Switzerland, Holland, Belgium, Luxembourg, Denmark and Norway, or Sweden, all acting together. What France and Britain could have done jointly against Nazi Germany in the 1930s could not have been done by any eight or ten other European nations acting either singly or in concert.

But the smaller democracies of Europe, had they read, watched, listened, and understood, would certainly have been in a position to assist the stronger powers by acting in concert. To them, no less than these greater powers, the door was open for the better part of a decade for all sorts of defensive and pre-emptive measures that would have impeded, and quite possibly thwarted, the murderous designs of the maniacal Fuehrer. Much could have been accomplished by political and military alliances, making it clear that Hitler was, or would be, facing a united front of nations determined not to allow him to set the world ablaze.

Smaller countries could have provided bases and transit rights to larger ones, and morally and politically could have done a great deal to put Hitler's Nazi Reich into a very unwelcome isolation tank in Europe. They could have co-operated in economic and humanitarian, as well as political and military matters, not only bringing great pressure to bear on Hitler, but indirectly also encouraging revolutionary opposition to Hitler's regime in Germany itself. All these things were possible and many would have been done, if indeed there had been an understanding and a will to do them. But alas, both understanding and will were lacking, precisely in those places where democratic-liberal apologists would have predicted the greatest abundance of understanding and will.

When one looks at the so-called "bottom line" of actual actions responding to the challenge of Hitlerism, the record of the world democracies was, in part, that of an ostrich hiding its head in the sand; in part, it was the record of the hysterical chicken, harmlessly and noisily flapping its wings, clucking, running round and about, and exhibiting a totally impractical state of agitation. The smaller nations sought refuge behind the facade of a pathetically futile neutrality; the larger ones did a lot a conferencing, dialoguing, and paper working, but, until the fateful September of 1939, they were not really ready to go beyond words and half-hearted measures to stem the tide of Hitler's campaign of domination.

The claim that the world external to Germany did not know (or could not know) during the 1930s what Hitler was doing in terms of all his major policies, especially, of course, rapid rearmament, is too frivolous to deserve serious consideration.

With respect to military affairs, Hitler, especially after 1935 when he had realized that the Western Powers would not punish him for his breach of the Versailles Treaty, delighted in emphasizing the new military prowess of his Nazi Germany.   There were air shows, exhibitions, parades, manoeuvres, unofficial statements, the Spanish intervention, and even motion pictures which, like *Triumph of the Will*, gloried in the renewed military exuberance of the "New Germany". If militarism in the Third Reich inspired fear abroad, if it intimidated Germany's opponents, Hitler welcomed it as an aid to his programme of European expansion.   One did not need to be a sleuth to appreciate in general what the Nazis were doing. Details of weapons, units, and operational plans were, of course, another matter.

Unlike Hitler's military policy and rearmament programmes, which, at least in their specific details and various particulars were closely guarded state secrets, Nazi policy toward the Jews of Germany was an open book to all the world. Actually, much of it was statutory in the form of decrees publicly made known to the people of Germany and simultaneously, of course, available to any newspaper reporter from around the globe.

Although not the first of these, the most important in this category were the so-called Nuremberg Laws of 15 September 1935 which defined "Jewishness"; deprived Jews, collectively as well as individually of their German citizenship; relegated them to the category of "state subjects"; and prohibited marriage or sexual intercourse between Jews and non-Jews. The Nuremberg Laws were constantly updated by the Nazis, and by the late 1930s the effect of these measures was to drive Jews out of the professions and the public service and generally curtail virtually all economic, social and cultural advantages and opportunities available to non-Jews. Jewish businesses were subjected to Nazi-organized boycotts and Jews individually to sporadic acts of violence.   The crescendo of Hitler's pre-war policy toward the Jews was achieved in the so-called Kristallnacht episode of 9 November 1938. This action, symbolically associated with the broken glass of Jewish residences, shops, and places of worship, was ostensibly a revenge by the Nazis for the murder of a German diplomat in Paris by a Polish Jew, Herschel Grynszpan. Kristallnacht involved nation-wide destruction and looting of Jewish property. Nazi-led mobs roamed the streets.   Nearly 200 synagogues throughout Germany were set on fire. Hundreds of shops and houses were destroyed.

Some 30,000 Jews were arrested and imprisoned in such concentration camps as Buchenwald and Dachau. Between 50 and 100 were killed. Hitler's cynical response to this night of officially inspired terror was to impose a 1 billion mark fine on the Jewish community of Germany, and, in effect, step up all his anti-Jewish measures.

The continually increasing persecution of Germany's Jews was not merely a matter of a more or less humanitarian interest, involving a relatively small group of people, less than 1 per cent of the population of the Third Reich. In the 1930s, the Jews were to the rest of the world as the canaries in a coal mine, a portent of Hitler's continuing adherence to the ideological direction set out in *Mein Kampf*. That direction transcended what in Nazi parlance would be termed the "Jewish Question".

To the rest of the world, Kristallnacht was, or should have been, another disturbing indicator about the nature of Hitlerism. It was a series of undisguised, even proudly acknowledged, crimes committed on behalf of the state. Arson, theft, and murder were here openly carried out at the instigation of the Nazi regime, with victims punished and perpetrators held blameless. That was Hitler's policy.

Was there likely a larger meaning in all of this, or was it merely a private matter between Hitler and some Jews in Germany? That was, in a sense, a test question for the court of world public opinion, and especially, of course, under conditions of freedom, for democratic public opinion.

Only one country responded to Kristallnacht by recalling its ambassador in Berlin -- the United States. The response of the world democracies to the unfolding Nazi persecution of the Jews of Germany in the 1930s could best be described as tepid, and officially all but indifferent. Very little was done by the democracies of the world to effect the rescue of Jews from Germany, or even to express to Hitler the moral disapproval of the international community. Between 1933 and 1939, in a period of six years, France admitted an average of 5,000 German Jews per year; Britain 6,700; and the United States 10,500. Because of British-imposed restrictions, only about 9,000 were able to emigrate annually to Palestine. One prominent effect of all these "inactions" was the availability in Germany of nearly a quarter-million Jews in 1939 to prospective annihilation in Hitler's gas chambers of 1942. Naturally, the indifference of the world democracies to what Hitler was doing at home and abroad greatly encouraged him in the pursuit of his reckless and murderous designs.

In fact, from the earliest days of his rule, Hitler pursued domestic policies which even "above the surface", that is in their publicly known aspects, evident to all onlookers, represented dire warnings about the meaning of his regime not only for Germany but for Europe and the rest of the world. These policies provided a certain verification of what Hitler was all about. One of these was Hitler's method of getting rid of the so-called Left wing of the Nazi Party led by Ernst Roehm and Gregor Strasser. Characteristically, Hitler's device for eliminating these people was neither political nor judicial. The method Hitler chose was sudden murder, without any pretence that depriving these formerly valued Nazi leaders of their lives required something more than a firing squad. Some of the victims were simply gunned down in their homes, others in prison cells and courtyards.

Stalin had taken 12 years from the death of Lenin in 1924 to the Great Purge Trials of 1936 to physically eliminate those whom he regarded as Party competitors and opponents. Hitler dispensed with patience and with pretence. The murders, carried out within a couple of days of 30 June 1934, occurred within 17 months of Hitler's assumption of the Chancellorship, and were audaciously acknowledged by Hitler in a speech to the Reichstag on 13 July 1934. He invoked "reasons of state" for the massacre -- no definite figure of killings was ever publicly ascertained; it may have approached 200. Hitler publicly declared himself the supreme Justiciar of the German people and warned that "everyone must know that in all future time if he raises his hand to strike at the State, then certain death will be his lot". Needless to say, there was nothing in the Weimar Constitution, even after the passage of the Enabling Act, which could be remotely construed to bestow this sort of power upon the Chancellor. But Hitler, characteristically, had great difficulty in controlling his violent urges, and his respect for the Constitution under which he was supposed to operate was probably only exceeded by his respect for the Versailles Treaty and the idea of law more generally.

Similarly unsettling were Hitler's policies in the field of German education with their tremendous emphasis on racialism and militarism. They certainly indicated that whatever diplomatic pronouncements Hitler might be making for the benefit of the gullible and the unwary, German cultural values would be fashioned on the basic pattern of *Mein Kampf.* These policies furnished some evidence to anyone willing to look and listen as to what Hitler really had in mind for his German subjects, and to what degree his speeches aimed at foreign audiences were credible. Much of Hitler's obviously disturbing domestic policy had open, public aspects understandable to virtually anyone interested. One example of this sort of policy was the Law for the Protection of Hereditary Health promulgated by the Nazis on 14 July 1933. It furnished the basis for Hitler's euthanasia programme justifying the killing of chronically sick and disabled people in the alleged interest of preserving the high racial quality of the Germans. This was simply one of many warnings uniting the past rhetoric of Hitler's doctrinal writings to the policies of the present and the future. But among the publics and leaders of the world democracies of Hitler's time there was much greater propensity to look the other way than to look and listen.

The real issue of the 1930s was not the lack of information, but the use or disuse of it, especially in societies where there were such large and sophisticated communication networks. One answer why so little was done is that political democracies often suffer from the phenomenon of cacophony. If different media and different interpreters of news events also differ in their interpretations of what they are hearing or seeing, and if this is compounded by simultaneous focus on many different questions or issues, it is obviously very difficult to crystallize an attentive consensus of public opinion. Cacophony is an aspect of division -- about what is important and about what people should believe or do. Naturally, badly divided electorates and legislatures cannot provide bold leadership and swift and decisive action. They tend to bicker rather than act.[3]

Beyond the fairly obvious phenomenon of division hides another more fundamental democratic problem: the propensity to self-indulgence. In a popularly-run political system, constituents are always looking for benefits for themselves, making life easier, more pleasant, less expensive, more secure, etc. Political parties and interest groups offer specific brokerage to citizens of democracies in terms of how precisely those benefits may be pursued and obtained. Usually, the "short-run" prevails over the "long-run", both for the constituents and the brokers. There are no interest groups looking to make sacrifices.

Winning the next election is tangible and important. The next 20 years less so. Policies of sacrifice and privation, especially if they are significant and long-term, and especially in response to physically unseen and unfelt stimuli, are as appetizing on the democratic election menu as is spinach amidst cookies and candy bars on a child's breakfast menu. The effect of this tendency among the democratic publics was to discount all news from and about Germany in such a way as to make any difficult, risky, or sacrificial actions unnecessary.

Self-indulgence promoted a policy of denial. It promoted simple indifference, which, in turn, saved people "information costs". Thus, substantial publics found comfort in the argument that Hitler was merely redressing the wrongs that were inflicted on Germany by the victorious powers of 1919. His pursuit of "fairness and equality" with other powers was "understandable" and therefore "justified".[4] Of course, Hitler's annexation of Austria in 1938 had nothing to do with the Treaty of Versailles. It also violated the principle of self-determination, since Hitler prevented the Austrians from staging a plebiscite on the question of their own independence. The argument of the "deniers" then became that, after all, Austrians were "German", and therefore, there was nothing to worry about here. Other forms of denial involved claims that reports of Nazi military power were greatly exaggerated, that Hitler lacked political support at home and that Germany lacked resources for a prolonged conflict.[5] A frequent form of denial was the projection of one's own set of values and attitudes onto Hitler and the Nazis. Thus, typically, appeasers argued that it just wouldn't make sense for Hitler to provoke war because, after all, wars were costly, risky, unpredictable, and, above all, "we wouldn't do it,[6] so why would Hitler?". Hitler's cover statements, the reassurances that he publicly issued after each aggressive action were often taken at face value.

A significant element in the public opinion of the democracies was pacifism, based on the memories of the great carnage and sacrifices of the First World War. To many people in Britain and France, regardless of Right-Left distinctions, the repetition of the horrors of 1914-1918 was simply unthinkable, no matter the cause or provocation. This aspect of democratic opinion not only undercut the option of militantly anti-Nazi foreign policies. (They were too risky.) It also handicapped the attempts to nurture programmes of rearmament and self-defence.

It was a matter of great interest and relevance, of course, that the kinds of memories and experiences which nourished pacifism in the West were also strongly represented in Germany. Millions of young Germans had been killed and wounded in the First World War. Millions of families mourned their losses. Under the Weimar Republic, pacifism was an important element of public opinion of Germany, reflected in its literature, art, and culture more generally, with especially significant influences among the political parties of the Left and Centre.

In promoting his massive rearmament programme, and his aggressive foreign policy, Hitler overcame the obstacle of German pacifism in a way that was not possible in the democracies of the West. Media controls and police surveillance made it extremely difficult for people in Nazi Germany to articulate pacifist values not only publicly but even privately. The regime promoted a kind of Orwellian "memory loss" among the people with respect to the many obviously very negative aspects of warfare, and also the various specific memories of German suffering in the First World War. Nazi propaganda glorified war, and effectively banished pacifism (with the help of the Gestapo and the concentration camps). Hitler's political system silenced, excluded and persecuted pacifists. It nullified their influence in every conceivable manner ranging from private conversations held in public places to all possible uses of media, meetings, associations, communications, and, above all, of course, elections. The dictator thus rendered the pacifists virtually powerless, something that no democratic political leader in the West could possibly do.

Democratic leaders who found it politically impossible to challenge Hitler sought to substitute denial and false hope for the untenable alternative of confronting the Nazis. At the end of 1938, in the wake of the Munich Conference, an editorial in *The New Republic* summed up an old liberal argument about the threat of Nazi Germany: "Again we must draw the lesson that the *New Republic* has never ceased to emphasize. The real danger from fascism to the great democracies is not a danger of conquest by German or Italian or Japanese armies. It is the danger of reactionary pressure and of political treachery from within; only the strengthening of democratic institutions can withstand it".[7]

When British Prime Minister Neville Chamberlain went to Munich in September 1938 to negotiate the concession of the Sudetenland by Czechoslovakia to the Nazis, he not only had ample access to all the threats and boasts that Hitler had made over the years but he also had behind him the experience of the Nazi march into the Rhineland in 1936 and the shocking take-over of Austria earlier in 1938.

But Chamberlain clung to the last vestige of hope. Why should Hitler be "unreasonable", if others were not? War might devastate Germany just as much as other countries. Chamberlain came to hope and believe that he could do business with Hitler. In the wake of his Munich journey, the Prime Minister explained his position in these seemingly reasonable terms:

> History teaches us that no form of government ever remains the same. The change may come by slow degrees or it may come suddenly like an explosion. But change in one form or another is inevitable and it would seem to follow, therefore, that we should be careful not to shut ourselves off from contact with any country on account of a system which in the course of time may well undergo

such modifications as to render it very different from what it is today.[8]

And, having met the Nazi Fuehrer, Chamberlain subsequently wrote in a private letter to his sister:

> ... in spite of the hardness and ruthlessness I thought I saw in his face, I got the impression that here was a man who could be relied upon when he had given his word.[9]

Hitler was very capable of eliciting a whole range of desirable public responses from the democracies. These involved, above all, considerations of self-interest, often predicated on deliberate or subconscious disregard of the totality of relevant information. Thus, many people in France who identified with the political Right viewed Hitler as a successful champion of the fight against Communism and the trade unions. They also sympathized, in many cases, with his anti-Semitism. They sincerely hated their own domestic Communists and Jews. They feared a social upheaval in France which Hitler, they thought, was able to stop in Germany. What many of them overlooked was the fact that Hitler was not only the sworn enemy of Communism and the Jews but also a sworn enemy of France. His plans called for the annihilation of France on the way to a Nazi hegemony in Europe. *Mein Kampf* was full of loathing and anger directed toward France. Typically, however, many people were selective in their perceptions, so eager for an anti-Communist champion that they were prepared to turn a blind eye toward the totality of what might be termed Hitler's "European programme". Of course, there were also many people on the political Right in France who knowingly and deliberately supported Hitler and endorsed Nazism because the issue of France's independence or even well-being in some general sense was simply not important to them.[10]

On the Left, and especially Far Left, Hitler and his ideas of anti-Bolshevism, imperialism, anti-Semitism, and all the rest, were viewed with complete disapproval. But here, too, there were certain problems. One of these was a characteristic underestimation of Hitler. Many Marxists believed the Nazi programme to be so "blatantly reactionary" that it was probably only a matter of time, not too much time, at that, until the "working class" of Germany would overthrow him. Some discounted Hitler's ability to even be in a position to do what he apparently said he wanted to do. In the view of some people on the Left, Hitlerism was something which should not interfere with the more immediate, and more important, local fights that the Left was waging: against the capitalist bosses and reactionary landlords of their own countries. They disliked being distracted from the traditional local conflicts they had been fighting for years. Hitler and Hitlerism could wait, or be subordinated to the task of defeating the Tories or the bourgeois Nationalists, or such like. Most importantly perhaps, many on the Left had a serious problem with the kind of struggle that might have been needed to defeat Hitler. They did not care for "militarism". They disdained war. They placed their faith in international comity and the League of Nations. The need to summon brute force and apply it on a large scale against Nazi Germany made these people distinctly uncomfortable. In practical terms, this made Leftist opposition much less effective than it might have been.

Heinz Pol, in his contemporaneous account, sums up the attitude of the French Left, its unique form of Hitler-denial, combining hostility with misperception and myopic pursuit of particularistic objèctives:

> The middle-class Left was passive and in part almost indifferent ... It underestimated Hitler, and thus it underestimated the significance of foreign affairs generally.

> The trades-union movement particularly, which since 1936 had experienced a growth unprecedented in the annals of France, became a retarding factor in the schooling of the masses in foreign policy. The masses began to have no interest other than the extension of social reform.[11]

> Their attitude toward Fascism and Nazism was one of unqualified hostility, but their pacifism made them underestimate the real danger. They were satisfied with the hope that both Hitler and Mussolini were colossi with clay feet who would never dare to back up their threats with action, or who would at least collapse instantly if they tried it.[12]

An important component of the democratic publics among all of Hitler's adversaries was a moderate centre made up of people for whom political concerns were more occasional than they were passionate. These people most closely approximated the mythical "average person", one who is as likely or more likely to read the sports or entertainment news in his or her local newspaper than to pay attention to party squabbles or international conflicts. The most important method for keeping these moderates at bay --

that is, uninterested in opposition to the ascendancy of Hitler -- was to cultivate the appeals of inertia. These people could be prevented from mobilizing politically against Hitler as long as they felt that nothing really drastic was happening in the international environment, nothing likely to affect their particular interests in any immediate or meaningful way; that most of the more revealing stories and accounts about Hitler and the Nazis were probably journalistic exaggerations, sensationalism intended to increase newspaper circulation; that whatever Hitler was doing was happening in places and to people with whom these solid local citizens had little, if any, connection.

It was also feasible to argue to this sort of "moderate" public that all politicians were more or less the same. They might like to call each other names perhaps, but this was just part of what political conflict in its most usual sense was always all about. As long as this politics, national or international, was conducted within some vaguely familiar, acceptable forms, the moderate public was likely to interpret actions and events occurring abroad in a complacently self-serving fashion, reinforced by the mores of western liberalism.

According to Franklin Gannon's account,

> The conservative quality-press adopted the line that Hitler's was a legal government recognized by and on at least ostensibly friendly terms with the British government, and considerably more stable than any of the other Central or Eastern European governments of the time. It held that the British government had no right to interfere in the internal policies of friendly states as long as they did not interfere with Britain.[13]

J. B. Priestley wrote in the spring of 1939 that the British people did not believe in appeasement and were "appalled by the Munich agreement" but he also thought that "a condition of military preparedness, a country that is like an armed camp, a people permanently mobilized -- all this suits dictatorship, which indeed cannot flourish in any other atmosphere. Not a democracy. It is terribly easy to lose your democracy by agreeing to defend it".[14]

While the Nazi Fuehrer offered periodic diplomatic reassurances to people abroad, the knowledge of his actions and the scale of his rearmament programme were, paradoxically, so "visible" as to give him another asset, the asset of fear.[15]

A recent author, Benny Morris, concludes in his study of British appeasement that fear of the Nazis was an important motive force. In a study of the English press during this period he writes that:

> ... all the weeklies showed acute awareness of British vulnerability. British resources were believed insufficient to meet [Britain's] commitments.

> Haltingly from 1933, and acutely from 1935, most of the weeklies exhibited a profound fear of British involvement in conflict in more than one area of the globe.[16]

> The belief in the Luftwaffe potency, which usually outran its actual strength at any given moment, was probably the single most important determinant of appeasement in the Thirties.[17]

Quite tellingly, Morris concludes that in Britain "liberalism sired appeasement" because "it precluded a full, early and unanimous appreciation of the nature and significance of Nazism. Nazism's postulates, like ideological politics in general, were too alien to the liberal outlook to be comprehensible to the exponents of liberalism".[18] Nazism challenged the liberal view that "men were basically good and that men and nations were essentially rational".[19]

Hitler also benefited in the eyes of moderate British public opinion in part because there seemed to be lots of other political villains on the political horizon. It was hard to single out Hitler, or make him "stand out". There was, for example, Mussolini "who had run amuck in Abyssinia in October 1935 and torn away the few illusions which still [attached] to the League of Nations. After 1936 there was a fighting war in Spain which involved the Left deeply and vocally. After 1937, there was an ideologically compelling war in the Far East. The Dollfuss and Schuschnigg regimes in Austria were considered fully as dictatorial and oppressive as Hitler's in Germany; and Poland's treatment of the Jews was admittedly more violent than Nazi Germany's".[20]

Gannon also emphasizes the belief, widely held in Britain, that Germany had valid territorial claims in Europe because of the "injustices of Versailles": claims which existed, or would exist, independently of the presence of Adolf Hitler.[21] There was even the interesting and somewhat pathetic view that there could be no lasting peace in Europe without German participation, and given the apparent domestic popularity of the Hitler regime, he presumably "had to be" cultivated by British policy makers.[22]

To all appearances, given the great trauma and cost of military confrontation, lots of people in Britain were looking for all sorts of more or less desperate excuses -- or reasons -- why it was possible and even necessary to "get on" with Hitler as with any other European or world statesman. The London *Times* argued in 1938 that while the "total conception of race had certain repercussions, such as the wholesale expulsion of Jews, yet the instinct is sound that there is in these differences of political creed alone no sane cause for armed conflict".[23]

Of course, Adolf Hitler thought a little differently about all these matters, but there again, peace and stability were so very clearly desirable that they required some people to indulge in political amnesia, overlooking all sorts of evidence which might have suggested to them much more alarming conclusions.[24]

A great asset to Hitler's image abroad, as it was at home, especially with the relatively moderate political opinion in all countries, was the legitimacy of his office. Whatever the events in Germany *following* 30 January 1933, i.e., his lawful installation as Chancellor by President von Hindenburg, Hitler was generally seen as the constitutional leader of his nation. This was a respected and prestigious position. The power of this high office allowed Hitler to gather the usual, great harvest of a characteristic human attribution or "projection" upon the position rather than the person.

Hitler became the beneficiary of the aura of his position. Thenceforth, he could nearly always count on the "benefit of the doubt". People who only recently saw him as an uncouth brawler and agitator now professed admiration for his important role in world affairs. Much was said and written about how the great responsibilities of his exalted station would likely "mature" Hitler if they had not done so already. In characteristic human terms, since Hitler was seen as having succeeded so greatly and so quickly to a position of such tremendous power, he was credited with many qualities he did not really possess. Among these were restraint, forethought, and undoubtedly more intelligence and what Westerners like to call "rationality" (often meaning simply disdain for violence) than he actually possessed.

With foreigners, as with Germans, once Hitler became Fuehrer, what a thrill and honour it got to be to shake his hand, or receive his smile, or merely be in his august (and conceivably in some way perhaps lucrative) presence! By accession to high office, Hitler had shed the attributes of a pariah and became the subject of cultivation and worship. To be sure, not everyone was taken in by Hitler in the resplendent plumage of Chancellor. Only the majority.

To his eternal credit, Winston Churchill, even then, even from moment one, did not succumb to the new authority Hitler exercised. Following Hitler's 1933 investiture, he told the House of Commons: "We watch with surprise and distress the tumultuous insurgence and ferocity and war spirit, the pitiless ill-treatment of minorities, the denial of normal protections of civilized society to large numbers of individuals solely on the grounds of race".[25] But relatively few people in Britain were interested at the time in Churchill's views.

In the early 30's, as William Manchester points out, Churchill was supported in his "alarmist" views about Nazi Germany by only "five MPs at the most".[26] This was a well-nigh incredible figure in a parliamentary body of over 600 members. Because of his adherence to these views, Churchill was estranged from the leadership and the rank and file of both major parties and the Liberals as well. For all his pains, he was reviled, ridiculed, and excluded from Cabinet office and all his past faults and miscalculations, his Dardanelles failure, his views about India, his party switches of earlier years, all these things were being used by opponents of his subsequent anti-Nazi position to undermine and discredit him.

He was an "erratic" man. He was "unreliable". He was a man of "doubtful judgment". He was an eccentric reactionary. He was a man whose political future, as some put it, was behind him. He was not a "team player". At best, he was a brilliant failure, hardly the sort of man whose judgment about serious policy questions should be respected. But Churchill, to his historic credit, persisted. Some have tried to rob him of the great magnitude of his sacrifice by pointing out that he was a well known writer and polemicist who, by the standards of the whole world, lived well by his wits. Even in the 1930s Churchill was what Americans would term a "celebrity". He was a former Cabinet minister and aristocrat; he was someone who certainly could, and did, earn a rather impressive living off his writings and his speeches.

But none of this could deny a sacrifice Churchill was willing to make that many, not to say most other, human beings would not make. He passed up the opportunity of official place and power to espouse what he believed to be right. His foresight of the 1930s earned Churchill the chance to lead Britain in 1940; and, in turn, despite all the British defeats and disappointments, his role in 1940-1941, before either the United States and the Soviet Union became involved in the Second World War, was critical to the ultimate defeat of Adolf Hitler.

Of course, to those who *wanted* to be deceived by Hitler, and to the obtuse everywhere more generally, the Fuehrer provided considerable gracious assistance in the form of the four P's, i.e., periodic, public, peaceful protestations.

Among some of the Hitler "gems", i.e., adroit public speeches delivered in Germany for international consumption, was this address to the Reichstag on 17 May 1933:

> We look at the European nations around us as undeniable realities. The French, the Poles, etc., are our neighbours, and we know that through no possible development of history can this reality be altered.
>
> No German Government will of its own account breach [the Treaty of Versailles] which cannot be removed without being replaced by a better one.[27]

In March 1935 Hitler violated the Versailles Treaty by announcing the rearmament of Germany. Within a few days of this action, he declared in the Reichstag:

> At no moment of my struggle on behalf of the German people have I ever forgotten the duty incumbent on me and on us all firmly to uphold European culture and European civilization.
>
> Why should it not be possible to put an end to this useless strife (between France and Germany) which has lasted for centuries and which has never been and never will be finally decided by either of the two nations concerned? Why not replace it by the rule of reason? The German people have no interest in seeing the French people suffer.[28]

In *Mein Kampf,* however, Hitler had said:

> We must be absolutely clear on the fact that France is the permanent and inexorable enemy of the German; the key to her foreign policy will always be her desire to possess the Rhine frontier, and to secure that river for herself by keeping Germany broken up and in ruins.[29]
> If the German nation is to stop the rot which threatens Europe, it

must ascertain who its most dangerous opponents are so as to strike at them with all its concentrated force.[30]

When Hitler marched his troops into Prague in violation of the Munich Agreement in March of 1939 he removed whatever was left of Czechoslovakia from that famous "etc." that he had listed in his speech of 17 May 1933.

But until the very eve of the Second World War, Hitler kept up his reassuring public statements intended to lull the opposition of the democracies.

On 26 September 1938 at the Berlin Sportpalast, Hitler declared:

> None of us want war with France. We want nothing from France; nothing at all! All territorial differences between France and Germany have now been settled. I can today conceive of no further differences between us! Here are two great nations wanting to work and to live, and they will live the better for working together![31]

On 9 October 1938, in a speech at Saarbrucken, Hitler said:

> As a strong state we are ready at any time for a policy of appeasement with our neighbours. We have no claims upon them; we want nothing but peace. There is only one thing that we wish for: that Great Britain would gradually dispense with some of the idiosyncrasies of the Versailles epoch. We cannot put up any longer with the moralizing of a governess![32]

In effect, Hitler was asking the Western Powers for a free hand in east-central Europe but all in the guise of faultless peacefulness. He seemed to be saying: "If I don't have any direct claims against you, why do you meddle in my activities directed at others?". In his speech of 6 November 1938 in Weimar, with the Sudetenland already swallowed up in Munich, Hitler said:

> It is all very fine to talk of international peace and international disarmament, but I for my part entertain grave doubts about the disarmament of those who are still fully armed in spirit.

Obviously, Winston Churchill's statements about the meaning of Munich irritated Hitler, and he reverted to the language of *Mein Kampf* saying that Mr. Churchill should "realize the complete folly and idiocy of his idle talk. This gentleman seems to be living on the moon. I can assure him: I shall prevent him from destroying Germany!"[33]

In a speech to the Reichstag on 31 January 1939, Hitler said:

> I have stated often enough that there is no German, and above all no National Socialist, who even in his most secret thoughts has the intention of causing the British Empire any kind of difficulties.
>
> It would be a blessing for the whole world if mutual confidence and co-operation could be established between the two peoples. The same is true of our relations with France.[34]

And again on 28 April 1939 he said:

> As the national leader of the German people, I have always admitted that, wherever the higher interests of the European community were at stake, national interests must, if necessary, be relegated to second place This attitude of mine is an absolutely sincere one.[35]
>
> I have never advanced a claim which might in any way have interfered with British interests.[36]

On 4 June 1939, in Kassel, Hitler made the following highly interesting statement:

> No nation and no regime will wage war merely for war's sake. Only in the brains of perverse Jewish journalists can the idea be conceived that anybody could resort to war from motives of pure delight in killing and bloodshed.[37]

This was probably the most candid of Hitler's statements, although the opinion he ascribed to "Jewish journalists" should have been, more accurately, ascribed to himself. It seemed to be a curious case of projection. Sometimes over his reassurances, Hitler's language reflected his natural impulses as if in odd analogy to the wolf's visit with Red Riding Hood.

The Fuehrer's more sinister aspects were actually more readily apparent in personal contacts, and most of the information about these was available through diplomatic channels to the democratic powers.

US Ambassador William E. Dodd, who had just arrived in Germany in the summer of 1933, recorded the report of a rather obscure American college professor relayed to him on 16 August 1933:

> [Professor Coar] ... came to describe his visit with Hitler. He had spent two hours with the Chancellor, with Hess as a witness. Coar reported that Hitler talked wildly about destroying all Jews, insisting that no other nation had any right to protest and that Germany was showing the world how to rid itself of its greatest curse. He considered himself a sort of Messiah. He would rearm Germany, absorb Austria and finally move the capital to Munich. There were other and equally important points, but Coar was not at liberty to mention them.[38]

Apparently within a few days of this date, two distinguished American business executives had had a conversation with the Chancellor and reported on it to Ambassador Dodd on 1 September. The envoy's diary records it as follows:

> Henry Mann of the national City Bank spoke of the conversation he and Mr. Aldrich had had some ten days before with the Chancellor at his summer palace. The ideas advocated by Hitler were the same as those he had advanced to Professor Coar. He is a fanatic on the Jewish problem. He has no conception of international relationships. He considers himself a German Messiah. But despite Hitler's attitude these bankers feel they can work with him.[39]

There was no comment from the Ambassador himself on any of these observations. There was probably very little interest in all this on the part of the US State Department. There wasn't anything surprising about Hitler's remarks: shocking and foreboding, yes, surprising, no.

Ambassador André François-Poncet, who had lived most of the 1930s in Berlin, keeping an eye on Hitler on behalf of France, recorded the following summary of his impressions:

> I labored under no illusions about his character. I knew him to be changeable, dissimulating, contradictory and uncertain, the same

man good-natured and sensitive to the beauties of nature, who across a tea table expressed reasonable opinions on European politics, was capable of the wildest frenzies, the most savage exaltation, and the most delirious ambition. There were days when, bending over a map of the world, he upset nations and continents, geography and history, like some demi-urge in his madness.[40]

According to François-Poncet, Hitler's "alternate states of excitement and depression, these fits mentioned by his familiars, ranged from the most devastating fury to the plaintive moanings of a wounded beast. Because of them, psychiatrists have considered him a 'cyclothimic'; others see in him a typical paranoiac. This much is certain, he was no normal being. He was rather, a morbid personality, a quasi-madman, a character out of the pages of Dostoevski, a man 'possessed'".[41]

According to the French Ambassador, Hitler could not actually distinguish between Germany and himself,[42] and, most importantly for the critical issue of peace, François-Poncet concluded: "Could he possibly have preferred to attain his ends without having recourse to warfare? Surely not. From the very outset, war figured in his forecasts and in his plans".[43]

In conversations with his German familiars and subordinate officials, there was nothing whatever to suggest that a new, post-*Mein Kampf* Hitler -- one interested in peaceful coexistence with his neighbours and the protection of the inviolability of international agreements -- had actually emerged. With respect to what Hitler had to say to his intimates, the Western Allies could not only rely on more or less conventional espionage; they were receiving quite a bit of relevant information from high-ranking German oppositionists to Hitler, largely, though not entirely, military. Shortly before Munich, the British received warnings from would-be anti-Hitler plotters that "the only real extremist" in Nazi hierarchy was Hitler himself, although Foreign Minister Joachim von Ribbentrop was characterized as an evil "Yes-man" to Hitler.[44]

This information was discounted in official British circles. German opponents of the Fuehrer wanted Britain and France to "get tough" with Hitler, the very last thing the Allies wanted to do. Apparently, they did not know of the meeting Hitler had held with his top military leaders and Foreign Minister Baron von Neurath begun at 4.15 p.m. on 5 November 1937 in Berlin. On this occasion, Hitler identified Britain and France as two "hate-inspired" states, and told the six individuals attending the meeting, that "Germany's problems could only be solved by force" and only the issues of "when" and "where" needed to be examined. In William Shirer's summary:

> Thus as evening darkened Berlin on that autumn day of November 5, 1937 -- the meeting broke up at eight fifteen -- the die was cast. Hitler had communicated his irrevocable decision to go to war. To the handful of men who would have to direct it there could no longer be any doubt. The dictator had said it all ten years before in *Mein Kampf*, had said that Germany must have *Lebensraum* in the East and must be prepared to use force to obtain it ...[45]

The participants in this conference were in addition to Hitler, Fieldmarshal Werner von Blomberg, General Werner von Fritsch, Hermann Goering, Admiral Erich Raeder, Baron Constantin von Neurath, and Hitler's military aide Colonel Friedrich Hossbach (who took minutes).

In addition to the problems of division and self-indulgence, the democracies also suffered from a certain "authority problem", ultimately implicit in the fundamental principles of political equality and pluralism. If all are, or should be, equal then perhaps no one, even in Government, is, or should be, "powerful". To the extent that in democracies power rests on persuasion, it is given today and perhaps just as likely withdrawn tomorrow. It is likely, therefore, to be somewhat tentative. And the distinction between "leaders" and "followers", even in formally organized bureaucratic and political hierarchies, may not be easy to sustain in the face of serious underlying conflicts. The very idea of "rule of law" is a concept which bureaucratic subordinates may use to variously oppose their nominal political chiefs when they happen to disagree with them.[46]

The weaknesses of the democracies were also the strengths of Hitler's authoritarian regime. People were much more likely to "jump" when Hitler ordered them to do his bidding than they were in response to the "suggestions" made to them by the likes of Edouard Daladier, Neville Chamberlain and Winston Churchill. The powers of the Nazi Fuehrer *vis-a-vis* his associates and subordinates were far more formidable. The leverage of "opposition" was much weaker.

Contrary to claims sometimes made, Hitler did not likely have the unanimous support of the German people for his policies throughout the 1930s. As late as March 1933, 48 per cent of the German people still voted against Hitler.[47] Dictatorship, however, was helpful in silencing and weakening domestic opposition to Hitler's policies and plans. Using terror and censorship to the hilt, Hitler was able to exact a high cost from any domestic source, group or individual, which might possibly want to challenge him in any way. By the virtual elimination of the Cabinet as a collective policy-making and administrative organ, and by the reduction of the Reichstag to an all-Nazi applause chamber, Hitler was able to make the government of Germany something that, in most of its critical aspects, could be conducted out of his back pocket -- secretly, privately, unaccountably and whimsically.

These actions were augmented, of course, by the abolition of the freedom of the press, rigidly centralized control of all media in Nazi hands, the abolition of the traditionally democratic freedoms of association, assembly, and petition, and the drastic diminution of the German judicial system by the introduction of the arbitrary agency of the Gestapo and the concentration camps. No one could publicly ask Hitler embarrassing questions and have them reported in the German -- and world -- media. It increasingly required the resolution of a martyr for anyone in Germany to challenge Hitler, especially if such a challenge had any public or quasi-public character. Hitler's brutality, even in the Thirties, made Italy's Benito Mussolini seem like a boy scout.[48] The principal policy which Hitler introduced in Germany -- apart from the persecution of the Jews and amassing of all forms of political power in the hands of the Nazis -- was a gigantic and, strictly speaking, unlawful scheme of military build-up. Hitler brushed aside Germany's international treaty obligations.

From the very beginning of his rule, it was quite clear that for Hitler the militarization of Germany had a distinctly offensive -- as opposed to defensive -- character. Hitler was not interested in a very gradual augmentation of German military resources, or in the design and manufacture of weapons of a principally defensive nature. The focus in Germany was on dive bombers not on building anti-aircraft shelters. True to his word in *Mein Kampf*, Hitler was anxious to make Germany the hammer, not the anvil of future international conflicts. Naturally, this kind of rearmament was consistent with the promise of *Mein Kampf*, envisioning, as it did, large expansion of German territory by violent means.[49]

While Hitler had assured himself of considerable leeway at home with respect to his incipient programme of aggression, the world community of states, and especially his European neighbours, constituted a different, and more serious challenge to his designs. Hitler could not, as yet, impose censorship and terror in France, or in Britain, or anywhere else outside Germany itself. Simultaneously, however, his Third Reich, emerging out of the restraints imposed on Germany by the Versailles Treaty, was still in 1933 militarily weak, and therefore to alert or to provoke his potential enemies too early would have been naturally risky, if not downright suicidal. Hitler needed, and deliberately pursued, a programme of deception, in which every one of his aggressive measures was always accompanied by public protestations of peaceful intent.

Still, what occurred between 1933 and 1936 with respect to relative strengths in Europe was not an accident of history. It was rather a collision between those who had the will to dominate and conquer, and those who feared and opposed conquest but were unwilling and unable to pay the costs of effective resistance.[50]

In 1932, the last full year before Hitler came to power, German military expenditures, still substantially "shackled" by the limitations of the Treaty of Versailles, amounted to the grand sum of 170 million US dollars. France was spending 455 million on her military or about 2.7 times as much. Britain was spending 535 million, or 3.1 times as much. Together, France and Britain were outspending Germany by a ratio of 5.83 to 1. But between 1933 and 1936 France actually decreased her military spending by about 20 per cent, while the British did not substantially increase their military spending until 1936.

Meantime, Hitler had managed to increase German military expenditures as share of the GNP thirteen-fold. The European arms race heated up in the late 1930s, i.e., from 1936 to 1939, but it heated up very unequally. By the end of 1939, the German share of GNP devoted to military purposes had increased from 1 per cent to 23 per cent, i.e., a twenty-three-fold rise. The British increased from 2 to 18 per cent or 9-fold. The French had increased less than 3-fold. The United States remained entirely static at 1 per cent of the GNP from 1932 to 1939.[51]

Where Hitler's ability to orchestrate intimidation, bluff, and deceptive reassurance proved especially effective was in the skilful co-ordination of diplomacy and military build-up. Hitler produced bloodless victories and acquisitions at a time when the total balance of power was still adverse to Nazi Germany. By 1939, however, Hitler had got his democratic opponents just about where he wanted them, that is, fighting him with forces which in a *de facto* sense -- though still not "on paper" -- were considerably inferior to his own.[52]

It is sometimes said that Germany had had a more robust birth rate than France or Britain in the 1930s. But that was only one of many elements in the pre-war equation of power. Obviously, it was not Germany but France and Britain which had a head start in the arms race in 1933. It was these two countries whose population exceeded significantly that of Germany at the beginning of 1938. It was these two nations which possessed extensive colonial empires and huge navies which Germany lacked. The combined industrial output of these two powers exceeded that of Germany at the beginning of 1938. Britain and France, not Germany, controlled, or were in a position to control, the supply of oil in the Middle East. And it was almost certainly Britain and France, not Germany under Hitler, which were likely to attract the diplomatic and military support of most smaller European nations fearful of Hitler's appetite -- if they only made a credible effort to enlist such support, not to mention at least the moral and political sympathies of America.

The failures of the democracies predated the regimes of Chamberlain and Daladier. They were actually not so personal as some would pretend. They rather represented more widespread, long-term, systematic collapse among the liberal democracies of that era. Chamberlain and Daladier were simply "the end of the line" in the democracies' long term bankruptcy of will, nerve, and capacity for sacrifice and endurance. One of the most obvious indications of the democracies' failure was the Nazi Reich's flourishing foreign trade. Looking at the figures of the 1920s, as well as the 1930s, it is clear that Nazi Germany maintained a more robust international commerce than did most European democracies. In consequence of the Great Depression, trade tended to decline among all countries but less so in Hitler's Germany than among many other states.[53]

Comparing trade averages for the 1920s and 1930s, British exports fell by nearly 38 per cent during the 1930s and the French by nearly 54 per cent, while the decline of Hitler's Germany was only 1.7 per cent. German imports fell by 23.2 per cent during the 1930s while the British fell by 36.8 per cent and the French by 40.6.

In 1939, Sweden's imports from Germany were larger than those from any other country, by a large margin.[54] They exceeded imports from Britain by 44 per cent and the US by 55 per cent. In Swedish exports, Germany ranked a close second behind the United Kingdom. Germany was also the largest trading partner of the Netherlands. In 1939, the combined volume of Dutch exports and imports with Germany was 42 per cent higher than that of the next largest trading partner -- Great Britain.

Between 1933 and 1939, Belgium's trade volume with Germany was second only to its main trading partner, France, and considerably exceeded trade with Great Britain and the United States. Denmark's trade with Germany was second only to that of her main partner, Britain. Indeed, Czechoslovakia's volume of trade with Germany was, by far, the largest of all her trading partners in the years 1933-1937, the last year of Czechoslovak independence and territorial integrity. In the foreign trade of Finland, Germany ranked a solid second behind the main trading partner, the United Kingdom. Between 1933 and 1939, Germany ranked easily first in the trade of Switzerland.

Among the European democracies, only France and Britain denied Nazi Germany the position of being either the number one or number two international trader in the years 1933-1939. Even in France, Germany ranked a close fifth behind, Britain, Belgium, the United States, and Algeria. Only in the case of the United Kingdom was Germany's trade exceeded by that of several countries, including the United States, Argentina, Canada, Australia, India, and New Zealand. Amazingly, even .in this case, Germany's trade volume with Britain during the pre-war Hitler years exceeded the trade with Britain's closest European ally, France, by more than 20 per cent -- £345 million to £283 million. And yet, Hitler managed to maintain all these lucrative ties while pursuing an unmistakably aggressive foreign policy right from the start.

Among Hitler's earliest international measures upon taking power in Germany was to step up Nazi terrorism in Austria which led to the outlawing of the Nazi Party in that country on 19 June 1933, scarcely five months after Hitler's investiture as Chancellor in Germany. In July, the Nazis concluded a concordat with the Vatican agreeing to respect the rights of Catholics, and on 3 September Hitler made a speech renouncing war as an instrument of policy, except, he said, with respect to "Bolshevism". These steps might have been reassuring to world public opinion, but on 14 October 1933 Hitler announced that Germany would quit the League of Nations and the multilateral Disarmament Conference alleging unequal treatment by the great powers. And on 1 January 1934, barely a year in office, Hitler ordered a huge expansion of the *Luftwaffe* in gross violation of the disarmament clauses of the Treaty of Versailles. There was no meaningful reaction to this Nazi measure from the Great Democracies, and Hitler took advantage of his new momentum by concluding a 10-year non-aggression pact with Poland on 26 January 1934. This was a signal to one and all that in view of the lethargic French and British attitudes, the new Germany needed to be courted by the smaller European countries and was open to making deals. On 25 July, however, Chancellor Engelbert Dollfuss was assassinated in an abortive Nazi attempt to seize power in Austria. Mussolini, not yet a Hitler ally, massed military forces on the

Austrian-Italian frontier to forestall a German take-over of Austria. In the upshot, Hitler backed off. (Given Mussolini's hesitations even in 1939, it is all but certain that if the great democracies had been able to stand up to Hitler, no Rome-Berlin axis would ever have developed.)

On 16 March 1935, Hitler formally declared that Germany would no longer be bound by the Versailles arms restrictions, that it would institute compulsory military service, and that it would create an army of 36 divisions. He told Hermann Rauschning:

> The struggle against Versailles is the means, but not the end of my policy. I am not in the least interested in the old frontiers of the Reich. The recreation of pre-war Germany is not a task worthy of our Revolution.[55]

The major response of the Western Powers was diplomatic in the form of the Stresa Conference of 11-14 April 1935, which protested and denounced "unilateral repudiation of treaties". The League of Nations added its condemnation of Germany. Hitler was being challenged by words, and, in effect, words alone. He responded with a Reichstag speech on 25 May which, without offering any concessions, sounded a reassuring and conciliatory note.

On 18 June 1935, an Anglo-German naval agreement was concluded allowing the Nazis to build up to 35 per cent of the tonnage of the British surface fleet and up to 45 per cent of the British submarine fleet. This was at once an official British "permission" for Nazi rearmament, all the earlier protestations notwithstanding, and a wedge in the Franco-British alliance. While official France was suspicious of Britain, the British resented the French for their allegedly chauvinistic, anti-German policies of the past, and were determined not to let France "drag Britain" into conflict with Germany.[56]

Hitler's next important initiative occurred on 7 March 1936, when in violation of two treaties -- Versailles and Locarno -- the Fuehrer ordered three German battalions to occupy the demilitarized Rhineland area. The troops were under orders to retreat should the French Army appear and attack them. Germany was still in no position to challenge the might of France. But the French did nothing, and the British, together with the French, also did nothing. Hitler got away with clearly his biggest bluff thus far.

The Western Allies seemed to find new uses for alliances in the Rhineland crisis. Consultations of the two governments were used not to initiate mutual action against Germany, but rather to reinforce the unwillingness of either party to take risks or bear costs in any kind of challenge to Hitler.[57] Considerable portions of British and French publics seemed to feel that the Rhineland was, after all, a part of Germany, and that the injustices of Versailles had to be appreciated in judging Hitler's behaviour.

The "lesson" was not lost on anyone in Europe, it seemed.[58] The League of Nations held a meeting about the German incursion on 14 March 1936 with no particular consequences. Hitler, as was his habit, submitted his latest initiative to a referendum by the German people -- held under the usual, Gestapo-controlled conditions. The annexation of the Rhineland was approved by 98.7 per cent of eligible German voters on 29 March 1936.

As William Manchester has observed:

> His triumph in the Rhineland had heightened the Third Reich's prestige throughout Europe and dealt England and France a deep wound, all the more painful because it was self-inflicted. The damage to Britain had been particularly grievous; in 1914 the French had gone to war because, facing invasion, they had no choice, but the British, who could have remained on the sidelines -- where the Germans had begged them to stay -- had fought to defend Belgian neutrality. Other small countries had assumed that they too could rely on the righteous might of history's greatest empire. Now that England had shown the white feather, recruits swelled the ranks of Nazi parties in Austria, Czechoslovakia's Sudetenland, western Poland, and the Free City of Danzig. New parties raised the hakenkreuz in Bulgaria, Rumania, and Hungary; and in May a Fascist plot was exposed in Estonia.[59]

In July, Hitler ordered Nazi transport planes to carry General Francisco Franco's insurgent troops from Morocco to the Spanish mainland. Other forms of aid to Franco and a major Nazi intervention in the Spanish Civil War ensued. (Nazi arms and troops were on international exhibition in Spain from 1936 to 1939.)

In September, Germany made public demands for the return of her colonies lost in consequence of the World War, and in October she negotiated with Italy the Axis alliance. German ambitions in Austria were given recognition by Italy in return for German support of the Italian conquest of Ethiopia. The following year, Hitler actually spoke publicly right out of the pages of *Mein Kampf*, declaring Germany's need for *Lebensraum*, allegedly to assure the nation's food supplies against unfavourable harvests. On 30

November 1937, France and Britain declared a position of "neutrality" on the question of colonies for Germany. They announced that the subject deserved "extensive study".

In December, when French Foreign Minister Yvon Delbos conducted a tour of East European capitals to bring about closer ties between France and such countries as Poland, Hungary, Romania, and Czechoslovakia, he discovered that there was already a good deal of scepticism there about the possibilities of containing Hitler's Germany.

On 20 February 1938, Hitler made a speech in the Reichstag demanding "self-determination" for the German people -- in Austria and in Czechoslovakia. On 9 March the Austrian Chancellor Kurt von Schuschnigg announced a plebiscite on the issue of Austrian independence to be held on the 13th. In response, Hitler amassed Nazi troops on the Austrian frontier, and called for a postponement of the plebiscite. The result might have embarrassed the Fuehrer even if the annexation to Germany won -- more or less narrowly. Nazis in Austria rioted. Schuschnigg was forced to resign, yielding the Chancellorship to the Nazi Dr. Arthur Seyss-Inquart, and on 12 March German troops invaded and occupied Austria. The Anschluss was complete. This time, Mussolini did not even object. Britain and France issued one more public protest about the use of force by Germany. In the American Congress there was virtually no reaction to the Anschluss.[60]

Interestingly, this Nazi incursion violated two principles that Hitler had been advancing to make his activities acceptable to the international community. The annexation of Austria had nothing to do with the alleged injustices of the Treaty of Versailles. Austria had never been part of the pre-war German empire. Hitler's invasion, pre-empting a plebiscite, was not an affirmation but rather a denial of self-determination. Neither of these facts made any significant impression on the great democracies of the time.

On 17 March 1938, the Soviet government, once again, reiterated the position it had held since 1933 that it was ready to co-operate in efforts to halt the Nazi juggernaut, if other European powers were prepared to join in such an effort. But there was not much interest in Stalin's offer. On 24 March 1938, the British government publicly rejected the Soviet overture as "inimical to prospects of European peace". On the same day, Prime Minister Chamberlain told the House of Commons that Britain would not unconditionally promise to come to the aid of France if a war broke out in Czechoslovakia. The loosening of the Franco-British links clearly depressed the French and encouraged the Nazis.

On 12 July 1938, the French government still insisted that its pledges of aid to Czechoslovakia were "indisputable and sacred". On 11 September 1938, Stalin told the French, the USSR would offer its military support to Czechoslovakia if France would honour its own mutual defence treaty obligations to that country. On 14 September, France officially reaffirmed its position. But within a few days, judging by some newspaper editorials, it seemed that the French attitude began to shift.[61]

On 15 September the British Prime Minister embarked on his visit to Hitler in Berchtesgaden looking for a mutually satisfactory deal to save the peace. By the 18th, both Britain and France were publicly demanding that the Czechs hand over Sudeten districts inhabited by a majority of Germans to the Third Reich.[62] On 19 September 1938, Russia declared that its willingness to help Czechoslovakia was -- still -- conditional on analogous French action, while on the same day France was publicly explaining its "cave-in" to Nazi Germany by the vital need to maintain British support. The implication was that Britain would not tolerate France's intransigence on the Sudeten question and would abandon her to her fate.

On 21 September 1938, Czechoslovakia, under duress from her allies, accepted Nazi demands -- whereupon Hitler increased these demands. He wanted all of Sudetenland, immediately. Again the Czechs sought to refuse, and fight, if supported by great-power allies. This led to the Munich Conference of September 29-30, which -- bringing together Britain, France, Germany and Italy without any Czechoslovak participation -- yielded to all remaining Nazi demands.[63] Russia had not been invited to the Munich Conference. Sudetenland became a part of the Third Reich and the remaining territory of Czechoslovakia received a new guarantee from Britain and France.

The Munich agreement was approved by the British House of Commons by a 366 to 144 vote. It was approved by the French Chamber of Deputies 535 to 75.

In his memoirs, Mr. Alfred Duff Cooper, who in September 1938 resigned his post as First Lord of the Admiralty in the British Cabinet over the policy of appeasement, recalled this public reaction to the Munich agreement upon Mr. Chamberlain's return to London.

> It was a wet evening but [Mr. Chamberlain] was received like a conquering hero and his journey from the aerodrome to Whitehall was a triumphal progress. At Downing Street friends and colleagues

were profuse in their congratulations. Even within the Cabinet no note of query or criticism was raised ...[64]

And when Mr. Cooper subsequently addressed the House of Commons to explain his own resignation from Chamberlain's Cabinet, he recalled that on that Friday evening he had been "caught up in the large crowd that were demonstrating their enthusiasm and were cheering, laughing and singing; and there is no greater feeling of loneliness than to be in a crowd of happy, cheerful people and to feel that there is no occasion in oneself for gaiety or for cheering". At that moment, Cooper also remarked that "the Prime Minister [was] more popular than he has ever been at any period"[65]

The Munich settlement produced the most dramatic swing in the balance of power since Hitler's assumption of the Chancellorship in 1933. Democratic Czechoslovakia represented an important military and industrial asset to the Western powers. Its loss to Hitler meant the reduction of Allied military capabilities by more than 30 modern, well-equipped divisions, positioned behind strong fortifications in the Sudeten region, and supported by a sizeable industrial establishment led by the famous Skoda works with its considerable military output and potential. What Britain and France lost, Hitler gained in terms of additional population, territory, and industrial capabilities. More importantly perhaps than even all this, the Czechoslovak crisis was probably the last realistic opportunity to involve the Russians in military opposition to the expansion of Nazi Germany and a clear signal to all the smaller European nations to fend for themselves as best they might.

A coalition including France, Britain, Czechoslovakia, and Russia in 1938 was almost certainly still too strong for Hitler to take on single-handedly. When the Western Powers, however, yielded to Hitler at Munich, Stalin began to give up on the West, and think seriously of a realignment, a realignment which eventually resulted in the Molotov-Ribbentrop Pact of 23 August 1939, opening the way for the Nazi attack on Poland.[66]

A new threshold had been reached in world politics. From now on, Russia would begin an abandonment of her anti-Nazi foreign policy. For whatever reasons, good and bad, no one seemed interested in her help. Hitler, though triumphant, was frustrated because his victory was a bloodless one. He was still spoiling for a fight and he would soon get it. As early as 24 October 1938, Nazi Foreign Minister Joachim von Ribbentrop told the Polish Ambassador in Berlin that Germany desired the return of Danzig to Germany and a corridor linking Pomerania and East Prussia. On 5 January 1939, Hitler himself renewed the Nazi demands on Poland in a conversation with Polish Foreign Minister Josef Beck.

But there was one more drama involving Czechoslovakia to be played out. After personally browbeating President Hacha, Hitler in March of 1939 sent in Nazi troops to occupy Bohemia and Moravia, while Slovakia, under a pro-Nazi government, declared its independence. The Munich agreement was dead. Prime Minister Chamberlain declared, with perhaps less than great credibility, that Allied guarantees to Czechoslovakia were not applicable here since there was no Nazi attack -- only a peaceful occupation by Nazi troops, though, of course, under the threat of force. For the first time in his term of office, Chamberlain was faced by a British public opinion seriously shaken in its faith about a policy of appeasement.[67]

The turn of Poland and the Second World War were rapidly approaching. On 25 March 1939, Hitler issued preliminary orders for the preparation of an attack on Poland. On 31 March 31, Britain and France issued a guarantee to Poland, offering her their unqualified support "in any action which clearly threatened Polish independence and which the Polish government accordingly considered it vital to resist with their national forces". On 28 April 1939, Hitler publicly repudiated the German-Polish Non-Aggression Pact on the ground that Germany was being subjected to a "hostile encirclement" in Europe. Apparently as late as 7 May, Russia inquired of Poland if the latter would permit the transit of Soviet troops on its territory in case she was attacked by Germany. Poland refused just as she had done on various previous occasions. On 3 May, the Soviets replaced Foreign Minister Maxim Litvinov with V. M. Molotov, a likely signal of their willingness to consider a critically new alignment in Europe. Hitler, too, was interested in securing his position in the east at the moment he might choose to devour Poland. A major new diplomatic deal was in the offing.

A number of other significant events occurred in the month of May. The French signed a military agreement with Poland on 19 May 1939, promising to launch an offensive against Germany with the main portion of their military forces on the fifteenth day following Poland's general mobilization -- in the event that the Nazis attacked Poland. (The failure to make good on this promise was subsequently rationalized by the French High Command on the grounds that the agreement was never officially ratified by the respective governments.)

On 22 May 1939, Germany and Italy concluded a military alliance, the so-called Pact of Steel. The next day, Hitler told his military leaders that he intended to attack and obliterate Poland with a view to obtaining for Germany necessary living space.

Hitler was blatantly self-contradictory in his statement to the Generals on how this Polish campaign would interface with Germany's relations with Britain and France. He said "the attack ... will only be successful if the West keeps out of it. If that is not possible it is better to fall upon the West and to finish off Poland at the same time".[68] Hitler did not say anything yet about the role Russia might have in all of this.

Beginning late in May and continuing well into the latter part of July there were still contacts between Britain and France on the one hand and the Soviets on the other, ostensibly directed toward finding some mutually acceptable formula for a defensive alliance against Nazi Germany. But the enthusiasm and trust on both sides seemed to be suspect at best.

When Britain and France agreed to discuss a political agreement with Russia, the latter demanded that a military mission be sent to Moscow by the Western Powers. On 27 July 1939, Britain and France agreed but sent relatively low-ranking military representatives, with no authority to enter into serious commitments, and, as if to emphasize the point, sent them on a leisurely voyage by ship through the North Sea, the Baltic, and the Gulf of Finland to Leningrad. The Nazi-Soviet Pact of 23 August 1939 was less than a month away.

On 22 August 1939, Hitler, greatly satisfied by the strategic easement offered him in the Soviet-Nazi Pact, addressed his generals at Obersalzburg. He said:[69]

> On the whole, there are only three great statesmen in the world: Stalin, myself, and Mussolini. Mussolini, the weakest, has not been able to break either the power of the crown or that of the church. Stalin and I are the only ones that see only the future. So I shall shake hands with Stalin within a few weeks on the common German-Russian border and undertake with him a new distribution of the world.

> ... History sees only in him a great state leader. What weak Western European civilization thinks about me, does not matter ... thus for the time being, I have sent to the east only my 'Death's Head Units', with the order to kill without pity or mercy all men, women and children of the Polish race and language. Only in such a way will we win the vital space that we need. Who still talks nowadays of the extermination of the Armenians?

... My pact with Poland was only meant to stall for a time. And besides, gentlemen, with Russia will happen just what I have practiced with Poland. After Stalin's death ... we shall crush the Soviet Union ... I saw our enemies at Munich ... They were miserable worms.

The occasion is favourable now as it has never been. I have only one fear and that is that Chamberlain or such another dirty swine comes to me with propositions or a change of mind. He will be thrown downstairs. And even if I must personally kick him in the belly before the eyes of all the photographers.

No, for this is too late. The invasion and extermination of Poland begins on Saturday morning. I will have a few companies in Polish uniform attack in Upper Silesia or in the Protectorate. Whether the world believes it doesn't mean a damn to me. The world believes only in success.

Be hard ... Be without mercy. The citizens of Western Europe must quiver in horror.

As the summer wore on, Nazi Germany continued to press its demands on Poland. On 23 August 1939, Hitler's pact with Stalin was publicly announced. What was not known was the secret bargain between the two dictators to divide the territory of Poland roughly in half, first by Nazi aggression from the West and then by Soviet aggression from the East.

There were also secret protocols about spheres of influence for each of the contracting powers. Hitler believed that this agreement gave him a free hand in Poland. When he was notified of the signing of the Pact by Stalin, he proclaimed exultantly that the way was now open for the soldiers.[70] It was also quite clear that Hitler did not contemplate parting with his booty for very long. He expected to recover the territories temporarily ceded to the Soviets by military means given appropriate future circumstances.

On 24 August 1939, President Roosevelt appealed to both Hitler and Polish President Ignacy Moscicki to resolve their conflict peacefully by direct negotiation or by arbitration. France urged the Poles *not* to resort to military action in the event Danzig declared itself part of Hitler's Reich. On the same day, however, Poland began calling up its military reserves. On 25 August 1939, Britain signed a 5-year mutual assistance treaty with Poland thus sending a seemingly unambiguous signal to the Nazis -- and to France -- that she would fight if Poland were invaded. On the same day, Mussolini informed Hitler that Italy was not yet ready to join Germany in a war with Britain and France because of her allegedly lagging military preparations. Mussolini said he needed more time. In response to these events, Hitler ordered a short postponement of the attack.

There was no question that with a little more patience on his part, a good deal was to be gained without firing a shot. On 26 August 1939, France urged the Poles to negotiate directly with Germany in order to avoid war. Britain suggested the Poles turn to the Pope to mediate the dispute, and subsequently also supported direct Polish-German negotiations. The wish to avoid war was still very strong in the west. But not so with the Fuehrer.

Hitler's state of mind may have been reflected in this recollection of the Swedish businessman, Birger Dahlerus, who visited Hitler, bringing with him last-minute British proposals intended to avert the Nazi attack on Poland on August 26.

> Suddenly he stopped in the middle of the room and stood there staring. His voice was blurred, and his behaviour that of a completely abnormal person. He spoke in staccato phrases: 'If there should be a war, then I shall build U-boats, U-boats, U-boats, U-boats.' His voice became more indistinct and finally one could not follow him at all. Then he pulled himself together, raised his voice as though addressing a large audience and shrieked: 'I shall build airplanes, build airplanes, airplanes, and I shall annihilate my enemies.' He seemed more like a phantom from a storybook than a real person. I stared at him in amazement and turned to see how Goering was reacting, but he did not turn a hair.[71]

Hitler postponed the date of his attack on Poland once, moving it from 26 August to 1 September, a matter of only six days. Having done so, however, he was unwilling to postpone it again even though the British, at the eleventh hour, had declared themselves willing to negotiate on his demands.

In the last days of August 1939 another Munich was still not entirely out of the question, and it was still possible for Hitler to exact substantial concessions from his latest victim -- Poland -- without going to war with anyone, least of all with Britain and France. The British were willing to pressure the Poles into direct negotiations with Hitler and into substantial concessions. The British Ambassador in Berlin, Sir Nevile Henderson, presented a note to Hitler on 28 August assuring him that Great Britain had already obtained Poland's consent for direct Polish-German negotiations.[72]

But on the evening of August 29 Hitler demanded of the British Ambassador that a Polish plenipotentiary arrive in Berlin the very next day, 30 August. This, especially in light of the past experiences of Austria, Czechoslovakia, and Lithuania, was interpreted as an ultimatum and declined in Warsaw as well as in London. In fact, Hitler communicated further specific demands upon the Poles to the British Ambassador on the night of August 30-31 when he knew that, short of instant capitulation, there was no time left in which to negotiate. His armies would cross the Polish frontier on 1 September.

The fact that Nazi Foreign Minister Joachim von Ribbentrop, who read the list of German demands to the British Ambassador (according to the latter so quickly that he was barely able to jot down a few of its main points) refused to transmit it to the Ambassador, strongly supports the suspicion that Hitler was not about to be cheated out of his war.[73] So does, of course, his oft-quoted remark on the eve of the attack expressing the hope that some *Schweinehund* would not make a last minute offer of mediation.[74]

This is how Hitler's ally, Italian Foreign Minister, and Mussolini's son-in-law, Galeazzo Ciano, assessed Nazi intentions in the final hours of August 1939:

> The [Nazi] decision to fight is implacable ... He [Ribbentrop] rejects any solution which might give satisfaction to Germany and avert the struggle. I am certain that even if the Germans were given more than they ask for they would attack just the same because they are possessed by the demon of destruction.[75]

Even Sir Nevile Henderson, not generally regarded as the most perceptive of diplomats, recalled that "... though Hitler was constantly talking of the hand which he had held out to England and complaining that England had rejected it, whenever definite advances were made to him, he always found some way of withdrawing and of refusing to meet us halfway. It is impossible to believe today that this was fortuitous".[76] The die was cast.[77]

NOTES

[1] General Sir Edmund Ironside, later Chief of British Imperial General Staff, recorded in his diary on 29 March 1938 his impressions of British military

preparedness at the time. "The paper on our rearmament ... is truly the most appalling reading. How we can have come to this state is beyond believing ... No foreign nation would believe it". See William R. Rock, *British Appeasement in the 1930's* (New York: W. W. Norton, 1977), p. 46. The shortcomings of British preparedness were even more appalling after the Nazis unleashed their Blitz on France. See also John T. Hendrix, "The Interwar Army and Mechanization: The American Approach," *The Journal of Strategic Studies*, Vol. 16, No. 1, March 1993, pp. 75-108. Note his conclusion: "Returning to the original question of why America entered the war against Germany so ill-prepared, it becomes clear that the US Army's doctrinal development had not kept pace with that of the Germans. Beyond a dearth of personnel, equipment and funds, the lack of an independent mechanized unit prevented American doctrine from naturally evolving separate cavalry and infantry missions into the combined arms approach embraced by the Panzer divisions. American industrial might would later produce tanks quickly and in great numbers, but the US Armored Force would not become proficient in the art of combined arms warfare overnight. Instead of perfecting the co-operation of artillery, tanks, and infantry, as the Germans did, the US Army wasted much of the 20-year peace trying to make the mechanized cavalry doctrine work. In disbanding the Mechanized Force of 1930, General MacArthur forced the Army to ignore what the most respected mechanized theoreticians had concluded after the Great War; tanks, artillery, and infantry had to be highly mobile and had to fight as one unit". (p. 95).

[2] See General Maxime Weygand, "How France is Defended", in *International Affairs*, Vol. XVIII, No. 4, July-August 1939, pp. 459-474, for a glimpse into official French misconceptions on the eve of the war. Note especially pp. 468, 470, and 474.

> [P. 468] My picture of the French Army would be incomplete if I did not say something of the spirit which animates it. Of what value are material considerations without a sound morale? The spirit of the serving soldier is excellent, no matter what may be his social background or political creed. ... I find it difficult adequately to describe the dignity and nobility of the spirit which animates all our cadres". [P. 470] "... I will now say a few words about the air force. Even though my main theme is the army, I cannot neglect it altogether". [P. 474] "... At an early state in 1914, operations on the Western front reached stalemate; from the battle of the Marne in 1914 onwards neither side made any real progress. This was accomplished with nothing but field fortifications, of earth, of wood, and of corrugated iron. What will happen in 19--? Armies face each other, even in peace-time, across fortified lines of steel and concrete. Though these fortified lines are not exactly the same, they are no doubt equally strong, and both are held by troops of equal fighting value, for I rate the German army very high. How can a rapid decision be reached on such a front? I believe we must broaden our strategic conceptions, and broaden them considerably".

3
Note Saul K. Padover, "France in Defeat: Causes and Consequences", *World Politics*, Vol. 2, No. 3, July 1950, pp. 305-377, with its extensive discussion of the great divisions in French political life and the "moral abdication" of a whole nation.

See also Hervé Schwedersky and John McJennett, "Democracy's Crisis in France", *Harper's Magazine,* Vol. 178, No. 2, May 1939, pp. 617-628. Very perceptively they observed:

"To America, France offers an extreme example of an inherent weakness in representative government to which we are also prey. For every French mistake, we can find an American counterpart", p. 628.

Obviously, these authors were not surprised by the events of 1940. But most observers in the West were.

"Admittedly, the 'easy-way' politicians are whipping boys -- as much victims of the system as they are exploiters of one of its few weaknesses", p. 618.

4
Note the view of Dean Acheson in a letter written in May of 1936 expounding the idea that Hitler's recent "initiative" was explained by, if not quite justified, by the wrongs perpetuated by the French on the Germans, especially in the Ruhr occupation of 1923. D. S. McLellan and D. C. Acheson (eds.), *Among Friends, Personal Letters of Dean Acheson* (New York: Dodd, Mead, 1980), pp. 27-28. Acheson, by 1939, in any case, strongly supported the President's foreign policy. See pp. 41-42.

5
Note Willson Woodside, "What Would Germany Fight With?" *Harper's Magazine*, Vol. 177, October 1938, pp. 426-437. This liberal expert briefly surveyed German ideas of a Blitzkrieg as expounded by Goering and others and sagely concluded: "All the experience of the Great War and of the Spanish and Chinese Wars cries out against this mad theory of the Blitzkrieg." (p. 426). He also argued that Germany had no raw materials adequate to the task of waging a European war, let alone a world war. He discounted the possibility that Germany could actually seize all the raw (and other) materials that she might need -- by Blitzkrieg. "Germany as we have shown, lacks adequate supplies of almost every kind to feed her guns and her people in a large-scale war". (p. 435).

See also his "Germany Would Lose", *Harper's Magazine*, Vol. 179, July 1939, pp. 113-125. In this article Mr. Woodside argued that in a war of attrition the totalitarian powers (i.e., Germany and Italy) would "fare very badly"; that the economic and psychological situation of Germany in 1939 was more like that of 1917 than of 1914; that the iron Germany would need was now *behind* the Maginot Line; and that the morale of the German population would be the Nazis' worst problem (p. 124). Woodside convinced himself that the one thing Hitler could not do was go to war (p. 125).

Cf. George F. Eliot, "If War Comes Tomorrow, The Strength and Strategy of European Powers", *The New Republic*, Vol. LXXXXIX, No. 1277, 24 May 1939, pp. 63-66. Major Eliot even believed that Poland "could fight a long, delaying war ... against Germany" although he conceded that she couldn't win it alone, p. 64.

See also Fritz Sternberg, "Germany and a Prolonged War", *The American Mercury*, Vol. XLVIII, No. 191, November 1939, pp. 296-303. Mr. Sternberg argued that all Britain and France had to worry about were a "war of nerves and political maneuvering" while Germany is overtaken by its economic weakness, p. 303.

See Louis Fischer, "America and Europe", *The Nation*, Vol. 149, No. 4, July 22, 1939, pp. 97-101. "If the fascist powers go to war they will be defeated. If they abstain from war they will enter a debilitating period of internal adjustment and unrest. Meanwhile economic difficulties are reducing their fighting strength, and, ominously, their ability to wait in uncertainty," p. 101.

[6]   Even Duff Cooper, who had earlier resigned over the appeasement policy from the Chamberlain Cabinet, as First Lord of the Admiralty, said in an August 1939 debate in the House of Commons: "If we can convince Herr Hitler that such an act [attack on Poland] will mean a European war I cannot believe he will commit it," *The Second World War: First Phase* (London: Jonathan Cape, 1939), p. 332. How British liberal culture overvalued Hitler's "rationality"!

[7]   *The New Republic*, Vol. LXXXXVII, No. 1253, 7 December 1939, pp. 113-114. The quotation appears on p. 114.

[8]   Neville Chamberlain, *In Search of Peace* (New York: G. P. Putnam's Sons, 1939), p. 243.

[9]   Quoted by Keith Feiling, *The Life of Neville Chamberlain* (London: Macmillan, 1947), p. 367.

Keith Middlemas in his *The Strategy of Appeasement: The British Government and Germany, 1937-1939* (Chicago: Quadrangle Books, 1972) observes that British ministers generally assumed that "even opposed nations had the same fundamental interest in peace, and proceeded to negotiate with them on that basis", p. 14. "War was regarded as an absolute evil". *Ibid.*

[10]   See Edward Tannenbaum, "The Reactionary Mentality of the Action Francaise", *The Historian*, Vol. XVII, No. 1, Autumn 1954, pp. 18-48. This author looks at the politics of the French Far Right not in terms of particular policy issues, but the underlying psychological foundation, to wit, a mentality which featured "clericalism, traditionalism, militarism, ethno-centrism, and hatred of democracy ... as an escape from a reality that has become intolerable, whether that reality involves personal, social, economic, or political, insecurity".

[11]   Heinz Pol, *Suicide of a Democracy* (New York: Reynel and Hitchcock, 1940), p. 266.

[12]   *Ibid*, pp. 268-269.

[13] Franklin Reid Gannon, *The British Press and Germany 1936-1939* (Oxford: Clarendon Press, 1971), pp. 290-291.

[14] *Harper's Magazine*, May 1939, Vol. 178, No. 2, pp. 580-587. Quotation appears on pp. 581 and 587.

[15] A fairly realistic and dispassionate article emphasizing the strength of British perception was published by Vera Brittain, "Will Young England Fight?", *The Atlantic Monthly*, Vol. 162, No. 5, November 1938, pp. 625-631. She argued that there would be less support for war against Hitler in the late 30s than there was in 1914 against the Kaiser (p. 631).

See Ian Colvin, *None So Blind, A British Diplomatic View of the Origins of World War II* (New York: Harcourt, Brace and World, 1965) who noted that propaganda in the 1930s had the greatest effect on those "most addicted to wishful thinking", p. 347. Apparently, 25 years later, Sir Horace Wilson, Chamberlain's ally in appeasement, evaluated Munich in these terms: "It was pretty clear Hitler had written off France, economically and militarily. You can add, of course, the decision of the USA. on non-involvement. The Dominions said no to war over Czechoslovakia. It was a perfectly English approach on the part of Mr. Chamberlain. He thought ... that if the situation was untidy, we should tidy it up ... and arrive at some conclusion", p. 285.

[16] See Benny Morris, *The Roots of Appeasement, The British Weekly Press and Nazi Germany during the 1930's* (London: Frank Cass, 1991), p. 179.

[17] *Ibid.*, p. 181. "Above all, for Britons in the Thirties war against Germany connoted the prospect of air attack and devastation", p. 180.

[18] *Ibid.*, pp. 3-4.

[19] *Ibid.*, p. 3.

[20] Franklin Reid Gannon, *op. cit.*, p. 301.

[21] *Ibid.*, p. 302.

[22] *Ibid.*, p. 295.

[23] *Ibid.*, p. 293.

[24] See R. J. Overy, "German Air Strength 1933 to 1939: A Note", *The Historical Journal*, Vol. 27, No. 2, June 1984, pp. 465-471. Overy discusses British knowledge in the 1930s of the extent of German air force rearmament and finds it generally accurate. The expansion was substantial and rapid but Overy says also that because of qualitative issues, "no realistic assessment of German air strength before 1939 can support the conclusion that Britain was ever 'at the mercy of a foreign power'." (p. 471).

See Keith Eubank, *The Origins of World War II* (New York: Thomas Y. Crowell, 1969) on Stanley Baldwin as forerunner of Neville Chamberlain in Britain. He "paid as little attention as possible to foreign affairs, preferring to postpone unpopular decisions on the chance that [problems] would solve themselves", pp. 74-75.

[25] William Manchester, *Last Lion: Winston Spencer Churchill Alone 1932-1940* (Boston: Little, Brown, 1988), p. 93.

See L. B. Namier, *Europe in Decay: A Study in Disintegration 1936-1940* (London: Macmillan, 1956), offers this vignette of Hitler gleaned from the recollection of his German diplomatic subordinates: "His ghastly lack of proper education, his imperfect mastery of the German language, especially of written German, and his complete disregard of logic were patent. No well-thought-out document ever came from his pen, merely vague directions", p. 231. Bluff and intimidation were two important Hitler techniques used with interlocutors and subordinates. Hitler lacked patience to read lengthy documents. "He would not do business in a committee, nor speak to more than two or three men at a time, unless he was addressing monologues to large gatherings. Government lost all collegiate character ... till no one knew his way through the maze of conflicting authorities and assignments", p. 232.

[26] Manchester, *op. cit.*, p. 86.

[27] German Foreign Office, *Documents on the Events Preceding the Outbreak of the War* (New York: German Library of Information, 1940), p. 49.

[28] See Alan Bullock, *Hitler: A Study in Tyranny* (New York: Harper, 1952), p. 314.

[29] See E. T. S. Dugdale (trans. and ed.), *My Battle* (Boston: Houghton Mifflin, 1933), p. 266.

[30] *Ibid.*, p. 270.

[31] German Foreign Office, *op. cit.*, p. 351.

[32] *Ibid.*, p. 236.

[33] *Ibid.*, p. 240.

[34] *Ibid.*, p. 257.

[35] *Ibid.*, p. 285.

[36] *Ibid.*, p. 325.

[37] *Ibid.*

[38] William E. Dodd, Jr., and Martha Dodd (eds.), *Ambassador Dodd's Diary, 1933-1938* (New York: Harcourt, Brace, 1941), p. 24.

[39] *Ibid.*, p. 31.

[40] André François-Poncet, *The Fateful Years, Memories of a French Ambassador in Berlin, 1931-1938* (New York: Harcourt, Brace, 1949), p. 286.

[41] *Ibid.*, p. 286.

[42] *Ibid.*, p. 291.

43 *Ibid.*, p. 292.

44 Keith Middlemas, *The Strategy of Appeasement, The British Government and Germany 1937-1939* (Chicago: Quadrangle Books, 1972), p. 275.

45 William L. Shirer, *The Rise and Fall of the Third Reich, A History of Nazi Germany* (New York: Simon & Schuster, 1960), pp. 307-308.

46 See the interesting and informative account by Yvon Lacaze in his *France and Munich, A Study of Decision-Making in International Affairs* (Boulder: East European Monographs, 1995) with much detailed information about specific defence measures, poorly designed, executed, and co-ordinated between France and Britain; great domestic disunity in France; lack of leadership and vision in the French government apparatus; and some corresponding advantages for Nazi Germany. All this was compounded by an overestimation of the alleged difficulties confronting Hitler (p. 357).

See Patrice Buffotot, "The French High Command and the Franco-Soviet Alliance 1933-1939", *The Journal of Strategic Studies*, Vol. 5, No. 4, December 1982, pp. 546-559. Note pp. 556-557. The author suggests that the French High Command's political distaste for Soviet Russia adversely affected France's foreign policy in Eastern Europe.

See Wesley W. Wark, "Baltic Myths and Submarine Bogeys: British Naval Intelligence and Nazi Germany 1993-1939", *The Journal of Strategic Studies*, Vol. 6, No. 1, March 1983, pp. 60-81. Note especially p. 78, conclusion on the substantial failures of British naval intelligence to anticipate conflict with Germany.

47 A. J. P. Taylor, *The Origins of the Second World War* (London: Hamish Hamilton, 1963). Taylor says that "Hitler was a sounding board for the German nation" and that "without the support and co-operation of the German people", he "would have counted for nothing". There is certainly a great deal of truth in this assertion, if not quite the whole truth since the "German people" is a collective concept, implying no exceptions. "He gave orders which Germany executed of a wickedness without parallel in civilized history", (p. 6). It is hard to disagree with this idea also, although "many Germans" would have been much better than completely generic "Germans". But when Taylor says that Hitler "aimed to make Germany the dominant power in Europe and maybe ... the world [but] other powers have pursued similar aims and still do ... In international affairs there was nothing wrong with Hitler except that he was a German", he exhibits the wonderful, modern propensity for obliterating all reasonable distinctions among actions, motives, means, ends, and ultimately all people and things. Illustratively, was British rule in India much the same thing as Hitler's rule in Russia (and his *Mein Kampf* programme for it, of course)? Is the record of American influence in Europe the same as Hitler's? Was Charles Manson a surgeon because he and his followers approached people with sharp objects? Like other liberal writers, Taylor underestimates the leverage of coercion.

[48] Among many sources, see Dante Germino and Stefano Passigli, *The Government and Politics of Contemporary Italy* (New York: Harper & Row, 1968), p. 41. "As has often been noted, terror of the scope and intensity employed in Nazi Germany or Stalinist Russia was unknown in Fascist Italy".

[49] See R. J. Overy, *War and Economy in the Third Reich* (Oxford: Clarendon Press, 1994). "For Hitler the object was not merely to make Germany capable of defending herself again ... or even to reverse the territorial clauses of Versailles, but to ... embark on a period of active expansion in Europe, and eventually the achievement of German world power status", p. 183. See also p. 188.

[50] Note the interesting article by Sean Greenwood, "Caligula's Horse' Revisited: Sir Thomas Inskip as Minister for the Coordination of Defence, 1936-1939", *The Journal of Strategic Studies*, Vol. 17, No. 2, June 1944, pp. 17-38, on how British democracy attempted to tailor defence needs to financial desiderata of a peaceful existence, instead of the other way around. Inskip's reputation was that of a "conciliator", (p. 19).

Note also Nicole Jordan, *The Popular Front and Central Europe: The Dilemma of French Impotence, 1918-1940* (Cambridge: Cambridge University Press, 1992). This account puts General Gamelin in the perspective of one little interested in halting Hitler and much more in minimizing France's costs and obligations, even if at the expense of Nazi hegemony in Europe.

[51] See Berenice A. Carroll, *Design for Total War: Arms and Economics in the Third Reich* (The Hague: Moulton, 1968), p. 184.

See also data presented in Walter P. Hall, *World Wars and Revolutions: The Course of Europe Since 1900* (New York: Appleton Century, 1943) and Pierre Cot, *Triumph of Treason* (Chicago: Ziff Davis, 1944).

[52] See P. M. H. Bell, *The Origins of the Second World War in Europe* (London: Longman, 1986) who says that the "rise of Germany was matched by the decline of France which at the beginning of 1933 still retained some strength but by the end of 1937 had fallen into weakness and passivity". This was in large measure caused by "internal problems -- social and political conflicts, unstable governments and a worsening economic situation", p. 221.

[53] See W. S. Woytinsky and E. S. Woytinsky, *World Commerce and Governments, Trends and Outlook* (New York: The Twentieth Century Fund, 1955), pp. 51-52, on Germany's foreign trade in the 1930s.

[54] See *European Historical Statistics 1750-1975*, pp. 528-601, for trade data on interwar Europe.

[55] See Robert Goralski, *World War II Almanac, 1931-1945* (New York: Bonanza Books, 1981), p. 29.

56 See the extremely perceptive, and in some respects, well-nigh prophetic article by Prof. H. N. Fieldhouse, "The Future of British Foreign Policy" in *International Affairs*, Vol. XVII, No. 3, May-June, 1938, pp. 408-417. Note especially pp. 411, 412, 415-416. Fieldhouse anticipated Britain's elimination from the ranks of great powers in the event of a European war. His views probably reflected those of many contemporaneous British "influentials".

57 Note Alexander J. Groth and Richard G. Randall, "Alliance Pathology: Institutional Lessons of the 1930s", *Political Science Quarterly*, Vol. 106, No. 1, Spring 1991, pp. 109-121.

See also R. A. C. Parker, "The First Capitulation, France and The Rhineland Crisis of 1936", *World Politics*, Vol. 8, No. 3, April 1956, pp. 355-373. He concludes that the "French tragedy ... notably in 1936 ... was the result not of a failure of vision, or logic or understanding but of absence of will-power, determination, and courage", p. 373. Of course, this was exactly what Hitler expected and he must be given due credit for his perspicacity.

58 See Piotr S. Wandycz, *The Twilight of French Eastern Alliances, 1926-1936 French-Czechoslovak-Polish Relations from Locarno to the Remilitarization of the Rhineland* (Princeton, NJ: Princeton University Press, 1988), pp. 477-478. "To be firm and resolute abroad, France had to be a different state from the declining, 'decadent' Third Republic. To adapt the alliances to the new post-Locarno realities, without emptying them of content, required a grandiose vision and élan, which were conspicuously absent, for Briandism was like a shadow without substance. Any bold vision naturally carries with it a risk ... France feared risks. Perhaps, in the final analysis, this was the main cause for the decline and fall of French eastern alliances", p. 478.

59 *Op. cit.,* p. 205.

60 See also Howard C. Payne, Raymond Callahan and Edward M. Bennett, *As the Storm Clouds Gathered: European Perceptions of American Foreign Policy in the 1930s* (Durham, NC: Moore Publishing Company, 1979) for the following apt observations: "While it is true that FDR and Secretary of State Cordell Hull were lacking in the qualities of firm leadership in the face of what FDR especially saw as real threats emanating from Germany and Japan, it must be admitted that timid American efforts at co-operation were not enthusiastically greeted by French and British leaders. They demanded firmer commitments. The words of Maxim Litvinov provide an accurate assessment of the roles played by these men: 'In the great transatlantic republic isolationism had made such great headway that one can hardly reckon on its eventual co-operation, particularly if in Europe itself there is not formed beforehand a firmly welded group opposing aggression with an appreciable chance of success'. There was no such co-operation in Europe. Instead many eyes were turned westward searching for a fair wind from the United States which would blow away the

gathering storm clouds, and though the wind finally came it was too late to prevent the clouds from first raining a devastating destruction over all of Europe for six long years", p. 167. In a sense, everyone was looking toward everyone else.

[61] For another illusion, see George Slocomb, "The Paradox of France", *The Atlantic Monthly*, Vol. 162, No. 2, August 1938, pp. 191-195. Said Solcomb: "It may be that in this knowledge of France's intention to go to war in certain circumstances lies her only strong card. Hitherto Hitler's aims have been achieved without fighting. The conviction that war with France would inevitably result from certain provocations may prove the ultimate deterrent in Germany's case. The leaders of the Reichswehr are familiar with France's fighting record, and have a healthy respect for it. The leaders of the French Army know that France will mobilize to the last man to defend her territory. And the leaders of the rival political parties in Parliament know that, whatever the feuds which now divide them, they will clasp hands and sing the 'Marseillaise' bareheaded in the Chamber of Deputies at the outbreak of war, as they or their predecessors did on that historic day in August 1914", p. 195.

[62] Political scientist Carl J. Friedrich had written in September of 1938, within a few days of Munich, that President Beneš of Czechoslovakia "will leave no question in anyone's mind that the Czechs are going to fight any attack upon them, even against overwhelming odds. That, no doubt is the best guarantee of peace. It forestalls bluffing". See his "Edouard Beneš", *The Atlantic Monthly*, Vol. 162, No. 3, September 1938, pp. 357-365. But even Beneš could not overcome his abandonment by the great democracies at Munich.

See John M. Haight, Jr., "France, the United States, and the Munich Crisis", *The Journal of Modern History*, Vol. XXXII, No. 4, December 1960, pp. 340-358. He notes that the "failure of Roosevelt's government to commit itself contributed towards Bonnet's acceptance [at Munich] of peace at any price. It also helped to weaken the spirit of resistance in France. Even when Roosevelt attempted to throw his weight behind Daladier's resistance policy, the President's messages were couched in such cautious terms that they were misread. The impact of American foreign policy upon France was therefore the opposite of what the majority of Americans and their leaders wished. Ironically the position of the United States was seen by many Frenchmen as one more justification for a peace that meant the 'sell-out' of Czechoslovakia", p. 358. Haight also makes this observation which gets to the root of much of the democracies' failure: "Apparently the premier [Edouard Daladier] believed it best to go along with Bonnet and his majority until France became strong enough to resist any further expansion of Hitler's Reich" (*ibid.*). Was there anything really happening in France, with its ossified military establishment, and its great political divisions, which promised greater strength anytime soon?!

[63] See also Barton Whaley, "Covert Rearmament in Germany 1919-1939: Deception and Misperception", *The Journal of Strategic Studies*, Vol. 5, No. 1, March 1982, pp.

3-39.   Note how despite all the technological gadgetry, Allied intelligence demonstrated a flip-flop tendency, and shifting focus from the alleged difficulties Hitler faced at home, it now succumbed to panic over German capabilities in 1938.

[64] Alfred Duff Cooper, *The Second World War, First Phase* (London: Jonathan Cape, 1939), p. 15.

[65] *Ibid.*, pp. 17, 18.

[66] See Georges Bonnet, *De Munich A La Guerre, Défense de la Paix* (Paris: Plon, 1967) for the argument that the Munich Agreement of 1938 provided Great Britain with one additional year for the build-up of its air forces, and that without it, the RAF victory over Germany in 1940 in the Battle of Britain would not have been possible. (p. 555).   M. Bonnet maintained a highly selective bookkeeping system in international affairs. He did not delve into the question of how much Germany gained during that year.

[67] See Eugene O. Smith, *The Dark Summer, An Intimate History of the Events That Led to World War II* (London: Macmillan, 1987) who recalls that Italian Foreign Minister Ciano called Hitler "unfaithful and treacherous" after the Nazi occupation of Czechoslovakia in 1939, while King Victor Emmanuel saw the Germans possessed by "insolence and duplicity"; they "were rascals", he said, pp. 135-136.

[68] William Shirer, *op. cit.*, p. 485.

[69] Text cited in R. Goralski, *op. cit.*, p. 87.

[70] See Gerhard Weinberg, "The German Generals and the Outbreak of War 1938-1939", in Adrian Preston (ed.), *General Staff and Diplomacy Before the Second World War* (London: Croom Helm, 1978). Hitler's statements to the Generals on 22 August 1939 not to allow a repetition of 1938 and his fear of some Schweinehund á la Chamberlain made it amply clear to his military that Hitler desired war, p. 37. They generally liked the idea of destroying Poland, if it could be done "cheaply", pp. 36-37.

[71] William L. Shirer, *op. cit.*, p. 571.

[72] *Ibid.*, p. 575.

[73] See Christopher Thorne, *The Approach of War, 1938-1939* (New York: St.Martin's Press, 1967) on "last-minute" British proposals to Germany (28 August 1939), which even included an offer of economic assistance to the Third Reich and promises of British friendship, p. 190. Note Chamberlain's position after the Nazi attack had begun (pp. 200-201). He was still prepared to "forget and forgive" and to start new negotiations as if Hitler's aggression had not occurred.

[74] See Walter Anger, *Das Dritte Reich in Dokumenten* (Frankfort: Verlagsanstalt, 1957), p. 107. Cf. Shirer, *op. cit.*, p. 531. Hitler made this remark in his address to the generals on 22 August 1939. Of course, this was not the only statement by Hitler indicating that war against Poland -- as opposed to, say "an advantageous settlement" -

- is what he really wanted. Note his earlier remarks to the generals of 23 May 1939 cited by Shirer, pp. 484-87. In this instance, he actually ended up by saying that the "aim will always be to force England to her knees" (p. 487).

[75]   Note Gerhard L. Weinberg, "A Proposed Compromise over Danzig in 1939?", *Journal of Central European Affairs*, Vol. XIV, No. 4 (January 1955), p. 338, and generally, pp. 334-338. See also H. Gibson (ed.), *The Ciano Diaries, 1939-1943* (Garden City, NY: Garden City Publishing Company, 1946), pp. 118-120, 130-131, and 136; and *Ciano's Diplomatic Papers* (London: Odhaus Press, 1948), pp. 297-304. Note pp. 306-309 on how much France still hoped to "make a deal" with the Nazis even after they had marched into Poland.

[76]   *Failure of a Mission, Berlin 1937-1939* (New York: G. P. Putnam's Sons, 1940), p. 110. "As I have said earlier, I am ready to believe that Hitler started by working sincerely for Germany. Later, he began to confound Germany with himself; and at the end Adolf Hitler was, I fancy, the sole consideration" (p. 56).

[77]   On this point, see Donald Cameron Watt, *How War Came, The Immediate Origins of the Second World War, 1938-1939* (London: Heinemann, 1989). "Britain entered the war in 1939, barely equipped for survival and in no position to help her allies; but in certain crucial respects she had the edge.   The combination of Spitfire and Hurricane fighters, radar and ground-to-air communication, not in place in 1938 and barely in place in 1940, enabled her to survive the onslaught of the Luftwaffe" (p. 621). Watt also noted that when Hitler realized that war with Poland would also mean war with Britain, he did not draw back. He postponed but did not stop his attack. "The only people who could have stopped [Hitler in 1939] permanently were those least conditioned to do so, his Generals, and their soldiers, if they had been ready to [act] by a *coup d'etat*, or an assassin capable of penetrating into the Reich's Chancellery", p. 624. Some of the discussion is based on the author's earlier "Bueno de Mesquita, Hitler, and Rationality in Statecraft", *The Political Science Reviewer*, Vol. XX, Spring 1991, pp. 286-311.

4 DEMOCRACIES IN DEFEAT: HITLER ASCENDANT, 1939-1941

The Nazi invasion of Poland on 1 September 1939 ushered in a two-year period of calamitous defeat for world democracies. Indeed, if it were not for the somewhat irrational, although heroic, resolve of Winston Churchill, and the clearly irrational mistakes of another man -- Adolf Hitler -- the Second World War would have ended in a spectacular and early Nazi victory. That victory would have occurred possibly sometime in 1940; certainly no later than 1942. In the practical world of waging a war, totalitarian Nazi Germany quickly proved itself overwhelmingly superior to its democratic opponents.

Despite all the mistakes and complacency of the democratic powers during the 1930s, Hitler did present two of them -- Britain and France -- with a small "window of opportunity" in September 1939. His attack on Poland denuded Nazi forces available for the defence of the Reich in the West.[1] Virtually all first-class units of the German army and air force were turned against Poland.[2]

Neville Chamberlain was probably wrong about many things in his life, but his judgment improved somewhat when he declared in the House of Commons on the afternoon of 1 September 1939 (the day Poland was attacked) that "the responsibility for this terrible catastrophe lies on the shoulders of one man, the German Chancellor, who has not hesitated to plunge the world into misery in order to serve his own senseless ambition".[3]

Of course, Chamberlain did not recall his own part in facilitating Hitler's truly senseless ambitions, nor did he even then declare, or ask the House to support him and his Cabinet in a declaration of war. Instead, he issued one more "warning" to Hitler and instructed the British Ambassador in Warsaw, Leon Noel, to approach the Polish Foreign Minister, Colonel Joseph Beck, about the possibility of another international conference to "resolve" Polish-German differences. Beck was surprised and told the British Ambassador that the time had come not for another conference (á la Munich?) but for the fulfilment of Franco-British pledges of military assistance to

Poland. Ambassador Noel left "sheepishly". The men of Munich were not yet ready to fight.[4]

Although the Nazi blitz was just that, an operation of only about one month's duration, the Poles put up a vigorous fight and they simultaneously created an opportunity for the French and the British armed forces to strike at the Germans in the West.[5]   Indeed, the Poles hoped and believed that their Great Power Democratic Allies would help them, partly, at least, on the basis of the military agreements concluded among Poland, France and Britain, and partly because common sense and human decency might well have advised this kind of action.

The French army alone possessed sufficient superiority along the German border in September 1939, to enable it to invade the Nazi homeland. If it had done so, the Germans might have been forced to divide their forces between East and West, possibly enabling the Poles to resist longer and resist more effectively. Stalin might have hesitated to invade Poland from the east, as he did on 17 September 1939.   There might have been political consequences inside Germany among high-ranking officers hostile to Hitler, analogous to what might have happened in 1938 at the time of the Czechoslovak crisis. In any case, it is virtually certain that a rapid advance by the French army into Germany's industrial heartland, located fairly close to the Franco-German border, would have gravely upset the possibilities of further Nazi operations. Whatever the ultimate results, it would have inflicted a tremendous psychological blow on the Nazis. They would have begun the war not with a lightning victory but instead with a huge defeat on their own soil.

Given the opportunity, however, the Western Allies succumbed to well-nigh unbelievable timidity and inertia.[6]   The French Army, at the time said to be the largest in Europe outside the USSR, remained in the Maginot Line positions.   Only a few light patrols were sent out into the Reich, and these, having met with hardly any resistance from the Germans, hastily withdrew to their own lines.   The French military leadership was spending most of its time explaining and justifying to its political superiors, and perhaps to itself, why it was not really possible -- yet -- to undertake any significant, offensive operations against the Germans.   The air forces of the two democracies likewise refrained from launching any major attacks on German positions and installations during this period.   There were a few air raids over Germany, some dropping pathetic propaganda leaflets, and some carrying out reconnaissance flights, but apart from a single, largely ineffectual, raid on naval installations in Wilhelmshaven, certainly no more.   The British and

French navies did not venture to attack the Germans in the Baltic Sea during Nazi operations against the Polish garrisons of Gdynia and the Hel peninsula. The two Western Powers were content to let Poland die alone, militarily abandoned.

One needs to remember, of course, that the British-Polish Agreement of Mutual Assistance of 25 August 1939, provided in its Article 1 that:

> Should one of the Contracting Parties become engaged in hostilities
> with a European Power in consequence of aggression by the latter
> against that Contracting Party, the other Contracting Party will at
> once give the Contracting Party engaged in hostilities all the support
> and assistance in its power.

The discrepancy between promise and performance was simply enormous, especially because the promise of help was reiterated in the Agreement's Article 5 which spoke of "mutual support and assistance immediately on the outbreak of hostilities"[7].

The Nazi victory over Poland featured some radically new aspects of warfare: tank units and mobile troops operating in large and independent formations, closely supported by the air force, launching rapid penetrating movements against a largely stationary enemy, with infantry following to mop up remaining pockets of resistance. Nazi dive-bombers and tanks wrought havoc with old-fashioned Polish infantry and cavalry. This was a very different style of warfare from the positional conflict of the First World War. Nazi air power -- some denial notwithstanding -- destroyed most of the Polish air force on the ground in the first few hours of the war. German bombing and strafing of the Polish transportation system and population centres spread terror behind the front lines, sowed panic among civilians, and impeded military movements by the Polish defenders. The issue was never in doubt, and on 5 October Adolf Hitler reviewed a parade of his victorious and highly capable troops in Warsaw.

The German military lost about 14,000 personnel killed and missing in Poland. This may not have been an exorbitant price to pay, from the Nazi perspective, in defeating a nation of about 35 million people in only about a month's time. But given the lesser size, equipment, and technological sophistication of the Polish armed forces as compared with those of France, Britain, Belgium, and Holland, the Polish performance against the Nazis was indeed very impressive[8].

A brief hiatus in the war on land followed Poland's defeat. The Nazis regrouped and prepared. On 9 April 1940, seven months after the beginning of the war, Hitler launched his attack on Denmark and Norway. Denmark had a land border with Germany, was a small country without a sizable military establishment, and its occupation was not a great challenge, but the German forces needed to get across open seas in order to strike at Norway. Moreover, they would need to cross the sea often in order to supply and to replenish their forces. This operation was clearly a major challenge to Britain's Royal Navy.

In the upshot, the British proved unable to stop the Nazis. By 3 May 1940, i.e., within about three weeks of the commencement of the operation, Nazi control over Norway was virtually complete (with a small Allied garrison still holding out at the northern port of Narvik and eventually evacuated on 9 June.) Germany lost 3 of its 8 cruisers and 10 of its 20 destroyers. These were significant losses for a still-small German navy, but the losses suffered by the Nazi army and air force were relatively quite light, and Hitler's objectives were attained rather fully and quickly. With respect to losses, it should be noted that German casualties in Norway included 1,317 killed and 1,604 wounded, with 2,375 missing or lost at sea. Allied losses were much higher with 4,400 British killed, and also 1,335 Norwegians and 350 French and Polish dead. All of this meant that the Allies not only failed to stop the Nazis but suffered almost 70 per cent higher fatalities in failing. At sea, the Nazis succeeded in sinking one British aircraft carrier, *Glorious*, one cruiser, seven British destroyers, and one French and one Polish destroyer. Admittedly, the British, with their much larger navy, could afford their losses more easily than the Germans. Some observers saw this balance of losses as crippling Germany's ability to invade Britain in the Fall of 1940,[9] but, more accurately, it was just one element in a larger picture.

While the German operation in Norway could be described with all sorts of favourable adjectives, adverbs, and nouns -- including brilliant, audacious, demonstrating ingenuity and well-nigh instant responsiveness to opportunity and circumstance, and certainly it was flexibly and skilfully carried out, the same could not be said of the responses of the democracies.

As Professor Olav Riste, Director of the Norwegian Institute for Defence Studies, relates the matter in a recent account:

> The surprise achieved by the Germans was due to three factors:
> first, the lack of real intelligence clues to the German operational
> plans and preparations [here credit needs to be given to Nazi ability
> to maintain secrecy, of course]. Second, the complete absence in

Norway of anything that could properly be called organs for the collection and analysis of military-political intelligence [here obviously we have an astonishing failure of foresight and watchfulness, indeed "responsiveness", on the part of a democracy, located a few hundred miles from the major aggressor in the second year of a world war]. Third, the inability of decision-makers to free themselves from the established perception that a major German assault on Norway was rendered unthinkable by the superiority of British naval power in the area and any small-scale attacks(!) would only be mounted in retaliation against major British violations of Norwegian neutrality. This perception, led to a concentration of attention by Norway on the actions and intentions of the Western Allies, and excluded consideration of the possibility that a German assault might occur independently of any Allied move. [Whatever happened to that wonderful, stimulating free market of ideas among the Norwegians? Obviously, it let a lot of people down ...]

As for Britain, Professor Riste notes that:

A combination of flawed intelligence and strategic prejudice also explains why the British were taken by surprise. Convinced, like the Norwegians, that a major German assault on Norway was impossible in the face of British naval superiority, they were predisposed to interpret incoming reports of large-scale moves of German warships as indicating a break-out into the Atlantic. The success of the German invasion was thus due to a double surprise: the strategic surprise of launching an operation which went contrary to the rules of naval warfare, and tactical surprise in the actual execution of the assault.[10]

To summarize Professor Riste's account, the democracies were fooled not just in one way but in at least a few ways.

After months of virtually no activity by either side, Hitler turned on France. On 10 May 1940 the Nazis launched their blitz westward smashing through Holland, Belgium, and Luxembourg (all of these states hoped that Hitler might respect their neutrality and their wish to avoid war), as well as France. The French and British forces confronting the Nazis were more than a match for the Germans in sheer numbers (especially if augmented by the armies of the three Benelux nations). But, once attacked, they all proved hopelessly incompetent in the face of the Nazi assaults.

With all the information one could possibly want available to the French and British military establishments on the methods of Nazi victory in Poland, no real learning took place between September 1939 and May 1940. In all respects, the Allies responded to the Nazi attack very badly. Little, if anything, was foreseen or anticipated.[11] At virtually all levels of military effort, involving intelligence, planning, co-ordination of allied activities, communications, transportation, adaptation to enemy initiatives, to name some, the Allied performance was a monumental failure.

Some recent authors have set out the reasons why the French -- and the British -- simply refused to believe that what happened in Poland would have direct relevance for them as well:

> The Allies studied that victory and many analysts and writers concluded that what happened in Poland could not happen in the west. After all, the Germans had surrounded Poland on three sides, and the Poles had depended on cavalry rather than tanks. Furthermore, the Allies knew that the Polish border was only thinly defended, and that the Poles had had no heavy border fortifications. Surely the West was better prepared, with the Maginot Line covering the entire frontier with Germany.[12]

On the other hand, the mentality of thinking oneself seriously inferior to the enemy prevailed with respect to any possible offensive operations. These were always out of the question because

> even though the Germans did not have a vastly superior air force, they had no more tanks than the Allied armies and most certainly had no field army greatly superior to that of the Allies ... both France and Great Britain were convinced that they did. Worse still, Germany's Axis partner, Italy, also had a significant military force which always remained in the back of the minds of Allied planners. The Allies felt their armies needed months or even years to prepare to fight their powerful adversaries, their air forces needed possibly the same amount of time, while [only] their navies were ready to do their jobs.[13]

Compounding Allied problems of co-ordination, communication, equipment, morale, training, leadership, and strategic-tactical understanding of the challenges confronting them, was the striking failure of intelligence which occurred despite the fact that the Belgian military captured Nazi Major Helmut

Reinberger with a briefcase full of Nazi plans in early January. The Major's plane crashed in Belgian territory, near the town of Mechelen; he carried with him a briefcase with German plans for the attack in the West (Case Yellow). The Belgians turned it over to the Allies who could not believe their eyes and suspected a "plant".

Although Hitler subsequently altered the plan, with the "Manstein Variant", neither the Belgians nor Dutch neutrality would be respected on 10 May 1940. Critically, however, the Mechelen incident failed to induce either the Belgian or the Dutch to co-ordinate their defence efforts more closely with the French and the British, or, indeed, each other.

> The Allies ignored many warnings of impending invasion including copies of the German plans for an operation through the Ardennes. In addition, reconnaissance and intelligence agents warned them of the German armoured build-up opposite southern Belgium. However, since they were also cognizant of the Schlieffen Plan, they refused to consider the possibility that the Germans might change their schemes, even after the Mechelen incident. They thought, instead, that the Manstein plan might be a trick. Furthermore, the Dutch military attaché to Berlin was told by a member of German military intelligence each time the code word "Danzig" was to be given. The attack was cancelled so many times that the Dutch ended up ignoring the warning when the operation actually took place Evidently, the Allies did not suffer from a lack of intelligence information but rather from an inability to evaluate and use it properly.[14]

The military capabilities of democratic France were tragically inadequate in the face of Nazi aggression. The failures of the French armed forces from top to bottom -- with a few individual and unit exceptions -- were so overwhelming in so many different aspects of military performance that the Battle of France turned into a rout within the first few days of the great German offensive. (France surrendered on 24 June, six weeks after the Nazi attack.) Surprise, confusion, timidity, indecision, and occasionally even panic and dereliction of duty were all variously descriptive of the French response to Hitler's attack in the west.

As Captain B. H. Liddell Hart wrote in his Introduction to Colonel Goutard's *Battle of France, 1940*:

The Germans managed to form and equip more divisions than the French did, but had no advantage in numbers over the total array of opposing divisions in the West ... The French had as many tanks, and more powerful tanks, but the greater part of them were scattered in packets instead of being concentrated for a powerful punch. The French generals still clung to the 1918 idea that tanks were the servants of infantry, while Hitler listened to Guderian, the leader of the new school ... Similarly, Hitler had gone all out for air power. Here he did have a big superiority in numbers, approaching 3 to 1 ... the French military chiefs had tended to underrate the value of air power until it was too late to remedy their prolonged neglect of the air arm ...

These errors in technical vision and organization made it difficult for the French to recover when thrown off balance by the strategic surprise which was the immediate cause of their defeat on the battlefield ...

... the pace of Panzer warfare paralysed the French staff whose minds were still moving at 1918 tempo. The orders they issued might have been effective but for being, repeatedly, twenty-four hours late for the situation they were intended to meet ...

The defeat of France started from the failure of military doctrine to keep pace with changing conditions.[15]

Describing the organization of France's top military command, Goutard tells us that at his headquarters, a 100 miles from the front, General Gamelin, "dwelt in an atmosphere very akin to a convent" with, amazingly, no radio communications with his armies facing the enemy. "He could neither receive direct information from the front nor listen to his army's signals nor get into direct contact with them".[16] According to some military wits, the General operated in a "submarine without a periscope". This was in marked contrast to Nazi practices where all units, especiallypanzers, were co-ordinated by radio.

In addition, the Commander-in-Chief compounded the problems of military management by certain characteristically democratic and liberal propensities. He was eager not to infringe upon the autonomy of his front-line commanders, and he was also eager to delegate his powers to various subordinates. He also liked to give his fellow generals "suggestions" rather than give them "orders". Confusion and irresponsibility flourished.[17]

When French troops, often including officers, abandoned their positions at the front without orders to withdraw, or without physical cause from enemy action, i.e., in consequence of sheer panic, no one thought of organizing on-the-spot court martials.[18] No doubt if anyone had, this would have been regarded as very undemocratic. Some might have even said that it contradicted the very ideals for which the Allies were fighting. In any event, desertions went largely unpunished. Official French policy of not defending large towns of over 20,000 population in order to limit economic, cultural, physical, and human losses, while in one sense humane and understandable, played into the hands of the Nazi aggressors. There were no Leningrads or Stalingrads in France in the summer of 1940. No Smolensks or Sevastopols. The race of Nazi panzers across the French countryside was made very much easier than it might have been.

With respect to the British, as Field Marshal Montgomery observed some years after the war:

> In September 1939 the British army was totally unfit to fight a first-class war on the continent of Europe ... In the years preceding the war, no large scale exercises of troops had been held in England for some time. Indeed the regular army was [even] unfit to take part in a realistic exercise.[19]

According to Ronald Atkin: "[Britain's] artillery had little more than half the range of the German guns; it was without any but the lightest armour, and pre-war training had to be undertaken with flags and dummies instead of batteries and tanks".[20]

Sometimes the portents of important things to come are reflected in relatively minor episodes. British General Sir Alan Brooke visited France in November 1939 and attended a parade of French troops marking the anniversary of the victorious armistice of 1918. He later recalled that:

> Seldom have I seen anything more slovenly and badly turned out. Men unshaven, horses ungroomed, clothes and saddlery that did not fit, vehicles dirty and complete lack of pride in themselves and their units. What shook me most, however, was the look in the men's faces, disgruntled and insubordinate looks, and, although ordered to give "Eyes left", hardly a man bothered to do so.[21]

While British morale and discipline may have been somewhat better, overall preparedness for a major conflict was deplorable. (The disparity in pay between officers and soldiers was much greater in the French army than in the British.) While preparedness lagged, the higher ranks of the French officer-corps lived exceedingly well.

Then General, later Field Marshal, Sir Alan Brooke, observed that French officers who took him to a meal shortly after his arrival in France treated him to a "champagne lunch consisting of oysters, lobsters, chicken, pheasant, cheese and fruits, coffee, liqueurs, etc. We sat down at 1 p.m. and got up about 3 p.m.".[22] (In Hitler's army, German soldiers and officers received the same food rations on combat duty.)

If "democracy" confers any practical advantages on human collectivities -- whether in processing information, co-ordinating, or energizing social action, or just about anything else -- those advantages were not much in evidence in the Allied military experience in France.[23] The sheer rapidity of France's defeat at the hands of the militarily innovative Nazis was a shock to Western public opinion. It was anything but expected.

In June of 1939, French writer and intellectual Andre Maurois had written in an American publication that France was "far more united than a year ago", that Franco-British unity was unbreakable, and that the two allies were both highly confident and strong.[24] Writing in *Current History* in November 1938, with Nazi conquest of Poland already accomplished, American journalist and scholar, Robert Strausz-Hupé, heaped praise on the French military: "General Maurice Gamelin, the Supreme Commander of all French armed forces, is a man who had the advantage of having been proved right". "Brilliant" and "prudent" were the adjectives bestowed by Strausz-Hupé on Gamelin. He concluded that "France does know that her army knows its job, husbands its strength, and can rely on the traditional valour of the French citizen-soldier".[25]

In January 1940, *The New Republic* published a commentary by a Paris correspondent, Genevieve Tabouis, which predicted Hitler's early and easy downfall in the war, even saying that Hitler will not attack anyone but sometime soon abdicate and give way to a government composed of soldiers and socialists".[26] In March of 1940, Mr. Fritz Sternberg was still insisting to his American readers that "today France would be in a fair position to continue the war with good chances for victory even after a successful German attack [broke] the Maginot Line".[27]

A point of great interest with respect to the German assault on France, especially in terms of any comparison between dictatorships and democracies, was that Hitler, unlike Chamberlain, Daladier and Reynaud, was able to bypass the bureaucratic chain of command in *his* military establishment. Hitler opted for a panzer attack across the allegedly impassable Ardennes, as originally devised by the then relatively junior General, Erich von Manstein, against the preferences of his nominally top military advisers.[28] The surprise attack proved brilliantly successful. In contrast, the French and British political leaders were far more deferential to their senior military advisers.

A factor of considerable importance among the liberal democracies was the relatively unwieldy character of their bureaucracies, military and civilian. Partly because of their legally safeguarded civil service status, and more importantly still because of the political vulnerability of democratic office holders, the bureaucrats could be, and often were, powerful nay-sayers in these regimes. Senior bureaucrats saw themselves as important decision-makers; they expected deference to their professional opinions from elected officials. They were the people with the technical expertise and experience. At the very least, they expected to be consulted and listened to. Often they would expect even more, because they had convinced themselves that their own specialized knowledge and years-on-the-job made them the best judges of what to do and how to do it. On the other hand, democratically-elected politicians were generally mindful of their own vulnerabilities. If one acted in accord with the advice of the bureaucrats, hopefully even a consensus of the relevant bureaucrats, one was "covered". If things went wrong, one would be better protected from any possible reproaches and recriminations.

"Playing within the channels" made a politician less vulnerable to hostile Parliamentary or press inquiries, or attack by one's colleagues; one was less likely to be accused of arbitrary, high-handed, and possibly even unconstitutional or at least incompetent conduct. It minimized the risks. It was also consonant with a kind of widely accepted culture of political-bureaucratic relations. What political executive in Britain or the United States would ever write or say to a senior bureaucrat: "I don't care what you think or why you think it. Just do what I tell you!"?

Hitler and Stalin could speak even more brutally to their subordinates and often did, but in the democracies this was not a practical option. Admittedly, all this made for more humane, gentlemanly, and kind personal relationships among politicians and bureaucrats. But it also made Western decision-making systems -- their political bureaucratic analogues -- playgrounds for the risk-adverse.

Career bureaucrats were always far more likely to explain why some course of action was too dangerous and impractical than to urge their political superiors to experiment in uncharted waters. Generally speaking, a safely collected pension was preferable to a blaze of glory, especially risky glory. And, of course, given the legal, cultural, and practical relationships among them, the bureaucrats were hardly in awe of their political superiors, coming and going with successive elections. They hardly feared the politicians. This often encouraged the substitution of one's own policy preferences for those of political leaders, especially in ill-defined situations. If one had to choose between the attitudes of awe and contempt, the latter would no doubt be more common among the top bureaucrats of democracies.

The great British military analyst Colonel Albert Seaton described the difference between the Nazi and Allied armies in the Battle of France as follows:

> ... the victory was due principally to the superiority of the *Luftwaffe* and then to the imaginative use of the new panzer arm ...

> ... the fact remained that much of the German Army equipment in 1940 was newer and better than that held by the western forces, and that its discipline and training, inadequate though it might have been by Prussian standards, was still better than that to be found at that time in the French and British Armies.

> ... The command on the field, particularly at the operative level, was infinitely better than that shown by the French and British senior commanders. The quality of the German tanks in armour and firepower was admittedly inferior to many of those in the Anglo-French armies, but this was more than compensated for by superior mobility, better optical, radio and fire control equipment and a high command that was determined to use armour *en masse* as an operative main arm. It was, in many respects, a victory of ideas, Lutz's, Guderian's -- even Hitler's.[29]

Apart from some fine performances by individual soldiers and commanders, there were no bright spots in the Allied disaster. The failure was general, quick, and thorough. Not only did the Nazis manage to defeat the allegedly greatest continental power in Europe in a month's time, but they did it all at a very low overall cost to themselves. The German armed forces, victorious in June 1940 over France, were hardly exhausted by their brilliant achievement. If anything, they had increased their capabilities by this experience, and the value of the experience easily outweighed their relatively modest losses in personnel and equipment.

Total German casualties in the Battle of France consisted of some 27,000 dead and 18,000 missing with about 111,000 wounded. The French, in a losing cause, suffered some 90,000 deaths and over 200,000 wounded, with 1.9 million soldiers going into Nazi captivity. Total British losses were 68,000; Belgian losses were 23,000; and Dutch casualties were about 10,000.[30]

Arguably, the authoritarian Polish regime of Marshal Pilsudski's heirs in 1939 had shown greater tenacity against Hitler's aggression than the larger, more advanced and richer democracies of the West in 1940. Nazi conquest in Poland gave Hitler 72,000 square miles of territory at a cost of some 14,000 soldiers killed and missing in action. From beginning to end of this operation, it took 35 days (1 September 1939 to 5 October 1939). Nazi conquest in the West, against Holland, Belgium, Luxembourg, and France, and also Britian, brought Hitler the capitulation of forces defending 239,000 square miles of territory in Europe at a cost of some 45,000 killed and missing in action. The military operation lasted 45 days from 10 May 1940 to 24 June 1940. It is noteworthy that the Poles resisted in a strategically hopeless position, surrounded on virtually all sides by Nazi Germany and the Soviet Union, and especially so after 17 September 1939. The capitulation of Belgium, Holland, and France, and the withdrawal of the British Expeditionary Force, all occurred while most of metropolitan France was still free with access to a 1,000 miles of coastline on the Atlantic and Mediterranean coasts and with Britain and French North Africa in close proximity.

In relation to time spent fighting in Poland and in the West, the German acquisition rate of territory was about 2,000 square miles a day in the former as against 5,300 in the latter. Even if one chooses to exclude Vichy France from the Nazi gains of 1940 (substantively, a dubious proposition) the territorial losses of Germany's opponents were still almost twice as extensive in the West for each day of warfare.

In dead and missing, German victory in Poland cost 0.19 casualties per square mile but actually 0.188 against the democratic Western Allies. Against the totalitarian Soviets, parenthetically, the analogous price for each square mile gained by the Nazis was 0.49 within the first 7 months of *Barbarossa*. The eventual price was 11.8, a 62-fold difference. In still other terms, the

Nazis' campaign against Soviet Russia lasted 36 times longer than their campaign against the Western Allies in 1940, and it produced German casualties in dead and missing that were 131 times larger.

Great as Hitler's 1940 victory was, it would have been very much greater if Hitler had not personally intervened on 24 May to halt the German panzers poised to wipe out the remnants of the British Expeditionary Force at Dunkirk. Some 380,000 Allied troops, mostly British, were encircled by Nazi forces around the city and port of Dunkirk. General Heinz Guderian was stopped by Hitler's order when he was close to a victory that might well have sealed the fate of Great Britain in the Second World War. During the last week of May, largely because of the Hitler-ordered diversion, the British were able to evacuate over 220,000 British troops from Dunkirk in addition to some 112,000 French and Belgian soldiers. The availability of these troops was crucial to the defence of England against a Nazi invasion in the autumn of 1940, or indeed later if the Nazis chose to pursue such a course.[31]

Of course, as Winston Churchill reminded people subsequently, the evacuation of Dunkirk was not a victory. It was more nearly a tragedy. The British left behind them 1,200 artillery pieces, 75,000 vehicles and 11,000 machine guns. Very little military inventory was left in the hands of the remnants of the British Army as it contemplated engaging the Nazis on the beachhead of southern England. If Hitler had chosen to attack within a few months of the fall of France, the British position would have been very difficult, at best.

Fortunately for Britain and the world, she was the beneficiary here of a strange ambivalence in Hitler's mind, a certain sympathy or admiration which he was never able to resolve completely. In 1926, in *Mein Kampf*, Hitler had had some distinctly positive things to say about Britain. Among these, he wrote with respect to the post-First World War situation:

> Not only did the English possess no interest in the total extermination of the German state; they even had every reason to desire a rival against France in Europe for the future.[32]

It was one of the more important aspects of the Second World War as a whole that Hitler's interest in destroying and invading Great Britain was always somewhat muted. Hitler did not seem to enjoy chasing and destroying the British nearly as much as various other people, especially the Russians.

Among other testimonials to Britain, or expressions of admiration, we find Hitler saying:

How hard it is to best England, we Germans have sufficiently learned. Quite aside from the fact that I, as a man of German blood, would, in spite of everything, rather see India under English rule than under any other.[33]

As Keith Middlemas describes it:

Towards Britain before 1936, Hitler showed a curious respect, based on his conception of racial affinity and that deduction from past history that she was a natural ally like Italy, just as France was a natural enemy. In the autumn of 1935, during the Abyssinian crisis, Speer heard him say: 'It is a terribly difficult decision. I would prefer to join the English. But how often in history the English have proved perfidious. If I go with them, then everything is over for good between Italy and us. Afterwards the English will drop us and we will fall between two stools'. The experiences of the First World War had convinced him that Germany had lost because she had been betrayed and because she had made the initial mistake of fighting the British Empire. This would not be repeated. In his *Second Book* he spoke of the significant value of Anglo-Saxon blood and traditions, and the sagacity of the British nation in its acquisition of an empire for the provision of raw materials and the colonization of surplus population. There was no essential conflict, he believed, between Germany and Britain, whose stable empire had now ceased to expand. Instead, Germany's animus lay against her inveterate encircling enemies, France and Russia.[34]

This Hitlerian lack of "killer instinct" with respect to Britain was undoubtedly the single most important cause of his undoing.[35] Victory was within sight in 1940 and 1941 but Hitler seemed to lose focus at the critical junctures.[36] The first occurred at Dunkirk; the second was his loss of interest in an invasion of Britain in 1940-41; the third was the failure to step up the war against British shipping by U-boats and air before and instead of attacking Russia; the fourth was his uncanny refusal to invest in the one theatre of operations where "investment" could have won the war for him even after 1941, North Africa.

In mid-July, the German General Staff directed the preparation of plans for an invasion of Britain some time after 15 August. But as early as 21 July, Hitler was already telling the Army leadership to begin planning the invasion of the Soviet Union. He reiterated his interest in attacking Russia on 29 July and again, in a speech to his military leaders, on 31 July. These statements reflected greater interest on Hitler's part in attacking Russia than in attacking Britain, despite the fact that major preparations for the latter were under way. On 8 December 1940 Hitler indeed finalized his orders to prepare *Barbarossa*.[37]

As one expert puts it:

> Informed sources in Great Britain believe to this day that had Hitler pressed the invasion, he would have penetrated the coastal defences, seized London or destroyed it, and taken one-by-one the other cities and ports of strategic importance. Tanks were sorely lacking, it is pointed out, as was artillery of sufficient calibre to stop the panzers. Resistance would have been stubborn, heroic -- and futile.
>
> With the British Isles under German occupation, the course of the war would have been materially altered, and quite possibly the direction of Western civilization for generations to come.[38]

A Nazi invasion of Britain in the summer or fall of 1940 would have been greatly facilitated not only by the lack of a properly organized and equipped British army (quite apart from its tactical skills), but also by the lack of formidable coastal defences in southern and south-eastern England. There was simply no time in June, July and August 1940 for the British to build an equivalent of the subsequent Nazi Atlantic Wall in northern France. Of course, no one in Britain had anticipated this sort of need in, say, 1939. Across the Channel, from Calais to Dover, the Germans were only about 20 miles from the English shore. They possessed at least ten types of shore-based artillery guns capable of firing across the Channel, and more than twenty types capable of denying British naval vessels passage through the middle of the Channel. The Royal Navy's failure in Norway (and, of course, subsequently at Crete) was not a good augury for the British.

The Luftwaffe, stronger than the RAF, whether before or after the "Battle of Britain", would have been able to operate at very short distances over south-eastern England. Hitler was passing up an historic opportunity. Even "heavy casualties" in an invasion attempt against the British in all likelihood would have been virtually inconsequential in comparison with the horrendous losses of the Russian campaign.

During the months of July, August, and September of 1940, the Nazi Luftwaffe carried out massive attacks on Britain, at times concentrating on RAF airfields and at times on London and other populated centres. During this period, now known to history as the Battle of Britain, 1,733 Luftwaffe aircraft are believed to have been shot down to 915 lost by the RAF. On 15 September, coincident with heavy raids -- and heavy losses by the Germans over Britain -- Hitler called off the invasion, first temporarily and then indefinitely. The apparent cause of Hitler's decision was the inability of the Luftwaffe to secure control of the skies over Britain, a condition seen by the Nazi military leadership as a critical prerequisite to any attempted cross-Channel attack. There is no reason to doubt that the immediate factor in the postponement was, at least in part, just as it has been historically understood. Hitler *was* probably discouraged by the Luftwaffe results. But should he have been?

According to Malcolm Smith, in an article published in 1994, "the figures of losses [in the Battle of Britain] remain controversial, but the best estimates suggest that, between 10 July and 31 October [1940] Fighter Command had lost approximately (!) 788 and the Luftwaffe 1,294 aircraft". In light of the total human and industrial potential available to each side, a 13 to 8 outcome in losses should have been downright encouraging to the Nazis.[39]

But, both explicitly and implicitly, the Battle of Britain has been mythologized into a victory it never was. There is a perception that in the three-month period from July to September, the RAF defeated the Luftwaffe so decisively that an invasion of Britain by the Nazis was no longer tenable once the Battle was concluded.

In fact, the losses on both sides could hardly be seen as decisive. In relation to the total production of military aircraft by either Britain or Germany during the Second World War, the casualties of the Battle of Britain were, relatively speaking, quite modest.[40] German losses, for example, constituted 4.3 per cent of the 40,593 aircraft which they produced in 1944 alone. Even in 1940, when German production was only 10,826 aircraft, the losses in the Battle of Britain amounted to 16.0 per cent of new output. In the case of Britain, the loss of around 900 aircraft was 6.0 per cent of production in 1940 and 3.5 per cent of the production of 1944. Given the total war output of each nation, German losses of July-September 1940 represented 1.4 per cent of their total. For the British, the loss was 0.7 per cent.[41]

A considerable and important victory at the time, the Battle of Britain was hardly a decisive victory. What had given it that appearance was Hitler's decision to abandon the invasion project in favour of the more appealing -- from his perspective -- attack on Russia. And it was undoubtedly because of that general orientation of the Fuehrer that the Luftwaffe did not move quite as quickly and as aggressively to recover from its losses and improve its capabilities as it might have done.

What is also clear is that many Western observers, eager to make the argument that Britain could "afford" its naval losses in Norway more than Germany could, did not keep this perspective in mind when they wrote about the Battle of Britain. In fact, by 1940 the Nazis controlled a population of ethnic Germans in Austria, Sudetenland, Alsace Lorraine, and western Poland, in addition to Germany proper, well in excess of 80 million people. They also controlled the bulk of European industrial resources.

Based upon the ratio of available population (about 45 million in Britain and over 80 million in Germany), it would seem that roughly 2-1 losses by the Luftwaffe were no worse than a draw. Given the fact that Britain depended on the import of so much of her food and raw materials from across the oceans, subject to U-boat attacks, it is quite realistic to think that Hitler could have worn down British resistance within several more months of battle, even with somewhat disproportionate losses by his Luftwaffe in the same way that a series of further one-against-one exchanges between the Kriegsmarine and the Royal Navy could have, in the short run at least, spelled the extinction of German sea power.[42]

None of this can, or should, deny the heroism of the young British and Allied pilots of the RAF. What they accomplished in the Battle of Britain was to show, for the first time, that Nazi Germany was not invincible, and Winston Churchill's celebrated, and inspirational, tribute to the RAF was undoubtedly understood throughout conquered Europe as a badly needed and justified message of pride as well as hope and faith.

One of the people who should have had Hitler's utmost attention in 1940 and early 1941 was Admiral Karl Doenitz. Simply put, the Nazi U-boat fleet had managed to put Britain on an inevitable road to defeat. The volume of shipping sunk by the U-boats significantly exceeded new tonnage constructed in British shipyards in the latter part of 1940 and early 1941. The picture still looked good from the Nazi point of view even in 1942. The challenge was to step up the effort. In the context of Britain's dire need for continuing the imports of food and raw materials, successful submarine warfare was a guarantee of strangulation for the British. The construction and deployment of more and better U-boats, as well as stepped-up aircraft operations in the Atlantic, the North Sea, the English Channel, and the Mediterranean, would have made the question of British defeat not one of *if* but only *when*.[43]

Perhaps Hitler could have invaded England in 1940 or 1941 and won.[44] The British army had yet to prove that it could offer really serious resistance to the Nazis. But Hitler did not need to risk an invasion and suffer some possibly high costs of carrying it out. All he needed was some patience and perseverance. The world was fortunate that the bloodthirsty maniac lacked those qualities. By explicit orders and directions of the Fuehrer, the seven-month period from September 1940 (when air attacks against Britain were called off) until 6 April 1941, when Germany attacked Yugoslavia and Greece, was largely wasted in preparing for a war that Nazi Germany could not win (against Russia) rather than in intensified pursuit of the war that it could win (against Britain).

The only constructive step Hitler took during this time, from the standpoint of securing a Nazi victory, was to send General, later Field Marshal, Erwin Rommel to North Africa with just two German divisions to help out the beleaguered Italians. On 12 February 1941 Rommel flew to Tripoli to take command of the German troops made up of the 5th Light Division (later named 21st Panzer) and 15th Panzer Division. The amazing effect which Rommel's few Nazi soldiers soon demonstrated on the fighting in Libya and Egypt should have told Hitler something very important about the proper priorities for winning his war.

Fortunately for the fate of the world, Hitler was often a completely unbalanced listener and observer. He had fallen victim to his Russian-Jewish-Bolshevik obsession. But, before launching *Barbarossa* on 22 June 1941, Hitler allowed himself a digression. He attacked Yugoslavia and Greece, in part to forestall a pro-Allied government in the former and another Italian military humiliation in the latter. On 14 April the Yugoslavs sued for peace, and on 23 April 1941, Greece concluded its final surrender. The British now executed one more of their evacuations, this time shipping out some 40,000 troops from the Greek mainland out of an original contingent of about 60,000 British soldiers. Apart from a demonstration of solidarity with Yugoslavia and Greece, British intervention in the Balkans was another huge failure. Not only did the Nazis accomplish their goals in three weeks, but their losses were trivial -- about 3,000 killed and missing. There was virtually nothing to show for a British loss of 15-20,000 troops.

The delayed final act of the Allied debacle in Greece occurred on 20 May on the island of Crete, defended by 42,000 Allied troops, 28,000 of them British, and protected, to all appearances, by the Royal Navy. The Germans, lacking any large surface naval vessels of their own in the Mediterranean, played their strong card -- air power. A force of 22,750 Nazi paratroopers was landed in the north-western part of Crete. At a cost of some 6,000 casualties, the Germans defeated the numerically superior British-Allied garrison within a period of just 10 days. Only 15,000 Allied troops were evacuated from Crete. Moreover, the Royal Navy sustained huge losses in the defeat. One aircraft carrier, three cruisers, and six destroyers were sunk by German aircraft.

The British defeat on and around Crete has been mythologized in much of the Western literature, many years after the fact, on the model of the Battle of Britain, i.e., by greatly underemphasizing one's own losses and greatly overemphasizing those of the enemy. Illustratively, we find William Klingaman writing in 1988:

> German losses during the invasion had been equally devastating(!) ... With *Barbarossa* only three weeks away, Hitler could spare no more troops for any further adventure in the Middle East. The Nazi Seventh Airborne Division, which had been so brutally slaughtered during the initial assault, was broken forever; the specter of a German airborne invasion of England vanished.[45]

By virtually all reputable sources, British manpower losses on Crete and around it were at least twice and possibly three times as great as the German, especially considering the many British prisoners of war as compared to all but nil for Germany; British naval losses had no German counterpart in surface vessels. Luftwaffe losses were greater than the British but at 250 aircraft hardly catastrophic. While one German division was perhaps "broken", that constituted a proverbial "drop in the bucket". Hitler was sending between 140 and 200 (by various estimates) Nazi divisions against Russia within less than a month of the Crete victory.

How hard would it have been for Hitler to reconstitute a single division? How could the absence of that division -- even a totally permanent absence -- *prevent* Hitler from "sparing", say, 5 or 10 divisions from his huge army on the Eastern Front? Any relationship between the Crete operation, of course, and a foregone invasion of Britain was, in late May of 1941, absurd. With the expenditure of forces Hitler made on the Eastern Front, a Nazi invasion of Britain was about as likely as a landing on Mars.[46] Meantime, while the British on Crete were being mopped up, Rommel's forces made their way across the Libyan border into Egypt.

When Hitler finally launched *Barbarossa*, he hurled an unprecedented array of military might at the Soviet Union. There were over 3 million Nazi soldiers and several hundred thousand allies, equipped with about 600,000 vehicles, 3,600 battle tanks and nearly 3,000 aircraft.[47] Ironically, if Hitler had allocated a mere 10 per cent of this force, let alone something like 15 or 20 per cent, to the Afrika Korps, Rommel would almost certainly have crossed the Suez Canal and seized the critically important oil fields of the Middle East. How Britain could have continued the war in these circumstances would be hard to imagine. What Hitler did not appreciate was that in the British he was facing an opponent who in all previous encounters was simply unable to hold ground against the Germans or even to inflict losses bloody enough to slow down the progress of the Nazi juggernaut.

In 1941, Hitler would have been encouraged even more if he had only paid serious attention to the debates of the House of Commons. In fact, the first three years of the war reflected continuing malaise. The underlying sense of weakness and of one's own inadequacy, reinforced by the terrible memories of the First World War, had not vanished from the British Parliament. It had its lingering effects; it continued to structure British actions and expectations after 3 September 1939.

No clue was more revealing in these respects than the three debates which followed Nazi victory over Poland, a country to which Britain, along with France, had promised military assistance. Not only was the quick, and unassisted, destruction of Poland subject to legitimate moral reproach against the British and French governments. It was also a matter of missed opportunity.

The first debate occurred on 20 September 1939 when isolated pockets of Polish resistance, especially in Warsaw, were still holding out against the Nazi siege. Mr. Chamberlain opened the debate with a frank recognition that the issue in Poland had already been decided. He said:

> If Britain and France have been unable to avert the defeat of the armies of Poland they have assured her that they have not forgotten their obligations to her nor weakened in their determination to carry on the struggle ... Our general purpose in this struggle is well known. It is to redeem Europe from the perpetual and recurring fear of German aggression and enable the peoples of Europe to preserve their independence and their liberties.[48]

Mr. Chamberlain recalled that Britain had been prepared to negotiate a peace settlement with Germany "even after the striking of the first blow", and then proceeded to give the House a rather challenging summary of what the Allies had been doing while Poland underwent her agony.

> On the western frontier the French have continued to make methodical and successful progress ... valuable strategic and tactical objectives have been secured ... in the face of increasingly severe German resistance.[49]

Mr. Chamberlain also told the House that "... our forces are stronger today than at the outset of any past war ...".[50]

This statement, if taken at face value, made the inaction of Britain and France all the more difficult to understand. The accuracy of Mr. Chamberlain's account as to what the French had been doing on the Franco-German frontier during September was easily open to the charge of gross misrepresentation.

As if to forestall possible objections, however, the Prime Minister enunciated a policy of military caution, saying that:

> We as a Government will not be rushed into courses which our military advisers, with whom we work in the closest possible contact and mutual confidence, do not approve.[51]

He elaborated on this proposition with what might be termed a "consensus doctrine" for military action. It would require, in Chamberlain's view, a consensus of the Government's "responsible military advisers", the Cabinet itself, and the French Allies -- presumably their Cabinet and their "responsible advisers" -- to initiate military operations.[52]

How did the House of Commons respond to Mr. Chamberlain's statement?

While several MP's deplored and regretted the fate of Poland, few actually reproached the Prime Minister either about his policy or the representations that he had made to the House. Not a single member of the House of Commons viewed British and French inaction as a missed opportunity in the war against Hitler.

Labour's Mr. Arthur Greenwood, Deputy Leader of the Opposition, declared:

... it lies on my conscience, and on that of other members of the House, that we did not do rather more for [Poland] before this terrible trial came upon her.[53]

Mr. Greenwood observed that:

It may be that what help we could have given to Poland would not have enabled her, successfully, to resist the terrific onslaught of both the Germans and the Russians ... [but] in the future such help as we give to our friends should be quick, certain and generous. He thought that the Government should show more courage and boldness ... than they have shown in the past.[54]

Sir Archibald Sinclair of the Liberals echoed Greenwood's general support for the war policies of the Chamberlain Cabinet. He seemed even more enthusiastic about the notion of not doing anything that the "responsible military advisers" were against ...".[55] He thought that Britain needed to prepare better. "We must prepare to be decisive ...".[56]

One of the conservative backbenchers expressed a sense of unease felt by some members in these terms:

There is the question why we were unable to bring more effective assistance to Poland in time. There may be formidable strategic reasons. But the ordinary man-in-the-street is asking himself that question all the time.[57]

Another member observed that Britain was now duty-bound to see the war through to victory inasmuch as Poland had earned British loyalty by her heroic stand against the Nazis.[58]

A rather more wistful attitude, though clearly a very important one in the House of Commons at the time, was represented by the view of Labour MP Vernon Bartlett who said:

It becomes increasingly clear that we shall not win this war unless we have the support of a great number of States which are now neutral.[59]

Characteristically, Bartlett argued that Britain should give the Indians political freedom so as to get them to support her cause, and participate in the war effort much more fully.[60]

A note reminiscent of the spirit of Munich was sounded by a Labour backbencher, Mr. Sloan, eager to negotiate a settlement with Germany:

> It is particularly sad to listen to speaker after speaker saying that the only thing that matters is that the war should be fought until we destroy Germany ... fight until we are all exhausted [with] millions of our youth slaughtered?[61]

> Having endured the past week, I think we can have very little confidence in the military authorities in this country. How they could stand aside, how they could encourage Poland to put up a resistance to Germany when it was common knowledge that we could not render her any assistance(!) is a rather disquieting feature in regard to the prolongation of the war.[62]

The debate on the conduct of the war was renewed on September 26th -- when the last embers of Polish resistance were being extinguished.

Mr. Chamberlain opened the discussion with another report about Allied activities:

> On the Western front, the French have continued to make progress in certain localities and have succeeded, notwithstanding increasingly energetic German reaction, in maintaining all their gains intact.[63]

Once again, no one sought to inquire into all those "activities" the Prime Minister attributed to the French. The Prime Minister's statement was followed by that of Mr. Clement Attlee on behalf of the Labour Party. Mr. Attlee confined himself to paying tribute to the heroism of the Polish people and expressed his admiration for the defenders of Warsaw. His remarks seemed to convey a sense of the regrettable inevitability of Polish defeat, and did not involve any recriminations or accusations against the Chamberlain Government. Attlee, as well as most of the subsequent speakers, emphasized largely domestic aspects of the conflict, issues related to economic mobilization, the proper organization of the War Cabinet, potential hardships faced by the British people and industries in the wake of war, the availability of various goods, and defence against German submarine warfare.[64]

Sir Archibald Sinclair expressed considerable satisfaction about the allegedly good reconnaissance work which the British and French air forces were carrying out on the continent.[65] One Conservative member, Commander Sir Archibald Southby, went so far as to suggest to the House that "our motto should be, as far as possible, 'business as usual' ".[66] Another member, more sensitive about the recent events in Poland, declared that:

> Many of us have felt ashamed that we have been able to do very little to prevent the terrible suffering through which Poland has passed in these early stages.[67]

But, Mr. Vyvyan Adams concluded that the sacrifice of Poland would still do some good because the Poles gave Britain time to "gather our strength for the blows of retribution".[68]

Once again, however, no one questioned the nature of British, and French, activities -- or non-activities -- during the German operations in the east. This was all the more remarkable in the face of assurances which Prime Minister Chamberlain had given the House of Commons on 1 September 1939, the very day when Hitler attacked Poland. Their importance justifies a full quotation. He had said:

> The thoughts of many of us must at this moment inevitably be turning back to 1914, and to a comparison of our position now with that which existed then. How do we stand this time? The answer is that all three Services are ready, and that the situation in all directions is far more favourable and reassuring than in 1914, while behind the fighting Services we have built up a vast organisation of Civil Defence under our scheme of Air Raid Precautions. As regards the immediate manpower requirements, the Royal Navy, the Army and the Royal Air Force are in the fortunate position of having almost as many men as they can conveniently handle at this moment ... The main and most satisfactory point to observe is that there is today no need to make an appeal in a general way for recruits such as was issued by Lord Kitchener 25 years ago. That appeal has been anticipated by many months, and the men are already available.[69]

The final debate in the wake of the Polish collapse took place on 3 October. Prime Minister Chamberlain spoke to the House of Commons on the war situation and reported upon the actions undertaken by the Allies while Poland fell. These were:

> On the Western Front some further progress has been made by the French which has enabled them to secure useful points for observation over German positions ...

> A large British Army has been transported to France ... We have reason to be proud of the efficiency with which [this was done] ... Reconnaissance flights both by day and by night are being made by the RAF units in France ...

> Aircraft of the Coastal Command have continued ... routine patrols ...

Some units of the German fleet have been attacked, he said, and anti-submarine warfare has been going on ...[70]

The ensuing debate reflected a mood of despair and an eagerness to terminate the conflict through negotiations with Germany to a degree not replicated in the whole 1939-1945 period. Indeed, when Mr. Gallacher, the Communist MP, demanded that Britain negotiate peace terms with Hitler forthwith, and wished to know why anybody should be afraid to talk about peace, his sentiments seemed to coincide with those of most other participants in the debate.[71]

A conservative backbencher, Mr. Buchanan, declared that there was no mass support for continuing the war in Britain, and, indeed, that if the Poles had known how little Britain was going to do for them, they would not have fought themselves.[72] Labourite Mr. McGovern expressed the view that Britain and France could not possibly defeat Germany and declared that, unlike 1914, there was no enthusiasm for the war throughout the country.[73] Mr. Lipson concurred. He viewed the destruction of Hitlerism as a hopeless quest. The real question was how one could get out of this war.[74] This was also the thrust of a speech made by Britain's last wartime Prime Minister, Mr. David Lloyd George, and several other members.[75]

No one suggested that, on Mr. Chamberlain's own showing, Britain and France, separately and jointly, had not done nearly enough to carry the war to Hitler and the Nazis, or indeed that seizing "good observation posts" and carrying out "routine patrols" was not the sort of thing which actually wins wars or stops a blitzkrieg. To anyone listening attentively, these debates had to be a valuable learning experience. To any staunch opponent of Nazism, they were bound to convey a mixed message, in some respects clearly disquieting. On 3 October 1939, the issue of how much Britain would do to defeat Hitler was competing in the House of Commons on somewhat unfavourable terms with a much more fundamental issue: was it really necessary and useful to go on with the war, and if not, how could it be ended?

Hitler's own intransigent brutality and his attacks on Denmark and Norway helped to quiet the doubters and paved the way for the 1940 Government transition from Chamberlain to Churchill. Much of the British "awakening to Hitler" clearly appears to have taken place after the beginning of the war. Nevertheless, anyone who had spent as many years in the Parliament elected in 1935 as Winston Churchill had was likely to be seriously influenced by its profound reluctance about war and fighting. If, given his own personal convictions about the threat which Hitlerism posed, Churchill searched his mind for an underlying formula with which Britain, Europe, and the rest of the world could be saved, and if he looked for clues in his immediate political environment, a primarily diplomatic-political formula, not a military one, was likely to suggest itself.

Given the state of German preparedness as Churchill knew it, or even suspected it at the outbreak of the war, the prospects of successful British military opposition to the Third Reich in land warfare would have required the adoption of domestically (politically) unpalatable measures. These would have involved some very high costs in lives lost, a Stalinesque, ruthless and painful mobilization on the home front, and also, almost certainly, some quasi-revolutionary shake-up of the British military establishment in order to adapt it to the techniques of warfare which the Nazis employed. It would have also required taking some very great risks.

In the First World War, Churchill had been severely punished for the blood-letting at Gallipoli.[76] It nearly cost him his political career. The attitudes of his colleagues at the beginning of the Second World War told him that, given the opportunity, he must seek solutions in another direction. Britain alone could not "outmuscle" Nazi Germany. Almost certainly, no British Prime Minister could fight the war with the ferocity with which Hitler could fight it. But Churchill could hope to rally the British people to self-defence; deny the Nazis entry and possession of the British Isles as long as the Royal Navy and Air Force remained reasonably intact. And he could use the time gained to create or perhaps simply gratuitously benefit by an international coalition, which -- particularly if led by the United States -- would be capable of defeating the Nazis in a prolonged conflict.

This strategy is described in a number of military histories and interpretations, most vividly in Trumbull Higgins' *Winston Churchill and the Second Front, 1940-1943* (New York: Oxford University Press, 1957). In the words of the author:

> ... from the start of the conflict in 1939, the future Prime Minister had thrown all his influence on behalf of that type of warfare so persuasively presented by Hart, Fuller and others in post-1918 Britain; a defensive warfare of limited liability on land, of blockade, of economic conflict, and of a small but elite army concentrated in Britain and the Middle East instead of France ...

After all, for so many years before 1939 British public opinion "was trained to put faith in every conceivable means of winning wars save by fighting battles and beating the enemy".[77]

Militarily, this formula would not be an alternative to the course pursued by Chamberlain. It would be more of the same, especially with respect to land warfare: low-profile, jab-from-outside, never-attack-first-if-you-can-help-it, minimal casualty-and-risk, usual-methods approach.[78] What was different was that Churchill, having much greater political skills and resources than Chamberlain, was more likely to employ this strategy successfully and with much less concern for domestic, Parliamentary opposition. Chamberlain's publicly acknowledged failure in the pursuit of appeasement rendered his Parliamentary support brittle and thin. The debacle in Denmark and Norway was enough to bring him down. Churchill, on the other hand, with his unique anti-Nazi credibility and peerless reputation, was capable of absorbing political blows at home which his predecessor simply could not.

All this became quite clearly evident when British forces suffered their first major setback at the hands of the Nazis in Norway in April and May of 1940. As First Lord of the Admiralty, Churchill shared the political and military responsibility for the Norwegian events with the Prime Minister. Here he quickly managed to prove himself both wrong and imprudent.

In a speech to the House of Commons on 11 April 1940, two days after the Nazi attack on Denmark and Norway, Churchill gave an oddly positive and up-beat appraisal of events. He said:

... it is the considered view of the Admiralty that we have greatly
gained by what has occurred in Scandinavia and in northern waters
in a strategic and military sense. For myself, I consider that Hitler's
action in invading Scandinavia is as great a strategic and political
error as that which was committed by Napoleon in 1807 or 1808,
when he invaded Spain.[79]

Why was that the case? Because Churchill thought that the people
conquered here would be able to offer "prolonged resistance to [Hitler's]
soldiers and his Gestapo", and because Hitler now had made commitments
which would require him to fight during a whole summer "against Powers
possessing vastly superior naval forces and able to transport them to the scenes
of action more easily than he can".[80] Churchill saw no advantages to the Nazis
and concluded that "I feel that we are greatly advantaged by what has
occurred". He assured the House that all German ships in the Skaggerak and
Kattegat would be sunk and said that "we are not going to allow the enemy to
supply their armies across these waters with impunity".[81]

While the value of adding Denmark and Norway to Hitler's dominions
could be, and was subsequently, disputed by military analysts, there was no
parallel here to Napoleon's invasion of Spain. The Norwegian and Danish
resistance did not prove nearly as troublesome to the Nazis as Churchill had
hoped and expected. There was no fighting over a whole summer because the
Allies were beaten in a few weeks. Although the Nazis had suffered some
substantial losses at sea, they faced no insuperable problem in supplying their
troops while the Allied and British loss in prestige was obvious and painful.[82]

When Mr. Chamberlain addressed the House on 7 May 1940, he said:

No doubt the news of our withdrawal from Southern Norway
created a profound shock both in this House and in the country.[83]

Restless interruptions momentarily stopped the Prime Minister's
remarks, but he continued,

If we had losses, the Germans had far heavier losses in warships, in
planes, in transport and in men [but] we have suffered a certain loss
of prestige ... a certain colour has been given to the false legend of
German invincibility on land ... some discouragement has been
caused to our friends ... and our enemies are crowing.[84]

In his reply to the Prime Minister, Mr. Attlee managed to reprove the First Lord of the Admiralty, too, for his "far too optimistic speech" and "hasty conclusions" on 11 April, but he saved the really heavy blows for Mr. Chamberlain. He reminded the Prime Minister that as recently as 2 May he had been saying "that the balance of advantage lies up to the present with the Allied Forces ....".[85]

Mr. Attlee proceeded to his own critical conclusion:

> We have to face facts ... It is not Norway alone. Norway comes as the culmination of many other discontents. People are saying that those mainly responsible for the conduct of affairs are men who have had an almost uninterrupted career of failure. Norway follows Czechoslovakia and Poland. Everywhere the story is 'too late'. The Prime Minister talked about missing buses. What about all the buses which he and his associates have missed since 1931? They missed all the peace buses but caught the war bus. The people find that these men who have been consistently wrong in their judgments of events, the same people who thought that Hitler would not attack Czechoslovakia, who thought that Hitler could be appeased, seem not to have realized that Hitler would attack Norway. They see everywhere a failure of grip, a failure of drive, not only in the field of defence and foreign policy but in industry ... There is a widespread feeling in this country, not that we shall lose the war, that we will win the war, but that to win the war, we want different people at the helm from those who have led us into it.[86]

Criticizing Chamberlain's methods, Sir Roger Keys declared that, "The war cannot be won by committees"[87] and in Mr. Amery's words, it could not be won on the basis of "the feeblest common denominator".[88]

The following day, Mr. Lloyd George bitterly assailed Chamberlain in the following terms:

> The Prime Minister must remember that he has met this formidable foe of ours in peace and in war. He has always been worsted ...

He called upon the Prime Minister to

> "sacrifice the seals of office" for the good of the nation.[89]

Churchill, too, was criticized in a number of speeches but usually with all sorts of "extenuating circumstances". He was apparently unable to do his best work in such a wretched Cabinet ...

When his turn came in the debate, Churchill began by accentuating the last positive aspect of the Scandinavian situation. He said that:

> We are now fighting hard for Northern Norway, and in particular for Narvik, and I will not attempt to predict how the struggle will go, nor will I give any information about it at all. I will content myself with saying that the conditions in that area are much more equal so far as ability to reinforce it is concerned -- much more equal and much more favourable than those which would have developed in Central Norway.[90]

Churchill defended the navy professionals who were his statutory advisers and he cautioned against turning out the government in a rash manner.

From a purely military point of view, he was once again raising false hopes. Narvik would soon be lost, too. Politically, however, he had made one of his most effective appeals to the House.

> ... I say, let pre-war feuds die; let personal quarrels be forgotten, and let us keep our hatred for the common enemy. Let party interest be ignored, let all our energies be harnessed, let the whole ability and forces of the nation be hurled into the struggle, and let all the strong horses be pulling on the collar. At no time in the last war were we in greater peril than we are now ...[91]

Churchill's words brought welcome reassurance to all those hundreds of MPs who only a year earlier had so strongly supported the policy of appeasement. His remarks were politically astute. Still, he insisted on some risky and faulty military judgments. He declared again that Hitler was worse off by seizing Norway than he was without it. Absurdly, he claimed that Hitler paid with ten lives for every one lost by the Allies ...[92] More reasonably, he pointed to the gain of hundreds of thousands of tons of new shipping gained from defecting Norwegians and Danes ...[93]

On 13 May 1940, Winston Churchill faced the House of Commons as Prime Minister and delivered some of the most memorable lines in the history of that institution:

... I have nothing to offer but blood, toil, tears and sweat ...[94] ...
We have before us an ordeal of the most grievous kind. We have
before us many long months of struggle and suffering ...[95] ... I feel
sure that our cause will not be suffered to fail among men ...[96]

The motion to welcome the new Government passed by the House by
a vote of 381 to none. Mr. David Lloyd George said that Britain was fortunate
to have a leader now who had "glittering intellectual gifts ... dauntless courage,
profound study of war and experience in its operation and direction ... at a
graver moment than any faced by any previous Prime Minister".[97]

But within a few days of the Nazi attack in the West, the House of
Commons had reason to wonder about the military competence of the new
leader. In a remark which reflected both on him and his professional advisers,
Churchill, on 19 May 1940 diagnosed the German Blitzkrieg against France in
uncomprehending terms:

> It would be foolish to disguise the gravity of the situation. It would
> be still more foolish to lose heart or courage, or to suppose that
> well-trained, well-equipped armies, numbering 3,000,000 or
> 4,000,000 of men, can be overcome in the space of a few weeks or
> even months, by a super-raid of mechanical vehicles, however
> formidable.

He went on to say that he had "invincible confidence in the French
Army and its leaders".[98]

Churchill presented the House of Commons with an appraisal of
events in France which was notable for its general inaccuracy. He said:

> When we consider the heroic resistance made by the French Army
> against heavy odds in this battle, the enormous losses inflicted upon
> the enemy and the evident exhaustion of the enemy ...[99]

Still, there could be no doubt about the Prime Minister's own resolve
and the compelling way in which he imparted his feelings to the British
people. When Churchill concluded with the sentence:

Let us therefore brace ourselves to our duty and so bear ourselves
that if the British Commonwealth and Empire lasts for a thousand
years men will still say, 'This was their finest hour'.

Mr. Lees-Smith, Labour member for Keighley, rose to convey a
response from his colleagues. He said:

My Honourable Friends on these benches ... wish to say to the
Prime Minister that in their experience among the broad masses of
the people of this country never in their lives has the country been
more united than it is today in its support of the Prime Minister's
assertion that we shall carry on right to the end.[100]

Within the framework of a militarily cautious and orthodox approach,
Churchill still faced more than two years of battlefield adversity. Until the
victory at El Alamein which coincided -- not accidentally -- with major
American and Soviet participation in the war, Britain had not managed to do
very well against her principal adversary. The same kinds of criticism which
had been levelled at the Chamberlain Cabinet were now being aimed at the
Churchill Government -- with two critical differences. Those who assailed
Winston Churchill did so, metaphorically speaking, on their knees. And not
too many were willing to indulge in any direct criticism of a man whom they
saw as the country's providential and indispensable leader.

All of this was already apparent in the first major public debate on the
war during the Churchill administration in August of 1940. France had fallen
and the Battle of Britain was well under way. The Prime Minister addressed
the House on 20 August 1940. He said that since his Government took over
"... a cataract of disaster has poured upon us ..." with Holland, Belgium, France
lost and the Nazis close by for air operations against Britain ... He soberly
said:

We cannot tell what lies ahead ... [perhaps] even greater ordeals ...
We shall face whatever is coming to us.[101]

On the other hand if Churchill meant to encourage the British, he did
so by several serious misrepresentations. He claimed that the British army,
navy and air force were all stronger than ever before -- all in the face of his
own admission of 18 June that the Army rescued from Dunkirk had lost
virtually all its vehicles, cannons and modern equipment. Churchill also

claimed that British fighters in France had inflicted losses in the ratio of 2 or 3 to 1 on the Nazis; even 3-4 to 1 at Dunkirk, and an even more favourable ratio was allegedly being achieved in the Battle of Britain.[102]

Given information now available, it is clear that these figures represented gross, if not preposterous, exaggerations. Perhaps appropriately under the circumstances, Churchill's claims were not only supported but even inflated by the Secretary of State for Air, Sir Archibald Sinclair, who told the House, that between 8 August and the 20th, 90 British pilots were lost as compared with more than 1,500 for Germany and that if one included British bomber losses, it was still less than 300 for Britain as compared with much more than 1,500 for Nazi Germany.[103]

In the remainder of his military review before the House, at a time when Britain stood so obviously alone against the full fury of Hitler's aggression, the Prime Minister indulged in a most unrealistic, perhaps even desperate, scenario of ultimate victory. He claimed that bombing military targets over Germany "... affords one of the most certain, if not the shortest, of all roads to victory".[104] Realistically, British air raids over Germany in the summer of 1940 possessed, at most, a very modest nuisance value. Nazi war production and assorted military capabilities continued to rise significantly for several more years -- even when the bombing of Germany was greatly escalated beyond the "demonstration levels" of 1940.

When the Government called for Parliamentary support on a motion of confidence on 6 May 1941, following defeats in Greece and Libya, the debate produced the usual mixture of specific criticisms of war policy coupled with disarming personal tributes to Winston Churchill. As one member (Mr. Kenneth Lindsay) put it:

> ... in spite of what the Prime Minister says, thousands of people are uneasy. It does not mean that they have not complete confidence in him. It is quite possible to have those two conceptions in your mind at the same time.[105]

Another Conservative, General Sir George Jeffreys, attempted to put things in perspective:

> There is no getting away from it, we have had setbacks in Libya and in Greece and ... may have [still more], but all war participants make mistakes ... Whoever makes fewer, as Napoleon urged, would win ...[106]

Labour MP Mr. Emanuel Shinwell, pointed out that:

> ... the dispatch of British forces to Greece failed to hold the enemy and, at the same time, weakened our forces in Libya, so that we failed on two fronts.[107]

He said that Government promises made in late October 1940 that Britain would overtake Germany in war production simply did not materialize,[108] and indicated that the Prime Minister misled the House on the quantity of shipping available or likely to be available for operations in Greece. He concluded by saying:

> I do not subscribe to the suggestion canvassed in certain quarters that our sole task in the present circumstances is to defend this country.[109]

Much of the reassurance that Churchill offered the House of Commons on this, as on various past and future occasions, was in his skilful emphasis of the constitutional continuity and legitimacy of his conduct. He said:

> We have succeeded in maintaining under difficulties which are unprecedented and in dangers which ... might well be mortal, the whole process and reality of Parliamentary institutions. I am proud of this.[110]

He assured the House that Britain could not have done more for Greece and that, consequently, "our honour as a nation is clear".[111] As for the question of how operations were conducted, Churchill -- even in the face of repeated charges of Government timidity -- fell back on the formula of political deference to professional expert opinion of the duly constituted bureaucracies. He said that in Libya and Greece "no violence had been done to expert military opinion ... all decisions have been taken unitedly and freely and in good will ...".[112]

This politically-appealing defence by Churchill was, however, once again coupled with some military pronouncements which very soon came back to haunt the Prime Minister. He told the House that while mistakes, shortcomings and disappointments must be added to his original 1940 list of promises, i.e., blood, toil, tears and sweat:

> We intend to defend to the death and without thought of retirement
> the valuable and highly offensive outposts of Crete and Tobruk.[113]

When these outposts were shortly afterwards lost to the Nazis, the manner of British defeat as well as the loss itself reinforced the sense of anxiety in the House of Commons.

The debate on the war situation after the fall of Crete on 10 June 1941 produced considerable acrimony. Several members recalled Churchill's pledge to fight to the death for the island and wondered how it could have been lost so very quickly and, in their view, so easily. Mr. Lees-Smith reminded the House that Britain had had bases on Crete including airfields at Malemi, Heraklion, and Retrino, for about seven months prior to the Nazi invasion, and yet the British air force was unable to cover and support Allied troops on the island.[114] He also wondered why these airfields could not have been destroyed, at least, so as to deny their use to the enemy.[115] Mr. Lees-Smith worried about the Nazis being able to do to Britain herself what they did to Crete, since they seemed to have conquered Crete in the face of British sea power controlling the surrounding waters of the eastern Mediterranean.[116] Nevertheless, he expressed the hope that all this disaster was perhaps merely a prologue to the following year (1942) when Britain would at last attain its material superiority over the Nazis.[117]

Churchill's perennial critic, the former Secretary of War, Mr. Leslie Hore-Belisha, dealt with the latest setback rather more harshly. He wondered why the Government had learned so little -- if anything -- about the need for air cover from its previous experience with Nazi operations in Norway as well as in the Low Countries, France, Yugoslavia, and Greece. He claimed that time was largely wasted in preparing Crete for the enemy attack. He vigorously denounced the political bureaucratic quagmire of British military decision-making. He said:

> As matters now stand the vital arrangements to be made by
> [commanders] before and during an action are for argument,
> negotiation and compromise between those who naturally take
> different views of the obligations and possibilities of their
> [different] respective services.[118]

The Army and Navy were left in the lurch by the Air Force, he claimed, and British supremacy at sea was completely nullified. More audaciously still, Mr. Hore-Belisha challenged one of the central myths of the Churchill Government, the notion that Britain was somehow well on its way to out producing Nazi Germany in all manner of military hardware. He cited an American source, Deputy Director of the US Office of Production Management, W. L. Batt:

> For us to suppose that Britain is growing stronger every day in relation to Germany is criminal folly.[119]

Since after 1940 Germany enjoyed a population base of about 80 million in the Third Reich alone, with a large initial lead in army and air force capabilities, and with all sorts of European resources connected by contiguous routes to Germany, the expectation that 45 million Britons, largely supplied by ships and planes from other continents, could outproduce the Nazis was nothing short of incredible. Such a shift in capabilities could have only occurred in consequence of a Nazi willingness to allow it. In the aftermath of the war, this notion -- propagated by the Churchill Government and to all appearances widely believed even by political sophisticates -- must be seen as a great monument to the human capacity for hope and self-deception in conditions of crisis.

Addressing the question of how military operations were conducted, Churchill said:

> His Majesty's Government in their responsibility to Parliament choose the best generals they can find, set before them the broad strategic objects of the campaign, offer them any advice or counsel necessary ... and then ... support them to the best of their power in men and munitions, and also, so long as they retain their confidence, they support them with loyal comradeship in failure or success.[120]

As William Shirer noted in his book, Hitler "did not fully realize what a blow [his Spring 1941 victories] had been to the British nor how desperate was the predicament of the Empire".[121] The Fuehrer was a victim of his own mindset, or madness. Grand Admiral Erich Raeder appealed to Hitler on 30 May to "prepare a decisive offensive against Egypt and Suez" and argued that such an operation "would be more deadly to the British Empire than the capture of London" but there was no reasoning with the great sociopath.[122]

While Hitler firmed up the preparations for *Barbarossa*, Winston Churchill was writing President Roosevelt:

> I adjure you, Mr. President, not to underestimate the gravity of the consequences which may follow from a Middle-East collapse.

He need not have worried. Hitler was about to let Britain off the hook at the proverbial five of twelve, perhaps five after twelve. The fatal mistake of his career and Second World War strategy was about to unfold. In March of 1941, when Rommel made his first visit to the Fuehrer's headquarters after taking command in Africa, he was told already that "there was no intention of striking a decisive blow in Africa in the near future" and that he should not expect to receive any reinforcements.[123] It was little short of amazing, given the successes that Rommel was able to produce within just a few months in Africa with a handful of troops, that Hitler was unable to change his mind and appreciate his opportunity of decisive victory.

Rommel's successes in North Africa were notable because they were achieved against an enemy who had (1) numerical ground superiority; (2) air superiority; (3) naval superiority in the Mediterranean and (4) logistical advantage because of the link-up of Suez Canal facilities with railroad lines to western Egypt, most of this, especially the Suez disembarkation areas, virtually free from air attacks by the Axis. Moreover, the supply and transportation "priorities", if they can be called that, accorded Rommel by the Hitler High Command were little short of scandalous. Yet, somehow, the Nazi Germans managed to get more out of their "human material" than did the democratic British -- for at least a year-and-a-half.

It should be noted that the supply difficulties which Rommel experienced in North Africa were easily solvable -- assuming an interest in solving them. The losses sustained by Italian and German convoys sailing on the Mediterranean to provision the Afrika Korps could have been virtually eliminated if Hitler had been willing to commit relatively modest air forces to patrolling the Straits of Sicily, where the distance between the African mainland and the island of Sicily was less than 100 air miles. German aircraft, operating from both shores, would have been easily capable of nearly round-the-clock surveillance of an area so relatively small. The British navy would not have been able to operate against this kind of air cover.

This shortest-distance route between Sicily and Africa, admittedly, lay across from the port of Tunis in Tunisia -- a potentially excellent disembarkation point for Axis vessels and aircraft. Tunis was under Vichy French control in 1941. The Nazis had the option of negotiating transit rights and base emplacements there with the regime of Marshal Petain, or, alternatively, taking it by force. In relation to the effort required for the war in Russia, such a task would have been a military equivalent of the proverbial "taking candy from a baby".

It is ironic to consider (in the light of the claims often made for "democracy ...") General Fritz Bayerlein's (Afrika Korps chief of staff) explanation of why it was that Rommel often succeeded while the British frequently failed:

> Contrary to the principle that one can never be strong enough at the centre of gravity and must concentrate everything at that point, every attack was made by part only of the [British] Eighth Army, and even the main offensive force, already too weak for its purpose, was thrown into battle dispersed.
>
> The result of these tactics of dispersal was that the British formations were either badly battered or destroyed one after another ... This fundamental mistake was one of the reasons why victory escaped them. Their unwieldy and rigidly methodical technique of command, their over-systematic issuing of orders down to the last detail, leaving little latitude to the junior commander, and their poor adaptability to the changing course of battle were also much to blame for the British failures.
>
> Immobility and a rigid adherence to pattern are bad enough in European warfare; in the desert they are disastrous. Here everything is in flux; there are no obstructions, no lines, water or woods for cover; everything is open and incalculable; the commander must adapt ... daily, even hourly. Everything is in motion ... he must be constantly on alert, all the time on the edge of capture or destruction by a more cunning, wide-awake or versatile enemy. There can be no conservatism in thought or action, no relying on tradition or resting on the laurels of previous victory. Speed of judgment, and action to create changing situations and surprises for the enemy faster than he can read, never making dispositions in advance, these are the fundamentals of desert tactics.[124]

Some British analysts agreed. This is how Hanson Baldwin described British military skills in North Africa at the end of 1941, more than two years after the outbreak of the Second World War:

> Tactically, the British had little to cheer about. Their men, rarely lacking in courage, lost engagement after engagement. Despite air superiority and the best air-ground support yet provided the British Army (not good), time after time the Germans exacted higher casualties with weaker forces, than they received. The British generals -- Cunningham and Ritchie -- did not command as Rommel did, on the scene' in person. They rarely controlled the battle: attrition and naval and air superiority won it for them. And the British expertise at armoured warfare was sadly lacking. Their dispositions were too scattered, and only infrequently were they able to meld the kind of fighting team the Germans usually presented: tanks, anti-tank guns, artillery and infantry.[125]

At the beginning of the war, the manpower, the economic resources and indeed the *aggregate* military capability even of Hitler's principal enemies -- Britain and France -- considerably exceeded those available to Hitler. Yet, notwithstanding this disadvantage, the Nazis managed to defeat and subdue Poland, Denmark, Norway, Belgium, Holland, Luxembourg, France, Yugoslavia, and Greece, in a period of about twenty months from 1 September 1939 to 1 May 1941. They all but destroyed the British army, causing it to flee the continent at Dunkirk with the loss of most of its weapons. On the eve of Hitler's fateful decision to attack Russia, the Nazis had brought Italy, Hungary, Romania, Bulgaria, Finland, and in some measure also Spain, into their sphere of influence. Only beleaguered Britain, and on the continent, Portugal, Switzerland, and Sweden, remained in uneasy independence from the Hitlerian New Order in Europe.

Moreover, as Hitler settled down to the full exploitation of his dominions, comparable to the EU today, he was in the process of waging highly successful submarine warfare against his one remaining active enemy -- the British. Any substantial intensification of that warfare, of which the Nazis were then easily capable, and conceivably even its mere continuation for another year or eighteen months, would have been sufficient to destroy Britain, literally starving her into surrender.[126]

In October of 1940, Admiral Doenitz had reported sinkings of British vessels exceeding by almost one 100 per cent the joint monthly construction capacity of both British *and* American shipyards; this pattern of British losses exceeding construction continued on an alarming scale well into 1941.

Reviewing Britain's position, Captain B. H. Liddell Hart has gone so far as to suggest that:

The industrialization of the island ... multiplied the menace of submarine power. By refusing to consider any peace offer the British Government had committed the country to a course that under such conditions was bound, logically, to lead through growing exhaustion to eventual collapse -- even if Hitler had abstained from attempting its quick conquest by invasion. The course of no compromise was equivalent to slow suicide.[127]

Winston Churchill recalled later that:

The only thing that ever really frightened me during the war was the U-boat peril. Invasion, I thought, even before the air battle, would fail. We could drown and kill this horrible foe in circumstances favourable to us, and, as he evidently realized, bad for him. It was the kind of battle which, in the cruel conditions of war, one ought to be content to fight. But now our lifeline, even across the broad oceans and especially the entrances to the island, was endangered. I was even more anxious about this battle than about the glorious air fight called the Battle of Britain.[128]

He returned to this theme in these words:

Amid the torrent of violent events one anxiety reigned supreme. Battles might be won or lost, enterprises might succeed or miscarry, territories might be gained or quitted, but dominating all our power to carry on war, or even keep ourselves alive, lay our mastery of the ocean routes and the free approach and entry into our ports ... The perils which the German occupation of the coast of Europe from North Cape to the Pyrenees brought upon us [were such that] from any port or inlet along the enormous front hostile U-boats, constantly improving in speed, endurance, and radius, could easily sally forth to destroy our seaborne food and trade.[129]

That Hitler was able to come as close as he did to achieving victory in 1940 and 1941, he owed, substantially and demonstrably, to certain superior capabilities of his dictatorial regime over those of the democracies opposing him.

Although the Nazi Fuehrer was not willing to demand total economic mobilization from the German people until a much later, and more desperate, period of the war, his regime was able in the 1930s to shift national resources from peaceful to military purposes much more quickly and substantially than did his opponents. (In 1938, the average work week of German industrial workers was 52 hours while it was only 40 hours in France.) Hitler could say "no" to German consumers as the democracies, especially in peacetime, never could.[130]

A related advantage which Hitler derived from his regime -- and one that was itself a substantial explanation of the first -- consisted in the overcoming of sizable domestic opposition both to the shift in resource allocation and to the policies of war and aggression more generally. Having suppressed all political opposition, Hitler was able to proceed with his rearmament programme and his assorted acts of aggression in a way that would have been impossible for his democratic opponents.

There were no outcries in parliament or the press; there was no opposition on radio. There were no public meetings, marches, vigils, demonstrations, or sit-ins organized by political opponents. There were no strikes, or slow-downs, or sick-outs, because Hitlerism did not tolerate any such things. There were no boycotts. There were no free elections, either. There was no such concept as inviolability of the mail, telephone, or any other form of communication or the sanctity of the home.

There was the Gestapo, with its hideous and quickly-established reputation, and there were concentration camps; and there was no judiciary in Nazi Germany which could as much as say "boo" to the political leadership. In the upshot, there could be no public counterweight to the appeals of the Nazi propaganda machine, and even private, whispered, comments adverse to the regime could be risky. Walls had ears. Neighbours could talk. If anyone were foolish enough to address a "letter of concern" to the Fuehrer himself on, say, the issue of German violations of international treaties, such an action would have been a well-understood invitation to the Gestapo to exercise its vigilance: with painful personal consequences to the offending party.

A factor of great assistance to Hitler was the strongly symbiotic relationship which he managed to establish (with considerable credit to two of his henchmen, Goebbels and Himmler) between propaganda and terror. The Nazi regime supplied lots of "motivation" and "information" through its orchestrated media to the fighting services and to the German population at large. There was no lack of "guidance". Much of it was blatantly false, vicious, and even absurd. But it enjoyed a legal monopoly rendered relatively effective by the skill and efficiency of the Gestapo. In Nazi Germany one could just possibly listen to news reports broadcast by the BBC from London, but only at the peril of one's own life, and perhaps those of one's family's. Discussing such reports with strangers would have been an invitation to a concentration camp or worse. The sanctions were just as predictable as the propaganda, and mutually reinforcing. To believe and to espouse the latter made one relatively safe from the former. It was, above all, in this respect that the Hitler dictatorship, like Stalin's, was vastly superior to that of Mussolini, and to that of many lesser dictators, or would-be-dictators. (Naturally, the word "superior" is used here without any positive moral connotations. The relationship, however, is very relevant to the issue of state "capabilities".)

Another Nazi advantage was in the ability to establish a qualitative orientation to the blitzkrieg strategy, so that not only could there be quick and massive rearmament, but the nature of that rearmament could be rather single-mindedly focused on a speedy attack with the co-ordination of various, appropriate to the task, weapons. This aspect of Nazi preparedness could only be realized if the political leadership knew what it wanted and could silence or overrule the all but inevitable discord, not only among various publics such as exist within democratic political systems, but, above all, within the military bureaucracies themselves, where differences in points of view and institutional and personal interests were just as likely.

There was also the advantage deriving from the coercive aspects of the Hitler regime, to disguise, camouflage, and keep plans and operations secret. This was helpful to the Nazis both at home and abroad. People at home might realize in some general way that big rearmament was taking place by what they saw, or heard from neighbours, or from their own experience if they were, for example, industrial workers. But they could never have more than a vague idea because no "numbers" or "facts" were published and made available to them. In domestic media, they would never hear or read any critical discussion of the subject with possibly adverse disclosures as far as the Nazi regime was concerned. In domestic media, they also could not possibly know what anyone outside Germany was doing. So perhaps, they could think, "The British and the French were arming twice as fast as we were, and we just needed to catch up".

As far as foreign opinion was concerned, Nazi Germany could keep it guessing, feeding it only such morsels of information as it might choose, and thereby add to the atmosphere of confusion, ignorance, and uncertainty among its designated enemies and victims. Secrecy, through a closed policy process, made it possible for Hitler to minimize embarrassing exposures and achieve the desired elements of preparation and surprise. The most important directives of Nazi policy, beginning with the clandestine rearmament effort of 1933 and culminating in the Final Solution decision on the extermination of European Jewry were issued orally, *in camera*, with utmost concern for secrecy. Thus at the outset of Hitler's rule:

> Goebbels was admonished never to allow the words 'General Staff' to appear in the press, since Versailles forbade the very existence of this organization. The annual official rank list of the German Army ceased to be published after 1932 so that its swollen list of officers would not give the game away to foreign intelligence. General Keitel, chairman of the Working Committee of the Reich Defence Council admonished his aides as early as 22 May 1933, 'No document must be lost, since otherwise enemy propaganda will make use of it. Matters communicated orally cannot be proven; they can be denied'.[131]

Another illustration of the Nazi procedures was furnished by Hitler in early 1938 when his then Foreign Minister Baron von Neurath, was fired from his job. Neurath, as we know now, baulked at the prospect of carrying out policies which Hitler had disclosed to him and a few top-ranking officers in certain private meetings (notably 5 November 1937). The announcement of von Neurath's departure from office was disguised with his simultaneous appointment to the presidency of a wholly fictitious entity, called the Secret Cabinet Council, created ostensibly for the purpose of advising the Fuehrer on the conduct of foreign policy![132]

Hitler's dictatorship also facilitated operational control which the Fuehrer could exercise over his military and bureaucratic establishments. That control was far more direct and much more brutal than was the case in the democracies opposing Hitler. The Nazi regime fatally undermined what might be termed, loosely, the "civil service concept" under which most democratic bureaucracies then, and since, have operated. In essence, Hitler was able to reward and punish his bureaucratic subordinates in more extreme ways than was possible for analogous "principal leaders" in the democracies, always restrained by law, rules, media, and opposition. Subordinates had much less recourse, or leverage, against Hitler than they would have had against his democratic counterparts.

The "civil service" concept provides for considerable autonomy within particular state bureaucracies. Bureaucratic duties and rights, and conditions of service, are regulated by administrative boards and by law and include appropriate appeal to the courts wherever violations, infractions, or disputes occur. Promotions, demotions, and transfers of officials are generally regulated partly by rules and partly by decisions of fellow professionals. Very importantly in the democracies, disgruntled bureaucrats have access to independent media, legislatures, opposition politicians, and ultimately the public at large. All this makes the control exercised by political leaders somewhat indirect and not nearly as irresistibly obligatory as it was in Nazi Germany. Obversely, a democratic bureaucrat who acts illegally or high-handedly opens himself to attack from the same quarters which might support him against an arbitrary political executive.

Some interventions by a democratic political leader with his or her bureaucracy could be regarded as illegal, let alone inappropriate, and therefore subject to public criticism, censure, and conceivably Parliamentary, congressional or legal proceedings. When President Nixon in the United States tried to get the Internal Revenue Service to audit the taxes of people he considered political enemies, a storm of public and legislative criticism broke out. The Watergate burglary, simply in the fact that the President *knew* of a criminal act and acted to *conceal* it, was enough to bring Nixon face to face with impeachment and removal from office and led to his resignation in 1974.

Hitler, on the other hand, could follow the path-breaking advice of a relatively junior General von Manstein and not worry about the proprieties of the official hierarchy and the ruffled feelings of the more senior Field Marshal Werner von Brauchitsch.

For purposes of deceiving public opinion, with perhaps the greatest impact at home, Hitler in August of 1939 engaged in a whole series of criminal acts when he ordered operation "Canned Goods". SS officer Alfred Naujocks was ordered to gather some concentration camp inmates, dress them in Polish army uniforms and have them shot on the premises of a German radio station at Gleiwitz to make it appear that they had seized the station as an act of Polish aggression against the Reich. None of those involved worried, or needed to worry, about exposure by the German press, by a possible Parliamentary inquiry, or by opposition criticism. Legally and politically they enjoyed a free hand.

The contrast between the two systems was illustrated nicely by an exchange between Prime Minister Churchill and his most famous commander, Field Marshal Montgomery, in a later period of the war. Shortly before D-Day, Prime Minister Churchill let it be known that he was dissatisfied with the balance of men and vehicles to be shipped with the invading forces onto the Normandy coast. As Churchill saw it, there were too many vehicles and too few fighting men. He apparently suggested that he himself would investigate the matter with Montgomery's staff. Montgomery pre-empted this initiative by asking the Prime Minister to have dinner at his (Montgomery's) headquarters and meet with his senior officers. When Churchill arrived on 19 May 1944, Montgomery ushered him into his private office and delivered the following statement to the Prime Minister:

> I understand, sir, that you want to discuss with my staff the proportion of soldiers to vehicles landing on the beaches in the first flights. I cannot allow you to do so. My staff advise me and I give the final decision; they then do what I tell them.

> The final decision has been given. In any case I could never allow you to harass my staff at this time and possibly shake their confidence in me .... You can argue with me but not with my staff. In any case it is too late to change anything. I consider that what we have done is right; that will be proved on D-Day. If you think it is wrong, that can only mean that you have lost confidence in me.[133]

The Prime Minister did not pursue the matter any further. Could anyone imagine a German General speaking in this fashion to Hitler or a Soviet one speaking in this manner to Stalin?

In the democracies, "status" and "autonomy" tended to reinforce one another in ways that were quite different from the realities of the totalitarian states. Generals, on occasion, developed a substantial political clout of their own, making it extremely difficult, if not impossible, for political superiors to exercise close control over them or, ultimately, even get rid of them. Indeed, this clout was probably reflected in Montgomery's haughty demeanour toward Churchill.

One must be careful not to confuse that which seems to us humane, decent, civilized, or for that mater, morally uplifting, with "effectiveness".[134]

Effectiveness, in many different meanings, historically has often resulted from the ruthless disregard of humanity, decency, civility, and morality -- among many other great virtues..

NOTES

[1] Warsaw surrendered on 27 September, while the last Polish troops offering organized resistance to the Nazis (in the Radzyn-Kock area) surrendered on 5 October. See Robert Goralski, *World War II Almanac: 1939-1945, A Political and Military Record* (New York: Bonanza Books, 1981), pp. 96-97.

[2] According to Cyril Falls, *The Second World War, A Short History*, Second Edition, (London: Methuen, 1948), the ratio of strength between Germany and Poland in mere numbers, apart from qualitative issues, in September of 1939 was 38 Nazi infantry divisions and 4 armoured divisions as against 16 Polish infantry divisions and 10 independent brigades of various sorts, p. 14. "It is hard to recall any campaign in which the odds against the weaker belligerent were so heavy. Position, strength, armament, air support, numbers -- in all these the Poles were hopelessly outmatched". He also describes the Allies' air war (p. 15) against Germany in 1939 and 1940 as "feeble and disappointing". Dispensing propaganda leaflets was an RAF favourite in the early stages of the war, p. 29.

[3] Leonard Mosley, *On Borrowed Time: How World War II Began* (New York: Random House, 1969).

[4] See Stephen Howarth, *August '39, The Last Four Weeks of Peace in Europe*, (London: Hodder & Stoughton, 1989) on how Ribbentrop refused, on 30 August 1939, to give the British Ambassador, Sir Nevile Henderson, a copy of Nazi Germany's 16 "conditions" allegedly demanded of Poland. He claimed it was "too late" for this sort of thing, since the Polish plenipotentiary had not shown up as the Nazis had demanded. Hitler was clearly in a rush to start the war as soon as possible. See Ritchie Ovendale, "Why the British Dominions Declared War" in Robert Boyce and E. M. Robertson (eds.), *Paths to War, New Essays on the Origins of the Second World War* (London: Macmillan, 1989), pp. 269-296. Note "Dominion opinion only confirmed Chamberlain on a course of action on which he had already decided", p. 293. The need to maintain the unity of the Commonwealth was considered, professedly, at least, an important factor in Chamberlain's appeasement policy.

[5] See Nicholas Fleming, *August 1939, The Last Days of Peace* (London: Peter Davies, 1979) for a description of the Allied failure to help Poland once the war had begun, pp. 209-213. He points out that such help was not merely a matter of honour, in light of past promises, or of great interest to Poland. It was actually a tremendously important opportunity to help their own cause that the Allies missed. What was also of great importance for all participants in the conflict was Soviet military intervention in Poland, which was still an open question in September 1939. The Nazis desired it,

so as to extricate themselves in the East as soon as possible. When it actuall. occurred on 17 September 1939, Nazi Foreign Minister Ribbentrop was taken by surprise, p. 218. More aggressive action by Britain and France in the West, possibly helping the Poles resist the Nazi attack more effectively, might have affected this action, too. Characteristically, Fleming concludes that what inspired Hitler's attack on Poland was no more than a whim, a whim which, "directly or indirectly, had brought about the deaths of no fewer than 50 million people", p. 221. See also Leonard Mosley, *op. cit.* (New York: Random House, 1969), pp. 443-444, on Allied guarantees to Poland.

[6]   See Anita Prazmowska, *Britain, Poland and the Eastern Front, 1939* (Cambridge Cambridge University Press, 1987), "... British military action decided upon and taken during September was in no way concerned with the situation on the German Polish front", p. 182. The first meeting of the War Cabinet, now even with Churchill and Eden included, "confirmed the general acceptance of this view", *ibid.* Dropping propaganda leaflets on Germany was the only measure the Cabinet authorized. In a letter Mr. Chamberlain wrote to his sister on 17 September he speculated on Nazis launching an attack in the West after defeating Poland, but concluded, "I see no possibility of [Hitler] scoring a major success in the West", p. 181. See also Col. A. Goutard, *The Battle of France, 1940* (London: Frederick Muller Ltd., 1958) who notes that the overriding French military principle when the Nazis attacked Poland "was to play for time", p. 66. Had the French taken the offensive, "the whole face of Europe would have been changed", p. 64.

Says Goutard: "While all the good German troops were occupied in Poland, our excellent regular divisions, our heavy-duty tanks, and our heavy guns remained silent in front of the Siegfried Line, which was of doubtful strength and was manned by very poor substitutes", p. 63. See also Jon Kimche *The Unfought Battle* (New York: Stein & Day, 1968). The French had a superiority of forty well-equipped divisions against a doubtful seventeen of the Germans. The French had 1,600 artillery pieces against the Germans 300 and 3,286 tanks against none for the Germans. British and French air forces had 934 fighter and 776 serviceable bombers against "virtually none" by Germany in the West, p. 142. "Had Gamelin executed his plan [of attack] it is the opinion of every senior German officer on that front that he would not only have broken through into the heart of Germany, in the direction of Mainz, but he would have trapped the hard core of the German army in the 'sack' in which it had been placed on the Saar Front", *ibid.* The military and political consequences would have been enormous. Cf. Roy Douglas, *The Advent of War 1939-40* (New York: St. Martin's Press, 1978), pp. 144-145. See Tom Shachtman, *The Phoney War 1939-1940* (New York: Harper & Row, 1982), pp. 69-70 on British and Allied reactions toward the events in Poland.

See William Manchester, *The Last Lion, Winston Spencer Churchill Alone 1932-1940* (Boston: Little, Brown, 1988), pp. 606-610, on the so-called Bore War in

Europe in the months between Hitler's conquest of Poland and his attack in the West. The only British casualty on the continent was a "corporal who suffered a flesh wound while cleaning his rifle", p. 606.

[7] German Foreign Office, *Documents on the Events Preceding the Outbreak of the War* (New York: German Library of Information, 1940), pp. 470-472.

[8] Telford Taylor, *The March of Conquest, The German Victories in Western Europe, 1940*, (New York: Simon & Schuster, 1958), p. 37 and p. 313.

[9] Telford Taylor, *op. cit.*, p. 153. See the interesting account by François Kersaudy, *Norway 1940* (London, Collins, 1990) which, unlike many British or Allied apologies, concludes that the only really positive element resulting from the Norwegian campaign for Britain was the replacement of Chamberlain by Churchill, for, as the author wisely observes, "no one can possibly say what would have happened if Neville Chamberlain had remained Prime Minister of Great Britain in the summer of 1940", p. 227. Kersaudy concludes that in human losses, the Norwegian campaign was about even between the Allies and the Nazis. Most interestingly, he finds the Nazi loss of 242 planes to the RAF loss of 112 a "relatively equal loss" given the strengths of each side (p. 225). He seems to think Hitler would not have made any significantly better use of the German navy if he had not suffered the losses that he did (roughly equal to the British but, in this respect, presumably more affordable to Great Britain than to Nazi Germany). "Economically, of course, victory in Norway was highly profitable for the Germans; once they had repaired Narvik harbour, they could receive an uninterrupted supply of both Swedish and Norwegian iron ore: 600,000 tons in 1941, 1.8 million tons in 1943" (p. 226).

[10] See Olav Riste, "Norway", pp. 818-823, in I. C. B. Dear and M. R. D. Foot (eds.), *The Oxford Companion to World War II* (Oxford: Oxford University Press, 1994) at p. 823.

[11] See Alexander Werth, *The Twilight of France 1933-1940* (New York: Harper and Brothers, 1942). Writing in 1942, Alexander Werth concluded that the "lessons of the [Nazi] campaign in Poland ... had been ignored and neglected on the easy assumption that the Poles are Poles and the French are French. Actually, everything tends to show that as an individual soldier the Pole was superior to the Frenchman", p. 352.

He also observed, interestingly, that "human life, generally, was prized too highly both by the French command ... and by many of the individuals directly concerned ... The old spirit of Verdun was lacking ... [The women] wept too much from the very day the Germans invaded Holland and Belgium", pp. 352-353.

[12] J. E. and H. W. Kaufmann, *Hitler's Blitzkrieg Campaigns, The Invasion and Defense of Western Europe, 1939-1940* (Mechanicsburg, PA: Combined Books, 1993), p. 106.

[13] *Ibid.*, pp. 106-107. In fact, apart from considerations of skill, quality of weapons, strategic and tactical abilities, and similarly less tangible factors, it was possible to say

in 1939 or early 1940 that France and Britain jointly exceeded the population of Germany (even after the seizure of Austria and Bohemia and Moravia by Hitler) and that without taking into account the colonies of either of these powers; that they jointly exceeded Germany in the manufacture of most industrial products; and that they also jointly exceeded Germany in the number of military personnel; the number of trained reserves; the number of warships; and even the number of tanks as well as artillery pieces. In aircraft, they were inferior by a ratio of about 3 to 4. See among others Hans Adolf Jacobsen, *Dokumente zur Vorgeschichte des Westfledzuges, 1939-40* (Goettingen: Musterschmidt Verlag, 1956).

[14]   *Ibid.*, p. 139.

[15]   Colonel A. Goutard, *The Battle of France, 1940* (London: Frederick Muller Ltd., 1958), pp. 10-12. See also Pierre Cot, *Triumph of Treason* (New York: Ziff-Davis, 1944). Cot was Minister of Aviation in pre-war France: "The war was badly conducted [by the French] because it had been badly prepared, and it was badly prepared because it had been poorly conceived", p. 231. How this could happen in a "democracy", obviously over a long period of time, is most distressing from the vantage point of liberal ideologues. As for General Weygand's view Cot says that "if there had really been any sincere desire to continue fighting, the means were not lacking. An important battle, not the war, was lost", p. 241.

[16]   Goutard, *op. cit.*, p. 99.

[17]   *Ibid.*, pp. 99-102. Elie J. Bois, *Truth on the Tragedy of France* (London: Hodder & Stoughton, 1941) describes General Gamelin in these terms:

> He had not the reflexes of a leader, but only those of a very intelligent, over-pliable, invertebrate, characterless military official, whose will power had been debased by twenty years of Government ... and political pettifogging. 'The front is broken! The German motorized divisions are on the road to Paris. Nothing will stop them!'. That is what he announced to the Government on the night of 15-16 May, advising it to leave the capital, p. 278.

[18]   *Ibid.*, pp. 135-137, 140. Cf. Perrett, p. 93, on Sedan panic. See also Tom Shachtman, *The Phoney War 1939-1940* (New York: Harper & Row, 1982), pp. 205-210.

[19]   Nicholas Harman, *Dunkirk: The Patriotic Myth* (New York: Simon & Schuster, 1980), p. 75.

[20]   Ronald Atkin, *Pillar of Fire: Dunkirk 1940* (London: Sidgwick & Jackson, 1990), p. 16. See also Basil Karslake, 1940, *The Last Act, The Story of the British Forces in France After Dunkirk* (London: Archon Books, 1979) for significant criticisms of

Allied, and especially British, conduct of military operations against the Nazis; see pp. 225-227.

[21] See Ronald Atkin, *op. cit.*, p. 21.

[22] *Ibid.*, p. 22.

[23] See Elie J. Bois, *Truth on the Tragedy of France, op. cit.* He speaks of a political-moral decay underlying the Fall of France in the following terms:

> ... successive French Governments, yielding to the wave of complacent optimism and unalloyed pacifism which submerged all the democracies, allowed [France's] military machine little by little to grow rusty: that the public, swept away in an impetuous current of demagogy, virtually lost its rational sense, even to the extent of displaying an indecent sense of well-being, on the morrow of Munich agreements, which were only excusable on the ground of the Western democracies' lack of preparedness: that Communist, Hitlerian and ultra-Conservative propaganda poisoned the soul of France and that the efforts at recovery in the military and aerial field, as in the moral, were not sufficiently energetic at a time when they should have been remorseless -- all this is but too glaringly apparent", pp. 26-27.

See Rene de Chambrun, *I Saw France Fall; Will She Rise Again?* (New York: William Morrow, 1940) who recalled a conversation with President Lebrun in which the latter expressed the view in May of 1940 that only the energetic "exercise of authority" by whoever might be the democratic leader could save the day against the Nazis, p. 184.

[24] Andre Maurois, "Why France Trusts England", *Harper's Magazine*, Vol. 179, June 1939, pp. 28-34.

[25] See Robert Strausz-Hupé, "France Goes To War", *Current History*, Vol. LI, No. 3, November 1939, pp. 22-26. Note also pp. 25-26. See also Vincent Sheean, "France at War", *Current History*, Vol. LI, No. 9, May 1940, pp. 13-14 and p. 62. In the very month of France's tragedy, Mr. Sheean wrote: "France ... is steeled to resist a great deal (!?) and cannot regard any defeat, as more than temporary", p. 13.

[26] Genevieve Tabouis, "France Looks Ahead", *The New Republic*, Vol. 102, No. 3, January 15, 1940, p. 79. The magazine didn't "wake up" until 17 June 1940 when the editor finally concluded that "It is hard to see how things could get much worse for the Allies", Vol. 102, No. 25, p. 807 ("The Darkest Hour").

[27] See Fritz Sternberg, "Sigfried Line vs. Maginot Line", *The American Mercury*, Vol. XLIV, No. 195, March 1940, pp. 286-293. Quotation is taken from p. 293.

[28] See Alexander Marwald, "The German General Staff: Model of Military Organization", *Orbis*, Vol. IV, No. 1, Spring 1959, pp. 38-62, with considerable information on the ostensible defects of German military planning and organization and Hitler's role in them. Note pp. 47-51 on the limitations of Hitler's role. On clearly ideological grounds, Marwald seems to have had a problem diagnosing the merits of Nazi military organization. Thus, we find him saying:

> "The battlefield performance of the German army, usually in the face of superior numbers and equipment, has been a professional achievement of the highest order" (p. 50).

But, on the other hand, he laments the fact that:

> "Whenever Hitler was called upon to make a decision, military or otherwise, he rarely acted upon the documentation prepared for him by the staff. He operated through snap judgments, relying on his superior gifts of "intuition". There is no other example of such a monstrous command arrangement. Surely, this pathological system sheds very little light on the theory and practice of military organization" (p. 48).

Marwald was apparently missing something important as he concluded:

> "Hitler abetted the tendency of the services to retain their full independence by often over-ruling his staff and by keeping the chief of the Füehrungsstab consistently at a relatively low rank. He never gave a job to an officer who could have asserted himself. Consequently, no joint, let alone unified, planning was done except on an occasional ad hoc basis" (p. 49).

Obviously, with whatever cost to bureaucratic-institutional tidiness, the Nazi Fuehrer exercised a highly flexible and simultaneously highly autocratic system of command. If the leader's ideas were bad, the results might well be disastrous. On the other hand, of course, if the leader's ideas ("intuitions") were good, there was much less chance of bureaucratic bottlenecks thwarting them.

[29] Albert Seaton, *German Army, 1933-1945* (New York: New American Library, 1982), pp. 140-141.

[30] Bryan Perrett, *A History of Blitzkrieg* (London: Robert Hale, 1983), p. 101. The Kaufmanns, *op. cit.*, give total Allied losses in killed-in-action at 106,915, p. 308.

[31] On Hitler's order to halt the German advance, see Norman Gelb, *Dunkirk, The Complete Story of the First-Step in the Defeat of Hitler* (New York: William Morrow & Company, 1989), pp. 129-132; Robert Carse, *Dunkirk 1940* (Englewood Cliffs, NJ: Prentice Hall, 1970), pp. 24-25. Note also p. 205; Ronald Atkin, *Pillar of Fire, Dunkirk 1940* (London: Sidgwick & Jackson, 1990), pp. 119-120. Some senior Nazi commanders, notably von Rundstedt, may have advised Hitler to halt the advance because they feared that their flanks were too exposed by the rapid advance of German armour. In this scenario, unlike many others, Hitler agreed with his cautious Generals. The real reasons for Hitler's decision are still unclear. See the extensive account by Col. Goutard, *op. cit.*, pp. 227-234. As Gen. Heinz Guderian was to write later: "After May 24 there was an intervention by the High Command in the conduct of operations which was to have an unfavourable influence on the whole course of the war. Hitler halted the left wing of the army ... No reasons were given for his order. The words used were: 'Dunkirk must be left to the Luftwaffe' ... We were dumb with astonishment", p. 230. Note Hitler's "appreciation-of-the-British" remarks made to various senior officers between 17 and 24 May, p. 233. Goutard himself says that the British "ought to light Hitler a large candle, for it was certainly his order to halt that saved their Expeditionary Force ... not the defeat of the Luftwaffe by the RAF nor the Royal Navy's evacuation ... [a] wonderful harvest ... was within [Hitler's] grasp". p. 234.

[32] Adolf Hitler, *Mein Kampf*, translated by Ralph Manheim (Boston: Houghton Mifflin, 1943), p. 673. Note also pp. 615, 618, picturing the French as more hostile to Germany than the British.

[33] *Mein Kampf, op. cit.*, p. 658. Note also p. 663, where Hitler says that pre-war Germany should have allied itself with England; also pp. 664-665.

[34] *Op. cit.*, p. 160.

[35] See Roger Parkinson, *Peace For Our Time, Munich to Dunkirk, The Inside Story* (London: Rupert Hart-Davis, 1971) who records the opinion of Neville Chamberlain on 10 May 1940, when he had already yielded the Prime Ministership to Churchill, that the reason for the Government's war failures was "the country's comparative weakness ...", p. 346. But why couldn't British democracy ever wake up between 1933 and 1940? That question Chamberlain never addressed.

In an otherwise somewhat sensationalized book, Louis C. Kilzer examines various facets of Britain's 1940-1941 situation; he records this rather reasonable view of Stalin's miscalculations of Hitler: "Since German border incursions on 5 April [1941] Josef Stalin believed that war with Germany was inevitable. But he was determined to postpone it for a year, believing Hitler would be accommodating. Certainly, Stalin felt, Hitler would not attack [Russia] before eliminating Great Britain. Instead he would do the logical thing: he would land his troops in Iraq and Syria and allow Rommel to checkmate Egypt. That done, Britain would be without oil or gas and would crumble. Then, Hitler would come to Russia". See *Churchill's Deception: The Dark Secret That Destroyed Nazi Germany* (New York: Simon & Schuster, 1994), p. 278. The author also says: "Did forcing the war east save Britain from defeat? It did, but only from a man intent on not defeating her. Hitler, as much as Churchill, saved Britain", p. 289.

[36] See Maxime Weygand, *Recalled to Service, The Memoirs of General Maxime Weygand* (London: William Heinemann, 1952). In his post-war retrospective, Weygand says that: "A just appreciation of the military situation in 1940 is, indeed, only possible if it is borne in mind that Great Britain no longer possessed forces in a condition to fight on the continent, that America did not enter the war until eighteen months later, and that for a year to come Russia was still allied to Germany", p. 210.

The following observation by General Weygand is also worthy of note:

> "Knowing the reduced resources then possessed by Great Britain, I thought in the first weeks of the armistice that if the Germans made a mass attack our friends would need good fortune, which I fervently wished them, for successful resistance", p. 249.

[37] See Martin S. Alexander, "The Fall of France, 1940", *The Journal of Strategic Studies*, Vol. 13, No. 1, March 1990, pp. 10-44; Hitler's easy victory over France, according to Alexander, gave him a false sense of invincibility and thus encouraged the mistake of *Barbarossa*, pp. 35-36.

See Andre Maurois, *Tragedy in France* (London: Harper and Brothers, 1940), Chapter II, "Why the First Eight Months of the War Were Wasted", pp. 27-61. Maurois cites in this order the causes of failure, 1) stupidity of industrial mobilization; 2) planning for a past war, not a present or future one; 3) political dissension; and 4) "a general lack of [popular] enthusiasm".

[38] Robert Carse, *Dunkirk 1940, A History* (Englewood Cliffs, NJ: Prentice Hall, 1940), p. 205.

See also *Foreign Relations of the United States, The Conference at Washington, 1941-1942* (Washington, DC: GPO, 1968), 4 December 1941, remarks by US Admiral Harold R. Stark to the effect that two US Marine Corps observers who had carried out inspections in 1941 thought that British defences against a possible invasion of England "left much to be desired", pp. 82-83.

[39] See Malcolm Smith, "Battle of Britain" in I. C. B. Dear and N. R. D. Foot (eds.), *The Oxford Companion to World War II* (Oxford: Oxford University Press, 1995), pp. 158-163. The quotation appears on p. 163. Note, e.g., Peter Townsend, *Duel of Eagles* (New York: Simon & Schuster, 1970), p. 433: The Battle of Britain ... would prove to be one of the most crucial battles in history".

Note William Shirer, *op. cit.*, p. 781: "Hitler's bomber losses over England had been so severe that they could never be made up, and in fact the Luftwaffe, as the German confidential records make clear, never fully recovered from the blow it received in the skies over Britain that late summer and fall".

By the time Hitler launched *Barbarossa* against Russia on 22 June 1941, the number of aircraft devoted to this operation was virtually equal to that employed against France on 10 May 1940, about 3,000.

[40] See Robert Goralski, *World War II Almanac 1931-1945, A Political and Military Record* (New York, Bonanza Books, 1981), p. 438.

[41] *The United States Strategic Bombing Survey*, Vol. I (New York: Garland Publishing Inc., 1976), pp. 148, 151, See also Telford Taylor, *The Breaking Wave: The Second World War in the Summer of 1940* (New York: Simon & Schuster, 1967), p. 187. "In the Battle of Britain the Luftwaffe was injured painfully but not mortally. In fact the Luftwaffe's total losses were higher during the two months of the Battle of France (May and June) than during the two crucial months (August and September) of the Battle of Britain. Fewer fighters were lost during the Battle of France (367 as compared to 668) but the bomber losses were slightly higher (521 to 508), and the Stuka (122 to 67), reconnaissance (166 to 46), and transport (213 to 11) losses were very much higher".

[42] It should be noted, of course, that once Hitler had conquered and subjected most of Europe to his will, as he did in June 1940, there was no reason why over the longer period of time, anywhere from three to five or six years, the Nazis could not have out produced the British in ship construction, too. Nevertheless, ship construction in the 30s and 40s was not as rapid as aircraft production, and therefore, even-loss-exchanges at sea were, for practical purposes, more damaging to Germany than even-loss-exchanges in the air.

[43] See B. H. Liddell Hart (ed.), *The Rommel Papers* (New York: Da Capo Press, 1953). As Field Marshal Rommel observed subsequently:

> In my opinion it was ... wrong not to risk a landing in England in 1940-41. If ever there was a chance for this operation to succeed it was in the period after the British Expeditionary Force had lost its equipment. From then on the operation became steadily more difficult to undertake, and undertaken it eventually had to be, if the war against Britain was to be won, p. 106.

[44] See Andrew Lambert, "Seapower 1939-1940: Churchill and the Strategic Origins of the Battle of the Atlantic", *The Journal of Strategic Studies*, Vol. 17, No. 1, March 1994, pp. 86-108. For a relatively favourable assessment of Churchill's understanding of sea warfare, allegedly offset by factors beyond Churchill's control. Note p. 86 and

p. 106. See also Jock Gardner, "The Battle of the Atlantic, 1941 -- The First Turning Point?", *The Journal of Strategic Studies*, Vol. 17, No. 1, March 1994, pp. 109-123. This essay attempts to put the "ultra hype" of recent years -- alleged British mastery of German communications -- into a more realistic and balanced perspective.

[45] William K. Klingaman, *1941, Our Lives in a World on the Edge* (New York: Harper & Row, 1988), p. 274.

[46] Colonel Albert Seaton reports German losses at 8,000, including the wounded: *The German Army, 1933-1945* (New York: New American Library, 1982), p. 171. Brigadier Peter Young in his *The World Almanac of World War II* (New York: Bison Books, 1981), cites a figure of 7,000 for the Germans and 17,000 for the British, p. 106. Goralski, *op. cit.*, gives a figure of 6,000 dead for the Nazis and 13,000 British and 14.5 thousand Greek troops lost, p. 160.

[47] Estimates of the original *Barbarossa* force differ. According to Marcel Baudot, *et. al.* (eds.), *The Historical Encyclopedia of World War II* (New York: Greenwich House, 1980), p. 42, the Nazis deployed 205 divisions.

[48] 351 H.C. Deb. 5s, pp. 977, 978. As Anita Prazmowska notes, the idea that Poland's ultimate fate "would depend on the final defeat, at some unspecified future time, of Germany ... was ... a piece of rhetorical ritual that effectively enabled Chamberlain to avoid the commitment that Britain had under the March guarantee to defend Polish territory from aggression", *op. cit.*, p. 192.

[49] 351 H.C. Deb. 5s, p. 978.

[50] *Ibid.*, p. 982.

[51] *Ibid.*, p. 983.

[52] *Ibid.*

[53] *Ibid.*, p. 984.

[54] *Ibid.*, p. 989.

[55] *Ibid.*, p. 991.

[56] *Ibid.*

[57] *Ibid.*, p. 998.

[58] *Ibid.*, p. 1013.

[59] *Ibid.*, p. 1004.

[60] *Ibid.*, p. 1006.

[61] *Ibid.*, p. 1020.

[62] *Ibid.*

[63] *Ibid.*, p. 1234.

[64] See *Ibid.*, pp. 1283-1308.

[65] *Ibid.*, pp. 1251-1252.

[66] *Ibid.*, p. 1270.

[67] *Ibid.*, p. 1275.

[68] *Ibid.*, p. 1274.

[69] *Ibid.*, p. 1312.

[70] *Ibid.*, pp. 1857-1858.

[71] *Ibid.*, pp. 1898-1899.

[72] *Ibid.*, pp. 1884-1886.

[73] *Ibid.*, pp. 1901-1906.

[74] *Ibid.*, pp. 1914-1916.

[75] *Ibid.*, pp. 1855-1922.

[76] R. W. Thompson, *Generalissimo Churchill* (London: Hodder & Stoughton, 1973). "When finally the tragic failure of the assault on the Dardanelles and the disastrous failure in Gallipoli overtook the British, Churchill became the natural scapegoat", pp. 33-34. See Robert R. James, *Churchill, A Study in Failure 1900-1939* (New York: The World Publishing Company, 1970): "All the evidence now available demonstrates the fact that Churchill initiated the Dardanelles project and pushed it with vigour, overruling or ignoring the doubts and criticisms of his service advisers", p. 78. Note also pp. 85-86. On the other hand, the campaign "was to cost the allies a quarter-of-a-million casualties before it was abandoned at the end of the year" (p. 85) and when "the crash came [Churchill] found himself -- like Lord Randolph in December 1886 -- completely isolated", p. 89. To believe that this was a sobering experience in Churchill's career is not unreasonable.

[77] *Ibid.*, p. 199. See also Higgins' subsequent *Soft Underbelly, the Anglo-American Controversy over the Italian Campaign 1939-1945* (New York: Macmillan, 1968), pp. 221-222: "Neither public nor professional military opinion in Great Britain was willing to endure casualties on the 1916-1918 scale for the sake of saving their European allies again or even to defeat Hitler more rapidly".

[78] See Martin Gilbert, *Road to Victory, Winston S. Churchill 1941-1945* (London: Heinemann, 1986), pp. 20-22, on the peripheral strategy of Churchill and the British Chiefs of Staff. In December 1941, Churchill wrote a note in which he indicated that "there was no need to fear any excesses of venturesome offensive action for 1943(!) ... I cannot, however, agree that all talk of this(!) must be postponed until Germany has been so weakened by night air-bombing as not to be able to offer any effective resistance to liberating armies", p. 21. Maxwell Philip Schoenfeld, *The War Ministry of Winston Churchill* (Ames, Iowa: The Iowa State University Press, 1972), pp. 128-129, on this "peripheral strategy" with the "all-important principle that the United States must be brought into the war", p. 128. Note also "Reliance on a small, specialized army and the hope of massive European defection from German rule

[implied] that direct military confrontation in overwhelming force was to be avoided", *ibid.* R. W. Thompson, *op. cit.*, p. 87, on Churchill's conviction that Britain could only overcome Germany's great military advantage through "the power of the bomber". On coalition strategy, see pp. 87-88. On his management of the Norwegian fiasco, scc pp. 58-65.

An image of Churchill, the dauntless warrior and adventurer, widely accepted and disseminated by various authors, obscures the cautious and limited strategy he really pursued.

[79] 359 H.C. Deb. 5s, p. 747. See Manchester, *op. cit.*, pp. 635-636, on Churchill's old-fashioned views about sea power with their characteristic underestimation of the role of aircraft. See also pp. 638-639, on his misjudgments concerning Norway.

[80] 359 H.C. Deb. 5s, p. 747.

[81] *Ibid.*, p. 748.

[82] Note George C. Herring, Jr., *Aid to Russia 1941-1946* (New York: Columbia University Press, 1973) on the effective use of Norwegian bases by the Nazis in deploying U-boats and aircraft against Allied convoys headed for the Soviet Union, pp. 43, 62-63, 65. See also W. H. Tantum IV and E. J. Hoffschmidt (eds.), *The Rise and Fall of the German Air Force* (Greenwich, Conn.: W. E. Inc., 1969), pp. 113-115, 116. See also M. A. Probert (ed.), *The Rise and Fall of the German Air Force 1933-1945* (London: Arms and Armour Press, 1983), pp. 103-115.

[83] 360 H.C. Deb. 5s, p. 1074.

[84] *Ibid.*, p. 1075. J. L. Moulton, *The Norwegian Campaign of 1940* (London: Eyre & Spottiswoode, 1966), gives Allied casualties in Norway at 1,355 Norwegians, 1,869 British and 533 French and Polish killed and wounded. German losses are given at 1,317 killed and 2,375 lost, p. 259. British aircraft losses were 112 compared to 200 for the Germans. The Nazis sank 7 British destroyers and 3 cruisers (*HMS Glorious, HMS Effingham* and *HMS Curlew*), p. 260. See Martin K. Sorge, *The Other Price of Hitler's War: German Military and Civilian Losses Resulting from World War II* (New York: Greenwood Press, 1986) who gives the following Nazi losses in Norway: total casualties 5,660 of whom 1,317 were killed and 2,375 lost "mainly when their ships were sunk" (p. 5). 200 aircraft were lost and 3 cruisers; 10 destroyers; 6 submarines and 1 torpedo boat (several large ships on both sides were damaged), *ibid.* The last Allied forces were evacuated from Norway, i.e., from Narvik, on June 9. Goralski, *op. cit.*, reports that Germany lost 3 of her 8 cruisers and 10 of her 20 destroyers; the Royal Navy lost 2 cruisers and 10 "destroyers and sloops" but out of a much larger naval force. (The British, e.g., had 58 cruisers in 1939, p. 89.)

The advantage in relative terms was thus clearly to the British, and, among other things, may have helped with the subsequent evacuation of the British and French from the beaches of Dunkirk, p. 110. See also Telford Taylor, *The March of Conquest, The German Victories in Western Europe, 1940* (New York: Simon &

Schuster, 1958), pp. 152-154. The long-term effects of Nazi naval losses and the overall value to the Nazis of the seizure of Denmark and Norway are a matter of controversy. Goralski and many other authors, sympathetic to Britain, usually forgot the usefulness of Norway for Nazi U-boats attacking convoys bound for Russia in 1942-1944.

[85] 360 H.C. Deb. 5s, p. 1087.

[86] *Ibid.*, pp. 1093-1094.

[87] *Ibid.*, p. 1129.

[88] *Ibid.*, p. 1148.

[89] *Ibid.*, p. 1283.

[90] *Ibid.*, p. 1357.

[91] *Ibid.*, p. 1362.

[92] *Ibid.*, p. 1360.

[93] *Ibid.*

[94] *Ibid.*, p. 1502.

[95] *Ibid.*

[96] *Ibid.*

[97] *Ibid.*, p. 1510. See Richard Collier, *1940: The Avalanche* (New York: The Dial Press, 1979) on the ouster of Chamberlain and the initial preference for Lord Halifax among some of the leaders of the major political parties, pp. 60-64. In May of 1940 the "men of Munich" felt understandably ambivalent about Winston Churchill.

[98] See 381 H.C. Deb. 5s, p. 530.

[99] Compare Telford Taylor, *op. cit.*, pp. 313-314. "Allied losses were ... much heavier than those of the Germans", p. 313. German casualties had been "extraordinarily light", *ibid.*

[100] 362 H.C. Deb. 5s, pp. 60-61.

[101] 364 H.C. Deb. 5s, pp. 1162-1163.

[102] *Ibid.*, p. 1166.

[103] *Ibid.*, p. 1273. It is appropriate to note, that if one uses the same "accounting method" in the Battle of Britain that many authors have used in evaluating British and Nazi naval losses in Norway, the conventional view of the results must be revised. Note Brigadier Peter Young, *The World Almanac Book of World War II* (New York: Bison, 1981), p. 54. He estimates Luftwaffe strength in May 1940 as 3 to 2 over both Britain and France. The population ratio between Germany and Britain in 1939 was 1.43 to 1 in favour of the former. It grew to 1.7 to 1 by 1940 with the various Nazi conquests.

Note Len Deighton *Battle of Britain* (London: Jonathan Cape, 1980), pp. 213-214, for a reasonable appreciation. Hitler probably would have attempted an invasion of Britain if the RAF had been destroyed. "At the very least, with Fighter Command ruined, the Luftwaffe would have been able to bomb Britain in daylight with impunity and ... ultimately [force] the British to surrender", p. 213.

The British victory has been exaggerated in response to certain, unrelated later events. As Derek Wood and Derek Dempster point out, in the aftermath of the Battle, the Luftwaffe did not make any substantial "changes in the structure of the [German] air force or its equipment", p. 409. This was, no doubt, far more serious than the actual losses it suffered. *The Narrow Margin: The Battle of Britain and the Rise of Air Power 1939-40* (London: Hutchinson, 1961). Compare Williamson Murray, *Strategy for Defeat, The Luftwaffe 1933-1945* (Washington, DC: US Government Printing Office, 1983), p. 55. "What was almost incomprehensible is the fact that the Germans paid so little attention to the attrition that had occurred in France and over Britain", p. 302.

[104] 361 H.C. Deb. 5s, p. 1167.

[105] 371 H.C. Deb. 5s, p. 798.

[106] *Ibid.*, p. 802.

[107] *Ibid.*, p. 786.

[108] *Ibid.*

[109] *Ibid.*, p. 788.

[110] *Ibid.*, p. 931.

[111] *Ibid.*, p. 932.

[112] *Ibid.*, p. 937.

[113] *Ibid.*, p. 940.

[114] 372 H.C. Deb. 5s, p. 65.

[115] *Ibid.*, p. 70.

[116] *Ibid.*

[117] *Ibid.*, p. 65.

[118] *Ibid.*, p. 65.

[119] *Ibid.*, p. 79.

[120] *Ibid.*, p. 151.

[121] William L. Shirer, *The Rise and Fall of the Third Reich, A History of Nazi Germany* (New York: Simon & Schuster, 1960).

[122] *Ibid.*, p. 829.

[123] *The Rommel Papers, op. cit.*, p. 105. Rommel himself believed that if he had been given another six mechanized divisions, and reasonably reliable supplies, he would have been able to defeat the British decisively in North Africa, but, as he noted:

> Basically ... there was no understanding of the situation, and thus no will to do anything.

And he concluded:

> With only three German divisions, whose fighting strength was often ludicrously small, we kept the British Army busy in Africa for eighteen long months and gave them many a trouncing, until our strength finally ran out at Alamein, p. 192.

[124] *Ibid.*, pp. 184-185. It is perhaps natural that at least among some British military commentators there has been great reticence in dealing with Rommel's exploits in Africa. A good example is Bryan Perrett's book, *A History of Blitzkrieg*, cited here earlier. The author devotes a whole chapter consisting of 19 pages to the discussion of warfare in North Africa with only 2 paragraphs devoted to the British experience with Rommel. All the rest was a much more comfortable discussion of fighting the Italian army. Note also Perrett's treatment of the Dunkirk episode, pp. 98-99.

[125] Hanson W. Baldwin, *The Crucial Years 1939-1941, The World at War* (New York: Harper & Row, 1970), p. 249.

See Lucio Ceva, "The North African Campaign 1940-43: A Reconsideration", *The Journal of Strategic Studies*, Vol. 13, No. 1, March 1990, pp. 84-104; the author discusses the performance of Italian troops in North Africa, finds some good performances but concedes that the Italian working class found it hard to hate the British .. and the Americans, even harder, pp. 101-102.

[126] See especially Daniel F. Gallery, *Twenty Million Tons Under the Sea* (Chicago: Henry Regnery Company, 1956), p. 35, for the following data reflecting the situation as of August 20, 1941:

Allied merchant vessels sunk	6,653
Tonnage lost	8,000,000
New construction	3,000,000
Net loss	5,000,000
New U-boats commissioned	153
Net gain	113*

* Plus 57 original boats = 170 total fleet

[127] Winston Churchill, *History of the Second World War* (London: Cassell, 1970), p. 141. See Edward P. Von Der Porten, *The Germany Navy in World War II* (New York: Crowell, 1969), pp. 175-176, on the opportunities of "strangling" Britain's shipping within one year of 1 January 1941, and pp. 178-179 on Hitler's failure to step up the resource priorities for submarine construction. See also W. D. Puleston, *The Influence of Sea Power in World War II* (New Haven: Yale University Press, 1947), pp. 67-68, who puts the peak of German submarine warfare at April 1941. On Hitler's failure to take full advantage of submarine capabilities, see Anthony Martienssen, *Hitler and His Admirals* (New York: E. P. Dutton, 1949), pp. 98 and 104, to same effect. Admiral Raeder protested the launching of *Barbarossa* before the decisive defeat of Britain. Also Captain S. W. Roskill, *The War At Sea 1939-1945*, Vol. I (London: Her Majesty's Stationery Office, 1954), pp. 362-365 and pp. 481-482. P. K. Kemp, *Key to Victory: The Triumph of British Sea Power in World War II* (Boston: Little, Brown, 1957), pp. 150-151, and p. 190. See also, Cajus Bekker, *Hitler's Naval War* (Garden City, NJ: Doubleday, 1974), p. 200, who sees U-boat successes against Britain matched by successful anti-submarine operations of the British navy and air force, but concurs in the potential of U-boat warfare for German victory which Hitler neglected with unrealistic and half-hearted plans for *Sealion* and then the diversion of resources to other enterprises, including *Barbarossa*. Construction of U-boats was relatively neglected, pp. 235-236; also pp. 337-338. "While the British authorities never wavered in their conviction that the war would be decided in the Atlantic, the German High Command, with its mind focused on the continent, was slow to reach the same conclusion   By the time the crucial importance of the U-boat arm was recognized the war was already lost". Note also Robert Cecil who observes that if Hitler had been really serious about "finishing off" the British in mid-1941, "skilled men should have been released from the army and put to work on the construction of U-boats and long-range aircraft, in order to cut Britain from her supplies. The rate of sinkings in October 1940 provided encouragement for this strategy though Admiral Doenitz estimated that it would not yield decisive results before the end of 1941 ... Hitler did not adopt this order of priority in production". *Hitler's Decision to Invade Russia 1941* (London: Davis Poynter, 1975), p. 79. See analogous views of Alan Bullock, in *The Origins of the Second World War: A. J. P. Taylor and His Critics* (New York: John Wiley, 1972), pp. 142-143.

[128] Winston Churchill, *The Second World War, Their Finest Hour* (Boston: Houghton Mifflin Company, 1949), p. 598.

[129] Winston Churchill, Vol. III, *The Grand Alliance* (1950), pp. 11-12. There were still other means of waging war which Hitler could have used with effective results. One of these, Battle of Britain notwithstanding, was air warfare. As Basil Collier reminds us, the British casualties in that battle were such as to "scarcely justify the

popular impression that the fighter force was stronger at the end of the battle than at the beginning ... The battle had been won, but by a margin whose narrowness was apparent only to those who had studied its progress in all its aspects and all its phases". *History of the Second World War: The Defence of the United Kingdom* (London: Her Majesty's Stationery Office, 1957), p. 250. Yet, as early as 6 February 1941, Hitler had issued a directive declaring that "we are unable to maintain the scope of our air attacks, as the demands of other theatres of war compel us to withdraw increasingly large air forces from operations against the British Isles". H. R. Trevor-Roper, *Blitzkrieg to Defeat, Hitler's War Directives 1939-1945* (New York: Holt, Reinhart & Winston, 1964), p. 56.

[130] There was a great paradox about Nazi military mobilization policies. Under Hitler's direction, Germany substantially outperformed the levels of military output among the Democracies during the 1930s. But once the war started, Hitler, whether out of overconfidence in response to the successes of his Blitzkrieg, or the desire not to strain the morale of the German home front, or perhaps both, did not resort to all-out economic mobilization.

In one of his more fateful mistakes of the whole war, Nazi all-out effort at home did not begin until after the Battle of Stalingrad. Thus, we find that in the peacetime period, between the end of 1932 and the end of 1936, the German share of GNP devoted to defence rose from 1 per cent to 13 per cent while Britain only went from 2 per cent to 5 per cent, and the United States remained stationary. But between 1939 and 1942 Germany's share of GNP given to war purposes rose from 23 to 55 per cent, while Britain rose from 22 to 64 per cent. The United States moved up from 1 to 31 per cent in the same period, and, despite its huge aggregate output, never exceeded 42 per cent of its GNP in the military sector. See Berenice Carroll, *op. cit.*, p. 184. According to Alfred C. Mierzejewski, *The Collapse of the German War Economy 1944-1945* (Chapel Hill: University of North Carolina, 1988) the respective belligerent populations c. 1943 were: UK, 42 million; Germany, 81.1 million; USSR, 170.5 million; USA, 137.3 million. Steel output was 13.2 million tons in Britain; 30.6 in Germany; only 8.4 in the USSR; and 82.1 in the US, p. 66.

[131] William L. Shirer, *The Rise and Fall of the Third Reich* (New York: Simon & Schuster, 1960), p. 281.

[132] *Ibid.*, p. 319, *Decree of Fuehrer*, 4 February 1939.

[133] Bernard Montgomery, *The Memoirs of Field Marshal The Viscount Montgomery of El Alamein, K. G.* (New York: World Publishing Company, 1958), pp. 213-214.

[134] See Alexander J. Groth and David W. Loebsack, "Regimes and Conflict Management: From World War to Cold War", *The Korean Journal of International Studies*, Vol. IX, No. 4, Autumn 1978, pp. 57-81, on some of the themes discussed here.

5   HITLER AND AMERICAN DEMOCRACY

Public opinion in the United States during the 1930s was at first largely indifferent to Hitler and Hitlerism. Only gradually, in response to various specific events and the assorted Hitler "initiatives" did it become more mobilized in the sense of becoming more concerned and attentive about foreign policy questions involving Nazi Germany. But, always, as it grew more attentive, it continued to be significantly divided in a variety of different ways.

The most fundamental cleavage in opinion was between isolationists and internationalists. The former generally viewed American involvement in the First World War as a huge, bloody mistake never to be repeated. They saw the failed League of Nations as an instrument for drawing the United States into dangerous and costly international adventures. The League was viewed by the isolationists not as an instrument of collective security (a favourite term among liberal internationalists) but rather as a sure road to war. The isolationists were, by and large, though not entirely, nationalists. (There was an important Leftist contingent, too.)

Their "civic religion" was based on George Washington's Farewell Address warning against American entanglements in Europe. They adhered to the Monroe Doctrine of keeping the New World, with its valuable American Experiment, safe from the wily predators of Europe. Their villain was Woodrow Wilson, who had dragged the United States into the bloody conflict of 1914-1918 (for America, of course, from 1917 to 1918) and then attempted to compound the mistake by supporting American membership in the League of Nations, an organization which would have legalized and institutionalized a most imprudent involvement by the United States in every quarrel of the whole world. Fortunately, of course, under the leadership of the Republican Party, the United States Senate rejected this Wilsonian folly by voting against the ratification of US participation in the new League in 1919.

The isolationists of the Left (including Communists after the Stalin-Hitler Pact) saw American involvement abroad as a perilous concession to greedy and unscrupulous munitions manufacturers. To them, all talk of political-military "preparedness" was either deliberate or an innocently foolish concession to the power of the big-money profiteers for whom war was a lucrative business. In this view, people needed to be on guard against the malevolent arms monopolists, the sinister interests described in Lenin's *Imperialism* of 1916, who converted the blood of the masses, especially that of poor working people, into gold for themselves.

Many isolationists wanted to cater to the fears and prejudices of small-town and rural America, profoundly suspicious of the goings-on in a seemingly strange and distant external world beyond their personal horizons. Anti-Roosevelt partisanship was very important. People who hated the New Deal and who saw Franklin Roosevelt as a would-be-dictator and a socialist revolutionary were likely to transfer their animosities and suspicions from domestic questions to those of foreign policy. This was especially true, and especially significant, because many of these people recognized -- not without reason -- that the management of foreign relations, especially in connection with military measures, would likely bolster the Chief Executive in his constitutional and historical capacity as the Commander-in-Chief. International interventions under Roosevelt meant a stronger Roosevelt, and this was anathema to many people on the political Right.

There were also important ethnic components supporting the power of American Isolationism. Among Italian-Americans and among German-Americans of the 1930s there was considerable opposition to measures directed against their old homelands -- for example, economic boycotts -- even if such measures might have been actually aimed at the governments of Mussolini and Hitler.

There were likewise isolationists who were more clearly and definably Fascist and Nazi sympathizers, especially among those who were also strongly anti-Semitic and strongly anti-Communist, because of the obvious ideological support which Fascism, and especially Nazism, provided for such orientations. There were also people who could be described as fervent pacifists, whether religious or not, and people who were "bandwagon followers" of Fascist Italy and Nazi Germany seeing in them successful, thriving social experiments, and believing also that any opposition to these regimes was not only risky but useless and foolish as well.

On the other side of the great divide, American internationalists were also far from homogeneous in outlook. Democrats, New Dealers, and Roosevelt supporters were more likely to be "internationalists", than were Republicans and political and social conservatives. Some ethnic groups were more interventionist than others, presenting a mosaic of attitudes which varied with the issue and the time related to every possible American involvement in foreign affairs. In the mid-1930s, the African-American population was increasingly mobilized on the side of internationalism by Mussolini's invasion of Ethiopia. Jews, assailed by Hitler's vitriolic anti-Semitism, were more likely than other ethnic groups to support anti-Nazi initiatives by the Roosevelt administration. People of British origins were also more likely to support the kind of interventionism Roosevelt promoted -- directed against the Axis powers -- than were people from other parts of Europe and the world. But within the loosely-defined internationalist coalition there were also differences in interest and outlook, especially with respect to the critical issue of how much intervention?   On whose behalf?   At what cost?   Under what circumstances?

Given all the division and the differences, the question, nevertheless, was, what stake did the United States possess in the incipient European conflict of the 1930s?   There were some powerful factors constraining American interventionism beyond the issue of personal predilections of individual citizens. Could the United States of the 1930s afford to see most of the economically, politically, culturally and militarily significant "world" outside its own borders dominated by a hostile power, or combination of hostile powers, denying it opportunities of trade and other interactions with that world? Could the United States afford in the 20th century to be reduced to a "fortress America", closed and self-contained, and isolated from the rest of the developed world?

That developed world outside the American border was clearly Europe, and especially so in combination with the rest of the "world island", that is, Asia and Africa, and, of course, the entire Middle East. On the very doubtful assumption that there could be a Fortress USA, with perhaps a few outliers such as South America and Australia, another question was, could this fortress maintain its integrity, independence, and prosperity, for any substantial period of time in an era of rapidly expanding technologies in all fields, but, above all, in communication, transportation, and military capabilities?

The problem, at least in abstract terms, was well expressed in a speech by US Secretary of State Cordell Hull, given in New York in February 1935 when he said:

> There was a time when the ocean meant, or could mean, a certain degree of isolation.   Modern communication has ended this forever.[1]

But, in the same speech, Hull also demonstrated America's inability to resolve the matter in a practical way when he concluded in this vein:

We have no direct concern with the political and economic controversies of the European states. We have time and again expressly disassociated ourselves from these disputes. Nevertheless, we are deeply interested in the peace and stability of Europe as a whole, and have therefore taken part in a number of multilateral efforts to achieve this purpose ...[2]

And in 1937, President Franklin Roosevelt said:

Innocent peoples and nations are being cruelly sacrificed to a greed for power and supremacy which is devoid of all sense of justice and humane consideration ... If those things come to pass in other parts of the world let no one imagine that America will escape, that it may expect mercy, that this Western Hemisphere will not be attacked, and that it will continue tranquilly and peacefully to carry on the ethics and the arts of civilization ...[3]

The practical problem in the United States was its democratic opinion in the most general sense. To what extent did the "sovereign people" share the Roosevelt-Hull view of America's inescapable entanglement in world affairs? And among those who might have agreed with it abstractly, how many might be genuinely prepared to support the costs and risks of a foreign policy designed to confront external challenges to American well-being and security? And to what degree, especially if the challenges were, to all appearances, at least initially, not direct but indirect?

In a 1931 survey of 19,372 American clergymen, 54 per cent expressed the view that it was their "present purpose not to sanction any future war or participate as an armed combatant". Interestingly, a prominent leader of the Jewish community in New York, Rabbi Stephen Wise, asked his congregation for forgiveness for having supported war in 1917 and pledged "without reservation or equivocation" that he would never again back "any war whatsoever".[4]

In 1935, a Gallup survey discovered that only 11 per cent of the American public identified some aspect of foreign relations as the most important problem facing the United States. In the midst of the Depression, the domestic economy was a much more pressing concern for most people. A Democratic Senator, Robert Reynolds of North Carolina, articulated what might be termed a prevalent American concern in 1935 when he publicly asked:

> What do my constituents care about spending money and time and energy and life and blood for the interest of Estonia, Ethiopia, Iraq, Latvia, or Liberia?[5]

The Congress responded to the strength of the anti-interventionist sentiment in the country with the passage of three successive neutrality acts in 1935, 1936, and 1937. In the mid-1930s, the Roosevelt administration, despite some presidential distaste for Hitler and Nazism, was being careful to discourage any overtly anti-German or anti-Nazi public activities. Caution, hope, and the desire for economically profitable relations with Germany all played a part.

What was of decisive importance for United States policy in the later 1930s and early 1940s was the fact that "the overwhelming majority of Americans consistently wanted to keep out of war",[6] and that much of the American public opinion about international affairs was both ill-informed and spectacularly wrong. In 1938 and early 1939, most people "believed that a major European war was not imminent".[7] In September 1938, 86 per cent of American respondents in a national poll expressed the view that if war came, Britain and France would be able to defeat Germany and 57 per cent thought the United States could stay out of such a conflict. Even as late as May 1939, only 32 per cent of the American public thought that a major European war would break out that year.[8]

Where public opinion of the late 1930s was seemingly more prescient was with respect to its lack of faith in Hitler's good intentions, and in substantial support for improving US defence capabilities. But even in 1939, only 31 per cent of Americans believed that it was a good idea to sell munitions to England and France. This figure grew with new alarming developments in Europe, but the "baseline" of Roosevelt's problem was that until the Japanese attack on Pearl Harbor on 7 December 1941, the share of American opinion willing to commit the nation to war against the Axis rarely crossed the modest threshold of 20 per cent.[9]

To be sure, there was a good deal of ambivalence in American public opinion. One month before Pearl Harbor, 68 per cent agreed that "defeating Germany was more important than keeping out of war". Nevertheless, the "baseline" view presented FDR with a problem which went beyond war itself, because in the context of American partisan politics and relations with Congress, the President needed to be very careful that his actions in the field of foreign policy not be construed as wilfully "dragging the nation into war". This charge was made against him by many opponents anyway, but caution was a virtual necessity if Roosevelt in office *and* democratic-constitutional politics were to continue in the United States.

Throughout the late 1930s and early 1940s, when people were asked whose cause they favoured in the European conflict, a large majority always sided with the allies, and after 1940, with Britain. If asked whether the United States would be, sooner or later, drawn into the conflict, most respondents believed, rather pessimistically, that it would be eventually involved. But on the crucial question of *approving* such participation, the 20 per cent threshold generally held firm. Among public opinion polls in the 1930s which indicated deep pockets of isolationist sentiment in the United States were three surveys, one in 1936 and two in 1937. In each case, large majorities rejected the idea that the American President should either initiate or participate in any international conferences called to promote world peace. The negatives ranged from 36 to 66 per cent.[10]

When the question was asked in 1939, whether people would like to see the US join in establishing an "international police force to maintain world peace", 46 per cent approved but 39 per cent opposed the idea, with the rest expressing no opinion.[11]

Of course, responses tended to fluctuate over time depending in part on events of the day, and they also tended to vary depending on how the questions were phrased. Nevertheless, with all due allowance for such possible and actual variations, it was clear in the late 1930s and early 1940s that the isolationist impulse in the United States was very strong indeed, and capable of being easily aroused. When in September of 1940 the public was asked whether the United States should take steps to "keep Japan from becoming more powerful" even if such action might involve the risk of war, 54 per cent disagreed while 46 per cent were willing to take the risks.[12] When in April 1941 the question was asked about the public's willingness to use American naval power to help Britain in case Singapore was attacked, 43 per cent opposed the idea and 38 per cent approved it. Even in response to a Japanese attack on the Philippines, 20 per cent believed that the United States should *not* declare war, and in the same month, an analogous question with respect to a Japanese attack on Hawaii disclosed a seemingly amazing 12 per cent of the public unwilling to go to war even over such a provocative event.[13]

In March of 1940, a survey conducted on the issues of the European war asked people what the United States should do if it appeared that Germany was about to defeat England and France. Those who opted for the war alternative constituted 8.7 per cent of respondents.[14] The same issue was addressed in slightly different language by another polling organization within three weeks of the earlier poll. This time the proportion of respondents willing to engage in war was 10 per cent.[15] Throughout 1940, in six national polls, the war alternative received the support of between 3 and 5 per cent of the public. In two polls in 1941, with France already defeated and Britain alone in the fight against Hitler, the proportion rose to 7 and 9 per cent respectively.[16] In May and June of 1940, coinciding with the Battle of France, 14 and 16 per cent of respondents in two national polls, respectively, were in favour of American participation in the war. One poll in July reached a figure of 17 per cent for the war-willing public.[17] In eight surveys conducted by the same polling organization during the latter part of 1941, the proportion of the war-willing rose to an average of slightly under 22 per cent.[18]

What is also important and appreciated by politicians, especially as savvy and experienced and as capable as Franklin Roosevelt, is the complexity of public opinion. Whether people wanted the United States to intervene on behalf of Britain or did not, represented only one dimension of many relevant aspects of public opinion. The Nazis greatly played up in their propaganda the allegedly excessive influence of Jews in the Roosevelt administration, as did the American Far Right. The New Deal was often referred to by people of that persuasion as "Jew Deal". The ambivalence of American opinion with respect to isolation and intervention had its counterparts with respect to the "Jewish question". To some, the issue was whether America would fight a war in the interest of the Jews. If this perception was, and continued to be, very widespread, isolationism was bound to be reinforced and American foreign policy conceivably handicapped.

It was a matter of some relevance, therefore, that in April of 1938, 58 per cent of Americans questioned in a national poll expressed the view that the persecution of the Jews in Europe was either wholly or partly their own fault.[19] In 1936, 14 per cent of Americans believed that Germany would be better off by driving out its Jews.[20] In April 1939, 33.2 per cent of respondents said that hostility toward Jews in America was increasing.[21]

Interestingly also, in three successive national polls in 1943, 1944, and 1945, in the United States when people were asked, "Do you think that Jewish people in the United States have too much influence in the business world, not enough influence, or about the amount of influence they should have?", the answer that they had "too much influence" received the support of 49.7 per cent, 57 per cent, and 58 per cent, respectively.[22] Even in 1943, 33 per cent of Americans believed that Roosevelt had appointed too many Jews to jobs in Washington.[23]

In a fairly detailed poll of public attitudes toward Jews in July of 1939, only 38.9 per cent of Americans expressed the view that Jews should be treated "in all ways exactly as any other Americans"; 31.8 per cent thought that "some measures should be taken to prevent Jews from getting too much power in the business world"; 10.8 per cent thought that Jews could "make respected and useful citizens so long as they don't try to mingle socially where they are not wanted". And, amazingly, or perhaps not, 10.1 per cent expressed the view that "we should make it a policy to deport Jews from this country to some new homeland as fast as it can be done without inhumanity".[24]

When at the end of 1938, Americans were asked if they approved of the "withdrawal from Germany of the American ambassador as a protest against the Nazis' treatment of Jews and Catholics", 28 per cent disapproved and 21 per cent expressed no opinion.[25] In November 1938, following Nazi Kristalnacht in Germany, 77 per cent of American respondents opposed allowing a large number of Jews to come to the United States; 57 per cent opposed US financial help to Jewish and Catholic exiles from Germany settling in other countries (outside the US).[26]

Not only were there many political varieties of isolationism; there was also a rich compendium of different personal perspectives converging on the ramparts of American isolation. Many isolationists were politicians; some were businessmen; some priests and journalists. One was unique and pre-eminent, the perennially youthful and heroic Charles Lindbergh, the man who had crossed the Atlantic from New York to Paris all by himself in 1927. Lindbergh married a woman of social prominence in Anne Morrow, the daughter of the American ambassador to Mexico, and soon became part of an American equivalent of the British Cliveden set, people who could be described as "old money" with very conservative and in some cases clearly reactionary and pro-Nazi attitudes.

Given Lindbergh's celebrity, he got to know a lot of important people all over the world and many of them wanted to know and cultivate him. One of those was Nazi Luftwaffe chief Hermann Goering, who invited Lindbergh to inspect Germany's new military aviation programme. Goering even let Lindbergh fly some of the newest Nazi planes, such as the subsequently

famous fighter Me.109. He also presented Lindbergh with an official German
decoration. Lindbergh was very impressed with the Nazi air force and aviation
programmes. He came to think, not without good reason, that the Nazis were
the best in Europe in the air department, perhaps even on the way to best in the
world. This gradually led him to the view that military opposition to Nazi
Germany on the part of Britain and France, and/or others, would be likely
futile and useless.

On 11 September 1941 Lindbergh also became convinced that if there was a menace out there
in the international environment, it was not Nazism but Communism that
needed to be stopped and opposed. He probably thought the Nazis could play
"a constructive" role in this respect. Given his celebrity, Lindbergh became
the single best-known, prestigious, and glamorous exponent of American
isolationism and of the America First Committee. He believed that the best
course for the nation was to rearm but otherwise remain completely neutral
with respect to the war in Europe.

On 11 September 1941 Lindbergh delivered a speech in Des Moines,
Iowa, in which, for the first time, he explicitly linked isolationism with anti-
Semitism in three critical paragraphs:

> It is not difficult to understand why Jewish people desire the
> overthrow of Nazi Germany. The persecution they suffered in
> Germany would be sufficient to make bitter enemies of any race. No
> person with a sense of the dignity of mankind can condone the
> persecution of the Jewish race in Germany. But no person of
> honesty and vision can look on their post-war policy here today
> without seeing the dangers involved in such a policy, both for us
> and for them.

> Instead of agitating for war, the Jewish groups in this country should
> be opposing it in every possible way, for they will be among the
> first to feel its consequences. Tolerance is a virtue that depends
> upon peace and strength. History shows that it cannot survive war
> and devastation. A few far-sighted Jewish people realize this, and
> stand opposed to intervention. But the majority still do not. Their
> greatest danger to this country lies in their large ownership and
> influence in our motion pictures, our press, our radio, and our
> Government.

> I am not attacking either the Jewish or the British people. Both
> races, I admire. But I am saying that the leaders of both the British

and the Jewish races, for reasons which are as understandable from their viewpoint as they are inadvisable from ours, for reasons which are not American, wish to involve us in the war. We cannot blame them for looking out for what they believe to be their own interests, but we also must look out for ours. We cannot allow the natural passions and prejudices of other peoples to lead our country to destruction.[27]

On the other hand, with the European war only months away, academician Charles A. Beard wrote:

To entangle ourselves in the mazes and passions of European conflicts and tie our hands to British and French manipulators on the remote contingency of a German and Italian domination in the Atlantic seems to me to embrace immediate calamities when the possibility of security and peace in this hemisphere is clearly open to us.[28]

A typical pro-Allied but isolationist assessment was offered by Major George Fielding Eliot in a June 1939 issue of *The American Mercury*. He concluded that "certainly we in the United States have little reason to fear either Germany's present power or any offensive by a Germany weakened and drained by the strain of war even though she might be victorious(!) ... our British and French friends are quite capable of taking care of their own interests if they have the will to do so ... the resources of Britain and France are ample to assure their success".[29]

One of the principal spokesmen for the liberal ideology of self-indulgence, Mr. Fritz Sternberg, wrote in the October 1939 issue of *The Nation*, notwithstanding Hitler's quick work in Poland:

"England and France, in the opening moments of this war, were less well prepared economically than Germany. But as the war continues, their superiority in necessary war materials, especially with the addition of American shipments, will become increasingly plain. America's contribution will in turn add to the British and French numerical superiority. Germany started the war at its highest point; the strength of the Allies is constantly mounting. They do not need to undertake heroic offensives. They can afford to wait".[30]

In October 1939, former President Herbert Hoover wrote in the *Saturday Evening Post*:

> "America must keep out of these wars ... It has nothing to fear for our own independence from these wars" (p. 8).

Hoover argued that American liberties at home would be lost by participation in the war, as they were, or at least as they were about to be, in the First World War. ("If we go into another World War, liberty will be lost in America" (p. 76.)

He advocated military preparedness but with strict neutrality. He also anticipated great American impoverishment at the conclusion of a war involving the United States. Interestingly, Hoover, like most Americans, assumed that Britain and France, powers deserving of American sympathy in his view, were together strong enough to win the war against Germany all by themselves.[31]

One of the loudest -- and most mistaken -- voices advocating American isolationism was that of the great Socialist leader Norman Thomas, a man who found himself in odd company politically with various elements of the Right. Mr. Thomas put forward many propositions for American neutrality in an emerging European conflict, practically all of them colossally wrong. "The danger of fascism can scarcely be exaggerated. But it is not primarily a military danger arising out of the strength of the fascist dictators". "... the minute America enters war, democracy will yield to the totalitarian state necessary for a totalitarian war". "The British and French orders for American bombers bode no good". "... any progress in democracy ... requires that we keep America out of war".

He also wrote that a proper American foreign policy was one which involved "maximum possible isolation from war". And he also proposed that a "sound programme of opposition to war will insist on clear-cut opposition to ... this militarism of the big navy and mobilization bills". [A war] would hasten, not check, the penetration of South America by fascist ideologies". And, finally, he argued democracy could not exist in a world of recurrent wars. Thomas concluded his essay with the idea that by keeping out of war, America might be able to develop new social techniques to make war everywhere unnecessary.[32]

On the Socialist-pacifist Left, Thomas opposed every one of Roosevelt's foreign policy initiatives. In 1940, he ran for President on the Socialist ticket and declared to the American voters:

To furnish supplies for other people's war is, to the profit seekers, a welcome alternative to supplying our own people with their daily bread. But the search for war profits and armament economics leads straight to war. War and frantic preparation for war means the totalitarian state, not Socialist Freedom.

To the whole world let America say:

We will not share in the collective suicide of your wars. We will, to the best of our ability, aid the victims of war and oppression. We will seek with all neutrals at the first appropriate occasion to mediate in behalf of negotiated peace. And to make that peace effective, we will co-operate in disarmament and in all economic arrangements which will lessen the strain of insecurity and exploitation upon the peoples of the world.[33]

Within a day of Pearl Harbor, Thomas was still writing to the *New York Times* proclaiming his opposition to American participation in the War, because, ultimately, it would make less likely a "constructive revolution of the people of Europe against ... the system that makes for war".[34]

Further on the Left, and prior to *Barbarossa*, there was the voice of the great African-American opera singer Paul Robeson, speaking out "continually against American involvement in the European conflict ultimately aimed, in his opinion, at destroying the threat of Soviet-inspired peoples' revolutions".[35]

In a book published in 1940, Earl Browder, the General Secretary of the Communist Party of the United States, wrote:

We denounce the present war as an imperialist struggle on both sides, in which the American people have no interest, and in which we should take no sides, economically, morally, diplomatically, or militarily.[36]

On 5 November 1939, veteran Republican Senator Hiram Johnson of California wrote his son about the repeal of the embargo in Congress:

It was a big victory for the President, and there is no question about that, but the way was made easy for him. The Jews, and every newspaper that they had an interest in -- and they are many -- were shouting for repeal of the embargo. Every fawning, crawling, inferiority-complex American ... was praising God that England was kind enough to govern us and direct our Congress how to act.[37]

On 25 May 1940, Senator Johnson was writing his son: "My sympathies, of course, are wholly with Britain and France, and I pray for their success; but this is a very different thing from taking us into the war, whither we are now drifting, and where we are bound to go".[38]

Senator Robert A. Taft, Mr. Republican as he was subsequently called, believed, as late as the beginning of 1941, that so far as the Nazis were concerned, "I don't see why the world isn't big enough to contain all kinds of different ways of life", and also that "war is worse than a German victory".[39] He had repeatedly put forward the view that: "The basic policy of the United States should be to preserve peace with other nations, and enter into no treaties which may obligate us to go to war. Our army and navy should be designed to provide an adequate defence against attack".[40]

In a post-war memoir, Republican Representative Hamilton Fish, one of isolationism's strongest supporters and FDR's most dedicated enemies, with all the benefit of hindsight, declared:

> I served as the ranking Republican member of the Committee on Foreign Affairs in the House of Representatives throughout the years leading up to the Second World War. During those years I tried to halt our step by step involvement in yet another of the eternal wars of Europe.
>
> There is, thank God, no blood on my conscience or on my hands, but I believe that a great deal of blood lies on those of Franklin Roosevelt. His deceitful policies cost this country a million casualties and three hundred billion dollars, and saw thirteen million Americans conscripted into an unnecessary war machine.
>
> ... At the time the President started his campaign to create war hysteria, the United States had never been safer from attack or invasion by any foreign power. We had, for example, the most powerful navy in our history, equal for the first time to that of Great Britain. Congress had also authorized appropriations that would make the American navy 50 per cent greater than the Japanese navy and three times the size of the German navy.[41]

Even in the very bosom of the administration, Joseph P. Kennedy, Boston Democrat, businessman, and US Ambassador to Great Britain, had written to the sympathetic Senator William Borah a few months before the Munich crisis:

> The more I see of things here, the more convinced I am that we must exert all of our intelligence and effort toward keeping clear of any involvement. As long as I hold my present job, I shall never lose sight of this guiding principle. I find that Mr. Chamberlain, Lord Halifax, and other high officials here understand thoroughly the state of public opinion at home. They have assured me, in private conversation, that they are going ahead with their plans without counting on the United States to be either for or against them. They have never given me the slightest impression that they want to or expect anything special from us. Having had this clearly understood from the beginning, I have been able to deal with them in a frank and business-like manner ... [42]

As popular a president as Roosevelt was, and the 1936 election clearly indicated that, with FDR carrying 46 out of 48 states, and over 60 per cent of the popular vote, he was nevertheless, vulnerable. Roosevelt could not have possibly forgotten 1937 when, following his triumphal reelection, he had unveiled his Supreme Court-packing measure. Actually, the proposal would have added up to 15 justices to the Court's 9, with one new appointee for every justice reaching age 70 and not retiring. This was, of course, Roosevelt's attempt to dismantle, or at least weaken, the power of a conservative Court to veto New Deal "welfare state" legislation. The proposal raised a storm of protests and objections around the country, and above all, in the Congress itself. In June of 1937, despite nominal control by Roosevelt's own party, the Judiciary Committee of the US Senate voted 10 to 8 to reject the Roosevelt scheme. Its report was replete with such phrases as "dangerous amendment of constitutional principle", "evasion of the Constitution", and "destruction of the independence of the judiciary". On 22 July 1937 the full Senate voted 70 to 20 to recommit Roosevelt's bill to the Judiciary Committee, thus burying it forever.[43]

The lesson could hardly have been lost on a President whose sensitivity to politics and public opinion undoubtedly ranked at the very top of those who ever served in the White House. Even the possibilities of impeachment and removal from office were not to be discounted when

Roosevelt confronted a Congress with perhaps half of his own party siding with most of the Republicans on the "war issue".

It may be pointed out that those strata of the American population least receptive to interventionism, small town, rural elements were also most strongly over-represented in the Congress, partly because of the nature of representation in the Senate, where New York and Pennsylvania, for example, were given equal voice with Wyoming, Iowa, North Dakota, Idaho, Nevada, Arizona, etc. Partly also this was a result of the seniority system as it then existed in the United States Congress, which, by and large, encouraged the longevity and, therefore also committee chairmanships and influence, for representatives of politically stable or even "stagnant" constituencies. These, more often than not, represented rural and small town America.[44]

Ralph Levering ably summarizes Roosevelt's dilemma as follows:

> One interpretation of the years leading up to Pearl Harbor holds that Roosevelt was indecisive and hesitant, that he overestimated the strength of non-interventionist sentiment, and that he failed to lead the nation toward more active resistance to the Axis powers as rapidly as public opinion actually would have permitted. While these charges may be partially valid for the period after the fall of France in June 1940, the fact is that Roosevelt had to move cautiously to allow time for the majority of both the mass and attentive publics to reach the conclusion that firmer steps to oppose Germany and Japan were justified. Roosevelt recognized the profound desire of most Americans to keep out of war, and he may also have understood better than some recent scholars the significance to foreign policy of the deep divisions within the public during these years.[45]

Indeed, Congressional revisions in 1939 of the 1937 Neutrality Act provided, predictably, all sorts of far-ranging restrictions on American efforts to aid the Allies. As Professor Alan Nevins described it:

> The new Neutrality Act, which became law on 4 November 1939, was frankly designed to keep us out of war. Loans to belligerents, American travel on belligerent ships, and the arming of American merchant vessels were still unlawful. The embargo was dropped but "cash and carry" was revived, making it absolutely safe for us to export even arms to belligerents. No longer could our ships approach their ports ... The country heartily approved. We would

not get into troublesome disputes with the British over the blockade of Germany; and, what was of much greater importance to us, we would give a wide berth to the Nazi submarines that would try to starve the British Isles into surrender. We, the only big neutral, were deserting the others. We were abandoning neutral rights in order that we might preserve our neutrality. We were throwing away our precious doctrine of the freedom of the seas, so that we might save our more precious peace.[46]

Although it may not fit well into a wholly heroic wartime and post-war mythology, it is fairly clear that Franklin Roosevelt, at least briefly in 1938, entertained the hope that Neville Chamberlain's method of personal negotiation with Hitler could open the way to a new stability in Europe. That this might be done at the cost of sacrificing Czechoslovakia to Nazi domination was implicit in this position.[47]

A considerable scholarly literature continues to dispute the inner state of mind of Franklin D. Roosevelt in 1938. Understandably, what the President may have said publicly was not necessarily what he thought privately. The best surmise is that he probably was attracted to the possibilities of a policy of appeasement but that he also retained substantial doubts about the chances of reaching a solid settlement with Hitler.[48]

In some views, Roosevelt's gestures of support for Chamberlain on the eve of the Munich conference were no more than a realistic response to the behaviour of two democratic European states which were not willing to act vigorously in their own defence. Under the circumstances, there was little else the President could do.[49]

It seems that the US State Department and American diplomats around the world were divided in their views about the value of the Munich agreement, and, more importantly, about the future course of American policy toward Nazi Germany.[50]

A remarkable message was sent to the US Secretary of State by the American Ambassador in Berlin, Hugh R. Wilson, on 5 October 1938, following the conclusion of the Munich Agreement:

> ... there is one characteristic of the situation in Berlin ... which I feel cannot be too much emphasized. It is the inadequacy which all of us have experienced here of any and all estimates of Hitler's character, in particular when venturing into the realm of what he

may be expected to do. He is a man apart whom it seems almost impossible to judge by customary standards. [51]

American Ambassador in Warsaw, Drexel Biddle, sent. a very pessimistic -- and also very realistic -- appraisal of Hitler's victory at Munich:

> Many signs point to the Munich Conference and its immediate sequels having already had far-reaching repercussions throughout the whole extent of the European continent. As in effect pointed out in my previous letter, in view of the apparent check suffered by the western powers, the smaller countries, such as those of the Oslo group, which had already decided upon neutrality and upon repudiation of the compulsory sanctions clauses of the League Covenant, are already congratulating themselves on their foresight and wisdom. Belgium, Holland, Switzerland, and the Scandinavians are more than ever determined not to be drawn into any conflict between the major powers.
>
> States east and south-east of Berlin, though rapidly falling in line with Berlin's orientation in an economic sense, are in many cases, still groping for some 'out' (a) from eventual German political hegemony, and (b) from becoming the potential victims of 'peaceful settlements' between the major powers. Poland is in this category.
>
> The Chanceries of eastern and central Europe are now apparently practicing a 'balancing policy', characterized by a search for the orientation whereby they may be the safest (at least temporarily so) and wherefrom they may acquire the most benefits.
>
> Having interpreted recent events to mean Britain's and France's 'evacuation' of eastern and central Europe, certain states, such as Poland, Yugoslavia and Hungary, have recently been evidencing an inclination to look to Rome in their pursuance of a post-Munich course of 'balance diplomacy' between Berlin and Rome. Due to Italy's politico-economic position in central Europe, these smaller states looked for Italy to adopt measures towards preventing German penetration and domination in a region which Italy had hitherto regarded as her natural and legitimate sphere of interest. Moreover, the smaller states felt Italy might be tempted by the prospect of acquiring for herself in these parts the leadership which France had apparently abandoned. [52]

I find it equally difficult at this writing to foresee any development which in final resort will not imply a variable degree of German hegemony over the various individual states east and south-east of Berlin -- a hegemony which certain economic and political arrangements between these states may mitigate, but not prevent. Moreover, as Germany's trade offensive effectively advances, the states in its path can hardly afford to quarrel with their best customer, from a trade standpoint.[53]

... an almost 'power drunk' and super-confident Germany intends to have no unsympathetic or undigested portions along the way towards its eastward goal.[54]

Whatever private doubts and vacillations FDR may have entertained with respect to Hitler and the possibilities of appeasement were probably dispelled by the end of 1938 and with even greater certainty by 1939.[55] Roosevelt would tip the scales of American foreign policy toward the Allies, but the question remained, how much and how fast? The tone of the President's Annual Address to the Congress on 4 January 1939 was indicative. Munich had already been concluded and it was not yet (entirely, at least) violated. FDR said:

A war which threatened to envelop the world in flames has been averted but it has become increasingly clear that peace is not assured.[56]

The President pointed to undeclared wars "raging around us", more deadly armaments and threats of new aggression. "There comes a time in the affairs of men when they must prepare to defend not their homes alone but the tenets of faith and humanity on which their [institutions] are founded". The President warned that "the world has grown so small and weapons of attack so swift that no nation can be safe in its will to peace so long as any other single powerful nation refuses to settle its grievances at the council table". And, perhaps most relevantly to Munich, the President declared that:

... nations cannot safely be indifferent to international lawlessness anywhere. They cannot forever let pass, without effective protest, acts of aggression against sister nations -- acts which automatically undermine us all.[57]

When Nazi troops marched into Czechoslovakia on 15 March 1939, the United States condemned the action and officially refused to recognize its legal validity.[58] A decisive change in American official attitude, matching the disenchantment of the European democracies with Munich, was now under way.

Still, in the words of Donald Cameron Watt, writing about 1939:

> Overtly, Roosevelt could only plead for peace. His aim was not the immediate deterrence of Hitler but the long-term education of American opinion. For him the reality of politics lay in Washington, Chicago, New York, in the valleys of the Ohio, the Mississippi and the Missouri, in the great plains of the Midwest, in the mountain states, in California, Texas and the Pacific states, not in Prague, Warsaw, Rome, Berlin, Paris, or London, still less in Bratislava, the Memel or Danzig, Nice, Corsica, Savoy, Albania, Athens, Belgrade or Ankara.[59]

On 1 September 1939 Nazi troops marched into Poland, and in his speech to the nation of 3 September 1939, Roosevelt outlined an approach which still sought to balance an international role for the United States and a "tilt" toward Britain and France with the American desire to keep out of the armed conflict:

> It is easy for you and me, to shrug our shoulders and say that conflicts taking place thousands of miles from the whole American Hemisphere do not seriously affect the Americas -- and that all the United States has to do is to ignore them and go about its own business. Passionately though we may desire detachment, we are forced to realize that every word that comes through the air, every ship that sails the sea, every battle that is fought, does affect the American future.
>
> Let no man or woman thoughtlessly or falsely talk of America sending its armies to European fields ...
>
> This nation will remain a neutral nation, but I cannot ask that every American remain neutral in thought as well. Even a neutral has a

right to take account of facts. Even a neutral cannot be asked to close his mind or his conscience.

I have said not once, but many times, that I have seen war and that I hate war. I say that again and again.

I hope the United States will keep out of this war. I believe that it will. And I give you assurance and reassurance that every effort of your Government will be directed toward that end.

As long as it remains within my power to prevent, there will be no blackout of peace in the United States.[60]

Whatever the President might have wanted to do, short of war, with obedience to "mind and conscience" had to be done very carefully because the public sway of American isolationism was still extremely strong. Roosevelt recalled, of course, the significantly negative reaction generated by his so-called Quarantine speech delivered in Chicago on 5 October 1937, where he first publicly attempted to move the United States away from a position of strict neutrality between the Axis on one hand and Britain and France on the other.[61]

Beginning with measures taken in the summer of 1940, the United States, under Roosevelt's leadership, quickly moved from neutrality to a partisanship just short of war. These measures included the sale of military equipment, especially aircraft, to Britain and France; the executive agreement of 6 September 1940, trading 50 American destroyers for British bases in the Atlantic and Caribbean; the sale of over 200 old tanks to Canada also in September; the sale of old merchant ships to Britain in December 1940; and certainly with great symbolic importance, the President's speech declaring the United States to be the "arsenal of democracy" on 29 December 1940; the passage of the Lend-Lease Act by Congress on 11 March 1941; the seizure of German and Italian merchant ships and their transfer to Britain in March-July 1941; the President's proclamation of an unlimited national emergency on 27 May 1941 in response to what it identified as an Axis attempt to destroy the existing democratic systems and establish their own world-wide domination of the peoples of the world by crushing all resistance to themselves; and finally the public announcement on 7 July 1941 of a new naval policy calling on US warships to fire upon Axis vessels believed to be threatening the northern

American continent and/or interfering with shipping between the United States and Britain.

It is instructive, of course, that between March and July 1941, Roosevelt had resisted the counsels of his more war-minded advisors who wanted the US navy to employ force in escorting shipping to and from Britain. But the President would only go so far as to permit American ships to run patrols across the Atlantic and pass information on Nazi submarines or other hostile vessels to the British navy. Caution was the watchword.

A critical development in the growing Anglo-American alliance was the Atlantic Charter issued on 14 August 1941, in consequence of the Roosevelt-Churchill meeting off the coast of Newfoundland. It was a declaration of mutually-held beliefs and mutually-desired goals ranging from the restoration of sovereign rights to those forcibly deprived of them to pledges of international co-operation and future disarmament and abandonment of the use of force.

From the Nazi point of view, this development made it clear that the United States and Britain were drawing ever closer together. It might have been seen as a harbinger of American participation in the war against Nazi Germany, perhaps sometime soon. But how soon? It was not yet intervention. No American troops were fighting the Germans, not even one battalion, let alone one division. And given the domestic situation in the US, it was not at all self-evident that, barring an act of aggression by one or more of the Axis powers, the United States *could* actually escalate its obvious conflict with Nazi Germany into full-fledged war.

What made all the pro-British measures possible in the first place was the preponderant, even overwhelming support and sympathy for Britain on the part of the American public. What made them dangerous politically for the President was the equally overwhelming desire of the American electorate to stay out of the war. Whatever may have been happening in Europe and the rest of the world, Roosevelt had to be prudent in order to forestall a revolt in the Congress and at the grass roots of American politics. There were disturbing precedents and portents.

Within four months of Pearl Harbor, the extension of military draft was approved by the US Senate on 7 August 1941, by a vote of 45 to 30. But the House of Representatives extended the measure by 203 votes to 202. Regionally, the most opposition to extension came from the Middle West. Politically, the Democrats voted 183 to 64 for it and Republicans 132 to 21 against it. As Wayne Cole says "a substantial majority of all congressmen outside the South opposed draft extension (196 nay, 102 yea)". And as he concludes: "Bolder leadership might have moved the United States to war against the Axis sooner. But that might have been accomplished only after a bitter battle that could have confronted the Axis states with a battered president leading a divided and weakened people; Presidents Lyndon B. Johnson and Richard M. Nixon were to do that a generation later in Vietnam, but that was not Franklin D. Roosevelt's way".[62]

The isolationists remained a strong political force right up to the Japanese attack on Pearl Harbor. When the Lend-Lease Act was passed by Congress in March of 1941, by a sizeable majority, it

> sparked a great debate on American foreign policy, a debate, Roosevelt later remarked, that was argued 'in every newspaper, on every wave-length -- over every cracker barrel in all the land.' A vocal minority of hard-core isolationists, mostly Republicans, opposed lend-lease vigorously. Certain that the war was not America's concern and that Hitler did not threaten the United States, they denounced lend-lease as a provocative and dangerous measure that would inevitably drag the nation into war and would destroy democracy at home by conferring dictatorial powers on the President.[63]

> ... Most Americans regarded Germany as an enemy and supported all-out aid to Britain even though it involved risks. But they were reluctant to accept the logical consequences of their own attitudes, and to take action that might draw them more deeply into the conflict. Roosevelt shared their hopes and fears. He was certainly aware when he conceived lend-lease that it might not be enough, that American troops might eventually be required to save Britain, and he was not entirely candid when he defended the Lend-Lease Act as a means of keeping out of war. But he sincerely hoped that intervention might yet be avoided. He realized that the United States was not prepared to fight, either physically or emotionally, and though he was anxious to assist the British, he was equally anxious to avoid steps that might lead to hostilities with Germany.[64]

One consequence of the confusion and division within the body of American public opinion was an appalling military unpreparedness of the United States, even as the war in Europe escalated to ever more dangerous levels. Some of the enormous difficulties of rearming America, closely related to its democratic public opinion, may be appreciated from statements made by

General George C. Marshall, arguably the most distinguished American military leader of the 1940s.

In a speech given to the American Historical Association on 28 December 1939 in Washington, DC, General Marshall declared:

> Everything in this country is expensive, in keeping with the high standards of living demanded by our people. Therefore, the military establishment is very expensive, and its maintenance on a sound basis is always endangered by the natural demand of the people for economy in government.[65]

In a speech he gave on 27 May 1940 to the National Aviation Forum in Washington, DC, General Marshall said:

> The public indifference of the past to our national defence requirements is a matter of fact which we are powerless to alter, and we must accept the resultant situation as our base of departure to remedy our deficiencies.[66]

In an appearance before a Congressional Committee in late May 1940, the General declared:

> We have one American standard, which we have to live up to. If we are going to maintain a volunteer Army, we must provide pay, food, shelter, and medical attention on a basis that is far beyond the requirements of other countries, particularly those with conscript or universal-service requirements.[67]

And in a memorandum to a subordinate of 22 July 1940, the General wrote:

> Today time is the dominant factor in the problem of national defence. For almost twenty years we had all of the time and almost none of the money; today we have all the money and no time.[68]

On 11 March 1941, in another such memorandum, the General referred to "quibbling and bickering, distracting arguments [and] the long debates in Congress, all of which ha[ve] produced so much confusion in the public mind ..."[69] As late as 19 August 1941, Marshall, in a letter to Bernard

Baruch, was complaining that "division of opinion in the country made it difficult to prepare the armed forces for war ...".[70]

When French Premier Paul Reynaud appealed to the President on 13 June 1940, for "clouds of warplanes from across the Atlantic ... to crush the evil force that dominates Europe", his appeal was, and seemed, pathetic. France was defeated, and it was too late to do anything about it. But given the failure of all the European democracies to stand up to Hitler when it was still possible to do so, America represented one of only two world cards, in addition to Russia, still left to play against Hitler.[71]

A measure of Winston Churchill's anxiety, and even despair was reflected in this message he wrote to Roosevelt asking for American help in June of 1940:

> Although the present government and I personally would never fail to send the fleet across the Atlantic if resistance was beaten down here, a point may be reached in the struggle where the present ministers no longer have control of affairs and when very easy terms could be obtained for the British island by becoming a vassal state of the Hitler empire.[72]

By 1940 and 1941, the kind of assistance the United States was providing to Britain was not nearly enough to stave off a British defeat, and a Nazi victory. Nothing short of American military intervention would have been enough. American aid extended to the Allied powers opposing Nazi Germany, including aid to Great Britain, generous as it may have been, was almost certainly in all respects too little and too late. But with some unintended assistance from Hitler it proved very important.

The United States' aid to Britain, especially following the collapse of France in June 1940, had double significance. It was important in the material sense, particularly with respect to American supplies, food, and fuel shipped across the Atlantic. Above all, however, it was important psychologically to the maintenance of British resistance to Nazism. It is clear that for both Winston Churchill and most British anti-Nazis of the bleak period of 1940-1941, American intervention represented the last, great hope of ultimate victory over Hitler. Alternatively, *if* it had somehow become clear in the aftermath of the Battle of France that the United States would *not* become involved in the war, the likelihood of a British collapse, probably through a negotiated peace, would have been overwhelming.

Together with Winston Churchill, it was to Roosevelt that the credit must go for doing what was necessary to forestall British failure during the critical period between the fall of France and the launching of *Barbarossa*. Even though British efforts in the war were only marginally hurtful to the Nazis during those critical months when Britain virtually alone opposed Hitler, ultimate victory and defeat were dependent precisely upon some slender margins.

As long as Britain stayed in the fight, Nazi Germany needed to maintain significant forces to prevent possible British incursions on the Continent. The unavailability of those forces in June of 1941 might have made a difference in the Nazi conquest of Russia. As long as Britain continued to fight Hitler, the several European governments-in-exile had a base of operations for themselves and both resistance and hope in the conquered countries could be plausibly maintained. The British dominions around the world were very unlikely to continue to fight if the "mother country" were to quit the war. A British collapse would have turned North Africa, the Mediterranean, and oil-rich Middle East to Nazi control and exploitation. There would have been no readily available bases for any conceivable American invasion of Europe in subsequent years, even if all sorts of changes had occurred in the United States' attitude concerning the desirability or necessity of American intervention against Nazi Germany.

The calendar year from June 1940 to June 1941 was the year of greatest vulnerability for the Allied cause. It was the period during which Hitler was most likely to win the war and the Allies most likely to lose it. It was a period during which it would have made the most sense -- if such a term can ever be applied to this transaction -- for Britain to seek a negotiated peace settlement with Nazi Germany. Because Churchill was able to withstand all the pressures of "going-it-alone" in 1940 and 1941, and because Roosevelt helped him materially and morally to continue the fight until Hitler would make his own fatal blunder, they earned themselves legitimately heroic reputations. Not all wars have had profound implications for the course of civilization, but the war against Hitler did.

Nevertheless, from the latter part of 1940 until Hitler's attack on Russia, everything depended on the possibility, and the hope, that Hitler might somehow make a mistake and fail to pursue his largely hapless victim to its all but inevitable doom. If Hitler chose to do so, Britain would have been defeated in all likelihood either in 1940 by invasion, or in 1941 without an invasion. Under that circumstance, the only potential challengers to Hitler's hegemony, the United States and the Soviet Union, would have found themselves in an all but hopeless situation. For the United States, there would have been no base in Europe from which to launch a strike against Hitler's empire. The isolationist sentiment would have been strengthened by the very magnitude and seeming futility of the task of opposing Nazi Germany alone.

The Soviet Union, alone against Hitler's power, understandably greater without Britain in the war than it was with Britain in the war in 1941, would have faced a task that it probably could not have handled, especially if Hitler chose to "settle scores" with Russia within, say, two or three years of his victory over the British. If the Nazis came as close as they did to Moscow and Leningrad in 1941 with at least a few divisions held out of the conflict to protect their flanks in the West, it seems unlikely that they would have failed given the chance to throw all their resources against Russia in the event of a fully one-front war.

Only what Machiavelli called "fortuna" saved the world from a Hitler victory after the defeat of France in June 1940, only the dictator's own failure and miscalculation. Instead of keeping up his pursuit of the British, Hitler let up the pressure and turned against Russia thereby fatally exhausting his military resources. And in the aftermath of Japan's attack on Pearl Harbor, he gratuitously obliged Franklin Roosevelt by declaring war on the United States and thereby giving FDR the opportunity that the isolationists at home had so far successfully denied him.

By then, the point of no return was, by all rights, already passed, unbeknown to the millions of Americans who had pressed upon their Chief Executive that he keep America out of war. Democratic public opinion in the United States failed to diagnose Hitlerism's fury and respond to it promptly. While no one could gainsay the courage of British airmen and sailors, or the stoicism of the Londoners under Nazi bombings, it was not their own foresight, or prudence but the vagaries of history that saved the world for the democracies in 1941.[73]

NOTES

[1] See Ruhl J. Bartlett (ed.), *The Record of American Diplomacy, Documents and Readings in the History of American Foreign Relations* (New York: Alfred A. Knopf, 1952), pp. 572, speech of 16 February 1935.

[2] *Ibid.*

[3] Address at Chicago ("The Quarantine Speech"), 5 October 1937, p. 577, *ibid.* Wayne S. Cole, *Roosevelt and the Isolationists, 1932-1945* (Lincoln: University of

Nebraska Press, 1983) says that FDR "was more nearly in tune with what the United States and the world were becoming", p. 556.

   See Robert E. Herzstein, *Roosevelt and Hitler: Prelude to War* (New York: Paragon House, 1989). Most of the reaction to FDR's 1937 Quarantine speech was negative; "the loudest voices" were opposed, p. 95. Roosevelt believed that he was fighting a public psychology which comes "close to saying -- peace at any price" (*Ibid.*). Even in the late 30s, to most Americans "support" for the Allies was not a *prelude* but *substitute* for US intervention (p. 117). In Herzstein's account, FDR was a mortal enemy of Hitler long before Munich, and in a more principled, and contextually-difficult situation (Britain being more directly threatened) than Churchill, pp. 412-414.

[4] See Ralph B. Levering, *The Public and American Foreign Policy 1918-1978* (New York: William Morrow, 1978), p. 49.

[5] See *Ibid.*, p. 56.

[6] *Ibid.*, p. 69.

[7] *Ibid.*, pp. 73-74.

[8] *Ibid.*

[9] *Ibid.*, p. 79.

[10] H. Cantril, *Public Opinion 1935-1946* (Princeton, NJ: Princeton University Press, 1951), p. 372.

[11] *Ibid.*

[12] *Ibid.*, p. 1076.

[13] *Ibid.*

[14] *Ibid.*, p. 971.

[15] *Ibid.*

[16] *Ibid.*, p. 971.

[17] *Ibid.*, p. 971.

[18] *Ibid.*, p. 973.

[19] Hadley Cantril (ed.), *op. cit.*, p. 381.

[20] *Ibid.*, p. 382.

[21] *Ibid.*, p. 383.

[22] *Ibid.*

[23] *Ibid.*

[24] *Ibid.*, p. 383.

[25] *Ibid.*, p. 382.

[26] *Ibid.*, p. 385.

[27] Wayne S. Cole, *Charles A. Lindbergh and the Battle Against American Intervention in World War II* (New York: Harcourt Brace Jovanovich, 1974), pp. 171-172. Even in 1974, Lindbergh "still believed that he and his fellow non-interventionists had been right before Pearl Harbor", p. 238.

See Justus D. Doenecke (ed.), *In Danger Undaunted, The Anti-Interventionist Movement of 1940-1941 as Revealed in the Papers of the America First Committee* (Stanford: Hoover Institution Press, 1990), pp. 110-112. Note letter of John T. Flynn to Robert E. Wood of 5 June 1941 expressing concern that America First may become a vehicle for "a powerful anti-Semitic undercurrent", p. 111. When America's hostilities began with the Pearl Harbor attack, Lindbergh sought to enter military service but President Roosevelt barred him from it, at least formally and officially. It was perhaps the measure of the character of this hero of winged flight that when he, coincidentally, came to visit a Nazi extermination camp in Germany in June of 1945, it did not cause him to reappraise his pre-1941 political views in the slightest. In 1954 President Eisenhower restored Lindbergh's commission in the Air Force Reserve and promoted him to brigadier-general. He died in 1974 at age 72 in Hawaii.

[28] *The American Mercury*, Vol. XLVI, No. 184, April 1939, pp. 388-399. Quotation appears on p. 399.

Note also Charles A. Beard, "Giddy Minds and Foreign Quarrels, An Estimate of American Foreign Policy", *Harper's Magazine*, Vol. 179, September 1939, pp. 337-351, in which the great academic warmly advocated the proposition that it was "folly for the people of the United States to embark on a vast and risky programme of world pacification", (p. 346). "We should stay clear of the hates and loves" (p. 347).

[29] George F. Eliot, "Germany Can't Win!", *The American Mercury*, Vol. XLVII, No. 186, June 1939, pp. 148-156. Quotation is from p. 156.

[30] Fritz Sternberg, "Time is With The Allies," *The Nation*, Vol. 149, No. 16, 14 October 1939, p. 409. Note also his earlier article "Will the Blockade Succeed?", *The Nation*, Vol. 149, No. 13, 23 September 1939, pp. 317-320.

[31] Herbert Hoover, "We Must Keep Out", *The Saturday Evening Post*, Vol. 212, No. 18, 28 October 1939, pp. 8, 74, 76-77, 78.

[32] Note Norman Thomas, "We Needn't Go To War", *Harper's Magazine*, Vol. 177, No. 4, November 1938, pp. 657-664.

[33] Murray B. Seidler, *Norman Thomas, Respectable Rebel* (Syracuse: Syracuse University Press, 1967), pp. 207-208.

[34] Bernard K. Johnpoll, *Pacifist's Progress, Norman Thomas and The Decline of American Socialism* (Chicago: Quadrangle Books, 1970), p. 231.

[35] Martin Bauml Duberman, *Paul Robeson* (New York: A. A. Knopf, 1988), p. 248.

[36]   Earl Browder, *The Second Imperialist War* (New York: International Publishers, 1940), pp. 213-214.

[37]   R. E. Burke (ed.), *The Diary Letters of Hiram Johnson, 1917-1945* (New York: Garland Publishing, Inc., 1983), 5 November 1939, p. 3.

[38]   *Ibid.*, 25 May 1940, p. 3.

[39]   See James T. Patterson, *Mr. Republican, A Biography of Robert A. Taft* (Boston: Houghton Mifflin, 1972), p. 243.

[40]   *Ibid.*, p. 196. It may be recalled that between them, Congress and the President did very little prior to 1941 in order to prepare the United States for a possible attack.

[41]   Hamilton Fish, *Memoir of an American Patriot* (Washington, DC: Regnery Gateway, 1991), p. 60.

See Hamilton Fish, *Tragic Deception, FDR and America's Involvement in World War II* (Greenwich, CT: Devin-Adair, 1983), for the view that FDR "pushed and prodded" Britain and France, and everyone else, into war with Nazi Germany, pp. 42-45. He also forced Japan to wage war against the US, pp. 14-15. Hardly any evil deed was not attributed to Roosevelt by Fish.

[42]   Marian C. McKenna, *Borah* (Ann Arbor: University of Michigan Press, 1961), p. 354.

Note Raul de Roussy de Sales, "America Looks At the War", *The Atlantic Monthly*, Vol. 165, No. 2, February 1940, pp. 151-159; he thought the war had become too boring from an American perspective; nothing much was happening, and perhaps it was time to get the "peace process" under way, pp. 158-159.

Note Frank C. Hanighen, "What England and France Think About Us", *Harper's Magazine*, Vol. 179, September 1939, pp. 376-385. As this author observes, "No one can avoid noticing that the American press tends to emphasize news from Europe indicating that Germany and Italy are breaking down internally. It also tends to overestimate the strength of the forces of Britain and France which are alleged to want a strong stand against the dictatorships", p. 384. Wishful thinking had its ample providers.

[43]   See Richard Hofstedter, *et al.*, *The American Republic, Vol. II* (Englewood Cliffs, NJ: Prentice Hall, 1959), pp. 531-532.

[44]   See Mack C. Shelley II, *The Permanent Majority, The Conservative Coalition in the United States Congress* (Tuscaloosa: University of Alabama Press, 1983), pp. 53-54, and also p. 11.

[45]   *Ibid.*, pp. 66-67.

[46]   Allan Nevins and Louis M. Hacker (eds.), *The United States and Its Place in World Affairs 1918-1943* (Boston: D. C. Heath, 1943), p. 455.

[47]   It is instructive to consider the view of this presented by William L. Langer and S. Everett Gleason at some length in their *The Challenge to Isolation 1937-1940* (New

York: Harper and Brothers, 1952): "Immediately after it was known in Washington that Mr. Chamberlain had accepted Hitler's invitation, the President instructed Ambassador Kennedy to transmit to the Prime Minister a laconic message: 'Good man'. This somewhat indiscreet step need not, however, be taken to mean more than approval of Mr. Chamberlain's decision to negotiate further, a decision which afforded the greatest relief on both sides of the Atlantic and unleashed 'a wild scramble for stocks' on the New York Stock Exchange. Mr. Roosevelt's congratulations had nothing to do with the specific terms agreed on between Chamberlain and Hitler on September 30, 1938".

FDR also sent Chamberlain a telegram on 5 October 1938, saying:

"I fully share your hope and belief that there exists today the greatest opportunity in years for the establishment of a new order based on justice and on law. Now that you have established personal contact with Chancellor Hitler, I know that you will be taking up with him from time to time many of the problems which must be resolved in order to bring about that new and better order".

One could say that, by implication, the text is morally disappointing, pp. 34-35.

[48] See David F. Schmitz, *The United States and Fascist Italy, 1922-1940* (Chapel Hill: The University of North Carolina Press, 1988), for substantial and persuasive discussion of the attempt by FDR, and the State Department, to pursue a policy of appeasement, especially economic appeasement, toward both Hitler and Mussolini, in order to lessen the potential conflict in Europe, pp. 176-190, especially. The idea of economic sanctions against Hitler was the very antithesis of this policy.

See also Frederick W. Marks III, "Fix Between Roosevelt and Hitler: America's Role in the Appeasement of Nazi Germany", *The Historical Journal*, Vol. 28, No. 4, Fall 1985, pp. 969-982. In this author's view, notwithstanding some rhetorical flourishes on FDR's part, he was seriously interested in pursuing appeasement of Hitler, if it would work, that is. If that strategy failed, "the United States must accept its fair share [of world responsibilities]" (p. 982).

Cf. Patrick J. Hearden, *Roosevelt Confronts Hitler, America's Entry Into World War II* (Dekalb: Northern Illinois University, 1987). 'Quest for Economic Appeasement', Chapter 4, pp. 88-122, discusses the hope of some State Department officials, including Sumner Welles and Adolph Berle, in the possibilities of appeasing German aggression through economic concessions. It is not clear how much of this was shared by FDR personally until, at least, Munich. See pp. 120-121.

[49] See Basil Rauch, *Roosevelt, From Munich to Pearl Harbor* (New York: Creative Age Press, 1950). "By the summer of 1938 the pattern of disunity among the nations threatened by the Axis was complete and Chamberlain was free to offer the Sudetenland to Hitler in return for a Four-Power Pact. Preparations for this immoral

deal deeply discouraged American internationalists and strengthened the position of the isolationists. They argued that the United States must avoid the sinister power politics of the "Old World", p. 66. See also pp. 78-79, where Rauch defends FDR from Beard's charges of complicity in Munich.

 C. A. MacDonald, *The United States, Britain and Appeasement, 1936-1939* (London: Macmillan, 1981), says that "The president was in a dilemma. It was difficult to persuade public opinion that an Axis danger existed while Chamberlain continued to talk about an Anglo-German agreement. Yet Roosevelt could not persuade Britain to take a stiffer line with Germany without widespread [domestic] support ... which would convince London that [the US could intervene in case of war]", p. 182. "The President was caught between the desire to play a larger role in world affairs and the necessity of preserving his political position at home", p. 182. See also his "Deterrent Diplomacy: Roosevelt and the Containment of Germany, 1938-1940", pp. 297-329. MacDonald sees the US State Department divided over the 1938 Munich agreement. Some saw it as a mere pause in Nazi expansion. Some saw it as a likely basis of a new settlement of the European situation. Cordell Hull and Under-Secretary George S. Messersmith sided with the former, while Under-Secretary Sumner Welles, his assistant Adolf Berle and Joseph P. Kennedy, US Ambassador in London, were among the latter group. "If Chamberlain succeeded in averting war and Hitler proved satisfied with German domination of central Europe, it might yet prove possible for Washington to summon a new 'Congress of Berlin' co-opting the Reich into a liberal-capitalist economic order dominated by the United States", p. 300. In a speech given on 20 October 1938, Ambassador Kennedy "called for co-operation between dictatorships and democracies to guarantee peace and end the arms race", p. 301.

 As for FDR, "Roosevelt's response to Munich seemed to reflect the optimism of the appeasers rather than the pessimism of their opponents .... In the weeks after Munich he even tried to assume some of the credit for the peaceful outcome of the crisis", (p. 301). "At the height of the Munich crisis Roosevelt preferred appeasement to war even at the cost of the 'terrible remorseless sacrifice' [of] Czechoslovakia. As he informed the British Ambassador on 20 September, if Chamberlain succeeded he would be 'the first to cheer' ". At the same time he had no doubt that if Hitler proved insatiable, American interests lay in supporting Britain and France. In the event of war, Roosevelt planned to adopt a policy of forward defence, throwing US industrial resources behind the democracies" (pp. 301-302).

 See William E. Kinsella, Jr., *Leadership in Isolation: FDR and the Origins of the Second World War* (Cambridge: Schenkman, 1978). FDR "never believed that a compromise peace would be possible with the proponents of fascism", p. 209. "Detestation and dread were the feelings engendered in Roosevelt by the appearance of the German dictator [in 1933]", p. 210. But, FDR "was constrained by isolationist sentiment, neutrality restrictions, and the appeasement solutions offered by other nations", p. 214. FDR always assumed that Hitler's aspirations would extend to the Western Hemisphere, p. 219. "The President had confided to a close associate that he wished to be dragged into the war through the accident of an incident", p. 223. He had earlier expressed to the same individual his desire to make decisions that would push the United States into global conflict", p. 223.

[50] See E. L. Woodward (ed.), *Documents on British Foreign Policy, 1919-1939* (London: Her Majesty's Stationery Office, 1955), Third Series, Volume VIII, No. 148. Telegram from British Ambassador in Tokyo, Sir R. Craigie, to Viscount Halifax, Foreign Secretary, 13 October 1938, 4.46 p.m.:

> "My United States colleague has formed the opinion that the Munich settlement has had a salutary influence here. He does not consider that war in Europe was desired by any but irresponsible elements in Japan ... The strengthening of our position out here becomes more apparent with every turn for the better in Europe", p. 134.

On the other hand, see E. L. Woodward and R. Butler (eds.), *Documents on British Foreign Policy 1919-1939*, Third Series, Volume III, 1938-1939 (London: His Majesty's Stationery Office, 1950), p. 89, for a memorandum of impressions by Sir Maurice Hankey to the Foreign Secretary indicating that, in the wake of the Munich Agreement, the American Ambassador in Paris, William Bullit, was urging the French to step up their rearmament programme, 3 October 1938.

Note also dispatch of British Ambassador to Washington, Sir R. Lindsay, of 18 November 1938, to Viscount Halifax, nine days after Kristallnacht in Germany, indicating that Under-Secretary of State Sumner Welles was not happy about Roosevelt's recall of the American Ambassador in Berlin, p. 279.

[51] See Department of State, *Foreign Relations of the United States, Diplomatic Papers, 1938*, Vol. I General (Washington, DC: US Government Printing Office, 1955), p. 715.

[52] *Ibid.*, p. 731.

[53] *Ibid.*, p. 732.

[54] *Ibid.*, p. 733.

[55] See Arnold A. Offner, *The Origins of the Second World War, American Foreign Policy and World Politics, 1917-1941* (New York: Praeger Publishers, 1975), on Roosevelt's initial approval of the Munich Agreement of September 1938. "Roosevelt rejoiced to Canadian Prime Minister Mackenzie King that war had been averted and told Ambassador Phillips, 'I am not one bit upset over the final result' ", pp. 126-127. As Offner says, "Roosevelt perpetually inclined toward appeasement, but soon after Munich he began to view Germany more harshly, became more resigned to the

196 Democracies Against Hitler

eventuality of a European war, and determined to prepare America accordingly", p. 127.

[56] See S. S. Jones and J. P. Myers (eds.), *Documents on American Foreign Relations, January 1938-June 1939* (Boston: World Peace Foundation, 1939), p. 26.

[57] *Ibid.*, pp. 27-28.

[58] See Sumner Welles' statement to the German Chargé d'Affaires in Washington of 20 March 1939, *ibid.*, pp. 302-303.

[59] Donald Cameron Watt, *How War Came, The Immediate Origins of the Second World War, 1938-1939* (London: Heinemann, 1989), p. 613.

[60] See William L. Langer and S. Everett Gleason, *The Challenge to Isolation 1937-1940* (New York: Harper and Brothers, 1952), p. 204.

[61] *Ibid.*, pp. 18-19.

[62] Wayne S. Cole, *Roosevelt and the Isolationists 1932-1945* (Lincoln: University of Nebraska Press, 1983), pp. 440-441.

[63] George C. Herring, Jr., *Aid to Russia 1941-1946: Strategy, Diplomacy, the Origins of the Cold War* (New York: Columbia University Press, 1973), p. 4.

[64] *Ibid.*, p. 5.

[65] See Larry I. Bland (ed.), *The Papers of George Catlett Marshall*, Vol. II, *"We Cannot Delay," July 1, 1939-December 6, 1941* (Baltimore: The Johns Hopkins University Press, 1986), p. 126.

[66] *Ibid.*, p. 227.

[67] *Ibid.*, p. 231.

[68] *Ibid.*, p. 274.

[69] *Ibid.*, p. 442.

[70] *Ibid.*, p. 591.

In a memorandum dated 22 May 1940, not addressed specifically to anyone but shown to FDR by the General, Marshall observed that "We cannot conduct major operations either in the Far East or in Europe due to lack of means at present and because of the resultant abandonment of the United States' interests in the area to which we do not send forces", p. 219.

[71] Thomas Parrish, *Roosevelt and Marshall, Partners in Politics and War* (New York: William Morrow, 1989), records that 5 days after taking over as Prime Minister on 10 May 1940, Winston Churchill, quite understandably, called Roosevelt to tell him that "the voice and force of the United States may count for nothing if they are withheld too long", p. 142. The American public shared FDR's "hopes" for victory over Hitler "but without an American army", p. 165.

[72] See Alan P. Dobson, *US Wartime Aid to Britain 1940-1946* (London: Croom Helm, 1986), p. 21.

Harold L. Ickes, *The Secret Diary of Harold L. Ickes, 1939-1941* (New York: Simon & Schuster, 1954). Ickes recalls discussing the consequences of British defeat at the hands of Nazi Germany with FDR as early as 26 May 1940, i.e., before the fall of France. They both feared the possibility of the British navy being handed over to Nazi Germany as part of a settlement that Hitler might offer Britain, p. 188.

[73] See Maurice Matloff (ed.), *American Military History* (Washington, DC: Office of the Chief of Military History, US Army, 1969), p. 435:

> After more than a year and a half of rearming, the United States in December 1941 was still in no position to carry the war to its enemies. On December 7 the Army numbered some 1,644,000 men (including about 120,000 officers), organized into 4 armies, 37 divisions (30 infantry, 5 armored, 2 cavalry), and over 40 combat air groups. Three of the divisions were overseas (2 in Hawaii, 1 in the Philippines), with other garrison forces totaling less than 200,000. By spreading equipment and ammunition thin, the War Department might have put a substantial force into the field to repel an attack on the continental United States; 17 of the divisions at home were rated as technically ready for combat. But these divisions lacked the supporting units and the training necessary to weld them into corps and armies. More serious still, they were inadequately equipped with many weapons that recent operations in Europe had shown to be indispensable -- for example, tank and anti-tank guns, anti-aircraft artillery, radios, and radar -- and some of these shortages were aggravated by lack of auxiliary equipment like firecontrol mechanisms.

> Above all, ammunition of all kinds was so scarce that the War Department was unwilling to commit more than one division and a single anti-aircraft regiment for service in any theater where combat operations seemed imminent. Only one division-size task force, in fact, was sent to the far Pacific before April 1942. Against air attacks, too, the country's defenses were meager. Along the Pacific coast the Army had only 45 modern fighter planes ready to fly.

6 HITLER'S WAR IN THE EAST

The attack on Russia was for Nazi Germany the most burdensome undertaking of the war, and the worst risk Hitler had run. This was clearly an enterprise which common sense, occasionally in very short supply with the Fuehrer, would have counselled him to avoid. A two-front war, voluntarily undertaken, was not a sound proposition. In orchestrating his huge, predatory attack on Russia, Hitler could count, as always, on the professional co-operation of his highly-skilled officer corps. Whenever he could offer these men the plums of promotions, commands, material rewards, and professional recognition, they could always rationalize his orders, however vicious and, on occasion, even senseless, so as to do his bidding.

When, on the eve of *Barbarossa*, an anonymous German official, perhaps a diplomat recently stationed in Moscow, attempted to persuade Field Marshal Fedor von Bock to help stop the Nazi attack at the eleventh hour, "Bock assured his listener that it was Germany's magnanimous destiny to erase the scourge of Communism from the world and to bring cultural and political freedom to the Russian people. No other time in modern history, Bock stated, was probably more appropriate to carry out this grand mission than now, and at no time would Germany be better prepared".[1] An amazing example of self-delusion! Was this what *Mein Kampf* suggested to the highly-cultured von Bock? Was this what Hitler personally suggested to him in his infamous 30 March 1941 briefing for the generals involved in *Barbarossa*?[2] But, then again, it was not a time for scruples. It was a time for spoils.

The initial assault under the blueprint of *Barbarossa* saw German units lash out at the Soviets primarily from positions in East Prussia and Poland. This was bound to create a wider front than any that the German army experienced thus far in the war. And unless the Red Army could be destroyed at one fell swoop, immediately somewhere behind the Nazi-Soviet frontier, the geography of the Soviet Union presented Hitler with even more daunting prospects.

The Left wing of the German attack would have to move north and north-east to capture the Baltic states of Lithuania, Latvia, and Estonia, and clear the path for an advance to Leningrad. The Centre would presumably be pointing towards Moscow, and the Right would advance towards the south-east with such destinations as the Black Sea, Crimea, the Don and the Volga, and the Caucasus in front of it. That sort of advance, even if largely successful, would create a front several times broader than anything that the Wehrmacht had experienced thus far, diluting necessarily the proportion of force-to-space, and it would also, quite inevitably, create a dangerous supply problem for the German armed forces.

The Russian road system was not nearly as well-developed as its western counterparts. The railroads operated on a different, broader gauge, and the density of the rail network was also not up to, say, French or Belgian or Dutch standards; the size of the country was such that, short of a spectacular victory at the frontier, the invading German force was likely to operate further away from its home base than in virtually all its previous campaigns. Here, in fact, the size of the attacking army and its distance from home would jointly handicap the whole effort.

The campaigns against Greece, against Crete, and also against the British in North Africa, were all long-distance campaigns, far from the German homeland, but they did not involve comparable logistical problems in terms of the number of troops and quantity of equipment that needed to be shipped, maintained, and resupplied.

This problem was compounded by natural conditions of land, topography, and, above all, climate. As the Nazi horde advanced deep into the Soviet Union, the likelihood of Russian roads, rivers, and fields becoming impassable either because of mud (the famous Russian rasputista) in fall and spring, and ice and snow in winter, was overwhelming. If the campaign could not be successfully concluded before the onset of winter, German troops were certain to face the hardships of bitter cold unlike anything they had faced so far on the European continent. Like Murphy's Law, all of these possibilities soon became facts for the invading Germans after 22 June 1941.

The challenges of nature -- which Hitler greatly underestimated and failed to anticipate in his planning -- were soon compounded by the great force of Russian resistance. This, too, had been grossly underestimated both by German intelligence services, and, characteristically, by the Fuehrer himself.[3]

There were some very early indications that the Nazi assault on Russia would prove a great disappointment to Hitler. One was a Swiss broadcast report of 18 July 1941, less than a month after *Barbarossa* had begun:

> There are no signs of waning morale or materiels in the Russian Army. In spite of the enemy's gigantic assault and gain in territory, the soldiers are fighting with an equanimity peculiar to the Russian

people, which even heavy losses and reverses cannot easily break. But both sides are doing their best to bring about a decision or finally to exhaust the enemy.[4]

More ominously still, Hitler's army chief of staff, Colonel General Franz Halder, made this entry in his personal diary on 11 August, the 51st day of the campaign:

> ... our last resources are depleted. From the overall situation, it is becoming increasingly clear that we underestimated the Russian colossus which had been deliberately preparing for war with complete unscrupulousness that is characteristic of a totalitarian state ... At the beginning of the war, we estimated about 200 enemy divisions. Presently, we are already counting 360. These divisions are certainly not armed or equipped in our sense; often they are tactically poorly led. But they are there. When a dozen of them have been smashed, another dozen replaces them. The Russians have the time to do so, because they are so close to their resources and we are always moving farther away from ours.[5]

The days of the free ride were over for the Nazis once they had entered Russia. Much of the reason for this was in Soviet policy, specifically Stalin's policy, both in preparing for war and in conducting it. Soviet war industries, even before 1941, were developed to a degree which the world found eventually quite surprising, both in terms of the quantity, and in many cases, quality of the weaponry produced. The outstanding example of quality was, no doubt, the Soviet T34 tank. It proved to be easily the most formidable armoured vehicle the Nazis had faced up to 1941.

Between the beginning of the war in June and the end of November, the Russians succeeded in evacuating eastward over 1,500 complete factories. Among these, nearly 90 per cent, over 1,300, were factories producing armaments. Virtually all these plants were relocated in areas well beyond the range of Germany's two-engined bombers and thus able to operate on an uninterrupted 24-hour-a-day schedule.[6]

Soviet reserves of manpower and mobilization capabilities greatly surprised the Germans. Somehow, to the consternation of Nazi generals, the reservoir of Soviet formations seemed practically inexhaustible. No matter how many Russian divisions the Nazi army destroyed, there were seemingly always new units to replace them. Despite staggering initial Soviet losses, the

Russians seemed not only able to replace what they lost; their armies actually kept getting bigger and more effective as the war continued.

Bryan Fugate in his book, *Operation Barbarossa*, points out that:

> ... between 22 June and 1 December 1941, the Soviet Supreme Command was able to send 194 newly-created divisions and 94 newly-created brigades to the various fronts ... The well-prepared Soviet plan for mobilization enabled the country's military forces to increase in size from 5 million men in June 1941 to 10.9 million in 1942, despite the large number of casualties sustained in the summer and fall of 1941. The German high command never dreamed that such feats would be possible.[7]

Despite the German capture of Soviet territory accounting for about 40 per cent of its pre-war population and almost 60 per cent of its industrial production in the summer and fall of 1941, the USSR was continuing to put up a vigorous fight. When Marshal Zhukov's Siberian divisions launched the great Soviet winter counter-offensive in the Moscow region on 5 December 1941, Nazi Germany suffered its first serious defeat in land warfare since the Second World War began. (Some would argue that the first serious reverse suffered by the Nazi Wehrmacht in ground action in the Second World War actually occurred at Rostov, liberated from the Germans on 26 November 1941 several days before the great Moscow counter-offensive.)[8]

There was, however, a very important prologue to that counter-offensive. Soviet resistance in the summer and fall of 1941 wore down the Nazi army far more seriously and far more rapidly than anyone or anything since the start of the War. Unquestionably, the heroism and selflessness of the Russian soldier fighting in defence of the motherland was an extremely important factor. But so was Stalin's policy which, ruthless and totalitarian, stood in marked contrast to the highly ineffective humane policies of the Western democracies.

The Soviet approach was rooted in a "scorched earth" defence, announced personally by Stalin in a radio speech to the Soviet people on 3 July 1941. All objects of sustenance, shelter, and possible assistance, were to be destroyed in the path of the advancing enemy. While the French and the British in the summer of 1940 gave up towns of 20,000 population or more to the Nazis without a fight, Stalin in 1941 demanded total resistance everywhere and a heavy price in blood and material from his Nazi adversaries.

Naturally, "scorched earth" asked for great sacrifices from the Soviet people. In one sense, it reflected Stalin's brutal indifference to the fate of the Russian civilian population which, through no fault of its own, may have fallen under Nazi control. How could those people live and work if their houses, farms, and factories, their whole, as we would nowadays call it, infrastructure, were completely destroyed? The answer, of course, is: not easily. Western democracies could not opt for such brutal policies. Stalin did. To deny shelter and comfort to the advancing Hitlerites, Stalin had to first deny it to his own people. The cost to the defenders was obviously enormous, but the Nazis, too, had to suffer and pay the costs of bleak desolation in a land over which they sought to move eastward. The time of "easy pickings" would never again return for Nazi Germany.

Apart from pitched battles, the German army in Russia found it all but impossible to find safe, comfortable havens for its troops on the way east, or, in retreat, on the way west. There was no equivalent here to the comfortable French hotels in undefended towns as in 1940. The Soviet leader demanded drastic means of defence and he did not hesitate to kill and punish those who failed to comply. Those who knew Stalin also knew that he meant business. No one was safe from the dictator's secret police and his firing squads or, alternatively perhaps, gulags. Not even Molotov's wife. And Stalin did not hesitate to deny the Soviet population in its millions the essentials of food, fuel, and shelter in areas conquered by the Nazis and to a lesser extent in those under Soviet control, too. To provide the enemy with an utterly hopeless, desolate, environment for hundreds and thousands of square miles between East Prussia and Moscow, Stalin had to deny, willy-nilly, the basic amenities of life to millions of people involuntarily left behind the Soviet lines. This policy was brutal but it was effective. Even in his successes, before the great Soviet counter-offensive, Hitler was made to pay a huge price for what he got, and in turn, of course, this "price" led to his undoing.

Stalin's conduct of the war, the epitome of totalitarian achievement, is to be sharply distinguished from his initial inability, and unwillingness, to recognize the portents of the Nazi attack. Wishful thinking, as so often in human experience, seems to have got the better of Stalin, especially throughout the early months of 1941, when he stubbornly refused to acknowledge information from many sources (including his own spy in Tokyo, Richard Sorge) that the Nazis were preparing to strike at the Soviet Union. Stalin received warnings from Britain and the United States; from his own agents; from German deserters; and even his own military, who reported suspicious German overflights of Soviet territory and concentrations of Nazi troops on the

Soviet border. But Stalin refused to believe all of them, refused to authorize defensive measures along the Soviet border, fearing allegedly to "provoke the Germans", and with characteristic paranoia suspected Allied intrigue to get him embroiled in a conflict with Hitler.

It is not clear what he actually thought. He may have projected his own brand of "rationality" onto the German Fuehrer. Why would Hitler want to invade the Soviet Union if he had not yet defeated Great Britain in the West? If Stalin wouldn't do it, why would Hitler do it? Perhaps Stalin had hoped that the conflict would come a few years later, when the Red Army would be in a more advanced state of readiness. Stalin almost certainly believed that his "friendship" with Hitler was not a permanent one; timing of the breach between them was the critical issue.[9] Whatever Stalin's illusions, he was deeply dismayed and depressed by Hitler's attack. According to some accounts, the Soviet dictator was willing to make huge territorial concessions to Hitler (à la Brest Litovsk in 1918) if the latter would only stop the panzer advance on Russia. The offer, allegedly made to the Bulgarian ambassador in Moscow, did not get anywhere.[10] But within a few days of *Barbarossa*, Stalin recovered his composure and began to manage Soviet defence efforts with his habitual focus, energy and brutality.

Despite all its preparations, the Soviet military was both at the beginning, and in some respects even in the later phases of the war, considerably inferior qualitatively to the German. The Soviet officer corps, led by Marshal Mikhail Tukhachevsky in the 1930s, had been decimated by Stalin's bloody political purges. The training and the technical skills of Soviet troops, not to mention experience, were not nearly as good as those of the Germans. Much of the Soviet equipment -- though not all, by any means -- was obsolete. For several months after the launch of *Barbarossa*, Hitler continued to reap the benefits of great tactical surprise. Soviet troop deployments were frequently ill-suited to flexible and effective resistance to the Nazis' well rehearsed panzer-Luftwaffe blows.[11]

British military analyst Hanson Baldwin gave this description of the Soviet military confronting the Wehrmacht:

> The Russian armed forces of June 1941 were, man for man, division for division, grossly inferior in military effectiveness to their German foes. The Red Army was distinguished then for mass, not quality. It was basically an Army of foot soldiers, with a few excellent professionals and natural leaders (most of them in subordinate positions at war's start) and many hastily armed

peasants ... Many of its units remained an 'armed horde' throughout the war. Though its arms and equipment were spotty -- the best and the worst, the most modern and the obsolete -- it had a lot of everything, and the production rate of the Soviet factories and the recuperative power of the Russian system proved to be surprising.[12]

Brigadier Young believed that the Nazis deployed 3,000,000 men, 3,300 tanks and 2,770 aircraft in the initial stages of *Barbarossa*, while the Soviets confronted this force with 24,000 tanks but

> only a quarter of these [were] in running order. The Red Air Force [had] about 800 aircraft facing the Germans but, again, many [were] obsolete or in poor repair. In all classes of equipment the most modern Soviet designs [were] simple and durable and at least as good as the German equivalent ...
>
> The Germans ... underestimate[d] badly the manpower the Soviets [had] available and [took] too little account of the speed with which the Soviets [would] prepare new army and militia units ... [The Soviet] KV type [tank] was almost invulnerable to the German tanks' guns ...[13]

It took Stalin a number of months to develop, and improve, his own proficiency of command. The Soviets suffered some cataclysmic defeats in 1941 and 1942 before the tide of war in the East clearly turned against the Nazis. There is little doubt that in the early stages of the war, the dictator was confused by the military situation facing him. He seemed unable to recognize the full impact of *Barbarossa*. The orders issued to, and through, Marshal S. K. Timoshenko, directing the Red Army to annihilate the German units invading Soviet territory were under the circumstances, absurd.

Stalin's posture of "no-retreat-anywhere" in the summer of 1941 helped ensure the liquidation and loss of huge Soviet armies, with millions of prisoners and masses of equipment captured by the Nazis. The execution of General D. G. Pavlov and some, or most, of his staff officers was an act of wanton cruelty; in all likelihood it was intended to shift the blame for the June debacle from Stalin to the military. But even this terrible period had a certain important "upside" for the Soviets.

Soviet resistance, though very costly, was nevertheless very effective in diminishing Nazi capacity for war. In the first eight months of the war, the Soviets inflicted 1 million casualties on the German armies -- according to

Nazi sources.[14] That meant that roughly one of every three soldiers who began *Barbarossa* had become a casualty. According to Nazi accounts, 243,790 soldiers and officers were dead or missing in action on the Eastern Front as of 20 February 1942.[15]

Since 1 September 1939, all German casualties until 31 August 1940 -- in the dead and missing categories -- had amounted to only 70,256. Rommel's losses in Africa prior to June 1941 are given at less than 2,000 dead and missing by Hanson Baldwin;[16] the conquest of Yugoslavia cost the Nazis an almost unbelievable 166 personnel killed and missing; and the conquest of Greece, apart from Crete, 1,100 killed with 4,000 "wounded and missing"; Crete itself was apparently more "expensive", with a figure of 6,116 casualties, although these consisted of killed, missing *and* wounded.[17] Thus, with all possible allowance for additional manpower losses at sea and in the air, it is still clear that German combat casualties in the two critical categories of dead and missing in action for all twenty months of war prior to *Barbarossa* were well under 100,000. Possibly, they were less than 90,000.

By February 1942, the rate of German losses in dead and missing per one month of fighting in Russia was at least 6 times as high as it had been against all other opponents elsewhere. Quite understandably, Winston Churchill subsequently observed that he would not challenge "in the slightest degree the conclusion which history will affirm that the Russian resistance broke the power of the German armies and inflicted mortal injury upon the life-energies of the German nation ...".[18]

Stalin's distinctive policy in war was the same as his principal policy in peacetime. Stalin was a leader who excelled in providing disincentives, or, perhaps one might say negative incentives. Soviet military and civilian bureaucrats lived in perpetual dread of Stalin and his not-so-secret, secret police. It has been said that Stalin made his subordinates more afraid of himself than they were of the Nazi enemy.[19] His command system was suffused with the notion that failure and death were close companions.

Stalin established a reputation for cruel and virtually unavoidable retribution for whatever in his eyes might seem a transgression, cowardice, slackness, or inadequacy. He combined this quality with intellectual prowess. A cruel but stupid leader could be outwitted. But Stalin cultivated great expertise in the affairs of state. His memory was legendary. Fooling him was both very difficult and extremely dangerous. Unlike Hitler, Stalin's interests in the business of state were so extensive that there were very few *carte blanche* refuges of delegated power in his decision-making system.[20]

Dmitri Volkogonov provides a good illustration from the experience of the Commissar of Transport, I. V. Kovalev. Kovalev was invited to the Kremlin shortly after the Nazi invasion of the Soviet Union and saw Stalin propose himself to the assembled group of political and military leaders as head of the Transport Committee attached to the State Defence Committee. Of course, Stalin also headed the Defence Committee. Many years later, Kovalev could still remember Stalin's words at the meeting:

> Transport is a matter of life and death. The front is in the hands of the transport. Remember, failure to carry out the State Defence Committee orders means the military tribunal.

When, on one occasion, Kovalev could not immediately account for a particular shipment to the front, Stalin said to him: "if you don't find it, general, you'll be going to the front as a private".[21] He also recalled that "it was no good giving [Stalin] only an approximate report; he would at once drop his voice ominously and say, 'Don't you know? What are you doing then?'." Stalin was "an incredibly cold person ... One felt oppressed by Stalin's power but also by his phenomenal memory and the fact that he knew so much. He made one feel even less important than one was".[22]

Another Volkogonov testimony deserves to be cited here in this connection even if at some length:

> Always, his response to a harsh situation was to make things harsher. For instance, Zhdanov and Zhukov, in reporting the situation in Leningrad mentioned the fact that, when attacking Soviet positions, the Germans had pushed women and children and old men ahead of them, placing the defenders in an even harder position. The women and children screamed, 'Don't shoot! We're your own people. We're your own people!'. The Soviet forces did not know what do. Stalin's immediate reaction was entirely in character.

> They are saying the German swine who are advancing on Leningrad are driving old folk and women and children in front of them. They are saying there are Bolsheviks in Leningrad who find it impossible to use their weapons against such deputies. I think that if there are such people among the Bolsheviks, then they should be destroyed first, because they're more dangerous than the German fascists. My advice is, don't be sentimental, smash the enemy and his willing or

unwilling accomplices in the teeth. Hit the Germans and their delegates, whoever they might be, with everything you've got, cut the enemy down, never mind if they are willing or unwilling enemies. Dictated at 0400 hours 21.9.41 by Comrade Stalin. Signed by B. Shaposhnikov.[23]

Going beyond what may be termed anecdotal accounts, it is clear that Stalin's approach to fighting the war against Nazism relied on the fundamental fear of death and severe punishment for every individual in Soviet society, and upon the collateral notion of collective responsibility. If one failed or fled, the risk of drastic punishment would extend to one's family and close associates as well. This policy was expressed with far-reaching significance, among other cases, in Stalin's Order 270 of 16 August 1941 which was read to all military units. It provided that any officer or soldier who surrendered to the enemy would be considered a traitor to the motherland and enemy of the people, subject to execution, and that families of such persons would be subject to punishment and deprivation of food rations. The order did not make exceptions on account of volition and capacity. It made no difference if one surrendered because one was physically unable to continue resistance, or if one surrendered because of direct constraint by the enemy. Under no circumstances could one honourably or lawfully surrender.

Another example of Stalin's policy was Order 227 issued on 28 July 1942, calling for the immediate execution, by shooting, of any officer or soldier who retreated from the front without official permission. It also provided that special detachments of a police character would be established in the rear of military units considered "unstable" with orders to shoot to kill those involved in panicky or disorderly retreat.[24]

Stalin, in fact, indicated what his policy would be as early as his 3 July 1941 speech to the Soviet people when he said:

... there must be no room in our ranks for whimperers and cowards, for panic-mongers and deserters; our people must know no fear in the fight and must selflessly join our patriotic war of liberation against the Fascist enslavers ... We must wage a ruthless fight against all disorganizers of the rear, deserters, panic-mongers and rumor-mongers; we must exterminate spies, [and] sabotage agents ...[25]

Indeed, one could argue that Stalin's pathological personality structure fitted him almost perfectly for the great task with which he grappled. He was remarkably lacking in human empathy.[26]

There are certain familiar "ifs" in Hitler's Russian campaign. The diversion of effort to Yugoslavia and Greece in the spring of 1941 delayed the start of *Barbarossa*, according to some sources, by a matter of weeks. This could have made a difference in the Nazi capture of Moscow and, conceivably in the whole campaign. A bigger "if" was Hitler's brutal treatment of the Eastern Slavs. How might have things turned out if Hitler had treated the peoples of the Soviet Union as a liberator rather than as an oppressor? On this issue, too, there are all sorts of possibilities, although Hitler's brutal persecution of the Soviet peoples was so firmly rooted in *Mein Kampf*, in who Hitler really was, that it must be viewed as one of the wilder speculations.[27]

There was also the factor of Western aid to Russia. How important was it in achieving Soviet victory over Germany? It was probably a good deal less than critical to Soviet survival, in part, because of its timing. On the other hand, it may have supplied the Russians with the crucial margin needed to push the Nazis all the way back to Berlin, quickly.

In the category of major weapons, the most significant item supplied to the Soviets by the US and Britain was aircraft, and these constituted only 12 per cent of the total employed by the Soviets during the Second World War. The proportion of tanks and artillery guns supplied from the West was well under 10 per cent of the Soviet totals. Trucks and jeeps, however, were a much more important item, as were communication and transport equipment, some scarce raw materials such as aluminium, and many other useful odds and ends. Most of the weapons the Soviets used in their war with Nazi Germany were home-built. All the soldiers were home-grown. As Ellsworth Raymond observes:

> Russia harvested at least 200 million tons of grain during the four years of the war, but received only 1 million from Lend-Lease. According to the US Department of Agriculture, American food filled no more than 5 per cent of the USSR wartime food requirements.
>
> ... Most Lend-Lease reached Russia in the later years of the war, when the Red Army was already winning on its own. Of the nearly 17 million tons of wartime supplies sent to the USSR by the United

States, Britain, and Canada, four-fifths came to Russia after the Battle of Stalingrad, the turning point in the European War.[28]

Is it possible, even likely, that the multi-billion dollar volume of American and British aid, especially in the years 1943, 1944 and 1945, made the difference between victory and stalemate on the Eastern Front? Of course! Wars, like business enterprises, are won and lost on the margins. If it takes one million dollars to succeed, eight hundred thousand is not enough. While no one could calculate this proposition exactly, it stands to reason that many a battle could have been won for the Soviets by having several hundred more trucks to sustain an advance, or lost for lack of transport at the decisive point or time.

Russia had lost about half of its European territory; about 40 per cent of its 1940 civilian population passed into Nazi control; and more than 20 million of her citizens lost their lives in battle, through casualties and Nazi executions, and all other causes linked to the war;[29] her lands were ravaged; her economy even in 1940 was, of course, not nearly as developed as that of Germany. Yet, remarkably, Soviet aircraft production rose from 10,565 planes in 1940, the last full year before the conflict, to 15,735 in 1941, to 25,436 in 1942, to 34,900 in 1943 and in the last full year of war to 40,300 in 1944. This was a typically huge increase over Russia's peacetime production under highly adverse circumstances.[30] Clearly, the Russians were doing a great deal on their own.

Bryan Fugate points out that while the Soviet Union produced only 18.3 million tons of steel in 1940 to Germany's 31.8, somehow, it managed to out-produce the Nazis in basic weaponry through the first year of the war. Thus, by the end of 1942 the USSR had produced 25,000 planes to only 14,700 for Germany; 24,700 tanks and armoured vehicles to Germany's 9,300; 29,500 artillery pieces to the Nazis' 1,200.[31] By 1944, Soviet armament factories had increased their production by 500-600 per cent; and their output of 30,000 tanks and 120,000 artillery guns between 1943 and 1945 exceeded that of Nazi Germany. All this was being done in a society whose males were conscripted by military draft from age 17 to 50. Obviously, Stalin managed to extract lots of valuable labour from a work population made up largely of women, children, and old men.

The Soviet economy may have sputtered and faltered under Brezhnev, Andropov, Chernenko, and Gorbachev but, somehow, it worked remarkably well under Stalin. It may not have been "efficient" in the various possible purely economic understandings of that term, but it was clearly "satisfying" in a period of unprecedented crisis in Soviet history. It supported the front, averted famine, and maintained high levels of military output.[32]

One critical aspect in which the Soviets surpassed all other combatants of the Second World War was in the ability to "squeeze" the domestic sector of the economy, to discipline and limit the civilian consumer to a greater degree than was the case in any other belligerent country. This can be inferred from the amount of military output -- in tanks, airplanes and guns -- for each million tons of steel produced by the respective belligerent economies. Analogous results are obtainable by using other indicators of economic development such as energy output or the production of electricity.

Unlike Western democracies, the Soviets were able to deny their civilian, consumer sector all kinds of basic amenities in housing, transportation, construction, appliances, and other goods of private and civilian consumption, while at the same time generating a huge effort on the battlefield. In this sense, the USSR actually out-produced and out-performed all combatants in the Second World War.

What is of great importance in the claims put forward by Western observers on behalf of American and British aid to Russia is an implicit assumption of equivalence. Stated in extreme form, the proposition is that weapons and supplies cannot win wars without soldiers to make use of them. That seems very reasonable. Soldiers without weapons and supplies cannot win wars either. That seems reasonable, too. In the upshot, we have two equal parts in the war-fighting equation.

In fact, however, the question is, would the United States and Great Britain, and/or anybody else, do to Germany what Russia did to Germany if Russia were not there to do it? Given the technology of the 1940s, when there were no smart bombs, guided missiles, lasers, computers, or nuclear-tipped ballistics, the only way in which the formidable German army could have been defeated on the continent of Europe was through brutal ground warfare of an extremely costly, i.e. bloody, kind. Not hundreds of thousands, but several millions would have had to die and bear wounds before the Wehrmacht of 1941 could have been decisively defeated. Would the Western Allies have been willing and able to conduct such a struggle against Hitler? Given the record of the democracies in the 1930s and the early 1940s, and, indeed, given the communications and decisions of Western leaders during the war itself ("an invasion of Western Europe is feasible only if the Russians are successfully engaging and wearing down the bulk of the German army in the east ...") this would have been a most unlikely scenario. The implicit claim of equivalence is profoundly misleading.

TABLE 1
AVERAGE ARMS OUTPUT IN 1941-44
IN RELATION TO AVERAGE STEEL OUTPUT

	1941-44 Avg Steel Output In Million Tons	Artillery Pieces Produced Per 1000 Tons Of Steel	Tanks Per 1000 Tons Of Steel	Airplanes Per 1000 Tons Of Steel	Avg Of 3 Weapons Per 1000 Tons Of Steel
USSR	11.35	35.15	7.41	10.25	18.27
USA	77.50	2.62	0.98	3.219	2.27
Ger	28.33	3.07	2.17	3.29	2.84
Brit	12.52	2.92	2.07	7.71	4.23

The Nazi-Soviet war, in effect, consisted of five phases. The first was from the launching of *Barbarossa* until Hitler's defeat at the gates of Moscow. In this phase, the Russians suffered a number of huge defeats and ceded great chunks of territory which followed the script of all of Hitler's previous aggressions, except for two factors. The Russians exacted a huge price from Hitler in Nazi casualties, far in excess of what had happened in the West. And their army was still very much alive at the conclusion of this phase of the war.

In December of 1941, two days before Pearl Harbor, the Soviets launched an offensive which shattered the myth of Nazi invincibility in land warfare, and forced very substantial, humiliating withdrawals on an hitherto unbeatable Wehrmacht. More than that, the Russians for the first time in the war raised the question of Hitler's ultimate defeat. Would Hitler suffer the fate of Napoleon in 1812 fleeing Russia pell-mell as the Great Corsican had done? In this instance Hitler's resolve not to retreat, while accepting great losses, is often credited with, temporarily, at least, saving the situation.

The third phase began in the spring of 1942 and may be termed the era of lessened Nazi advantage. In this period, the Germans did not renew their attack on Moscow and instead concentrated their forces in new, successful thrusts largely toward the south-east in the direction of the Caucasus and the Volga. In this period the Nazi advance was not nearly as rapid as in 1941 and it ended with the second calamitous Nazi defeat at Stalingrad, involving the loss of Field Marshal von Paulus' 300,000 strong army at the beginning of February 1943. For many people inside Germany and out, Stalingrad was the final, decisive indication that ultimately Hitler would lose the war. It was undoubtedly the single most painful German defeat of the Second World War

After Stalingrad, the question was no longer could Hitler defeat the Russians, but rather how long could he hold them off? Could the Nazis establish a viable defensive front strong enough to withstand new and certain Russian attacks? It is at least probable that very able generals, like Erich von Manstein, believed that this might still be possible, and undoubtedly some high-ranking German officers still believed that Manstein, or someone like him, might be able to hold the Russians on shortened and flexible defence lines.[33]

Not without reason, most German military leaders still regarded their own army as qualitatively superior to the Russians, even if they were out-numbered and out-fought. This fourth period, however, was very short. It came to an end in July in consequence of Hitler's fateful decision to try one more huge offensive gamble in the East, this time in the battle of Kursk. In this debacle, German losses in men and material, especially panzers, were so severe that from July 1943 onwards there simply were not sufficient resources with which to hold off the Russians more than temporarily and locally.[34]

Given the new balance of power, the road to the West was now substantially open for the Red Army. It was now up to Stalin and his military chiefs to choose their points of attack, smash the enemy, regroup and prepare, and attack again. From now on, it became a question of "when" and "how long" rather than "if". In the analogy to the *Titanic* disaster, the German army had hit an iceberg and the gash it sustained was so critical that there could no longer be any reasonable hope of recovery. If truth were told, it was time to think about life-boats. The Soviet Union was on its way to victory in the Second World War.

Two very important indicators of the Soviet contribution to Allied victory in the Second World War were battle casualties sustained by the Nazis, and the proportion of German divisions engaged on the respective fronts. A reasonable indicator of the first measure is that about 85 per cent of German battle deaths occurred on the Eastern Front. Out of a total of 3.3 million Nazi fatalities in the Second World War, sustained in battle, 2.8 million were inflicted by the Russians. Measures of proportion-of-forces engaged are also very much in favour of the Soviets.[35]

When Hitler unleashed *Barbarossa* on the Soviet Union, the German army, by some accounts, deployed 205 divisions, among them 152 infantry divisions; 11 motorized infantry divisions; 20 armoured divisions and 5 SS divisions. "The fighting forces in the east -- which included practically all the motorized infantry, armoured, and SS divisions -- accounted for about 75 per cent of the field troops, with a total of 3,050,000 men".[36] On 16 June 1942, 77 per cent of German divisions were still facing the Soviets. On 1 July 1943, 69 per cent of German divisions were fighting in the East.[37]

In October 1943, the German Army, in consequence of all its losses, was reorganized into units of reduced numbers and strength. The Army was divided into 371 divisions of which 287 or nearly 77 per cent were stationed on the Russian front.[38] According to Baudot *et al.*, the Nazis had a total of only 57 divisions in France and the Low Countries to confront the Allied invasion of 6 June 1944.[39]

According to Brigadier Young, at the beginning of *Overlord*, the Germans in France, Belgium and Holland "[had] 60 divisions including 11 armoured. These figures [were] somewhat misleading, however. About half of the infantry divisions [were] not equipped for mobile warfare and all [were] understrength. Some [were] in France simply to refit after heavy losses on the Eastern Front and [were] hardly fit for action".[40]

A still more realistic view of the relative contributions of the various participants takes into account the number of divisions actually engaged in battle in relation to the time of conflict. Even here, the quality of the forces involved is not assessed. Nevertheless, under this rubric, one discovers analogous disparities. For example, between mid-1941 and mid-1942, the Soviets faced an average of at least 170 Nazi divisions (including 5 deployed in Finland) while the British faced 3. After the 1943 Allied invasion of Italy at most 27 German divisions were engaged with no appreciable change in the East. Only in the last year of the war did the Allies engage a maximum of perhaps 80 German divisions simultaneously in the West and in Italy. Allowing for both the variables of force (divisions) and time (days of warfare) the ratio of Nazi engagement on the Eastern Front was at least 6 times as substantial as that against the Allies, west and south.

Part of the "secret" of Russia's successful defence lay in the tremendous tenacity of its forces even in situations where, locally, little advantage, let alone any kind of "victory" was possible. What apparently was always possible, however, from the Soviet point of view, was a successful war of attrition reducing Nazi manpower and war resources, ruthlessly, brutally, nearly always at great cost to oneself, but also to the enemy. This kind of warfare was not reflected in highly publicized attacks and counter-attacks or the capture of prominent cities. It was a matter of many small-scale engagements eating out the heart of the German Army, its resilience and it reserves. Much of this kind of fighting occurred in urban settings, a classically in Stalingrad, where the fighting was conducted on a house-by house, and sometimes even room-by-room basis.

A German lieutenant left this memoir of his experiences and impressions in the city:

> We have fought during fifteen days for a single house with mortars, grenades, machine-guns and bayonets. Already by the third day fifty-four German corpses are strewn in the cellars, on the landings, and the staircases. The front is a corridor between burnt-out rooms; it is the thin ceiling between two floors. Help comes from neighbouring houses by fire escapes and chimneys. There is a ceaseless struggle from noon to night. From storey-to-storey, faces black with sweat, we bombard each other with grenades in the middle of the explosions, clouds of dust and smoke, heaps of mortar. Pools of blood, fragments of furniture and human beings. Ask any soldier what half-an-hour of hand-to-hand struggle means in such a fight. And imagine Stalingrad; eighty days and eighty nights of hand-to-hand struggles. The street is no longer measured by metres but by corpses ...
>
> Stalingrad is no longer a town. By day it is an enormous cloud of burning, blinding smoke; it is a vast furnace lit by the reflection of the flames. And when night arrives, one of those scorching, howling, bleeding nights, the dogs plunge into the Volga and swim desperately to gain the other bank. The nights of Stalingrad are a terror for them. Animals flee this hell; the hardest stones cannot bear it for long; only men endure.[41]

Without the softening-up of the Nazi military establishment in the years 1941-1942, the great victories of 1943 and 1944 and 1945 would not have been possible. Soviet operations represented a different style or mode of war from that conducted by the liberal democracies in the West. The closest Western approximation to the grim Soviet practice of tying up and using up enemy forces at high cost to oneself was probably the American defence of Corregidor in the Philippines against the Japanese. (The German siege of Bastogne in 1944 was, fortunately, too brief to test the ability and willingness, of the United States to engage in this kind of enterprise.) American troops, commanded by General MacArthur and after his departure on 11 March 1942, ɔy General Jonathan Wainwright, with little hope of relief, held out on Corregidor for more than four months, and, counting from the earliest Japanese attack, almost five. They capitulated on 6 May 1942.[42]

This episode, however, was more than offset on the Allied side by the collapse of the British position and alleged fortress of Singapore. British and other Allied forces, including Indian and Australian troops, numbering over 100,000, capitulated to numerically inferior Japanese attackers on 15 February 1942. The actual Japanese siege of the city and harbour of Singapore did not ɔegin until the beginning of February, and resistance folded in less than two weeks. Desertions and lack of discipline were a major problem for the British. Ironically, Singapore's surrender occurred just as the Japanese attackers were about to run out of ammunition and other resources. Postwar accounts indicate that the alleged lack of water in the city was not the problem making surrender inevitable (as officially alleged).[43]

By way of comparison, in Leningrad, the Nazi siege lasted for more than two-and-a-half-years. The Soviet regime was willing to accept losses of perhaps 700,000 lives in its course, and tremendous destruction of a city which was the cultural and architectural jewel of Russia, both old and new. Stalin would not easily yield the city of Lenin to the Nazis. He demanded that, in case of the Germans breaking into Leningrad, all buildings be blown up and the defenders fight the enemy in its ruins until no one was left alive.

Meantime, even relatively small children were required to help build anti-tank ditches and other fortifications, and were refused meagre food rations if they did not show up for those duties. Hunger, even cannibalism, were not unknown in the city during the siege, as was virtually every other deprivation ever experienced by humanity. But the Soviet regime did not show pity. When Stalin sent Zhukov as his plenipotentiary to Leningrad, the latter, à la Stalin, threatened people with executions if they failed to carry out his orders.[44]

An important perspective on the Nazi-Soviet conflict is presented by the work of Glantz and House who point out that, whatever the losses on either side, the Germans were much less effective in providing replacements, and thus the balance of manpower on the Eastern Front continually widened in favour of the Soviets. Thus, by 1 April 1943, Nazi troops numbered 2.7 million men or between 300 and 600,000 fewer than at the beginning of *Barbarossa*, depending on different estimates, while the Russians increased their troop strength to 5.8 million, probably about 2 million more than in June 1941. By 1 August 1944 German troop strength declined to 1.99 million while the Red Army increased to 6.5 million. While specific troop figures usually differ among several authorities, there is no doubt about the general tendency described by Glantz and House.

These authors also point out that the Germans were actually somewhat better in replacing lost equipment than lost manpower but even in this area of military performance the Nazi replacement, or even weapon increases, did not keep pace with the Soviets. Thus, Soviet armour, i.e., tanks and self-propelled guns, rose from 7,753 on 1 June 1944 to 8,300 on 1 January 1945, while over the same period, the Nazi inventory increased from 2,608 to 3,700. Quite importantly, obviously, by November 1944 German artillery disposed of 5,700 guns while the Soviets employed 114,600 guns.[45]

In a more general perspective of the conflict, between 1941 and 1943, through stubborn resistance, the Soviets had tied up Hitler's huge military establishment, simultaneously denying it victory, grinding it down beyond repair, and also, of course, denying it alternative opportunities of conquest. After 1943, it became largely a question of time: how long would it take the Soviets to defeat Nazi Germany altogether?

But while it is possible to speak of a final Soviet victory over Nazi Germany *without* an Allied invasion of Europe, such a victory was at least conditional on the continuing engagement of the Western Allies against the Third Reich at least at the levels in effect prior to D-Day. About two-thirds of the German air force in 1944 was busy fighting off Allied raids over the German homeland and at least 60 Nazi divisions, admittedly of varying strengths, were employed in anticipation of an Allied landing in Western Europe, as well as in defence of southern Italy. If the Nazis were free to use all these forces against the Russians, and if the flow of trucks and other supplies from the US to the USSR were stopped, Soviet victory would have been much more problematical.

In Seaton's estimate:

> The Soviet Union's success in halting the German invasion was due in the first place to the accident of geography, to the vastness of the Soviet Union, to its undeveloped road and wide-gauge railway system, to the vagaries of its climate and the bitterness of its winter. The second most important factor was probably Stalin's brutal determination as a war leader and the third the resistance put up by the Red Army during this first year of war.[46]

There was nothing that Stalin contributed to Russia's geography, but the resistance of the Red Army was, in large part, at least, due to the leadership at the top and from the top.

> As head of the Soviet state there was little of real importance which escaped Stalin's attention. The direction of foreign and home affairs, of Soviet industry and economy, all were under his tight control. He alone was the supreme controller and co-ordinator. As a war leader Stalin dwarfed all his contemporaries.
>
> In addition he was, like Hitler, the Commander-in-Chief of the Armed Forces, a military and field commander, following, and sometimes directing, operations. The control he exercised over the General Staff and subordinate field commanders was personal, close and threatening, for as the *de facto* Supreme Commander he was greatly feared and his wish was law. The words 'you will answer for it with your head' and 'or we will shorten you by a head' were commonplace adjuncts to his orders. No joke was intended. None dared to disagree, far less argue, though, if the opportunity occurred and the occasion was auspicious, some might discuss or plead their case.[47]

In retrospect, it is clear that for the Soviet Union, victory in the war stemmed from its ability to overcome its great initial losses, specifically by reorganizing and increasing its military production, by mobilizing a huge army and deploying it effectively with good weapons and good leadership, and by giving it the requisite logistical base of support. All of these things could only have been done if Stalin was able to maintain control over the country.

This was an enormous, well-nigh horrendous task, given the flight of so many people from the western part of the USSR and the relocation of thousands of industrial plants from west to east. Without order and discipline, there could have been no effective mobilization, no war production, and no steady support of the armies in the field. Stalin's system of internal controls had much more in common with that of Hitler than with Roosevelt's or Churchill's. Given the Russian position of 1941, with great defeats everywhere, grave danger of further conquest and invasion by the Nazis, and a very difficult internal situation in terms of resources for private consumption, whether in food, fuel, housing, clothing, and virtually all other amenities, the single most destructive alternative would have been to tell people: "Do whatever you like and don't do anything you do not like".

If the Soviet regime announced these things as its policy, the outcome of the Nazi-Soviet conflict almost certainly would have been swift and certain and analogous to what occurred in France in 1940. Flight and panic would have quite naturally -- and, above all, quite understandably -- ruled the day. There were very few positive incentives for people in Russia to "stay put", to work around the clock in her war factories for meagre wages under military discipline, and to serve in her armies, with a great chance of being killed or maimed.

The best individual option in Russia would have been flight, almost anywhere, to Iran, to Turkey, to Vladivostok and beyond, to anywhere but home. And the number of people dislocated by the German advance was so large that, without drastic controls over the movement of people, what happened in France in 1940 would have been the proverbial picnic compared with the probable events in Russia. Hunger and riots would have ruled the day. Private traffic would have overwhelmed Russia's transport system. Apart from such factors as propaganda, patriotism, and hatred of Nazi invaders, Stalin's police state apparatus with its -- by 1941 -- legendary evil reputation was all but indispensable to the achievement of Soviet resistance and ultimately to Soviet victory.

Stalin's police-state apparatus was not only similar to Hitler's. It played an analogous role in Nazi Germany, within the more narrow limits of Hitler's possibilities. By 1944, contrary to Allied expectations, Nazi war production continued to increase. Nazi resistance on the battlefields, east and west, even if not generally successful was still fierce. Even as late as 1945, the Western Allies recognized the German armed forces as formidable, even often fanatical, opponents. And yet, Germany was being bombed night and day by the British and the Americans. There were no victories to boost domestic morale. German families were receiving news of the deaths of their fathers, husbands, brothers, nephews, and uncles, in ever-increasing numbers. The war seemed, after Stalingrad and after D-Day, a lost cause to more and more Germans.

But neither military performance on the fighting fronts nor the volume and quality of Germany's war production seemed affected. The American Army executed one soldier for desertion. The Nazi army executed possibly between 25 and 30,000 soldiers and officers. The Soviets may have killed even more, though no such numbers are known. But, of course, pervasive, efficient, and above all, highly credible police controls in Germany, as in Russia, were instrumental in the suppression of panic, doubt, dissent, disaffection and opposition; and if truth be told, these controls clearly and greatly helped the respective regimes, Communist and Nazi, to some very impressive military performances in the Second World War.

It was, no doubt, one of the great ironies of history, and perhaps of the human condition, that in the task of destroying one of the most evil figures ever -- Adolf Hitler -- hardly any one proved quite as useful as another evil man -- Joseph Stalin. Each was a ruthless dictator and each deserved the title of mass murderer. If Hitler was the master of the Final Solution and many other horrendous crimes, Stalin was the perpetrator of the most massive, bloody political purges, violent collectivization, and the Katyn massacre, just to name a few of his "conspicuous accomplishments".

In the Second World War there was an opportunity to destroy only one of the great oppressive and menacing political systems, Hitler's, because without Stalin's help the democracies would have been most likely unable to do it on their own. Given Stalin's far greater prudence and restraint, as compared with Hitler's, in the conduct of foreign relations, the Allies' choice of evils-to-be-eliminated-by-the-use-of-force, was, it would seem, historically vindicated with the largely non-violent "fall of communism" in 1989.

NOTES

[1] Alfred W. Turney, *Disaster at Moscow: von Bock's Campaigns 1941-1942* (Albuquerque: University of New Mexico Press, 1970), pp. 43-44.

[2] *Ibid.*, pp. 35-37.

[3] See Richard Muller, *The German Air War in Russia* (Baltimore: The Nautical and Aviation Company of America, 1992) for an insightful, critical discussion of the tremendous dispersal of forces and objectives which the Luftwaffe suffered with consequent decline in its effectiveness. See especially pp. 230-235. Note also the memoir of General Karl Koller, Chief of the German Air Staff, published in H. A. Probert (ed.), *The Rise and Fall of the German Air Force 1933-1945* (London: Arms and Armour Press, 1983), pp. 407-409. The political failure to invest more resources in the Luftwaffe in 1940 and "the folly of the Russian war" were his principal explanations for Germany's overall failure and, of course, the decline of the Luftwaffe itself. Wrote Koller: "We were smothered by the enormous superiority of the American and Russian material, because the German High Command undertook too much on the ground in the East, and because it did not direct the main weight of armament right from the beginning towards air supremacy...", p. 408.

[4] See Janusz Piekalkiewicz, *Moscow 1941: The Frozen Offensive* (Novato, CA: Presidio Press, 1981), p. 49.

[5] *Ibid.*, pp. 58-59.

[6]   See Barry A. Leach, *German Strategy Against Russia 1939-1941* (Oxford: Clarendon Press, 1973), "the size of the Soviet tank forces and the quality of its new tanks also came as an unpleasant surprise ... the amount and thickness of armour of these new types came as a shock to the Germans", p. 202. Leach puts the Soviet tank total at close to 24,000. He also notes that the Nazis seriously underestimated the Soviet Air Force, p. 202. Cf. Mark Harrison, *Soviet Planning in Peace and War, 1938-1945* (Cambridge: Cambridge University Press 1985). Note also Earl F. Ziemke and M. A. Bauer, *Moscow to Stalingrad: Decision in the East* (Washington, DC: Center of Military History, US Army, 1987), p. 514, "... in 1942 Soviet output already surpassed that of Germany in tanks and other armoured vehicles ... in aircraft ... in infantry rifles and carbines ... and in artillery ... Soviet accounts attribute this remarkable feat entirely to the Communist system's ability to overcome adverse circumstances, but it also appears likely that stocks of strategic materials, particularly steel and other metals, had been accumulated before the war". These authors also indicate that "Despite the Germans' best efforts, the Soviet strength at the front grew from 2.9 million in June 1941 to 4.2 million in December 1941 and then to 5.5 million in June 1942 and to 6.1 million in November 1942", p. 514. On Nazi underestimation of Soviet strength, see pp. 47-48.

[7]   Bryan I. Fugate, *Operation Barbarossa, Strategy and Tactics on the Eastern Front, 1941* (Novato, CA: Presidio Press, 1984), pp. 57-58.

[8]   See S. M. Shtemenko, *The Soviet General Staff At War 1941-1945* (Moscow: Progress Publishers, 1975), p. 49.

[9]   There is widespread, multifaceted, one might say, speculation in the scholarly literature on the reasons for Stalin's failure to take note of what, in retrospect, seems obvious. Among various sources, see, for example, Geoffrey Roberts, *The Soviet Union and the Origins of the Second World War, Russo-German Relations and the Road to War, 1933-1941* (New York: St. Martin's Press, 1995): Stalin probably viewed Nazi build-up in the East as precursor of some as yet unknown demands on Russia (ultimatum) rather than war. After all, "who would believe that even Hitler would be mad enough to launch an invasion of Soviet Russia"?, p. 141. See William Carr, *Poland to Pearl Harbor: The Making of the Second World War* (London: Edward Arnold, 1985) who views Stalin's policy of alliance with Hitler as a piece of *realpolitik* based on the notion that the Western powers either would not or could not help Russia against Germany. War with Germany needed to be delayed and this was the best way to do it, pp. 64-65. Obviously, he could not get it delayed enough.

See Richard K. Betts, "Surprise Despite Warning: Why Sudden Attacks Succeed", *Political Science Quarterly*, Vol. 95, No. 4, Winter 1980-81, pp. 551-572. The author maintains that the Stalin failure of 1941 was by no means unique or confined to authoritarian political systems. Note also A. J. Groth and J. D. Froeliger, "Unheeded Warnings: Some Intelligence Lessons of the 1930s and 1940s",

Comparative Strategy, Vol. 10, No. 3, Fall 1991, pp. 331-346. See John Erickson and David Dilks (eds.), *Barbarossa, The Axis and the Allies* (Edinburgh: Edinburgh University Press, 1994), pp. 43-44, on differences between the British Government and British intelligence services, at least in the first few months of 1941, as to whether Hitler would attack Russia in 1941. Churchill professed certainty of it as early as March 1941, p. 55. See *"Barbarossa and the Soviet Leadership, A Recollection"* by Stepan A. Mikoyan, pp. 123-133.

See James Barros and Richard Gregor, *Double Deception: Stalin, Hitler, and the Invasion of Russia* (DeKalb: Northern Illinois University, 1995) who observe that both Stalin and also the British Government could not bring themselves to believe that Hitler would attack Russia. It seemed "irrational" to them! "It was surprising that someone in Whitehall at this time did not discern the thread of irrationality that ran through the fabric of Nazi Germany ..." (p. 109). "Like it or not, the British were ensnared in what might be called, for want of a better phrase the "rationality syndrome" (*ibid.*).

As for Stalin, the authors say: "How Stalin persevered in his belief that Hitler would play a rational role remains a mystery in view of mounting evidence to the contrary after Hitler's assumption of power in 1933 and certainly after the outbreak of the war in 1939", p. 224.

Stalin did not lack intelligence data before *Barbarossa*, just the ability to make sense out of it, as Barros and Gregor point out. Stalin's views of Germany and of Hitler were excessively "respectful", according to these authors, overestimating Hitler's rationality; they were also very hostile to Britain and the British. The "structural" problem which worsened the Soviet position was that Stalin's power was well-nigh absolute and the sycophants around him feared to challenge his views and perceptions, pp. 223-225.

Of course some of these structural factors also worked in the opposite direction, both before and after the war began. If the thrust of Stalin's policy happened to be "right", there was less likelihood of anyone interfering or thwarting it. If the preferences of "everyone" in Russia had really counted, it is doubtful that the kind of brutal war of resistance Stalin imposed on his people would have been feasible.

See H. W. Koch, "Hitler's 'Programme' and the Genesis of Operation 'Barbarossa' ", in *The Historical Journal*, Vol. 26, No. 4, December 1983, pp. 891-920, for an A. J. P. Taylor-like discussion of the Russo-German war. In this scholar's view, the Russians forced Hitler to attack them, p. 920. The war is said to have grown out of old ambitions, Russian and German (*ibid.*). As usual in such treatments, many relevant factors are left out to bolster the case, such as *Mein Kampf* avoidance, or Hitler's March 1941 briefing of the commanders.

See the article by Marshal M. V. Zakharov, first published in 1970, "On the Eve of World War II (May 1938-September 1939)" in *Soviet Studies in History*, Vol.

XXIII, No. 3, Winter 1984-85, pp. 83-122. This author, many years after Stalin's death wrote that in 1938 -- before Munich -- the Soviet Union followed the thesis that the "World is One" and "made every effort to create a system of collective security in Europe". The Western democracies, however, "remained deaf to Soviet appeals", p. 120.

[10] See the account presented by General Dmitri Volkogonov in his *Stalin: Triumph and Tragedy* (New York: Grove Weidenfeld, 1991), pp. 412-413. If the story, as told by various important personages of the time, is accurate, the Bulgarian Ambassador, whom Stalin and his Politburo colleagues approached, refused to transmit the offer of territorial concessions to Hitler. He professed faith in an ultimate Soviet victory.

[11] See David M. Glantz and Jonathan M. House, *When Titans Clashed: How the Red Army Stopped Hitler* (Lawrence: University of Kansas Press, 1995). They say that: "In retrospect, the most serious Soviet failure was neither strategic surprise nor tactical surprise, but institutional surprise. In June 1941, the Red Army and Air Force were in transition, changing their organizations, leadership, equipment, training, troop dispositions and defensive plans. Had Hitler attacked four years earlier or even one year later, the Soviet forces would have been more than a match for the Wehrmacht", p. 44.

[12] Hanson W. Baldwin, *The Crucial Years 1939-1941, The World At War* (New York: Harper & Row, 1970), pp. 311-312. See B. H. Liddell Hart, *The German Generals Talk* (New York: William Morrow, 1948). As Field Marshal von Kleist said of the Russian soldiers, "[they] were first-class *fighters* from the start, and we owed our success simply to superior training. They became first-rate *soldiers* with experience", p. 220. "As the war went on, the Russians developed an increasingly high standard of leadership from top to bottom", p. 222. Barry Leach points out that despite frequently inferior strength, German Panzer forces achieved remarkable victories: "Their success was due to the superior tactics and leadership that resulted from their training and experience, especially in the use of radio communications for the co-ordination of supporting fire and in the tactical use of the ground. Thus, they were frequently able to outmaneuver and defeat even the Soviet units equipped with KV and T34 tanks", *op. cit.*, p. 203.

[13] Peter Young (ed.), *The World Almanac Book of World War II* (New York: Bison Books, 1981), pp. 109-110.

[14] See Klaus A. Maier, *et al.*, *Germany and the Second World War, Volume II, Germany's Initial Conquests in Europe* (Oxford: Clarendon Press, 1991), Table V, VI, p. 304.

[15] See Louis P. Lochner (ed.), *The Goebbels Diaries 1942-1943* (New York: Doubleday and Company, 1948) for German casualties in the East until February 1942, pp. 112-113. Note W. Victor Madej, "Effectiveness and Cohesion of the German Ground Forces in World War II", *Journal of Political and Military*

Sociology, Vol. 6, No. 2, Fall 1978, pp. 233-248. The author says that "just in the third quarter of 1941, losses in dead and missing nearly doubled the losses of the entire preceding period from 1939", p. 235; he also notes that "over 80 per cent of unit commitment and casualties occurred on the eastern front", p. 233. Note also p. 240, where 84 per cent of German battle deaths between 1941 and 1945 are assigned to the Eastern Front.

Madej questions the earlier Shils and Janowitz study attributing fighting effectiveness of the Wehrmacht to "group cohesion". Madej says that "the army continued its struggle because a totalitarian government promised that such struggle would benefit Germany". Also important were "lack of information about strategic situation"; "fear of Russian vengeance"; and also the "skill and efficiency of experienced soldiers", p. 246. (Note that coercion is not even mentioned here!)

See also Basil Collier, *The Second World War: A Military History* (New York: William Morrow, 1967): "By Christmas [1941] the Russian adventure had cost the German Army three-quarters-of-a-million casualties [and] permanently blunted the striking power of the German long-range bomber", p. 224. Russian losses were "staggering but their manpower was immense, their factories were at full blast far from the fighting front, and the Americans and the British could not afford to allow them to be defeated if they hoped to see the German Army beaten in the field", p. 224.

[16] Hanson W. Baldwin, *The Crucial Years 1939-1941, The World At War* (New York: Harper & Row, 1970), pp. 231, 234-235.

[17] *Ibid.*, p. 279.

[18] Winston S. Churchill, *The Grand Alliance* (Boston: Houghton Mifflin Company, 1950), pp. 394-395. See S. P. MacKenzie, "The Treatment of Prisoners of War in World War II", *The Journal of Modern History*, Vol. 66, No. 3, September 1994, pp. 487-520. The author gives a total of 3,150,000 Germans as POWs of the Soviet Union during the whole of World War. At least 1 million of these died in captivity, p. 511. He estimates the death rate of German POWs at about 90 per cent in the 1941-42 period (*ibid*).

See Hans von Luck, *Panzer Commander* (New York: Praeger, 1989) for the account of a Nazi officer's journey in Russia from an early state of optimism in the summer of 1941 to the despair of the Great Winter. Ultimately, von Luck recorded that "only the will to reach safety in the prepared positions kept the men going [in retreat westward]. Anything to avoid being left behind and falling into the hands of the Russians", p. 65. See H. F. Richardson (ed.), *Sieg Heil! War Letters of Tank Gunner Karl Fuchs 1937-1941* (Handen: Archon Books, 1987) for an absorbing account of one man's illusions. The diary records the observations of an enthusiastic Nazi tankman from the euphoric early days of the Russian campaign to the harsh days of winter in front of Moscow. Killed in November 1941, he believed until at least the beginning of November that the Russians must be "all but finished": see pp. 150-151.

In a work published twenty odd years after the War, the official Soviet history recorded that at Stalingrad alone, between 17 July 1942 and 18 November 1942, Nazi Germany suffered the loss of 2,100 planes. See M. N. Kozhevnikov (ed.), *The Command and Staff of the Soviet Army Air Force in the Great Patriotic War 1941-1945* (Moscow: Nauka, 1977), p. 92.

[19]   Note Albert Seaton's evaluation of the military hierarchy under Stalin in his *The Fall of Fortress Europe 1943-1945* (London: Batsford, 1981). "The position of the Red Army general was little different from that of his German counterpart. His feared, and sometimes hated, commissar was his shadow, and he was reported upon by both the commissar and by the secret police special sections set to watch him. Mindful of the consequences of disobedience, he did what he was told, however barbarous or unlawful the orders": p. 206.

Even when the commissar system was abolished in 1942, accountability-to-the-top was not. Seaton's vignette concerning Marshal A. M. Vasilevsky is worth quoting: "Vasilevsky, the first deputy head of the operations department and later Chief of the Red Army General Staff, in closest touch with Stalin, has told how his aged father, a preceptor or choirmaster in a Russian church and therefore a Soviet undesirable, used to write to him. Vasilevsky did not dare to answer the letters but thought it safer to inform the responsible commissar on the Red Army General Staff and ask for advice whether or not he should reply to his own father. The commissar thought it wiser not to do so. One may well assume even from this little incident that neither Vasilevsky, nor Shaposhnikov, his predecessor, educated and humane though both were, would protest at the atrocities and barbarities that they saw about them": *ibid.*

[20]   Note Albert Speer, *Inside the Third Reich* (New York: Macmillan, 1970), p. 365. In late 1943, "[Hitler] spoke admiringly of Stalin, particularly stressing the parallels to his own endurance. The danger that hung over Moscow in the winter of 1941 struck him as similar to his present predicament. In a brief access of confidence, he might remark with a jesting tone of voice that it would be best, after victory over Russia, to entrust the administration of the country to Stalin, under German hegemony, of course, since he was the best imaginable man to handle the Russians".

See John Erickson, *The Road to Stalingrad, Stalin's War With Germany* (Boulder, CO: Westview Press, 1984), especially pp. 125-126. Note also Robert H. McNeal, *Stalin, Man and Ruler* (London: Macmillan, 1988). McNeal calls Stalin "an immensely gifted politician", p. 312, and cites the view of Marshal Vasilevsky that "Stalin's remarkable memory ..." was "the best he ever encountered"; Stalin used it in reshuffling the commands of the Red Army: p. 243. Compare also W. Averell Harriman and Elie Abel, *Special Envoy to Churchill and Stalin 1941-1946* (New York: Random House, 1975), p. 535, and G. R. Urban, *Stalinism: Its Impact on Russia and the World* (London: Maurice Temple Smith, Ltd., 1982), p. 41.

[21] Dmitri Volkogonov, *Stalin, Triumph and Tragedy* (New York: Grove Weienfeld, 1991), pp. 418-419. For a very uncomprehending study of the subject, with delightfully "liberal" assumptions, see Amnon Sella, *The Value of Human Life in Soviet Warfare* (London: Routledge, 1992). This author provides a Pollyana-ish approach to the subject, offering the opinion that "Armies cannot afford to waste the lives of their soldiers. This has nothing to do with the regime and the government, nor with the political leadership. It is strictly a utilitarian approach": p. 195. Whose approach? Mr. Sella's? Note also: "It is impossible to assess how many lives were lost because of these harsh measures and how many were saved as a result of Soviet stiff resistance that might have been influenced by such measures", p. 170. Was Stalin really interested in "saving lives"? Were Soviet casualties the principal test of the Stalin war effort? This author would probably do well analysing the parallels between the Red Cross and the Gestapo.

[22] *Ibid.*, p. 419.

[23] *Ibid.*, p. 420.

[24] See Walter Laqueur, *Stalin, The Glasnost Revelations* (New York: Charles Scribner, 1991), pp. 219-221.

[25] Quoted by J. T. Murphy, *Stalin 1879-1944* (London: John Lane and the Bodley Head, 1945), pp. 223-224.

[26] See Gustav Bychowski, "Joseph V. Stalin: Paranoia and the Dictatorship of the Proletariat" in Benjamin B. Wolman (ed.), *The Psychoanalytic Interpretation of History* (New York: Basic Books, 1971), pp. 125-126.

Stalin once told Khrushchev: "I don't trust anyone, not even myself". On Stalin's psyche, note also Roy Medvedev, *Let History Judge: The Origins and Consequences of Stalinism,* Rev. Ed. (New York: Columbia University Press, 1989), pp. 541-543. The section is titled "Was Stalin Mentally Ill?". Medvedev's conclusion was that Stalin was mentally competent although characterized by psychopathic traits, p. 543. See also Edward E. Smith, *The Young Stalin; The Early Years of an Elusive Revolutionary* (New York: Farrar, Straus and Giroux, 1967) and Daniel Rancour-Laferriere, *The Mind of Stalin, A Psychoanalytic Study* (Ann Arbor: Ardis, 1988) on Stalin's personality.

[27] See, however, Alexander Dallin, *German Rule in Russia, 1941-1945; A Study of Occupation Policies* (New York: St. Martin's Press, 1957); also Walter Goerlitz, *History of the German General Staff, 1658-1945* (New York: Frederick A. Praeger, Inc., Publishers, 1953), "The fact that the destruction of Bolshevism began soon to mean simply an effort to decimate and enslave the Slav people was the most fatal of all the flaws in the whole campaign", p. 397; and J. F. C. Fuller, *A Military History of the Western World, III* (New York: Funk and Wagnalls Company, 1956). "What is astonishing is that Hitler, a man of exceptional political perspicacity, who had reckoned on the collapse of the Soviet regime as the fruits of the invasion, made no

effort to win over the subjugated peoples of western Russia, but deliberately set out to antagonize them. This colossal political blunder lost him his 1941 campaign and added insuperable difficulties to those that followed". (p. 434). This theme is developed more fully in pages 434-438; also Donald W. Treadgold, *Twentieth Century Russia* (Chicago: Rand McNally and Company, 1972), pp. 362-366. "Hitler's political errors were perhaps no less decisive in the long run than his military miscalculations", p. 366. See also Matthew Cooper in his work *The Nazi War Against Soviet Partisans 1941-1944* (New York: Stein & Day, 1979). He concludes that the outcome of the war in Russia was ... affected very little by the activities of Soviet guerrillas" (p. 162), but he also observes that the Nazis' brutal war against the Soviet partisans helped ensure the hostility of Russia's peoples toward Nazi Germany thus, ultimately, helping to defeat the Third Reich (p. XI).

[28] Ellsworth Raymond, *The Soviet State* (New York: Macmillan, 1968), p. 130. See article by Mark Harrison "The Soviet Economy and Relations with the United States and Britain, 1941-1945" in Ann Lane and Howard Temperley (eds.), *The Rise and Fall of the Grand Alliance 1941-1945* (London: Macmillan, 1995), pp. 69-89. Harrison, sensibly enough, attributes Soviet capacity for "the destruction of Germany's offensive power in 1941-42 ... largely to "domestic supply" but capacity for advance westward "significantly upon western resources", p. 70. See Martin Kitchen, *British Policy Towards the Soviet Union During the Second World War* (London: Macmillan, 1986) who says that on the eve of *Barbarossa*, the British Government "expected the worst" ... "saw little chance of giving the Soviets any real assistance and did not want to find themselves allied to the Soviet Union". The British feared loss of American support.

If the worst happened, i.e., Russia was defeated, the British Middle East position and all else presumably would be lost. It seemed that nothing could be done but to wait and hope for the best, pp. 54-55. He points out that there was a reluctance in Britain to help Russia because it was widely felt that after Russia was defeated, Hitler would return to an invasion of Britain. Also, there was much British sentiment as expressed by a general who said in June 1941 that "it is good to see the two biggest cut-throats in Europe, Hitler and Stalin, going for each other": p. 65. Apparently, Eden, but not Churchill agreed with this line of thinking: p. 57.

Churchill was much more "taken" personally by Stalin than is, or was, generally realized: p. 250 and p. 270. "After the Teheran Conference the second front was no longer an issue and the question of the postwar settlement became the central concern of Anglo-Soviet relations", p. 272. "As the war drew to a close it was obvious for all to see that the Soviet Union was by far the strongest power in Europe ... By now it was such a great military power that even the most patronizing of the British generals viewed it with awe, respect and considerable alarm": p. 273.

[29] Note D. Glantz and J. House, *op. cit.*, give a figure of 29 million killed, p. 285.

[30] Robert Goralski, *World War II Almanac, A Political and Military Record* (New York: Bonanza Books, 1981), p. 438.

[31] Fugate, *op. cit.*, p. 32.

[32] Note Robert V. Daniels, "Stalin: Revolutionary or Counterrevolutionary?" in *Problems of Communism*, Vol. 3, No. 5, September-October 1989, pp. 81-86. Daniels discusses recent studies which suggest that Stalin's economic policies in the 1930s were "an absolute detriment to economic growth", p. 84. Colossal waste, inefficiency, and collapse of quality are charged from various sources. Somehow, all of this was not inconsistent with a magnificent war effort in the 1940s.

[33] One commander on whom many Germans indeed might have pinned their hopes -- assuming that Hitler would allow him some freedom of action -- was Field Marshal Erich von Manstein. See especially Dana V. Sadarananda, *Beyond Stalingrad, Manstein and the Operations of Army Group Don* (New York: Praeger, 1991) for a glowing account of Manstein's military genius.

[34] Whatever may be said of the irresistibility of the Soviet advance *after* the Battle of Kursk, the outcome of that contest was, like most battles, not quite so certain and predictable as it appears in retrospect. According to Paul Carell, Soviet success "hung by a thread". See his *Scorched Earth, The Russian German War, 1943-1944* (Boston: Little, Brown, 1966), p. 96. See also Bryan I. Fugate and Sev Dvoretsky, *Thunder On The Dnieper, Zhukov-Stalin and The Defeat of Hitler's Blitzkrieg* (Novato, CA: Presidio, 1997), pp. 335-337.

[35] As Christopher Duffy says in his *Red Storm on the Reich, The Soviet March on Germany, 1945* (London: Routledge, 1991):

> Essentially, the Second World War was won and lost on the Eastern Front. Only nations which were spared the experience of that holocaust have been able to regard the Second World War as somehow more light-hearted than the Great War, and a fit subject for adventure stories and comedies.
>
> Statistics by their nature carry little emotional impact, but a few figures bear some repetition. Russian deaths in the Great Patriotic War exceed 27 million. This makes up about 40 per cent of all the people killed in the Second World War, and equates to at least ten souls for every metre of ground between Moscow and Berlin. At least seven million of the Russians who died were civilians, and 3.25 million were soldiers who perished in German captivity.
>
> On its side, the Soviet military effort accounted for the greater part of the 3.25 million German military fatalities in the war.

Approximately 3 million further German troops were captured by the Russians, and about one-third of them did not survive the ordeal. Altogether the German human sacrifice on the Eastern Front came to around 10 million killed, missing, wounded or captured, and the loss of equipment amounted to some 48,000 tanks, 167,000 artillery pieces and nearly 77,000 aircraft: p. 3.

See the more extensive analysis by Erickson and Dilks, *op. cit.*, pp. 257-262, especially.

[36] Robert Goralski, *op. cit.*, p. 270. Cf. Albert Seaton, *The German Army 1933-1945*, *op. cit.*, p. 353. According to his data, 70 per cent of German tanks and 71 per cent of their assault guns were on the Eastern front, most of them around Kursk: see p. 205. Seaton assigns 75 per cent of German divisions to the Russian front but as he points out, even these figures understate the concentration of Nazi resources in the East. "In reality the strength of the German army committed in the east was much higher than the 75 per cent of its field formations appear to indicate, for the divisions in France and in the Balkans had been reduced to skeletons and were in no way battleworthy": *ibid.*, p. 175. George E. Blau, *The German Campaign in Russia, Planning and Operations (1940-1942)* (Washington, DC: Department of the Army, 1955) gives a total of 147 German divisions in the *Barbarossa* attack, p. 10. This is probably the lowest, or at any rate, lower end of the scale reported by scholars.

[37] See Marcel Baudot, *et al.* (eds.), *The Historical Encyclopedia of World War II* (New York: Greenwich House, 1980), p. 42. See Henri Michel, *The Second World War* (London: Andre Deutsch, 1975), who, in his monumental history of the great conflict, gives the following estimates of Nazi forces (in terms of divisions), committed in the East: June 1941--70 per cent; November 1942--72 per cent; July 1943-66 per cent; May 1944--53 per cent; May 1945--60 per cent: p. 477. These figures underestimate the Soviet contribution in four of the five periods mentioned, because they do not take into account the per centage of German forces actually *engaged* in action. On the other hand, his appraisal of the Stalin role in the Soviet war effort is undimmed by characteristic, western-liberal sentimentalism: p. XXI.

[38] Baudot, *et al., op. cit.,* p. 355.

[39] *Ibid.*

[40] Brigadier Young, *op. cit.*, p. 268.

[41] Alan Clark, *Barbarossa, The Russian-German Conflict* (New York: William Morrow, 1965), p. 238. See also pp. 220-238. A thorough and interesting account is provided by the man who led the Soviet forces in the city itself, Marshal Vasili I. Chuikov, *The Battle for Stalingrad* (New York: Holt, Rinehart & Winston, 1964): "Firing never died down on the Army's front, day or night": p. 178. See Bernd Wegner, "The Road to Defeat: The German Campaigns in Russia 1941-43", *The*

Journal of Strategic Studies, Vol. 13, No. 1, March 1990, pp. 105-127; "After Stalingrad there was no longer any ... hope for victory in the East": p. 123. Among detailed accounts of the Stalingrad battle, see William Craig, *Enemy At The Gates, The Battle for Stalingrad* (New York: E. P. Dutton, 1973); Louis C. Rotundo (ed.), *Battle for Stalingrad The 1943 Soviet General Staff Study* (New York: Pergamon-Brassey's 1989); also a very interesting study by Ronald Seth, *Stalingrad Point of Return, The Story of the Battle August 1942-February 1943* (London: Victor Gollancz, 1959); David M. Glantz, *From the Don to the Dnieper, Soviet Offensive Operations December 1942-August 1943* (London: Frank Cass, 1991).

According to Seth, Field Marshal von Paulus exhibited the same kind of propensity to rationalize the "unthinkable" which was shown earlier by Field Marshal Fedor von Bock. When in Soviet captivity, Paulus claimed that as soon as he met Hitler in 1942 to discuss the Stalingrad operation assigned to his Army, he realized Hitler's complete unwillingness or inability to modify his military designs regardless of adverse facts or circumstances. But he took on the assignment anyway, because he believed (or professed to believe) that the project would go ahead in any case, and he (Paulus) might do more for the troops than someone else would. See Seth's Conclusion.

Alexander Werth, *The Year of Stalingrad, A Historical Record and a Study of Russian Mentality, Methods and Policies* (New York: A. A. Knopf, 1947) quoted General Vasili Chuikov as saying "Why did we hold Stalingrad? Simply because we had to!". Even though Chuikov denied it "there has remained a conviction among many people in Russia that Stalin was, at one time or another, at Stalingrad during the battle", p. 462. Stalingrad was "a mincing machine, a meat chopper", p. 465. In Werth's more "traditional" view, after Stalingrad victory "had become a matter of time", p. 475.

[42] See Gerard M. Devli, *Back to Corregidor* (New York: St. Martin's Press, 1992), pp. 6-23.

[43] See Peter Elphick, *Singapore: The Pregnable Fortress A Study in Deception, Discord and Desertion* (London: Hodder & Stoughton, 1995), p. 364 especially. See also Noel Barber, *A Sinister Twilight, The Fall of Singapore, 1942* (Boston: Houghton Mifflin, 1968) who reports that Winston Churchill sent a message to General Wavell, area commander, on 13 February 1942, informing him that "he was sure it would be wrong to enforce needless slaughter and without hope of victory to inflict the horrors of street fighting on civilians", p. 246. A more closely "official" British account of the matter, with a foreword by Earl Mountbatten, puts a positive face on the Singapore disaster, to wit: "In the circumstances that existed in Singapore City by the middle of February 1942, [General] Percival was quite right to have surrendered, for the disaster to the million Asians in the city and to the troops would have been very great had the surrender been delayed by even a few hours ... the control of Singapore passed from Britain to Japan with amazing smoothness(!)".

[44] See Harrison Salisbury, *The 900 Days, The Siege of Leningrad* (New York: Harper & Row, 1969), see pp. 447-459 and especially p. 343. Note also Boris Voyetekhov's *The Last Days of Sevastopol* (New York: A. A. Knopf, 1943) for a vivid account of the battle-to-the-end of resources and life itself waged by the Soviet garrison of Sevastopol. Here, the Nazis were forced to sacrifice valuable manpower and precious time in the effort to reduce the fortress defences. Given various phases of German "attention", Sevastopol held out from the end of September 1941 until the end of June 1942 -- nine months in all.

[45] Glantz and House, *op. cit.*, p. 215.

[46] Albert Seaton, *The Battle for Moscow 1941-1942* (London: Rupert Hall-Davis, 1971), p. 289.

[47] *Ibid.* See Richard Overy, *Why the Allies Won* (London: Jonathan Cape, 1995) who says about Stalin that "it is difficult to imagine that any other Soviet leader at the time could have wrung such efforts from the population", p. 259. "There is a sense in which the Stalin cult was necessary to victory", *ibid.* As for Hitler, Overy credits him with fanatical will-power and willingness to take risks, but says he "was more Custer than Clausewitz", p. 275.

Overy does credit the Allied bombing campaign over Germany as one of the "decisive elements in Allied victory", p. 133. But his data are more "qualitative" (people became tired) than "quantitative" and he avoids the subject of arms output which by his own showing (pp. 331-322) tended to increase in Germany despite the bombings until late in 1944. See also Geoffrey Jukes, *Hitler's Stalingrad Decisions* (Berkeley: University of California Press, 1985), pp. 242-243, on the comparison of Hitler and Stalin as military leaders of their respective armed forces, with considerable margin of advantage to the latter. Albert Seaton in his *Stalin as Warlord* (London: B. T. Batsford Ltd., 1966) observes that: "Stalin alone was responsible for the heavy losses of 1941 and 1942. But if he is to bear the blame for the defeats of the first two years of war, he must be allowed the credit for the amazing successes of 1944 ... in Belorussia, Galicia, Rumania and the Baltic ... Some of these victories must be reckoned as among the most outstanding in the world's military history"; p. 271. Compare Francis B. Randall, *Stalin's Russia, An Historical Reconsideration* (New York: Free Press, 1965). Randall found Stalin's war leadership much better than Hitler's (pp. 282-283) although the outcome of the war was probable from the beginning, he thought, because of the initial ratios of strength between Germany and Russia. According to Randall, "Stalin's later conduct of the war was quite sufficient, if unnecessarily costly", p. 284.

On Stalin's role more generally, see Alexander J. Groth, "Russia's Stalin Dilemma", *Political Crossroads*, Vol. 5, 1997, pp. 123-142.

7 DEMOCRACIES AND THE FINAL SOLUTION

Since the time of the Great French Revolution of 1789, political democracy has been associated with universal human ideals. In the understanding of the late eighteenth century, liberty, equality, fraternity were not just the ideals of France; they were the ideals of all mankind. They defined the universal mission of the Great Revolution as the ultimate liberator of all peoples.

But in the twentieth century, in the 1930s and 1940s, political democracy, in all its different shapes and sizes around the world, sustained a great moral failure when it turned a blind eye toward the fate of the Jews, pretending not to see, not to hear, not to know. It demonstrated great creativity in only one area: the production of alibis and excuses.

Hitler's war against the Jews was not a war against nation states, either near, or far, or both. It was a war against a people defined by Hitler in completely worldwide terms: the fight against international Jewry. And it was a war which, in Hitler's own definition, was not fought against "some Jews" or "particular Jews" or "certain kinds of Jews". It was a fight to the death against all Jews, without distinctions and qualifications, by the terms of *Mein Kampf.*

If there could have been any doubt with respect to Hitler's universal animus toward Jews in 1933, Nazi laws and policies of the interwar period should have been sufficient to dispel it. Nazi legislation and administrative practice in Germany between 1933 and 1939 did not admit of the sort of distinctions which might have offered hope to the optimist. While the build-up of Nazi rules, regulations, and practices with respect to the Jews of Germany was gradual in the 1930s, there could hardly be any doubt by, say, 1935 or 1936, if not earlier, that the policies were categorical andascriptive.

No Jew could be a German citizen, not even one whose family roots in Germany extended over many generations; not even one who had never been charged with any crime; not even one who fought for Germany in the First World War and bore wounds, or received military decorations. No attempt was made by the Nazis to distinguish, by any criteria, between the meritorious and the unmeritorious; between those who had given faithful and distinguished service, and those who had not. The war against the Jews in Germany, such as it was in the 1930s, was a total, categorical war. What still remained an issue of some doubt was how far Hitler would carry this war: would he proceed to the physical liquidation of Jews?

The distinguished Jewish scholar, Yehuda Bauer, illustratively, concluded that "contrary to the claims of some historians, it is by no means clear whether [Hitler] meant murder or forced emigration [of Jews] from German soil. In his book *Mein Kampf*, as in his talks with Rauschning and in his speeches, with all their extreme anti-Semitism, there is no clear indication of an actual murderous design".[1] Rauschning claimed that Hitler had told him, privately, in response to his question as to whether Jews should be exterminated completely (How interesting! Where could he possibly have got that idea?!) that "one needs a visible enemy not an invisible one", and if Jews did not exist they would have to be invented.[2]

Granting that Hitler, privately, told Rauschning precisely what Rauschning later claimed that he had told him, the public record of *Mein Kampf* was not in any way affected by it. The formula of *Mein Kampf*, contrary to Bauer's or anyone else's claim, was as clear as a syllogism. It was a formula for the murder of the Jews. It was the answer to Hitler's question: "What was one to do against one's mortal, implacable enemy if one was to survive in this world?". The generic Hitler answer always was, (i.e., repeatedly) destroy or be destroyed, kill or be killed.

What was not discussed in *Mein Kampf* was the precise time, or the manner, or the place or places, where such destruction might be consummated. And, admittedly, what *Mein Kampf* could not settle definitively were such issues as: Would Hitler want to adhere to his own views in subsequent time? Would he have an opportunity to pursue his goals? Would he be prevented from realizing them by the actions of other people, possibly in Germany itself and perhaps throughout the world?

The central fact about Hitler was that he was probably the greatest criminal madman in the history of statecraft, a man totally lacking in conscience and moral feeling, the darkest of souls driven by profound impulses of violence and destruction. Hitler, however, was not mentally dysfunctional in any clinical sense. He could not only cope with the daily routines of life; he was capable of all sorts of (some would say brilliant) insights in political and military affairs, and above all, he was enormously capable in impressing people with his leadership abilities (the essence of charisma). But the core of the Hitler personality was dominated not by the muses of Reason but by the muses of Fury. He was a man obsessed.

Granted that there could have been, indeed should have been, say in 1933 or 1935 some considerable uncertainty as to what ultimately would happen, the weight and direction of Hitler's murderous intentions should not have been overlooked. And as he continued to succeed within Germany and Europe, the odds on his ability to realize his aspirations increased.

It is probably not coincidental that in his attempt to obscure Hitler's intentions toward the Jews, Yehuda Bauer chose to give greater weight to an alleged private remark by Hitler than either to the Fuehrer's doctrinal writings, or for example, to the Fuehrer's public declaration in the Reichstag on 30 January 1939. And, even if he were interested in private remarks only, the balance (as illustrated by the two citations offered here earlier) would have been clearly against him. In any case, what is involved here, is a characteristic attempt to exonerate from responsibility those who should have known better -- including even, and especially, prevalent Jewish public opinion in the freest of democracies in the 1930s. Jews too, in common with everyone else, greatly underestimated Adolf Hitler.

After all, how could anybody really contemplate such terrible deeds? It simply exceeded the bounds of conventional, liberally conditioned, expectations about humanity and such like. It was also more convenient and comfortable for people -- Jews included -- to believe the less terrible rather than the more terrible prospects. It just upset things a lot less. The *Mein Kampf* formula strongly suggested what Hitler might do, if he could. But, as is the case so often with terrible and unpleasant things, prevailing democratic public opinion, even Jewish public opinion, chose not to recognize Hitler's killing syllogism.[3] It could not bring itself to face such a horror. It indulged every conceivable illusion to avert its eyes.

Still, leaving the future prospects aside, Hitler's policies up to 1939, such as they were, constituted a great affront to some of the most fundamental principles of Western civilization. They challenged the notions of humanity, justice, and the rule of law as well as the ideals of human equality and individual freedom. There was certainly plenty here to invoke all manner of moral indignation and solidarity with the unjustly persecuted.[4] Yet, in the light of all these developments, the democracies of the world showed themselves astonishingly indifferent to Hitler's self-evidently criminal policies. This indifference was an encouragement to Hitler. The passivity of his opponents and victims was never lost on the Fuehrer.

Bauer's view of official American and British policies toward Jews is, unfortunately, that of an uncritical, "co-opted" apologist. Note the following (with my annotations).

> Even a cursory glance at the attitude of the major Allies to the Jews under Nazi rule makes clear that we are dealing with a complicated phenomenon.   In America there were people of the ilk of Breckinridge Long, but there were people like John W. Pehle as well. [There were all sorts of people everywhere!] In Britain, the Prime Minister himself intervened a couple of times to impress upon his officials the need to do something, but even a Prime Minister could not break through the barrier of officialdom. [Why not? It's a good thing he could get through to the RAF in 1940!] The motivations for the largely unhelpful attitude of both powers differed in details, but there appear to me to exist some common elements.   Anti-Semitism was a more important factor in the United States than it was in Britain.   Nor can the British attitude be properly termed apathetic. The term apathy would fit the American attitude much better.   Official Britain was concerned with the possibility that the Jews might be unloaded onto her in large numbers [that would have been catastrophic?!], about the possibility of Nazi infiltration into Jewish refugee transports [never actually demonstrated], and about the danger that any action concerned with alleviating the lot of Jews might prolong the war. [Did helping Tito's partisans prolong the war?] The refugee question generally, and the Jewish problem specifically, was a bothersome minor point that was endangering Anglo-American co-operation on the major issue, which was the defeat of Nazi Germany.   [What was this danger? Where was the split?] When the Holocaust became known in the West in 1943 (?!) and 1944, this became just another reason to defeat the Nazis quickly. [These are the most absurd of Bauer's propositions since (a) the Allies acknowledged the Final Solution in 1942 and (b) there is no evidence whatever that the Allies sought to speed up operations against Hitler because of this.][5]

Once again, in dealing with the Holocaust we are confronted by the seemingly puzzling liberal democratic anomaly. There is an abundance of information.   There are all sorts of communication media available to distribute this information. There is general freedom and security for those who might want to either purvey or to receive information and, of course, engage in the analysis and discussion of it. The relevant publics are, generally speaking, literate and well-educated. But, somehow, no learning, especially learning toward some sort of social action occurs.

In her fine book dealing with the American Press' response to the Holocaust, Deborah Lipstadt concluded that both the Final Solution and the bystanders' equanimity were beyond belief. She found that while the American "press had access to a critically important and unprecedented story ... it reacted [to it] with equanimity and dispassion".

> There is no way of knowing whether the American people would have even been aroused enough to demand action to rescue Jews. But we can categorically state that most of the press refused to light its 'beacon,' making it virtually certain that there would be no public outcry and no 'common activity' to try to succour this suffering people.[6]

Alas, here was a problem which transcended the question of how the press (or "media", more generally) was organized, whether it was free of government censorship and control, or whether it was autonomous in the sense that the various press organs were independent of one another. The problem lay with the human qualities of those disseminating news and opinions and those making or receiving them. And in this respect, news of Nazi persecution of the Jews and the Holocaust especially, even after the official Allied Declaration, met a wall of denial.

Denial was, and is, a great human capability of avoiding whatever is unpalatable, unpleasant, inconvenient, dangerous, or odious -- under all sorts of guises.[7] One of those, of course, was, and is, the formula "I cannot possibly believe that something this bad could actually happen". Another version of it is "I cannot believe that civilized human beings, rational, and, or compassionate beings, could possibly do such things". Other forms of denial take on the forms of indifference. "I know but I don't care" or better yet "I know, and it is all pretty terrible, but there are so many other more important, or immediate, things to worry about".

There is all manner of suffering in the world. War is hell. There is also the old ruse of not challenging the moral meaning of the message but raising doubts about its authenticity or accuracy. "It would be terrible if the Nazis were doing all this to the Jews, but how can we be sure of it?". The reports of Jews may be discounted because they are, after all, an "interested party", trying to promote sympathy for themselves, etc.[8] In fact, of course, if the will is there, virtually every conceivable source of information can be questioned on one ground or another, and some people are even very good at questioning many, different, and ostensibly independent sources of information. What better example of this would we want than by now the fairly sizeable literature in many democratic countries of the world denying the very occurrence of the Holocaust?

Finally, there is the more refined tactic of acknowledging "the facts" and offering sympathy, yet providing effective denial by skilful handling of the implications of what is acknowledged. In this version of denial, no possible assistance to the victims can be rendered because it would interfere with carefully prepared military operations; it exceeds the capabilities of the bystanders; there may be secondary consequences of such assistance (alleged infiltration of Nazi spies among the refugees is an example) so that the risk cannot possibly be run, etc.

On the other hand, it should be noted that Lipstadt's work documents press coverage which, however limited in relation to the actual Jewish catastrophe, was more than sufficient to act as a clue for officials who might have been interested -- if they had been interested -- in doing something about it.

Moreover, the coverage raises interesting questions about mass opinion, too. Why would people believe the news on page one but refuse to believe it on page three or four? This line of analysis suggests that the ability of people to comprehend and respond to information is shaped not so much by its substantive contents but by such criteria as how loudly, how frequently, how colourfully, etc., the information is presented.[9] This points to an analogy with advertising, where the rational content of the message is often completely irrelevant as long as people can identify the product sold in some favourable way.

Before 1939 there were two principal, peaceful, ways in which the nations of the world -- democracies presumably in the forefront -- could have counteracted Hitler's policies. The first would have been to offer sanctuary to his victims. In the 1930s the Nazis were still quite willing to let go all the German Jews who wanted and were able to emigrate. The second response, which would have forced Hitler to re-examine his course, would have been sanctions, especially trade and economic sanctions. In both areas, immigration and sanctions, the democracies could have acted both unilaterally and in concert.

Clearly, countries like Luxembourg and Sweden were not in a position to offer all the refuge necessary to the half-a-million Jews in Germany, much less to the millions conquered or threatened by Hitler in places like Austria, Czechoslovakia, or Poland, or other areas of East-Central Europe, targeted by Nazi lebensraum policies. But each of these countries, even the smallest, would have been in a position to make a dramatic gesture of sympathy, solidarity and humanity: above all, toward the persecuted Jews of Germany. Certainly, the several democracies of the world, acting in concert, could have done a great deal to offer refuge to the Jewish victims of Hitlerism in Germany.

What the world democracies did produce with respect to this problem was, characteristically, a lot of conversation in the form of conferences, meetings, speeches, and the like. But very little meaningful action. The meetings and the conferences produced a lot of explanations, suggestions, interchanges, pronouncements, and, above all, excuses. But hardly anything to help the victims was ever done either singly or multilaterally by the great and small democratic states.

After all, there was a world economic depression. There were important domestic needs. There were pressures from domestic constituencies opposing Jewish immigration. There was truth to tell, considerable domestic anti-Semitism in many cases. There were all sorts of other problems to worry about. As for economic sanctions against Germany, especially multilateral sanctions, these were hardly even considered by the world democracies. The needs of business and the economy could not be risked. Under Hitler's rule, Germany's trade with the democratic nations of the world continued at respectable levels right up to the beginning of the Second World War. If Hitler had got the idea, by the late 1930s, that he could do pretty much whatever he wanted with the Jews as far as the external world was concerned, he was right on the mark.

One of the most important preconditions of Hitler's Final Solution in the 1940s was the availability of the victims to the executioner. In that respect, the policies of the world democracies greatly facilitated Hitler's objective. There were other important preconditions once the programme of mass killings was launched. Two of these were rescue and reprisal. Obviously, even after the mass murder of Jews had begun, it was still *possible* to conduct some types of rescue operations which would remove at least a portion of the intended victims from the clutches of the murderers. And it was similarly possible to confront Hitler with costly reprisals which might have caused him to stop or at least suspend, the murder programme.

In all these respects, the democracies of the world contributed to the final terrible result of Hitler's killing operation. In war, as in peace, they excelled in conferencing, communicating and discussing, but not in acting. In some cases, even "speaking out" would have been enough to put some serious impediments in Hitler' path, but in those cases nothing was said -- usually for fear of some allegedly enormous political and practical difficulties.

The Conference at Evian-les-Bains held in July 1938, originally promoted by President Franklin Roosevelt, and attended by the several major world democracies, aimed to resolve problems of emigration and resettlement of political refugees, many of them Jews. In substance (apart from the joys of "discussion"), the Conference was a failure, or put more accurately, its results, to the extent that they were positive, were of the Band-Aid variety. Illustratively, Australia declared its willingness to admit 15,000 refugees in the ensuing three years, a proverbial drop-in-the-bucket.

One gets a realistic perspective on the Conference and the situation at the time from a memorandum prepared by the third secretary of the American Embassy in London in November 1938, Mr. Theodore Achilles. Under the heading "Future", Mr. Achilles wrote: "It is easy to discuss the whole problem by saying 'nobody wants any more Jews'. That is unquestionably true, but the problem remains to be solved and this Government is committed to solving it". Achilles observed that the United States would need to exert pressure upon other countries if anything really serious were to be accomplished. He noted that 500,000 people (mainly Jews) needed to be rescued from Germany and observed that the US was taking in between 27,000 and 30,000 annually, which amounted to "only one-fiftieth of one per cent of our population". If the rest of the nations represented at Evian were willing (even) to absorb a proportionally equal number, Achilles wrote, 100,000 Jews and/or other refugees could be rescued annually. He noted wistfully that "almost any country can profit from the absorption of the skills and brains of a reasonable number of these people, especially if they bring in a certain amount of new capital". Still, no one was really interested.[10]

British anti-Semitism in the 1930s was almost certainly less powerful that its American counterpart, but it was, by no means, trivial. In fact, scholarly literature locates reservoirs of anti-Semitic attitudes in Britain not only on the political "far Right" where perhaps they might be most expectable, but on the Left, and also among the middle-class, roughly liberal, strata as well. There were also important pockets of *institutional* anti-Semitism in Britain, ranging all the way from the Foreign Office and other official bureaucracies, to universities, business establishments, social clubs, and even trade unions. Winston Churchill's Cabinet could quite reasonably feel a political concern with this stratum of British opinion, latent and overt, and not wish to "unduly provoke it".[11]

It is certainly of great interest -- and relevance to the argument about the alleged capabilities of democracies -- that Joseph Stalin, a harsh despot if there ever was one, permitted the influx of more Jews onto Soviet territory in less than two years (the period between 17 September 1939 and 22 June 1941) than most world democracies, the United States included, in the whole post-1933 period. Twelve world democracies absorbed a total of 260,000 German Jewish refugees in a 5-year period from 1933 through 1938.[12] The United States accepted 102,222 Jewish refugees; Britain accepted 52,000; France and the Netherlands each 30,000; Canada 6,000; Australia 8,600; Belgium 12,000; Sweden 3,200; Norway 2,000; Switzerland 7,000; Czechoslovakia 5,000; Denmark 2,000. With virtual certainty, the USSR exceeded this twelve-nation total by perhaps at least a third in less than 2 years from 1939 to 1941.

It is especially remarkable that the Soviets allowed this huge influx of a destitute Jewish population into areas where, before the war and during the war, anti-Semitism was an extremely strong presence among resident Poles, Ukrainians, and Byelorussians. The controlled Soviet media did not report any such activity to the local inhabitants. One can only wonder what would have occurred if a free press had operated in these areas and reported on the Jewish influx. Riots and demonstrations would have been very likely. None occurred under Stalin's rule.

Several hundred-thousand Jews from western, Nazi-occupied, Poland fled eastward to Soviet-occupied Poland and received asylum or domicile there, without any concern on the part of the Russians about either skills or assets which such persons might possess or the number of children they might bring with them.[13] In many cases, those escaping to the East were so confused about Jewish prospects under Nazi rule that after a while they voluntarily returned to western, German-occupied Poland. A great many of those who did go East and stayed there were content to remain within the borders of the pre-war Polish state and did not seek entry into the deeper recesses of the Soviet Union. This lack of prescience generally cost them their lives as Hitler's *Einsatzgruppen* moved into Russia on the heels of the Wehrmacht in June of 1941.

Those Jews who were fortunate to find themselves deep within the USSR in 1941, either because they had been forcibly deported there by the

Russians, or because they had managed to get there on their own, faced harsh living conditions and little, if any respect, for their identity as Jews. But they also faced excellent odds of survival. It would probably be a conservative estimate to say that between 80 and 90 per cent of such Jews managed to live through the war. In contrast, for Jews remaining on Polish territory occupied by the Nazis, before and after 1941, the odds of survival were roughly one in seventy.[14]

What is remarkable and ironic about the contrast between the asylum provided Jews by the world democracies on the one hand, and Stalin's Russia on the other, is that it ran contrary to rhetorical expectations. Winston Churchill and Franklin Roosevelt, especially, had made many favourable public references to the Jewish people; at various times they condemned their persecution, and, indeed, offered them more corporate recognition as a unique, cultural, religious, and ethnic entity than did Stalin; this was especially the case after 1929 when Stalin consolidated his one-man rule in Russia, and also during the 1941-1945 so-called Great Patriotic War, when Stalin publicly talked about "fascism" and "German-fascist atrocities" but virtually never about Jews, anti-Semitism, or a Final Solution specifically aimed at Jews.

Stalin's regime had also subjected Jewish religious and cultural life in Russia to a degree of persecution very hard to imagine in Britain, or the United States, or any of the other world democracies.[15] His political murders of Jews, Leon Trotsky, Lev Kamenev, Gregory Zinoviev, and Polish Bundist leaders, among many thousands, were well known.

Western politicians often made statements during the War indicating their wholehearted willingness to help Jews in their terrible predicament. These statements generally turned out to be misleading and empty. Stalin made no promises to Jews, and, to be sure, showed no interest in their fate after 1941.

Of course, Stalin would have been an oddly anomalous moral pacesetter for the liberal democracies of the West. In any case, Soviet indifference to the Final Solution could be readily explained by liberal theory about information, communication, and politics. The Russians, as a whole, were simply deprived of information by their political leadership. If they did not know, how could they respond? They were denied "all the facts". But, clearly, this was not the case in the Western liberal democracies. Here, even during the War, no one was really censoring the *New York Times*, and the *Chicago Tribune*, or the *Washington Post*. The West was brimming with multiple, autonomous, sources and conveyors of information. If it could only figure out what it all meant, and if it could only get itself to act on it!

A great shell game has gone on in the Western world in recent years about what-was-known-when concerning the Holocaust. Attention is often focused on the earliest reports of German liquidations of Jews following the invasion of Russia. In recent years, the *New York Times* has published many delightfully titillating articles and letters on the subject of "what was known when". Most of these discussions constitute intellectual cover-ups. Information was not the democracies' problem, and the focus on the *Einsatzgruppen* or the Wannsee Conference of January 1942 is something of a redundancy. There were much earlier indications of what Hitler and the Nazis were doing to the Jews, and where they were headed, and these were not even actually "secret".

The single most important warning of Nazi designs for the physical liquidation of the Jewish people came from the capital of Poland, Warsaw, a city of over 1 million population even before the War. It came with the establishment of the largest ghetto under Nazi control, closed to exit by Jews and entry by non-Jews on penalty of death on 16 November 1940. Here, within a year of its establishment, more than 400,000 Jews, men, women and children, not only from Warsaw itself but from various other destinations, were herded into an area of less than 2 square miles, with somewhere between 9 and 13 persons per every room of inhabitable space.

By an official Nazi decree, the food ration for each ghetto inhabitant was set at 184 calories per day. Even though fuel and medicines were also in very short supply, one needs to go no further because this ration, strictly administered, would have resulted in the termination of human life in the Ghetto within a relatively short time. It was in itself a slow-strangulation death sentence. The official food ration was literally a *death* ration on which no human being could survive more than say, a month, even with the body at rest. And it was a ration which was publicly, officially announced to the Jews of Warsaw. It was one of the official documents of the so-called General Government of Poland. In 1940 and 1941 it was still mitigated to some extent by Nazi toleration of smuggling of food into the Ghetto, often with the corrupt connivance of German authorities. Smuggling, however, was potentially, and in some actual cases as well, punishable by death. Also, occasionally at least, the Nazis allowed food packages from abroad to be sent to individuals in the Ghetto. Still, more than 10 per cent of the Ghetto population died during the first winter of incarceration in 1940-1941. The mortality rate was 15 times greater than the pre-war figure for the Jewish quarter of Warsaw.[16] The streets of the Ghetto were littered with bodies of emaciated victims of starvation, exposure, and disease, especially, of course the typhus epidemic of that first winter. What is of particular interest here is that the reality of this deathly existence, as it were, of the Warsaw Ghetto was not a deeply hidden secret.

Life in the Ghetto could be observed by naked eye or binoculars from the windows of hundreds of apartment buildings in the Polish sections of Warsaw adjacent to the Ghetto. For some months, streetcars from the Polish part of the city passed through the Ghetto. Some Polish employees of German factories operating within the Ghetto periodically entered and left the area. Some Jewish workers were routinely used in Nazi-operated plants in the Polish part of Warsaw and could share their knowledge with outsiders. Amazingly, even the pre-war telephone network between the two parts of Warsaw, Polish and Jewish, was still partly operational. One could call up to ask, or tell, about the conditions in the Ghetto not only in 1940 and 1941 but even as late as 1942 at a time when the deportations to the gas chambers had already begun.

TABLE 1

LIST OF MAJOR STREETS IN "ARYAN" WARSAW, NORTH TO SOUTH, CLOCKWISE, WHOSE SECTIONS FACED DIRECTLY UPON THE GHETTO, 1940-1943

STAWKI	ŻABIA
POKORNA	KRÓLEWSKA
KONWIKTORSKA	PRÓŻNA
LAPIEŻYNSKA	WIELKA
FRANCISZKAŃSKA	SIENNA
BONIFRATERSKA	TWARDA
ŚWIĘTOJERSKA	ŻELAZNA
OGRÓD KRAŚINSKI	PAŃSKA
NALEWKI	ŁUCKA
PRZEJAZD	GRZYBOWSKA
TŁOMACKIE	LESZNO
RYMARSKA	ŻYTNA
ELEKTORALNA	KACZA
ŻIMNA	MIRECKIEGO
MIROWSKA	OKOPOWA
CHŁODNA	DZIKA
KROCHMALNA	KONARSKIEGO

Did it really require a brilliant, super-secret, James Bond-style, intelligence network for the British and the Americans to find out about the Nazi treatment of the Jews? Was there a profound intellectual difficulty in trying to figure out what a 184 calorie per day food-ration meant? It should be remembered, of course, that the British government had continuous contacts with the Polish underground movement through the Polish Government-in-Exile, based in London. The United States had an Embassy in Berlin until December 1941, about 300 miles west of Warsaw, and a Consulate in Breslau (Wrocław) even closer. Britain continued to have full-scale diplomatic representation in 1940 and 1941 in much of eastern Europe, including Yugoslavia, Bulgaria, Hungary, and Rumania. Of course, so did the United States. The Allied disclaimers of knowledge about the fate of the Jews, whether before 1942 or after 1942 always had a hollow ring about them.[17]

The reality of the democracies' response to the tragedy of the Holocaust is a combination of prejudices officially denied but privately accepted; no less importantly, intimidation by the prejudices of others; and, above all, great timidity by political leaders about the attitudes of domestic and foreign constituencies believed to be important to keeping one's job or carrying out one's duties in the relatively easiest possible manner: all of it nicely garnished by moral callousness camouflaged in the slogan about keeping one's focus on winning the war.

The notion that the Allies had a choice -- win the war or help the Jews -- is an assault on simple logic. There is nothing inherently contradictory about combining these objectives. Under some circumstances (e.g. helping the Russians or the Yugoslavs) one can see them as symbiotic. The notion would be true if "helping the Jews" actually *replaced* the goal of winning the war which would be absurd. And it would also be true if Allied leaders believed that helping Jews would so undermine their standing with their respective publics, that resistance to the Nazis would disintegrate; or that such help would so offend the Grand Mufti of Jerusalem and other Arab extremists that the Allied position in the Middle East would become untenable.[18] Though one could never expect an official acknowledgement of the latter two (mutually compatible) alternatives, they form the unspoken, unarticulated, but highly important subtext of the tragedy of the Holocaust.

John Martin, former Principal Private Secretary to the Prime Minister, recorded this interesting observation about Winston Churchill in August of 1940:

> One day I lunched with Dr. Weizman, Chairman of the Jewish
> Agency ... He was of course aware of Churchill's sympathy with
> Zionism, but must also have been conscious of the Prime Minister's
> wish to keep aloof at a time when he could not give practical effect
> to that sympathy (apart from opposition to the policy of withholding
> arms from the Jews in Palestine) or enter into any commitments
> regarding arrangements to be made in any postwar settlement.[19]

Obviously, the "keeping aloof" mentioned here needs to be construed
very broadly as far as Mr. Churchill, and for his own analogous reasons, Mr.
Roosevelt, were concerned!

Anti-Semitism, overt and latent, was not only a significant public
attitude in both the US and Britain. Anti-Semitism, as a weapon of Nazi
propaganda, was aimed at both Britain and the United States with its constant,
day-in and day-out, barrage of charges about Jews allegedly controlling state
policies and the war being fought at the direction and on behalf of Jewish
interests. Officials in both countries were seemingly sensitive to such charges
and eager to avoid situations which might bolster the plausibility of Nazi
claims.[20]

There was also a common Anglo-American platform of appealing to
the sensibilities of Arab public opinion, first clearly by the British and then
secondarily by the Americans. The latter acted in apparent agreement with and
support of the British position that Arab goodwill was essential to maintaining
an Allied hold in the Middle East and that the Middle East itself was crucial to
overall Allied strategy.

In the upshot, Allied Governments exhibited all but total indifference
to the plight of the Jews under Hitler's rule, transmuted, to be sure, into a
number of analogous excuses for the failure to help. There were: the need to
focus single-mindedly on victory over Hitler; lack of resources, or better
alternative uses of resources, which might have been employed to help Jews;
the danger of setting bad precedents, creating obligations to other entities
which might make the same claims of persecution that Jews did and ultimately
strain Allied resources; the uncertain or doubtful chances of success for any
initiatives intended to assist Jews. These were among the more common.

There is no doubt that some proposals for the rescue of or assistance to
Jews were impractical or ill-advised. Allowing the Nazis to blackmail the
Allies, giving them money or weapons of war in exchange for Jews, or giving
Jews assistance which one would not offer one's own nationals or POWs
would have been in that category. But many possible measures were not of

that nature, and their possible liabilities were grossly exaggerated by officials who were simply unwilling to act.

The roots of Allied failure to help the Jews of Europe grew out of the actions of Neville Chamberlain's Cabinet. On 17 May 1939 it reversed a long-standing British commitment to the Balfour Declaration which in 1917 had pledged the establishment of a Jewish national home in Palestine. This decision was taken on the eve of the War, and in the midst of drastic Nazi persecution of Jews in Germany, Austria, and what used to be Czechoslovakia. It constituted an enormous tilt toward the position of Arab nationalism. Henceforth, Britain pledged itself to the creation not of a Jewish state but rather of an independent unified Palestinian state with a severe limit of 75,000 Jews to be allowed to emigrate to Palestine in the five year period following the Cabinet's decision. After the five years, all further Jewish immigration into Palestine was prohibited unless by consent of the Arabs. Thus, Britain simultaneously reduced the most likely place of refuge for Europe's Jews, and, given the demographic realities of 1939 Palestine, awarded the future independent state of Palestine to likely Arab control.

In rendering its decision, the Chamberlain Cabinet showed a well-nigh unbelievable indifference to the fate of European Jewry. Even if one wholly agreed that no one could possibly have foreseen Hitler's Final Solution, the fate of Jews under Nazi rule in the years 1933-1939 was an open book. About 319,000 Jews had fled Nazi Germany in response to Hitler's persecutions, the most dramatic and recent one being the 9 November 1938 so-called Kristalnacht. By May of 1939 war with Hitler was already more than a possibility; it was a likelihood. Britain, and France, had given Poland a guarantee of military assistance in the event of German attack at the end of March after Hitler's triumphal entry into Prague. And in May, Hitler's campaign for Danzig and the Corridor was in full swing.

Chamberlain's gesture toward the Arabs was, under the circumstances, a singular act of weakness, a gratuitous case of overkill. There was no tangible indication in 1939 that Britain would not be able to maintain security in the areas under its control. The concession was not one to fact but to fear. Even if one assumed, somehow, a British need to appease the Arabs so as to promote stability and security in the Mediterranean and Middle East British outposts, many more moderate alternatives were available than the one chosen. One of these might have been some sort of reaffirmation of the *status quo*, promising nothing new to either Arabs or Jews, neither affirming nor repudiating the Balfour Declaration. Another would have been a decision to defer definitive action concerning the future of Palestine until some unspecified or more remote time in the future. Finally, there could have been less drastic immigration concessions to the Arabs, with, critically, some emergency escape provisos.

In the 7-year period of 1933 through 1939 about 224,000 Jews immigrated to Palestine, an average of over 30,000 people per year, notwithstanding British restrictions even then. In the single year of 1935 the number of Jews entering Palestine was nearly 62,000. The 5-year 75,000 person ceiling was an act of cruel indifference on the part of the British Government, especially in light of the known difficulty of finding alternative outlets for Jewish emigration, and the likely impact on Jews of any further European conflagration. The ensuing chapter of British policy from 1939 to 1942 was one of unbelievably harsh enforcement of a policy of preventing Jewish "illegals" from entering Palestine.

In 1939, British officials were actually giving serious consideration to firing with live ammunition on ships seeking to bring illegal refugees to the shores of Palestine. British policy reached its nadir with the December 1941 episode of the *SS Struma* which carried 769 Jewish refugees fleeing from Rumania through the Black Sea and the Dardanelles with the hope of reaching Palestine. The *Struma*'s captain was a Bulgarian (Captain G. T. Gorbatenko) and it flew the flag of Panama. It was an old, creaky vessel, not genuinely seaworthy. When it arrived in Istanbul, its engine broke down and it required repairs before it could proceed -- anywhere. The ship remained for two months off the Turkish coast. The Turkish authorities would not allow the passengers to disembark on their territory. The conditions of the passengers were, in all respects, appalling. Meantime, Britain made every effort through its official and diplomatic channels to have the Turks send the ship back into the Black Sea. Eventually, this is what happened. In February of 1942 the *Struma* sank with the loss of virtually all on board.[21] It had been apparently sunk by a torpedo of unknown origin.

It is little wonder that British policy inspired venomous hatred in many segments of Palestine's Jewish community. (It was in the context of this policy and climate of opinion that the assassination of Lord Moyne, Deputy Minister of State for the Middle East, earlier Secretary of State for the Colonies, and chief advocate of Jewish exclusion from Palestine, took place in Cairo in November of 1944.) Two of the reasons most often (*openly*) cited by British officials for not allowing any Jews to disembark in Palestine was that there might be Nazi spies and agents among them. Not one was ever found. Another reason was that any breach in British policy of no-illegal-admissions would likely produce a wild flood of refugees descending upon them. Given the realities of Nazi policy toward European Jews, beginning with the ghettos and ending up with the extermination camps, these British anxieties were little short of absurd. Needless to say, the British Government did not provide any alternative outlets to whatever Jewish emigration could still materialize in Europe.

Winston Churchill, who was not yet a member of the Chamberlain Cabinet when the 17 May 1939 White Paper on Palestine was issued, professed opposition to it until he was appointed First Lord of the Admiralty in September 1939. But he was unable to change British policy, even after he had replaced Chamberlain as Prime Minister on 10 May 1940. His responsibility for the fate of the *Struma* and all the collateral issues is both constitutionally and factually unquestionable. An anti-Jewish and pro-Arab majority of the Cabinet led by the rather anti-Semitic Anthony Eden prevailed, but it prevailed with the acquiescence of Winston Churchill. If anyone in the world knew the meaning of collective responsibility under the British Constitution, Churchill did.[22]

The United States, which in 1940 and 1941 was supplying Britain with the most vital military, economic, and political assistance, exerted no leverage on the British with respect to their management of refugee questions in Palestine. And since the United States itself had not done much on its own to relieve the plight of Hitler's Jewish victims, the executioner's crop was bound to be a bountiful one.

The most critical threshold ever in Allied policies toward the Holocaust occurred on 17 December 1942 when British Foreign Secretary Anthony Eden made a formal declaration about it in the House of Commons. This statement was made on behalf of eleven entities, the Governments of Belgium, Czechoslovakia, Greece, Luxembourg, the Netherlands, Norway, Poland, the United States, the United Kingdom, the Soviet Union, Yugoslavia, and the French National Committee.

The statement included the phrase that the attention of the above parties:

> ... has been drawn to numerous reports from Europe that the German authorities, not content with denying to persons of Jewish race in all the territories over which their barbarous rule has been extended the most elementary human rights, are now carrying into effect Hitler's oft-repeated intention to exterminate the Jewish people in Europe. From all the occupied countries Jews are being

transported, in conditions of appalling horror and brutality, to Eastern Europe. In Poland, which has been made the principal Nazi slaughterhouse, the ghettos established by the German invaders are being systematically emptied of all Jews ... None of those taken away are ever heard of again ... The number of victims of these bloody cruelties is reckoned in many hundreds of thousands of entirely innocent men, women and children.

Eden prefaced his statement by declaring that the reports upon which the Allied declaration was based were "reliable", and that they had reached His Majesty's Government "recently". In the conclusion of the official declaration, Eden said that the Allied Governments (1) condemned the "bestial policy of cold-blooded extermination", (2) were strengthened in their resolve to "overthrow the barbarous Hitlerite tyranny", and (3) resolved to ensure that "those responsible for these crimes shall not escape retribution".[23]

Nothing was said about any possible assistance to the victims. Nevertheless, in response to several questions asked in the House following his statement, Eden did promise help to Jews although in language which suggested considerable discomfort on his part. MP Silverman asked Eden whether he was consulting with his colleagues and other Allied governments "as to ... constructive measures of relief [that might be] immediately practicable". To this question Eden replied that "my honourable friend knows the immense difficulties in the way of what he suggests, but he may be sure that we shall do all we can to alleviate those horrors, though I fear that what we can do at this stage must inevitably be slight". Another MP asked Eden if efforts could be made to "explore ... co-operation with non-belligerent and neutral Governments to secure the emigration of Jews, say, to Sweden or to some other neutral country". To this Eden replied that "naturally I should be only too glad to see anything of the kind but the Honourable member will understand the circumstances". Eden was also asked by one MP the following question:

> May we take it from the right hon. gentleman's statement that any persons who can escape from any of the occupied territories will be welcomed and given every assistance in the territories of the United Nations?

Eden replied to this question as follows:

Certainly we should like to do all we possibly can. There are, obviously, certain security formalities which have to be considered. It would clearly be the desire of the United Nations to do everything they could to provide wherever possible an asylum for these people, but the House will understand that there are immense geographical and other difficulties in the matter.[24]

Eden also volunteered a statement which may have represented the greatest of his lies that day, to wit:

I may also say that all the information we have from the occupied countries is that the peoples there, despite their many sufferings, trials and tribulations, are doing everything in their power to give assistance and charity to their Jewish fellow-subjects.[25]

Had he been candid, Eden would have said that while some, generally very few, people in the occupied countries were helping Jews at great risk to themselves, many more, especially in eastern Europe, were literally murdering Jews, often even before the Nazis would begin to do the killings themselves. Nor did Eden tell the House how the officials of His Majesty's Government in Palestine had been doing their "level best" to send the few escaping Jews back to the inferno from which they had just miraculously fled.

However Eden may have misrepresented his own attitude and that of the British Government, the fact of the Nazi Holocaust against the Jews was now, at last, officially and publicly declared on behalf of all the major Allied powers as well as several governments-in-exile. Henceforth, anyone pretending "not to know what was happening to the Jews of Europe", whether in government, media, military, or otherwise (and also pretending to be at least a regular newspaper reader and/or radio listener) was engaging in blatant denial. To be sure, quite a few people fell into that category, so seemingly at odds with the liberal faith in the rational human being.

One of these was US Supreme Court Justice Felix Frankfurter, himself Jewish, who was briefed on the tragedy of the Jews of Poland, and especially of Warsaw, by the Polish underground emissary, Jan Karski, early in 1943. This was obviously *after* the Eden declaration. Frankfurter's response to Karski was that he just could not believe what he had been told. When asked if he thought Karski a liar, Frankfurter denied thinking that but insisted that he simply could not believe him. When Karski gave his account to President

Franklin Roosevelt, the latter responded to the effect that Karski should tell his people that the United States was intent on winning the war.

Besides shuffling memoranda and holding meetings and conferences, there was not very much that the democratic leaders of the world were willing to do for the Jews of Europe: even in situations where action was feasible; even when it would have cost very little to act; and even in cases where it would have cost virtually nothing to act by symbolic pronouncement, by instructive demonstration, by salutary warning. Why? To all appearances for fear of the Arabs; for fear of their own anti-Semites; for fear of European anti-Semites; for fear of taking risks; even, to all appearances, for fear of opposing the judgments of their own subordinates.

Historian Richard Breitman offers this vignette of Franklin Roosevelt's response:

> There is little question that the President was aware of the Final Solution by November 1942, if not earlier. Given Roosevelt's unwillingness to stir up additional trouble over European Jewry with Congress, certain lobbies, and Middle Eastern nations, he likely resisted believing the early reports of Jews being killed en masse in death factories. If Felix Frankfurter, a Jew, could not force himself to believe them, why should FDR have been different?
>
> [Rabbi] Stephen Wise asked the President to receive a delegation of Jewish leaders at the White House in early December as part of an international day of mourning (2 December) for European Jews. The Jewish leaders wished to give FDR specific information about the Final Solution. FDR did not wish to see the group and tried to avoid the meeting. He suggested that the delegation go to the State Department instead. Wise persisted, and, with the assistance of Presidential Adviser David Niles, he obtained an appointment for a small group of Jewish leaders with the president on Tuesday, 8 December, at noon.
>
> ... After Wise read the delegation's declaration and presented a detailed memorandum about the Final Solution, he appealed to FDR to bring the extermination programme to the world's attention and 'to make an effort to stop it'. The President said that the government was familiar with most of the facts, but it was hard to find a suitable course of action. The Allies could not make it appear that the entire German people were murderers or agreed with Hitler's actions. He agreed to release another statement denouncing Nazi mass killings.

When the delegation wanted some statement that it could release immediately, FDR authorized the re-release of his statement to July's Madison Square Garden rally, which, he said, had to be quoted exactly. That meant no specific emphasis of Nazi crimes against Jews. The delegation press release exceeded the President's instructions and quoted FDR as saying that he was shocked to learn that two million Jews had, in one way or another, already perished as a result of Nazi rule and crimes.[26]

The most flagrant case, symbolic of the general Allied failure to help the Jews of Europe, occurred with respect to the Warsaw Ghetto rising of April and May 1943. But the scope of the Allied failure could only be appreciated by those cognizant of the parallel case of the Polish Warsaw uprising of August and September 1944, so that, in reverse chronology, one needs to consider it as background to the Ghetto episode.

In July of 1944, as the Red Army moved rapidly westward, Radio Moscow called on the people of Poland to help in the liberation of their country. In the expectation that the Soviets would soon reach the nation's capital, the leadership of the largest underground organization, the so-called Home Army (Armia Krajowa), politically controlled by the London-based Government-in-Exile, began an armed uprising against the Nazis in Warsaw. Since the Russians had already installed a Communist-led authority of their own in the nearby town of Lublin, the uprising, if successful, would have had great political significance.

Presumably, Soviet armies advancing westward would encounter the presence of the London-supported group in charge of the liberated capital of the country; this could be seen as a powerful claim to its recognition as the true and legitimate government of Poland. Since this was, arguably, the precise opposite of what Stalin had in mind for the future, the advancing Red Army stopped just short of Warsaw, in fact occupying the suburb of Praga on the right bank of the Vistula, a distance of yards rather than miles from the besieged capital. And there it rested giving virtually no real help to the badly outgunned resistance fighters across the river. The Nazis, largely undisturbed by any Soviet action in, near, or above the Polish capital, proceeded to reduce the Polish forces in the city with horrendous ferocity over a period of two months; estimates of deaths in Warsaw range up to 200,000, through bombing, artillery and mortar barrages, the use of armour, and also through the work of execution squads moving relentlessly with and behind Nazi troops. The Poles appealed for international help, and while the Russians remained fundamentally unco-operative, at first even denying that any fighting was occurring in Warsaw, the West responded at the highest levels of power.

Prime Minister Churchill and President Roosevelt appealed to the Russians for help. Because of their physical proximity, they were obviously in the best position to help. When that proved unavailing, Western leaders requested landing rights for British and American aircraft on Soviet-occupied territory to enable the Allied air forces to assist Warsaw. The Allies sent some aircraft to Warsaw from their own, more distant bases in southern Italy, dropping supplies and arms to the insurgents below in what proved to be a costly mission but one that certainly provided encouragement and made clear Allied support for the Polish cause. Some missions were flown from England and planes landed on Soviet airfields after completing their tasks. To those confined in the dark cellars of the city of Warsaw, to all of Poland, and to the world at large, the BBC and the Voice of America beamed numerous broadcasts during these two months of Polish agony, publicizing, lauding, and extolling the heroism of Warsaw's freedom fighters. Finally, when Polish resistance was no longer equal to the task, the Western Powers played one last, important card. Foreign Secretary Eden issued a statement in London expressing the Allies' wish and expectation that Warsaw's surrendering freedom fighters would be treated as combatants and accorded all the rights pertaining to prisoners of war under the Hague and Geneva international conventions.[27]

Naturally, the Nazis might well have construed such a statement as an implicit threat of Allied reprisal against their own POWs. The surrendering soldiers and officers of the Home Army were, by and large, accorded the appropriate rights. The leader of the Polish uprising, General Tadeusz Bor-Komorowski, survived the war in a German prisoner of war camp and lived to write his memoirs. He died in 1966 in London, a free man.

It is only against the backdrop of the 1944 events that one can fully appreciate what had happened to the Jews of Warsaw in 1943. On 19 April, coinciding with the Jewish holiday of Passover, the Warsaw Ghetto, by then reduced to perhaps 60,000 inhabitants through relentless Nazi deportations of Jews to the gas chambers of Majdanek and Treblinka, rose in armed defiance of its executioners. The uprising was led by a young man, barely 23 years old, Mordecai Anielewicz, who headed the Jewish resistance movement, the ŻOB or Jewish Fighting Organization. Armed with the most rudimentary of weapons, largely Molotov cocktails and pistols, with a few rifles here and there, the Jewish fighters of Warsaw stood off the challenge of Nazi military power for a period of 28 days, until 16 May, when the last centres of resistance in the Ghetto were at last destroyed by the forces of SS General Jurgen Stroop. Mordecai Anielewicz had already been killed at his command post on 8 May. (By some accounts, he committed suicide to avoid capture.)

Although no exact, reliable figures have ever been made known, the Nazis almost certainly suffered several hundred casualties in dead and wounded. With the exception of a few hundred Jewish resistance fighters who escaped through the canals of the city to the Polish side of Warsaw, and a very few hidden in deep bunkers that escaped Nazi detection, all the remaining inhabitants of the Ghetto were murdered and all buildings destroyed by fire and explosives.

What was remarkable about the valiant fight put up by the Jews of Warsaw -- especially in light of criticisms often made about Jewish passivity toward the Holocaust -- was that its duration exceeded that of the resistance of several nation-states Hitler had conquered in Europe. Calculated in terms of time from beginning of hostilities to official capitulation of their armed forces, Belgium, Holland, Luxembourg, Denmark, Yugoslavia, and Greece, all put up a shorter resistance to Nazi attack than did the Warsaw Ghetto. And the Ghetto did it under the most unfavourable possible conditions. According to Polish Home Army sources, likely to overstate the help that they actually offered to the Jews of Warsaw, one can form a reasonable impression of the resources available to the Jewish resistance.

> In the spring of 1943 the Polish Home Army had 600 heavy machine-guns at their disposal; none were supplied to the Jewish Fighting Organisation in the ghetto. Of the Home Army's 1,000 light machine-guns, one was supplied to the Jews; of 25,000 rifles, the Jews were given ten; of 6,000 pistols, the Jews received ninety; out of 30,000 hand-grenades the Ghetto was assigned five hundred.[28]

It is, however, this very circumstance which draws attention to the sordid record of the Western Democracies in the unfolding and the consummation of Hitler's Final Solution in Europe. The fact of the Ghetto uprising was reported by the American and British press shortly after it had begun in April. Its general significance, of course, was already implicit in the statement made by Anthony Eden in the House of Commons on 17 December 1942. It was not exactly an event occurring in some "unknown context". Allied leaders had often publicly expressed their willingness to do whatever they could to help the persecuted Jews of Europe. Certainly, Eden did so in response to questions in the House of Commons on 17 December.

What could the Allies have done for the Jews of Warsaw in April and May of 1943? To suggest that they could have done nothing, was, and is, absurd. Even some scholars and observers, however, who should know much better have accepted this well-nigh unbelievable line of thought. Thus, we find Bernard Wasserstein declaring in his 1979 book:

> But, in the spring of 1943, there was little beyond words of comfort that the Allies could offer Jewish resistance in Eastern Europe. Communications with Poland from the west were extremely limited until the start of regular supply flights to Polish underground forces from the airfield at Brindisi in the spring of 1944. Nor did the Polish underground forces outside the ghetto (strongly impregnated with anti-Semitic feeling) offer much help from the resources at their disposal.[29]

Actually, there was a world of effective measures of assistance readily accessible to Allied leaders, had they been willing to use them. Naturally, they all involved some risks, as do most actions, especially in war. The most obvious mistake of people like Wasserstein and other apologists for the Western democracies has been to underestimate the power of words. There would have been not only comfort, but great leverage in the spoken word, if only the appropriate people were willing to utter it, publicly *and* privately. Prime Minister Winston Churchill, who, after all, hosted the Polish Government-in-Exile in London needed to call in the Polish Premier, General Wladyslaw Sikorski. He needed to insist that, as a matter of the highest state urgency, with effects upon all future Anglo-Polish relations, the Polish Home Army (a) immediately provide weapons and other logistical support to the Jewish resistance fighters in the most ample amounts possible subject to radio-verified approval of the recipients and (b) stage appropriate and prompt military actions in the vicinity of the Ghetto to bring relief to the ŻOB and hopefully to facilitate and assist the escape of as many Jews as possible. President Franklin Roosevelt might well have taken some time off his busy schedule to convey an analogous message to Sikorski.

It might have been possible (as was done in 1944) to send a small number of long-range aircraft from the south-eastern coast of England to Warsaw, partly to cause distraction among the Nazis on the ground, and, far more importantly, to demonstrate Allied solidarity with and support for the defenders of the Warsaw Ghetto. The psychological and political importance of such an act, even if it turned out to be a material failure, would have been immense, above all for the Jews, who would no longer see themselves as utterly forgotten and abandoned, and whose willingness to resist elsewhere would have been encouraged. It would have been very important for Poles, too. Here after all, most of the Final Solution was taking place -- as Anthony Eden had acknowledged on 17 December 1942. It would have made an enormously important impression on Polish public opinion that in the view of Britain and America -- countries with which that opinion very much identified -- Jews were indeed human beings whose fate was of great importance to the Allies.

Naturally, some might suggest that any Allied air force mission over Poland would have required considerable time to prepare. They might be reminded perhaps of how Adolf Hitler called General Nicholas von Falkenhorst to his headquarters on the morning of 21 February 1940, and ordered him to report by 5 p.m. of the same day with an operational plan for the invasion and occupation of Norway. The General had never been to Norway but he was ready with the appropriate plan by the appointed hour.[30] Although one could hardly describe such a mission as "easy" considering the distance and the enemy defences across Europe, the Western Allies did possess planes which were capable of a round-trip flight to Warsaw in April of 1943. Both the British Lancaster bomber and the American B-17 were operational in early 1943 on British soil and had a range of about 2200 miles or 300 miles in excess of the London-Warsaw trip by the shortest possible air route. If, as is suggested here, a mission over Warsaw in 1943 was to be flown primarily for moral-political demonstration purposes, rather than for the achievement of some strictly military objectives, additional fuel could have replaced some or most of the bomb load. If there had been a genuine interest in any such mission in the West, a few planes could have been flown off a carrier deck in the North Sea (à la Jimmy Doolittle in 1942) cutting down considerably on the length of the round trip.

Of course, the "bottom line" in the discussion of technical possibility in all these matters was probably best expressed by the late Andrei Vishinsky when he served as Soviet Ambassador to the United Nations. He once invoked a Russian proverb to the effect that he who wants to hit a dog will always find a stick. It is both easy and natural to find all sorts of excuses when one doesn't want to act, and not unusual to show great ingenuity when one is truly interested in acting. Certainly, the B-17 bomber which appeared in large numbers in 1943 could fly a maximum distance of 3,400 miles at a cruising speed in excess of 200 miles per hour. The plane was capable of carrying up to nearly eight tons of explosives and by reducing its bomb load, its range (within the 3400 mile limit) could be expanded.

Clearly, unless one had in mind a typical bombing mission, here was one instrument, at least, which could have been used for a politically and psychologically important mission over Warsaw in mid-1943. In the launching of the raid on Japan by General Jimmy Doolittle in April 1942, the United States sacrificed a number of planes and crews knowing that, under the best of circumstances, they would perhaps land somewhere in China after flying over and bombing Japan. A return to the launching carrier was precluded by circumstances. Sixteen planes could not have seriously damaged Japan's military and economic power but the psycho-political implications of the audacious attack, the demonstration of Japan's vulnerability, were enormous.[31]

In the vital sphere of moral support, which so often translates into all sorts of very practical consequences -- like people's willingness to take some risks in helping more Jews to escape or hide -- much could have been done, and nothing was done. President Roosevelt and Prime Minister Churchill did not utter one public word during the 28-day agony of the Warsaw Ghetto. Foreign Secretary Eden and US Secretary of State, Cordell Hull, were both busy with their routine duties, and not one sentence for public consumption passed their lips. The BBC and the Voice of America, until after the fact, had nothing to say about the heroic, unequal struggle fought within the walls of the Warsaw Ghetto, a struggle which, after all, could have been, and should have been, seen as a struggle on behalf of all victims and opponents of Nazism, not merely or only Jews.

The last message from the Warsaw Ghetto received in London declared that the "world of freedom and justice is silent, does nothing". And on 12 May 1943, the Jewish (Bundist) deputy to the Polish National Council in London, Shmuel Zygielbojm, committed suicide in protest of world passivity toward the murder of the Jews. He left a letter, memorable in history, but hardly noticed by Western public opinion at the time:

> The responsibility for this crime -- the assassination of the Jewish population in Poland -- rests above all on the murderers themselves, but falls indirectly upon the whole human race, on the Allies and their governments, who so far have taken no firm steps to put a stop to these crimes ... My companions of the Warsaw Ghetto fell in a last heroic battle with their weapons in their hands. I did not have

the honour to die with them, but I belong to them and to their common grave. Let my death be an energetic cry of protest against the indifference of the world which witnesses the extermination of the Jewish people without taking any steps to prevent it.[32]

It is little wonder that given Allied policies toward the Jews, as opposed to rhetorical representations, Dr. Goebbels was led to make his famous observation:

The question of Jewish persecution in Europe is being given top *news* priority by the English and the Americans ... At bottom, however, I believe that both the English and the Americans are happy that we are exterminating the Jewish riff-raff.[33]

Is it really credible to argue, as so many implicitly have, that the possible loss of ten or fifteen bombers on a mission to Warsaw would have jeopardized Allied chances of victory in the Second World War? Would the expenditure of gasoline necessary for such a mission "break" the Allied war budget? Finally, there was the very helpful measure which the Allies employed on behalf of the *Polish* Warsaw resistance of 1944. They could have -- and should have -- publicly insisted that the Ghetto fighters, if captured, be treated as combatants by the Nazis with the obvious implication of Allied reprisals on German POWs. (Coincidentally, over 100,000 German soldiers were taken prisoner by the Allies in Tunisia on 12 May, just 4 days before most of the last Warsaw Ghetto insurgents were killed.) Because of the effect of such a measure on the morale of German troops and also on families at home, Hitler would have been severely pressed.[34] We know that in 1944 he resisted his natural inclination to kill the captured Polish "bandits" for these obvious reasons.

As Michael Cohen points out, a year later, with scarcely any hope of eventual success, the Allies flew 22 night missions to Warsaw from bases in southern Italy between 8 August and 20 September. Among the 181 bombers used on these missions 31 were lost. The Americans also flew missions to Warsaw from Britain -- obviously over the same distance in 1944 as they would have been in 1943 -- and on 18 September they dropped 1,284 containers of arms and supplies over the city of which only 288 reached the Polish insurgents with the rest falling to the Nazis.[35]

Analogously, in 1944, there were all sorts of excuses about the alleged technical difficulties of bombing Auschwitz -- or railroad tracks near it --

belied by numerous previous allied bombing raids over several locations in Silesia, some of them less than five miles away from the infamous Nazi death camp.[36] What might have been accomplished by such a mission, or even more than one mission? The implementation of the Final Solution at one of its major centres might have been disrupted; some Nazi killing facilities might have been destroyed or damaged; some SS guards and officers might have been killed and hopefully many wounded; some prisoners, Jewish and non-Jewish, might have been enabled to escape; many prisoners might have been, and, in fact, almost certainly would have been, killed.

Allied interest, the willingness to risk and sacrifice, on behalf of the victims, and the damage and trauma inflicted on Hitler's killers would have lifted a lot of hearts in Auschwitz and elsewhere. Would any such action have put a complete and definitive stop to the programme of the Final Solution? Most unlikely! But it did not need to do that, anymore than *any* bombing mission anywhere could not be expected to win the war for the Allies. In fact, the relationship between much, if not most, of Allied bombing of Germany during the Second World War and the victory of the Allies was far from an obvious, straightforward proposition. (See *infra* Chapter 8.) Hundreds of planes and thousands of lives were lost on many missions whose effectiveness was marginal and sometimes close to nil.[37]

In looking back on Allied responses to the Holocaust, it is important to distinguish particular events and actions from the more obvious general tendencies. The extermination of the Jews was a long-term Nazi effort begun even before the summer of 1941. Amidst many atrocities committed by them in many places, it was singular in its aim of a systematic liquidation of a whole people. The ostensible Allied idea of dealing with all Nazi atrocities "equally" and without preference to Jews was a political dodge useful to the evasion of recognizing as "different" that which was "different". Many actions, loudly symbolic and also significantly substantive, could have been undertaken during those years. Until the latter part of 1944, none were. Auschwitz was no more than an episode among many episodes.

Nevertheless, Bernard Wasserstein's account of this affair is a wonderfully revealing testimonial to scholarly, human, and liberal gullibility. It would almost seem that Prime Minister Churchill was out of town when the Holocaust happened. He was too busy with world politics to assure, personally, any possible measures of rescue and aid in a catastrophe that he himself described in 1944 as the worst in human history.[38]

A number of years ago, a prominent American pugilist, Mohammed Ali, described certain ring tactics designed to mislead, confuse, and entrap opponents as "ropadope". Politicians have engaged in these tactics since time immemorial. They could always count on substantial publics, including the most learned, to be taken in by them. Churchill and Roosevelt were both great masters of the craft. Thus, Wasserstein describes the attempt, seemingly approved by Churchill, to formulate a British plan to bomb Auschwitz:

> The result was a striking testimony to the ability of the British civil service to overturn ministerial decisions: although it had secured the explicit backing of the Prime Minister and the Foreign Secretary, the scheme was rejected. Churchill was abroad in August 1944 and does not appear to have been told of the decision. Eden, greatly preoccupied with the severe crisis in relations with the USSR as a result of the Warsaw Rising and the Soviet refusal to grant landing rights to British or American supply planes, assigned the task of dealing with the Jewish Agency bombing proposal to the Minister of State, Richard Law. Letters announcing that the scheme had been rejected were signed by Law and dispatched to Weizmann and Sir Archibald Sinclair. A subtle difference in formulation marked the two communications. The letter to Weizmann stated that 'in view of the very great technical difficulties involved' the Government had decided it had 'no option but to refrain from pursuing the proposal in present circumstances'. No reference was made to any other reason for the decision. But the letter to Sinclair placed the technical objection in a secondary position: 'For the last month our reports have tended to show that Jews are no longer being deported from Hungary. In view of this fact and also because we understand from the Air Ministry that there are serious technical difficulties in the way of carrying out the suggestion, we do not propose to pursue it'. [39]

The present author has a good deal of sympathy for Wasserstein's argument insofar as bureaucratic obstruction and foot-dragging are concerned. This is undoubtedly a problem in all political systems, and in the constitutional democracies it is perhaps especially acute when people can hide behind their statutory protections. But projected over the whole period of the Second World War, with respect to the Jews, it is little short of absurd. It is an Alice in Wonderland argument.

Winston Churchill couldn't do anything about bombing Auschwitz because his bureaucratic underlings would not follow up on his directives. Perhaps also as Prime Minister he did not know about his Government's policy with respect to Jewish refugees in Palestine. He had never heard of the *Struma* episode. He had never heard of the slow strangulation of the Jews of the Warsaw Ghetto between 1940 and 1942. He never received any reports from the London-based Polish Government-in-Exile. He was personally briefed by the Polish Underground Emissary Jan Karski, but he either could not understand what he was being told, did not believe it or instantly forgot it. His own government publicly acknowledged the Holocaust on 17 December 1942 in the House of Commons but he either did not know it, did not believe it, or simply could not remember it. He noticed the Polish uprising in Warsaw in 1944 but he did not notice the Jewish uprising in Warsaw in 1943, even though it had been reported by the press of the Allied nations. He was not too busy to help insurgents in Warsaw in 1944 but he was too busy in 1943. In 1943 he was too absorbed in "fighting the war" but in 1944 he was not. In his six-volume history of the Second World War he never mentioned the Holocaust in the *text* of his work, probably because it was not sufficiently important even from the perspective of 1950.

The above is, of course, only a partial and sketchy list of the strange lapses and omissions of Winston Churchill. Except for the matter of the memoirs, the case is identically the same for Franklin Roosevelt. Collecting excuses for these two leaders is like asserting that Adolf Hitler had no idea whatever that Jews in his empire were being somehow mistreated. He was too busy with the war!

An overall assessment of the Hitlerite destruction of European Jewry requires the recognition that it was only in part a crime of commission; in large measure, it was also a crime of omission. It occurred not only because the Nazis willed it and carried it out. It occurred because people who could have prevented it, or thwarted it, or even obstructed or limited it, did not do what they could have done to interfere with Hitler's policy toward the Jews.

Even though no document exists, or at least none has been found thus far, linking Hitler directly to the Final Solution (by detailed and specific instructions to subordinates), it is amply reasonable to identify him as the instigator of the policy. This follows from several publicly-known facts. To begin with, Hitler repeatedly, publicly and privately, advocated the extermination of the Jews. His power over the German political system, especially party organizations and auxiliaries such as the SS and Gestapo, was enormous and in the years between 1939 and 1944 entirely unchallenged.

The Final Solution was an operation of great magnitude, requiring a considerable period of time for its execution and a significant diversion of resources, especially transport, for its consummation. Its oblique treatment by Nazi media indicated that it was recognized as a subject of considerable political sensitivity. There is evidence that Hitler both knew about it and approved of it from various sources, especially, for example, the diaries of Dr. Joseph Goebbels. Under the circumstances, it is all but impossible to believe that Hitler was *not* the source of the policy, let alone its principal supporter.[40]

Analogously, the public record strongly suggests the personal complicity of Churchill, Roosevelt, and Stalin in the success of the Final Solution. They all knew what was happening by their own collective public admission of 17 December 1942. There is a great deal which they either knew or should have known much earlier. Allied disclaimers of knowledge about the killing of Jews prior to December 1942 are overwhelmingly lacking in credibility. Stalin's callous behaviour, his indifference to the extermination of a whole people, fit in with his character and his own methods of dealing with human beings, or even whole categories of human beings, whom he regarded as opponents.[41]

The leaders of the great democracies in the Second World War operated under a pretension of humanity and benevolence, and at various times gave misleading, not to say untruthful, pledges of support and assistance to the Jewish people.[42] Given both the opportunity to act, and from time to time all sorts of means to act, they failed to intervene on behalf of the Jews in what Winston Churchill himself called the greatest crime in the history of humanity. Assuming that they, unlike Stalin, had consciences, the public record testifies not only to their complicity in the crime of the ages but also to a pathetic effort to conceal their true roles.

How accidental is it, one may ask, that Winston Churchill in his six-volume *History of the Second World War*, mentions the Final Solution only in one footnote of Volume Six. Why does he never mention, let alone discuss, Eden's declaration in the House of Commons of 17 December 1942? Was it not authorized by the British Cabinet over which Churchill presided? Was there not a Cabinet discussion preceding it? Perhaps even more than one? Were there perhaps any private discussions before or after Cabinet meetings? Was there any concern with some sort, any sort, of action on behalf of the victims *after* the Declaration?

There is much that Churchill has to say about the Warsaw uprising by the Poles. But he never in his *History* mentions the 1943 uprising of the Jews.

The subject of British policy in, and concerning, Palestine was never touched upon in the several volumes (outside of some correspondence concerning the raising of a Jewish fighting force). Why not? The fiction that Churchill was simply too busy running the war effort is just that, a fiction. The Prime Minister's style of life, even in the midst of war, generally permitted him all sorts of time for refreshment and reflection. It was hardly all work and no play. Much the same was true of Franklin Roosevelt and the principal subordinate colleagues of these leaders.

Anthony Eden's treatment of the Final Solution in his *Reckoning* published in 1965 is nothing short of amazing in the haste with which he "walks away" from the subject after briefly mentioning his famous 1942 House of Commons statement. There is neither prologue, nor postscript, nor reflection, attached to it. It appears as if out of a void and disappears into a void. Could this be accidental? Not very likely. Wasn't the Final Solution known to Eden *after* 1945 as it must have been to Churchill? Why the reticence? Was it not a subject of great public interest in the 1950s and 1960s?

Secretary Hull's memoirs are quite similar to Eden's on this issue. He makes the briefest possible reference to knowing about the fate of the Jews in 1942. After all, since the 17 December Declaration was made on behalf of the US Government, how could he do any less? Hull manages a studious avoidance of any discussion, commentary, or reflection on its origin. It is rather interesting, however, to read his assertion that he had discussed the plight of the Jews with the President "many times" and that the latter never reproached him for what he was doing, or not doing, to help the Jews of Europe.[43] He was probably right. The subject seems generally to have been too painful to men whose main concern was always to get through the war with as little trouble, risk, or challenge, as was humanly possible.

The references to Jews made by General Eisenhower when he and his forces landed in North Africa in November 1942 are illustrative of the amazingly defensive and timid attitude of the Allied high command on the general subject of "Jews".

> One complication in the Arab tangle was the age-old antagonism between the Arab and the Jew. Since the former outnumbered the latter by some forty to one in North Africa, it had become local policy to placate the Arabs at the expense of the Jews; repressive laws had resulted and the Arab population regarded any suggestion for amelioration of such laws as the beginning of an effort to

establish a Jewish government, with consequent persecution of themselves ... it is easy to understand that the situation called for more caution and evolution than it did for precipitate action and revolution. The country was ridden, almost ruled, by rumor. One rumor was to the effect that I was a Jew, sent into the country by the Jew, Roosevelt, to grind down the Arabs and turn over North Africa to Jewish rule. The political staff was so concerned about this one that they published material on me in newspapers and in special leaflets to establish evidence of my ancestry. Arab unrest, or, even worse, open rebellion, would have set us back for months and lost us countless lives.[44]

And also:

An important point was that we could not afford a military occupation [in North Africa] unless we chose to halt all action against the Axis. The Arab population was then sympathetic to the Vichy French regime, which had effectively eliminated Jewish rights in the region, and an Arab uprising against us, which the Germans were definitely trying to foment, would have been disastrous.[45]

The real issue before Eisenhower in 1942 was not whether to persecute Arabs or establish Jewish domination over them. It was a matter of restoring equal rights to Jews along with everybody else in North Africa. The Vichy regulations were only a little more than two years old when the Allies got to Morocco and Algeria. And yet, with all his troops ashore, the General was terribly worried about having to give up any offensive operations against the Axis, and about the loss of "countless lives", if only status quo ante-1940 were to be restored. In effect, Eisenhower indicated the need to deal rather gingerly with the matter of everyone's civil rights so that the local Arab population should not get the wrong idea about Allied policies being pro-Jewish.

There is little doubt, of course, but that the General reflected the less-than-sympathetic views of his political master, President Roosevelt. In a conversation with the Vichy French General Charles Nogues, on 17 January 1943 at the President's villa during the Casablanca Conference, the following exchange took place.

> Mr. [Robert] Murphy [President's political representative in the region] remarked that the Jews in North Africa were very much disappointed that 'the war for liberation' had not immediately resulted in their being given their complete freedom. The President stated that he felt the whole Jewish problem should be studied very carefully and that progress should be definitely planned. In other words, the number of Jews engaged in the practice of the professions (law, medicine, etc.) should be definitely limited to the per centage that the Jewish population in North Africa bears to the whole of the North African population. Such a plan would therefore permit the Jews to engage in the professions, at the same time would not permit them to overcrowd the professions, and would represent an unanswerable argument that they were being given their full rights. To the foregoing, General Nogues agreed generally, stating at the same time that it would be a sad thing for the French to win the war merely to open the way for the Jews to control the professions and the business world of North Africa. The President stated that his plan would further eliminate the specific and understandable complaints which the Germans bore towards the Jews in Germany, namely, that while they represented a small part of the population, over fifty per cent (sic!) of the lawyers, doctors, school teachers, college professors, etc., in Germany, were Jews.[46]

Nowhere in Eisenhower's book, or in analogous memoirs of top Allied commanders, was there any reference to the humanitarian aspects of their military mission in Europe, the need, or desirability at least, of shortening the war in order to save many innocent lives threatened by Hitler.

At the apex of political power, Winston Churchill and Franklin Roosevelt led their respective countries to a great victory, one which Roosevelt did not live to see in 1945. They both, each in his own way, made critically important contributions to the defeat of Hitler's Germany, a deed of enormous value and significance in human history. But human beings are very imperfect, often virtuous and far-sighted on some things but not on others. Perhaps Roosevelt and Churchill overestimated the political constraints on them, at home and abroad, on the issue of helping the Jews. But they were savvy politicians. They responded to aggregate constituency constraints, foreign and domestic, within the political and cultural conditions of their time. Their own attitudes were probably much less sympathetic than what they publicly pretended. The attitudes manifested in the American Congress and the British House of Commons during the War on the issue of sheltering escapees from Hitler's Europe clearly signalled to these leaders: "careful about the Jews!". In their own minds, though this is conjecture, they may have thought that the greater objective of defeating Nazism fully justified their silence and their betrayal of the six million.[47]

What capabilities, then, did the democracies of the world demonstrate while Hitler slaughtered the Jews of Europe (with their official knowledge since 1942)? Not even symbolic ones, let alone any that could be called "substantive". Those vaunted powers of disseminating and absorbing information in order to distill "truth", and then act upon it, did not seem to be much in evidence in those days.

NOTES

[1] *The Holocaust in Historical Perspective* (Seattle: University of Washington Press, 1978), pp. 9-10. Note also p. 17.

[2] *Ibid.*, p. 10.

[3] *Ibid.*, pp. 58-60, on the attitudes of partisans of different persuasions toward Jews. Bauer believes that even Hitler did not know what to do with the Jews "until fairly late"; that the Nazis did not have a "clearly preconceived" plan; there was only one clear idea -- to get rid of Jews in Germany: pp. 10-12. Bauer believes Hitler himself "probably" pushed his colleagues into "Final Solution" in March of 1941 anticipating war with Russia, p. 13. The opportunity arose, p. 14. He sees Hitler's earlier statements as just "rantings and ravings".

[4] See Shaul Esh, "The Dignity of the Destroyed: Towards a Definition of the Period of the Holocaust", pp. 346-366, in Yisrael Gutman and Livia Rothkirchen (eds.), *The Catastrophe of European Jewry* (Jerusalem: Yad Vashem, 1976). This author argues that the Holocaust as "organized war against the Jews" really began in 1933, p. 346.

[5] Yehuda Bauer, *op. cit.*, p. 85.

[6] Deborah E. Lipstadt, *Beyond Belief: The American People and the Coming of the Holocaust 1933-1945* (New York: The Free Press, 1986), p. 278.

[7] Seymour Maxwell Finger, *American Jewry During the Holocaust* (New York: Holmes and Meier, 1984), an excellent source on the issue of what was known about the Holocaust by Western public opinion, governments, and Jewish audiences as well, in effect, all that ever needed to be known. It is also excellent on the subject of human propensity for denial. As the author says about some of the most recent books: "These volumes are very informative and shed some new light on the sequence of events, and the psychology of people often subconsciously incapable of comprehending the nature and meaning of things they *knew*. They also tell a lot about the failure of the Western powers to do anything substantial to rescue great numbers of Jews doomed to the gas

chambers. For all their very considerable merits, these books are not vital instruments for our purpose. The governments of the democratic nations and the USSR, the international organizations of great prestige and moral power like the Vatican, the International Committee of the Red Cross, and the leadership of major Jewish organizations did not need, in the late 30s and all through the war years, to read Wyman, Braham, Friedman, Laqueur, Gilbert, *et al.,* to be informed of what was happening": p. 42.

There is something wonderfully self-indulgent about the claim of being at once horrified and yet unable to believe the reports about the Holocaust. It almost invites our sympathy for the psyche of the people oppressed by these terrible reports that they could not possibly bring themselves to believe.

[8] Note *ibid.,* pp. 170-171, on how *The New York Times* during the 1930s and 1940s seemed to make every effort not to appear "too Jewish". The paper's publisher, Arthur Sulzberger, was part of a group in 1939 seeking to dissuade FDR from naming Felix Frankfurter to the Supreme Court because that would "generate anti-Semitism", note, p. 171. Roger Manvel and Heinrich Fraenkel, *The Incomparable Crime, Mass Extermination in the Twentieth Century: The Legacy of Guilt* (New York: G. P. Putnam's Sons, 1967): "Inability to understand the magnitude of the tragedy facing the Jews affected even the Jewish organizations themselves in the free world ... At a special conference of thirty-four Jewish organizations in America convened in January 1943, three weeks after the Allied declaration had been made, the letter calling the meeting made no reference to the crime of genocide, nor put forward any proposal, however desperate, to try to stop it": pp. 228, 299. "The Nazis took a cynical, satanic advantage of [the Jewish] tradition of peaceful endurance", p. 231. These authors also speculate that the "great majority" of Jewish victims of the Holocaust "did not accept that they faced death through extermination", p. 232. Among members of the German Wehrmacht who did learn of the work of the *Einsatzgruppen* and Jewish "liquidations" more generally, denial was facilitated by the idea that "partisans" and "bandits" were being executed: p. 237. Reichsmarshal Goering denied at Nuremberg any knowledge of the extermination of the Jews, pp. 233-234.

Speaking of Germany and Germans in the 1960s, the authors concluded that "no one you met had ever supported Hitler let alone been a Nazi. It was always the others who were guilty": p. 251. See also Arthur J. Goldberg and Arthur Hertzberg, "Commentary from Commission Members on American Jewry and the Holocaust" in Appendix 3, pp. 1-4 in Seymour Maxwell Finger (ed.), *American Jewry During the Holocaust* (New York: Holmes and Meier, 1984): "The evidence is incontrovertible that American Jewish leadership did know what was going on in Nazi Europe and that the Allied governments to which they were appealing knew even more precisely than the Jewish leaders the details of the horror. In England, the now-famous decoding operation in Bletchley produced daily lists of the transports to the slaughter, and in Washington American intelligence sources were hardly less well-informed. Certainly everybody knew what was going on before the war in the 1930s, openly before the eyes of the world. Why, then was so little done?": p. 6.

Note Haskel Lookstein, *American Jewry's Public Response to the Holocaust, 1934-1944: An Examination Based Upon Accounts in the Jewish Press and Periodicals* (Yeshiva University, New York, 1979).

[9] We may recall that, according to public opinion polls, "even as late as December 1944, 12 per cent of Americans believed that the mass murder accounts were untrue, 27 per cent believed only about 100,000 people were involved and only 4 per cent believed the truth -- that over five million Jews had already been put to death". S. M. Finger, *op. cit.,* pp. 43-44. Note also Monty Noam Penkower, *The Jews Were Expendable: Free World Diplomacy and The Holocaust* (Urbana: University of Illinois Press, 1983), pp. 292-293, on widespread refusal of Jews in Europe at the beginning of the liquidation to believe the worst. "Incredulity stemmed from a deeply rooted belief of many [Jews] in the culture and conscience of the West", p. 294.

[10] The text of the relevant portion of Achilles' memorandum is reproduced in Volume 6 of *The Encyclopedia Judaica* published by the Keter Publishing House Jerusalem Ltd. in 1972 at page 990. See Henry L. Feingold, *The Politics of Rescue, The Roosevelt Administration and the Holocaust 1938-1945* (New York: Holocaust Library, 1970). Writing of the late 1930s, he says: "Although Roosevelt cast a statesmanlike eye on the future refugee problem, there seemed little that the Administration was willing to do to relieve immediate distress", (p. 89).

[11] See especially Colin Holmes, *Anti-Semitism in British Society, 1876-1939* (New York: Holmes and Meier, 1979); Grisela C. Lebzelter, *Political Anti-Semitism in England, 1918-1939* (London: Macmillan Press, 1978); and Tony Kushner, *The Persistence of Prejudice, Anti-Semitism in British Society during the Second World War* (Manchester: Manchester University Press, 1989).

[12] I. C. B. Dear (ed.), *The Oxford Companion to World War II* (New York: Oxford University Press, 1995), p. 366.

[13] See Don Levin, *The Lesser of Two Evils: East European Jewry Under Soviet Rule 1939-1941* (Philadelphia: Jewish Publication Society, 1995), p. 6; Lucjan Dobroszycki, *Survivors of the Holocaust in Poland* (New York: M. E. Sharpe, 1994), pp. 18-19. About 500,000 Jews escaped from West to East in these years but only between 300 and 350,000 managed to flee deep into Soviet territory before *Barbarossa*, and of those at least 240,000 returned West after the War. Yehuda Bauer in his *The Holocaust in Historical Perspective* (Seattle: University of Washington Press, 1978), p. 55, gives a figure of 264,000 Jews actually deported into the USSR. See Shimon Redlick (ed.), *War, Holocaust, and Stalinism, A Documented Study of the Jewish Anti-Fascist Committee in the USSR* (Luxembourg: Harwood Academic Publishers, 1995), who reports that 400,000 Jews from Soviet-annexed areas "mainly refugees from German-occupied Poland" were deported to the interior of the USSR,

and another 85,000 fled there voluntarily for a total of about "half-a-million Jews who had not been Soviet citizens in 1939": pp. 29-30. Note Keith Sword, *Deportation and Exile, Poles in the Soviet Union, 1939-1948* (London: St. Martin's Press, 1994), who gives a figure of 198,000 Jews in the so-called "refugee" category removed to the USSR between 1939 and 1941, p. 26. He also gives a figure of 136,500 Jews returning to Poland from the USSR "during the first half of 1946", p. 195. Jeff Schatz in his *The Generation: The Rise and Fall of the Jewish Communists of Poland* (Berkeley: University of California Press, 1991) reports a figure of 157,420 Jewish repatriates from the USSR registered with the Central Committee of Jews in Poland, p. 203. It should be noted that many Polish Jews who left the USSR after the war went to countries other than Poland, and also that many Polish Jews remained in Russia after 1945. Arkady Vaksberg, *Stalin Against the Jews* (New York: Alfred A. Knopf, 1994), provides an otherwise interesting catalogue of Stalin's anti-Semitic attitudes and actions; nevertheless, he engages in a curious misrepresentation of history when he provides the following account of the Jewish exodus to the east in 1939-1941, to wit: "Taking advantage of the porous new border [between Germany and the USSR] ... Jews from western and central regions of Poland tried to cross over as quickly as possible to the areas of Soviet military units. Knowing he would be sending them to Germany and not wishing to waste time or money on this unwieldy operation, Stalin gave orders not to allow Jews onto Soviet territory.' They were shot at from both sides": p. 105. On the whole, this is one of the more remarkable fantasies to be found in what professes to be serious literature.

14   See Lucjan Dobroszycki, *Survivors of the Holocaust in Poland, A Portrait Based on Jewish Community Records, 1944-1947* (London: M. E. Sharpe, 1994), Table 4.2 'Number of Jews Living in Poland by Provinces and Regions' (15 June 1945), p. 68, gives a total of 73,955 Polish Jews, including persons from Displaced Persons camps in Germany and the Polish Army organized in the USSR There were 13,000 Jews coming into Poland with the Soviet-sponsored Polish Army. Thus, the total of Jews saved in Poland and in German camps was about 60,000. Virtually identical number is given in Table 4.3, p. 69, which gives the analogous figure for 15 August 1945. Later figures reflect the substantial influx of Jewish civilians returning from exile in the USSR. Naturally, no completely accurate numbers are possible since at least some Jews who survived the war probably chose not to register with any Jewish organizations. The 60,000 given by Dobroszycki constitute less than 2 per cent of Poland's pre-war Jewish population and, allowing for about 300,000 who may have fled beyond Nazi reach to the USSR before 22 June 1941, still less than 2 per cent of the 3.2 million Polish Jews who in 1941 lived under Nazi rule.

15   See Louis Rapoport *Stalin's War Against the Jews, The Doctors' Plot and the Soviet Solution* (New York: The Free Press, 1990),. Rapoport describes Stalin's anti-Semitism, the many murders of Jews, and the conspicuous Soviet silence on the Holocaust. While Rapoport mentions Stalin handing over 600 German Communists

to the Nazis (p. 57), most of them Jews, presumably in 1940, and many other undoubtedly genuine, bloody Stalinist persecutions of Jews, he does not mention the hundreds of thousands of Jews allowed entry into the USSR between 1939 and 1941 from western Poland. His chapter titled "Rescue Denied, Stalin and Hitler Sacrifice the Jews" contains no acknowledgement of it. Curiously, his book does make reference to the twenty-odd generals of the Red Army of Jewish extraction, including a relatively major figure, Colonel General Ivan Cherniakovsky, killed in East Prussia in early 1945.

[16]   See Yisrael Gutman, *The Jews of Warsaw, 1939-1943, Ghetto, Underground, Revolt* (Bloomington: Indiana University Press, 1982), who reports that the peak population of the Ghetto was 445,000 in March 1941, and that the rate of mortality was such that within 10 years all the inhabitants would have been dead, without any additional, violent measures; 43,000 or 10 per cent of the population died in 1941 alone: pp. 63-64. Lucy S. Dawidowicz, *The War Against the Jews, 1933-1945* (New York: Holt, Rinehart & Winston, 1975), on Ghetto conditions, pp. 207-222. On the ŻOB and the Uprising of 1943 see pp. 332-339. Note Raul Hilberg, *The Destruction of the European Jews* (New York: Holmes and Meier, 1985), pp. 83-84; at first, there were 28 points of entry into the Warsaw Ghetto and 53,000 persons with passes to enter and leave for various purposes. Subsequently, there were 15 gates. In March 1941, Hilberg reported a Jewish population of 445,000 in the original Ghetto, in a 1.3 sq. mile area, a density nearly 20 times greater than in the rest of Warsaw, with 920,000 people for 53.3 sq. miles area.

[17]   See Stefan Korbonski, *The Jews and the Poles in World War II* (New York: Hippocrene Books, 1989), who presents a defence of the Polish role in the catastrophe of the Holocaust. Note pp. 5-56, where Korbonski discusses, quite understandably and properly, the failure of the Allies to render assistance to the Jews when informed repeatedly and extensively (as by Jan Karski in November 1942 and thereafter) by the Polish Underground and Government-in-Exile. Note his detailed and impressive account of all the information about Nazi atrocities against Jews passed on to the Allies and "Jewish representatives in London and New York" by the Polish Government-in-Exile, beginning with reports in 1940, and periodically repeated in 1941, 1942, and 1943. These were all received with reactions ranging predominantly from disbelief to indifference, pp. 329-332. See also Tadeusz Bór-Komorowski, *Armia Podziemna* (London: Veritas, 1950), p. 100. The General reports sending *daily* reports to London about Warsaw ghetto deportations in 1942 -- and the complete silence of the BBC!

[18]   The Grand Mufti of Jerusalem, Hajj Amin al Husseini (1895-1974), was a Palestinian Arab who became a Nazi collaborator and active supporter of the Final Solution policy. In 1943 he provided leadership in organizing Bosnian Muslim battalions in Croatia integrated into the SS and involved in rounding up Jews for

270 Democracies Against Hitler

extermination. He, in effect, out-Eichmanned Adolf Eichmann, by directing requests to both Nazi and Nazi satellite-state authorities opposing the escape or release of any Jews in their custody through emigration permits. He also founded in 1943 the Arab Institute for Research into the Jewish Question in Berlin along the lines of a similar Nazi project of Alfred Rosenberg. For obviously "political" reasons, none of the Allied Powers, Soviet Union included, chose to prosecute the Mufti after the War. See article by I. Abramski-Bligh in Israel Gutman (ed.), *Encyclopedia of the Holocaust* (New York: Macmillan, 1990), Vol. II, pp. 703-707.

[19] Sir John Martin, *Downing Street, The War Years* (London: Bloomsbury, 1991), pp. 19-20.

[20] Note the report of 31 March 1938 by Under Secretary G. S. Messersmith to Secretary of State Cordell Hull on the formation of an inter-governmental committee on refugees. The report says, in part: "Rabbi Wise has been to see me and he agrees with all others I have seen that the activities of Jewish organizations must be kept in the background. A number of members of Congress have been in touch with me and I have gathered uniformly from them that ... any proposed changes in our immigration laws might lead to more restrictive rather than liberal practice on our part". See John Mendelson (ed.), *The Holocaust, Selected Documents, Jewish Emigration from 1933 to the Evian Conference of 1938*, Volume 5 (New York: Garland Publishing Company, 1982), p. 173. Also note Fred L. Israel (ed.), *The War Diary of Breckinridge Long, Selections from the Years 1939-1944* (Lincoln: University of Nebraska Press, 1966). Long recorded in his diary that in December of 1940 he had drafted a statement about US policy on refugee matters and that on 18 December FDR "has approved our entire policy". He also speaks of the "small element in this country which wants to push us into war," and which has been attacking the Department of State, p. 162. On 13 July 1944 Breckinridge Long was telling his diary that he had been "thrown to the wolves" and took the brunt of all the worst media criticism, implying that Hull and Roosevelt wanted him to do what he did, and take the heat for it, too: p. 366.

[21] Bernard Wasserstein, *Britain and the Jews of Europe 1939-1945* (Oxford: Clarendon Press, 1979), p. 152.

[22] *Ibid.*, p. 34, pp. 351-351. See Dalia Offer, *Escaping The Holocaust, Illegal Immigration to the Land of Israel, 1939-1944* (New York: Oxford University Press, 1990), on British policy toward Jewish emigration to Palestine adhering to the restrictive principles of the May 1939 White Paper, a policy obviously maintained by the Churchill Cabinet of 1940-1945. See especially pp. 7, 148, 220, e.g. "As the situation worsened, the Zionist leadership in Palestine appealed to Britain to display compassion for the plight of Rumanian Jews and accept a greater number of immigrants from that country. Repeated requests were sent to the British High Commissioner in Palestine and to the Colonial Office, beginning in December 1940.

Weizmann also appealed directly to Churchill on 5 December 1941. He described the 'inhuman' situation in Rumania and asked that Britain help find some way to relieve the suffering of Jews there, lest the issue cloud future relations between Britain and the Jewish people": p. 148.

As Bernard Wasserstein, *op. cit.*, notes: "During the early part of the war, when the German Government openly tried to dispatch large numbers of Jews beyond the borders of the Reich, every practicable tactic was employed by the British Government to prevent significant numbers of Jews reaching Palestine (or, indeed, anywhere else in the Empire, including, as will be seen, Britain itself). Only the restraining influences of Churchill, of American Jewish opinion, and of potential Jewish unrest in Palestine stopped the policy being *enforced* even more stringently. As the escape routes were sealed so too was the fate of the majority of the Jews imprisoned in Nazi Europe": p. 80 [italics mine].

Interestingly, also: "In May 1941, in the wake of the pro-Nazi Rashid Ali Gailani coup in Iraq (in which the Mufti of Jerusalem played a prominent role), Colonial Office officials again considered drastic expedients to counter a potential 'flood of Jewish refugees by means of wholesale expulsions'. One measure which received serious consideration was a proposal that the policy, abandoned in 1939, of firing on illegal immigrant ships in order to drive them away from Palestinian ports should be revived. J. S. Bennett minuted: 'It is an ugly business having to fire at a ship load of 'refugees'. But the present serious state of the war in the Middle East justifies strong measures' ": pp. 79-80.

[23] Parliamentary Debates, Fifth Series, Volume 385, *House of Commons Official Report* (385 H.C. Deb 5s), p. 2083.

[24] *Ibid.*, p. 2086.

[25] *Ibid.*, p. 2085.

[26] See Richard Breitman, "Roosevelt and the Holocaust", pp. 109-127, in Verne W. Newton (ed.), *FDR and the Holocaust* (New York: St. Martin's Press, 1996), p. 116-117. Michael R. Marrus in his "Bystanders to the Holocaust", *ibid.*, pp. 151-158, takes note of "... the indifference of Franklin D. Roosevelt to the Jewish tragedy ... Although periodically informed about mass killings, FDR was prepared to run no risks for the Jews, [and] thought that action on their behalf meant trouble politically ...": p. 155.

[27] See Frank P. King, "British Policy and the Warsaw Uprising", *Journal of European Studies,* Volume 4, No. 1, March 1974, pp. 1-18, who notes that "during the course of the rising, the RAF dispatched 196 aircraft to Warsaw on 22 nights at a cost of 39 aircraft. Out of the 149 drops made over Warsaw, the insurgents received but 44". Note also how the British Cabinet authorized a declaration "making the Home Army an allied force in an effort to guarantee their treatment by the Germans as regular soldiers", p. 11. See Stanislaw Mikolajczyk, *The Rape of Poland, Pattern of*

Soviet Aggression (New York: McGraw Hill, 1958), p. 90. "The declaration of British and American governments recognizing the combatants' rights of the Polish Underground had forced the Germans to regard the Home Army as prisoners of war and to treat the civilian population as human beings. The Germans only partly carried out their pledges ...". See Mark J. Conversino, *Fighting With the Soviets: The Failure of Operation Frantic 1944-1945* (Lawrence: University Press of Kansas, 1997), discusses flights by US and Allied air forces from Italy and Britain in support of the Warsaw insurgents during the August-September Polish Uprising in that city. In this case, Allied planes either returned to Italy or landed on Soviet territory after completing their missions.

[28]   See Bernard Wasserstein, *Britain and the Jews of Europe 1939-1945* (Oxford: Clarendon Press, 1979), p. 305 and fn. 119. Anti-Semitism was a powerful force isolating the Jews of Warsaw in the 40s. Note Emanuel Melzer, "Anti-Semitism in the Last Years of the Second Polish Republic", pp. 126-137, in Y. Gutman, *et al.* (eds.), *The Jews of Poland Between Two World Wars* (Hanover: University Press of New England, 1989). He concludes that "the atmosphere prevailing in the last years [in Poland before the Second World War] was characterized by a radicalization of anti-Semitism in all its various manifestations ... [with] serious implications for the relations between Poles and Jews during the Holocaust": p. 137. See Jerzy Holzer "Polish Political Parties and Anti-Semitism", pp. 194-205, in A. Polonsky, *et al.,* (eds.), *Jews in Independent Poland 1918-1939* (London: The Lithman Library of Jewish Civilization, 1994). Holzer notes that, by the late 30s, "... anti-Semitism constituted a kind of psychosis at the end of the Second Republic, disabling a healthy political sense and obscuring an awareness of the genuine threat to the life of the Polish state ...": p. 205. Cf. Josef Banas, *The Scapegoats, The Exodus of the Remnants of Polish Jewry* (New York: Holmes and Meier Publishers, 1979), pp. 42-44, on pre-war Polish anti-Semitism, and also pp. 48-49 on the relative unwillingness of Poles to assist the Ghetto insurgents of 1943. Note also Yehuda Bauer, *The Holocaust in Historical Perspective* (Seattle: University of Washington Press, 1978), especially pp. 52-55, and p. 77 on Polish and other East European attitudes.

[29]   *Loc. cit.*, p. 300.

[30]   Note account in William L. Shirer, *The Rise and Fall of the Third Reich, A History of Nazi Germany* (New York: Simon & Schuster, 1960), pp. 680-681.

[31]   See Carroll V. Glines, *The Doolittle Raid, America's Daring First Strike Against Japan* (New York: Orion Books, 1988), especially pp. 215-220. A few British or American planes flying from London to Warsaw might even have been ordered to land in neutral Sweden on completion of their mission.

[32]   See Wasserstein, *op. cit.*, pp. 304-305.

[33]   L. P. Lochner (ed.), *The Goebbels Diaries 1942-1943* (New York: Doubleday, 1948); 13 December 1942 entry on p. 241. Italics are mine.

[34] It is appropriate to note here a measure taken by a great President of the United States 80 years earlier. The following Order of Retaliation was signed by Lincoln on 30 July 1863, in response to rumours of the Confederacy's incipient measures against the Union's black soldiers: "The government of the United States will give the same protection to all its soldiers, and if the enemy shall sell or enslave anyone because of his colour, the offence shall be punished by retaliation upon the enemy's prisoners in our possession. It is therefore ordered that for every soldier of the United States killed in violation of the laws of war, a rebel soldier shall be executed; and for every one enslaved by the enemy or sold into slavery, a rebel soldier shall be placed at hard labour on the public works and continued at such labour until the other shall be released ....". See Roy P. Basler (ed.), *The Collected Works of Abraham Lincoln* (New Brunswick, NJ: Rutgers University Press, 1953-1955), Vol. VI, p. 357.

[35] Michael J. Cohen, *Churchill and the Jews* (London: Frank Cass, 1985), p. 302.

[36] *Ibid.*, p. 301. See Martin Gilbert, *Auschwitz and the Allies* (London: Michael Joseph, 1981). He reports John J. McCloy's refusal to bomb Auschwitz and other Allied failures to help. Note conclusion, pp. 339-341. As Michael J. Cohen says: "The test of the Allied response came in the summer of 1944, when the British and American policymakers were asked to bomb Auschwitz. At the time of this request the American Government possessed a great deal of information about Auschwitz, including both its location and its function, together with the technical ability to bomb both the railway-lines leading to the camp and the gas chambers in the camp itself. The British policymakers had, in addition, Churchill's personal authority to examine a bombing scheme with a view to positive action. Yet even then, a few individuals scotched the Prime Minister's directive because, as one of them expressed it at the time, to send British pilots to carry it out would have then risked 'valuable' lives. At that very moment however Allied lives were being risked, and risked willingly by volunteer crews, to drop supplies on Warsaw during the Polish uprising: and during these missions, these very same pilots had actually flown across the Auschwitz region on their way to Warsaw". *Churchill and the Jews, op. cit.*, p. 341.

[37] See James H. Kitchens III, US Air Force archivist, "The Bombing of Auschwitz Reexamined", in V. W. Newton, *FDR and the Holocaust* (New York: St. Martin's Press, 1996), pp. 183-217. Kitchens severely challenges David Wyman in *Abandonment of the Jews* (1984), and others, who believe that the Allies could have bombed Auschwitz in the latter part of 1944. Those included in the purview of his criticism, are, among others, Arthur D. Morse, *While Six Million Died: A Chronicle of American Apathy* (1968), and Martin Gilbert, *Auschwitz and the Allies* (1981). Kitchens' critical conclusion is that "an objective look at targeting possibilities, available intelligence, operational constraints, and the realistic allocation of military resources ... shows that the effective use of air power against Auschwitz is a

chimera(!) having little to do with War Department policies, indifference, military ineptitude or negative ethnic attitudes" (p. 191).

Says Kitchens: "In the instance of Auschwitz, military policy was driven by availability of intelligence, operational possibilities, asset allocation, the rules of war, and conventional morality": p. 204.

It is interesting to consider, for a moment, who or what decides "asset allocation"; and even more interesting to know that the rules of war and conventional morality had no difficulties over Dresden, and Hamburg, or Hiroshima, or Nagasaki (or Mers el Kebir) though somehow, insuperable moral military objections arose with respect to bombing Auschwitz.

In war, results cannot be guaranteed in advance. See J. Dugan and C. Stewart, "Ploesti", in I. C. B. Dear and M. R. D. Foot (eds.), *The Oxford Companion to World War II* (Oxford: Oxford University Press, 1995), p. 890. They report the first raid on the oil fields of Ploesti by the Western Allies as early as 12 June 1942, by 12 American bombers. The first major raid occurred on 1 August 1943 by 178 American bombers from North African bases. Since Ploesti was heavily defended, and the Nazis were not surprised by the attack, losses were enormous, 54 bombers and 532 crew members were lost to all causes. Five Congressional Medals of Honor were awarded to participants. However, "the raid destroyed 42 per cent of Ploesti's capacity [and since the refineries] had only been running at 60 per cent capacity ... within weeks [Ploesti] was producing at a higher rate than before the raid".

[38]   Winston S. Churchill, *The Second World War, Vol. VI, Triumph and Tragedy* (Boston: Houghton Mifflin, 1953), p. 630: "There is no doubt that this [persecution of Jews in Hungary and their expulsion from enemy territory] is probably the greatest and most horrible crime ever committed in the whole history of the world ..." This note, addressed to Eden, was dated by Churchill 11 July 1944. The parenthesis appears to have been inserted by Churchill when he prepared the manuscript for publication because the reference seems more appropriate to all of Nazi extermination of the Jews.

[39]   Wasserstein, *op.cit.*, pp. 316-317.

[40]   See Gerald Fleming, *Hitler and the Final Solution* (Berkeley: University of California Press, 1982), on the lack of a written order from Hitler. "Adolf Hitler's Final Solution ideology represented in stark reality a cult of the irrational bordering on lunacy yet [it] advanced under the guise of ice-cold reason, a cult whose founder saw himself as the benefactor and savior of his German Reich": p. 188. Saul Friedlander in his Preface says: "Destruction was [Hitler's] constant leitmotif. As long as there was no concrete possibility of realizing this destruction, Hitler allowed various policies to develop; but once the appropriate moment arrived, the constant theme became policy": p. XXIX. Interesting corroborative testimony on the Hitler question was provided by the Commandant of the Auschwitz Camp when he was awaiting trial

in Poland in 1946. Obersturmbannfuhrer Rudolf Höss wrote that: "In the summer of 1941, I cannot remember the exact date, I was suddenly summoned to the *Reichsfuhrer SS*, directly by his adjutant's office. Contrary to his usual custom, Himmler received me without his adjutant being present and said in effect: The *Fuehrer* has ordered that the Jewish question be solved once and for all and that we, the SS, are to implement that order. The existing extermination centers in the east are not in a position to carry out the large actions which are anticipated. I have therefore earmarked Auschwitz for this purpose, both because of its good position as regards communications and because the area can easily be isolated and camouflaged. At first I thought of calling in a senior SS officer for this job, but I changed my mind in order to avoid difficulties concerning the terms of reference. I have now decided to entrust this task to you. It is difficult and onerous and calls for complete devotion notwithstanding the difficulties that may arise. You will learn further details from *Sturmbannfuhrer* Eichmann of the Reich Security Head Office who will call on you in the immediate future. The departments concerned will be notified by me in due course. You will treat this order as absolutely secret, even from your superiors. After your talk with Eichmann you will immediately forward to me the plans of the projected installations. The Jews are the sworn enemies of the German people and must be eradicated. Every Jew that we can lay our hands on is to be destroyed now during the war, without exception. If we cannot now obliterate the biological basis of Jewry, the Jews will one day destroy the German people". See Jadwiga Bezwinska and Danuta Czech (eds.), *KL Auschwitz Seen By The SS, Höss, Broad, Kremer* (New York: Howard Fertig, 1984), p. 109.

[41] Although the Soviets under Stalin never gave explicit recognition to the murder of the Jews, the punishment of those involved in it was, in all likelihood, more certain and severe under their rule than it was in the West. Between 1945 and 1949 the Western Allies managed to convict 5,025 persons of war crimes. Among these, 486 were executed. The German Federal Republic from 1949 to 1962 added another 5,426 persons to those convicted and of these 3 were executed. In contrast, from the end of the War until the early 1960s, the Russians sentenced 24,000 Nazis for war crimes. The Poles sentenced another 16,819 and the East Germans 12,807. Judging by newspaper accounts, a far greater proportion of all these sentences involved executions. Note Manvel and Fraenkel, *op. cit.*, pp. 249-250.

[42] Speaking of specific instances, Winston Churchill promised to help the Jews in a July 1943 message to South African Prime Minister Jan Smuts. Note Michael J. Cohen, *op. cit.*, p. 251. The Smuts telegram to Churchill stated that "Jewish sufferings and massacres make their reasonable requirements a first charge on Allied statesmanship [and should] take precedence over efforts to placate Arabs or the like". Churchill responded that this "expressed his own views exactly", p. 251. Cohen does not give the date in July 1943 when this exchange occurred. On 1 August 1946 in the House of Commons, Churchill declared "that [he] had no idea, when the war came to

an end, of the horrible massacres [to which Jews were subjected]": pp. 266-267. Obviously, he just was not aware of his own Cabinet's official statements! Monty Noam Penkower, *op. cit.*, records President Roosevelt's statement to a delegation of Jewish organizations on 17 December 1942: "We shall do all in our power to be of service to your people in this tragic moment": p. 86.

[43] See Cordell Hull, *The Memoirs of Cordell Hull* (New York: Macmillan, 1948), Vol. II, pp. 1538-1539. Hull notes that with respect to refuge for Jews "we did all that the law allowed", and that in the Middle East, Arab and Jewish interests had to be "balanced" against one another.

[44] See Dwight D. Eisenhower, *Crusade in Europe* (New York: Doubleday, 1948), p. 128.

[45] *Ibid.*, p. 108.

[46] See Department of State Publication 8414, *Foreign Relations of the United States, The Conferences at Washington 1941-1942, and Casablanca, 1943* (US Government Printing Office: Washington DC 1968), p. 608. The President's figures reflected some wild anti-Semitic stereotypes. At the beginning of 1933 Jewish physicians constituted about 11 per cent of all German physicians; Jewish lawyers were 16 per cent of the German total. See Saul Friedlander, *Nazi Germany and the Jews Volume I, The Years of Persecution* (New York: Harper Collins, 1997), pp. 29-30.

[47] A perusal of FDR's wartime speeches and statements reveals only one occasion, in late March 1944, when the President mentioned, very briefly, the plight of the Jews and appealed for the world's sympathy and help on their behalf. By that time, however, most of Hitler's Jewish victims were already dead. Churchill made no such speeches at all.

8 DEMOCRACIES AT WAR, 1942-1944

The democracies' response to Hitler's demagoguery, violence and aggression was full of failures and catastrophes. But not entirely so. After Pearl Harbor, the United States gave the democracies something to cheer about. One of America's great achievements was the well-nigh unbelievable step-up in military production. Where others crawled, America leaped, and there was simply no comparing that leap to what all the other powers were doing. American production sustained the defence, and offence, of its allies and equipped what in 1944 became the largest military establishment in the world - - the United States armed forces at 14.8 million total personnel. This exceeded the Soviet 11.2 million, the German 9.1 and the Japanese 5.3 million, as well as the British at 5.0 million.

Perhaps most impressive was America's leap from 5,856 aircraft produced in 1939 to 96,318 turned out in 1944. This was an increase of 16.4 times in five years. During the same period, Britain increased its aircraft output by 3.3 times; Germany by 4.8; Japan by 6.3, and the Soviets by 3.9. The aggregate American output was more than twice as big as the German or the Soviet; almost 4 times as large as the British, and three-and-a-half times greater than Japan's (28,180 aircraft).

In 1943 the United States produced 2,654 major naval vessels. This was more than ten times as much as Britain; ten times as much as Germany, and nearly 22 times as much as Japan (122). It was more than 200 times the Soviet output of only 13 major naval vessels. American tank production was less impressive in the aggregate, since in 1944 the US total of 17,565 was exceeded by Germany's 22,100 and the Soviet's 28,963. Nevertheless, the American rate of increase, from a mere 400 vehicles in 1940, was a 44-fold leap, a much faster rate of growth than anyone else's.

The United States also vastly increased its production of energy sources and many other industrial materials with great relevance for the war effort of its allies as well as its own. Illustratively, between 1939 and 1944, American output of aluminium rose from 163.5 thousand tons to 776.4, where the British advanced only modestly from 24.9 to 35.4; the Germans from 199.4 to 245.3 and the Japanese from 29.5 to 110.3 thousand. The Russians increased their output from 51.7 thousand in 1942 to 82.7 thousand in 1944.

America's most impressive performance in battle was actually reserved for the Japanese. Here, unlike the European theatre, the Americans were not seriously constrained by what the British demanded of them. Douglas MacArthur and Chester Nimitz were not much concerned with British conceptions about how the war in the western Pacific might be fought. This was quite understandable since the British did not furnish -- as they did in Europe -- the principal base, or at least one of them, for any major attack on the enemy and did not provide any large-scale resources in this theatre.

Once the Americans got past the fiasco of Pearl Harbor (itself, of course, hardly a testimonial to the intelligence capabilities of American democracy or any democracy) they pursued a vigorous and extremely well-designed strategy for the defeat of their Japanese enemy. In the vast reaches of the Pacific Ocean, the Japanese could project their power against the Americans only with the critical assistance of sea and air power.

But within six months of the defeat at Pearl Harbor, the American navy, displaying bravado rarely evidenced by the democratic participants in the Second World War, inflicted a grievous defeat on Japan.

Beginning with the Battle of the Coral Sea in May 1942, the United States demonstrated a new technique of fighting a war at sea, and it demonstrated it more effectively than did the Japanese. In the words of Admiral Ernest J. King, Chief of Naval Operations:

> Thus ended the first major engagement in naval history in which surface ships did not exchange a single shot. Although the loss of *Lexington* was keenly felt, the engagement in the Coral Sea effectively checked the Japanese in their advance to the southward.[1]

Between 4 June and 8 June 1942 in the battle of Midway, a great naval and aerial duel took place. Through a combination of American skill and courage, a larger force was defeated by a smaller force. American carriers commanded by Admirals Raymond Spruance and Frank Fletcher destroyed four Japanese carriers of the much larger naval contingent commanded by Japanese Admirals Isoroku Yamamoto and Chuichi Nagumo, losing only the *Yorktown* to the Japanese. Critical to the battle was the heroic sacrifice made by US naval pilots who first attacked Japanese carriers on 4 June. Out of a total of 41 torpedo planes launched by the Americans only 6 made it back. But the Japanese carriers, busy fighting off the initial attack, were prevented from launching and deploying their own fighters to deal with a subsequent launch of US bombers, and these soon reduced the Japanese carriers to smoking hulks. Without taking any credit away from the brave and brilliant pilots of the RAF, it must be appreciated that Japan's defeat at Midway was a much more genuine victory than was the Battle of Britain.

The Battle of Britain was an action in which the Germans lost more planes than the British but the "victory" resulted not from this fact but rather from what Hitler chose to do or not to do following this Battle which was concluded at his initiative. Had he so wished, the Battle of Britain might have been a prelude to Britain's total defeat in the Second World War. Attacks could have been continued, modified, strengthened, and redirected. The losses to Germany were hardly catastrophic in any reasonable perspective. Midway was quite different. Japan was not able to replace its carrier losses within a few weeks or months under the circumstances of 1942, quite apart from the painful loss of experienced airmen and sailors. Her navy was dealt an enormous blow. The tide of the Pacific War was decisively turned, never to be reversed.

In the memorable words of Walter Lord:

By any ordinary standard, they were hopelessly outclassed.

They had no battleships, the enemy eleven. They had eight cruisers, the enemy twenty-three. They had three carriers (one of them crippled); the enemy had eight. Their shore defenses included guns from the turn of the century.

They knew little of war. None of the Navy pilots on one of their carriers had ever been in combat. Nor had any of the Army fliers. Of the Marines, 17 of 21 new pilots were just out of flight school -- some with less than four hours' flying time since then. Their enemy was brilliant, experienced and all-conquering ...

They took crushing losses -- 15 out of 15 in one torpedo squadron ... 21 out of 27 in a group of fighters ... many, many more.

They had no right to win. Yet they did, and in doing so, they changed the course of a war. More than that they added a new name -- Midway -- to that small list that inspires men by shining example. Like Marathon, the Armada, the Marne, a few others, Midway showed that every once in a while 'what must be' need not be at all. Even against the greatest of odds, there is something in the human spirit -- a magic blend of skill, faith and valor -- that can lift men from certain defeat to incredible victory.[2]

Whatever may have been said of the ego, self-promotion, and perhaps other less admirable attributes of General Douglas MacArthur, the forces under his command pursued an extremely effective plan of attack against Japan. And there was no doubt that the Americans, from mid-1942 onward, were always on the attack, somewhere, making their way across the Pacific in huge leaps to the ever-closer, vulnerable core of Japan's home islands.

MacArthur explained his strategic concept of fighting the Japanese in the following succinct formula:

> My strategic conception for the Pacific Theater contemplates massive strokes against only main objectives, utilizing surprise and air-ground striking power supported and assisted by the fleet. This is the very opposite of what is termed 'island hopping', which is the gradual pushing back of the enemy by direct frontal pressure with the consequent heavy casualties which will certainly be involved. Key points must of course be taken, but a wise choice of such will obviate the need for storming the mass of islands now in enemy possession. 'Island hopping' with extravagant losses and slow progress is not my idea of how to end the war as soon and as cheaply as possible. New conditions require for solution, and new weapons require for maximum application, new and imaginative methods. Wars are never won in the past.[3]

American Marine and Army units, supported by the tremendous firepower of the US navy and air force, worked collaboratively to maximize their advantage against the Japanese. In rapid succession, they bit one chunk after another from the newly-conquered Japanese empire. More importantly, the United States simply chewed up the two elements of force that Japan vitally needed to defend that empire -- air power and sea power. The roughly six-to-one ratio of fatalities suffered by the Japanese in fiercely opposing the Americans was indicative of the fatal tearing-down process that the Americans had developed against them.[4] Its most graphic illustration was the so-called Great Marianas Turkey Shoot of June 1944 when over 400 Japanese carrier planes were shot down by US forces at a cost of about 130 American aircraft. Within a year of the Battle of Midway, Japan's fate in the Second World War was all but sealed. Japanese military leaders were probably cognizant of impending defeat, in a fairly general way, by the time of the June 1944 Battle of the Philippine Sea. All that remained to be determined -- and these turned out to be very important, sensitive political questions -- was how long would it take to bring Japan to final surrender, and what the price in human lives and treasure for the achievement of that purpose would turn out to be.

It goes without saying that by attacking the United States in 1941, Japan had made itself part of the Hitler coalition; and obviously without defeating, or at least substantially containing Japan, the United States would not have been in a position to concentrate and contribute its resources for the defeat of Hitler. But while doing well in the Pacific, the United States encountered some disappointments in the European theatre. Here, the British role was extremely important in the joint Anglo-American effort.

America's entry into the war did much to convince Winston Churchill that the global conflict would ultimately end in an Allied victory. But it also produced a problem for him: how to keep his American, not to mention Russian, allies from involving Britain in costly land warfare of the sort he had always hoped to avoid. The Prime Minister was consistently looking for "inexpensive" ways to victory.

This expressed itself in a rather peculiar "peripheral strategy" advanced by Churchill in the second part of the conflict. It sought to minimize British losses and British involvements at the expense of others, primarily, of course, the Russians. Part of the strategy was to have the Russians do the bulk of "heavy lifting" against Nazi Germany on the eastern front, and to pay for it by having the Americans supply the Russians with the bulk of material aid needed to both sustain and encourage them in their efforts. It also entailed, for practical purposes, the willingness to make political concessions to the Russians at the expense of others, primarily in eastern Europe. On the purely military side, the Churchillian strategy was a nebulous scheme of assorted "pin pricks" aimed at Nazi Germany and totally lacking the seemingly critical ingredient of engaging and destroying the German Armed Forces on the ground.[5]

The professional head of the American military establishment, General George C. Marshall, opposed the Churchill scheme and promoted the idea of a massive, concentrated attack on the Nazis in Western Europe, the sooner the better.[6] But in the United States, understandably, the political leadership, exercised by President Franklin Roosevelt, prevailed in favour of a compromise. The massive, concentrated blow in the form of a cross-Channel invasion of Europe was not abandoned. But it was postponed. It was postponed until mid-1944 by which time the issue of the war in Europe was largely settled and the real question was how much influence on the European continent the Western Powers would be able to maintain.

Churchill and his service chiefs, from the very beginning of the Anglo-American wartime alliance, steered common strategy toward relatively "inexpensive" and also "time-consuming" objectives. The British idea was to avoid massive engagements anywhere, allow the Russians to bear the brunt of the fight as long as possible, and prevent the Americans from stampeding Britain into any costly and dangerous ventures on the European continent. In the 1930s and in 1940-1941, Winston Churchill was a lion in the wilderness. The Churchill of the 1942-1945 period was a man who, not without reasons, to be sure, sought the cheapest possible victory for Britain, no matter how long it might take and no matter how much suffering it might entail for Hitler's victims in Europe.

By the early 1940s, Britain was weakened and impoverished by her efforts. The willingness to bear heavy casualties at home was, understandably, a serious difficulty for the leader. The memories of British defeats at Nazi hands between 1939 and 1942 were clear and painful. If the British were to preserve any kind of position for themselves after the war, they needed to husband their strength and their resources very carefully. If in the process of defeating Hitler, Russia were to be further weakened this would not have been disadvantageous from the British perspective, by any means.

On the other hand, there was a certain balance here that Churchill needed to recognize, and to a degree he did. If Russia made a separate peace with Hitler, that would not have been good news for Great Britain. That alternative needed to be, if at all possible, avoided. And it would not have been good for Britain either if Russia were to conquer most of Europe all to herself in consequence of her war with Hitler. That was also an issue of some importance for Britain, although implicitly Churchill seemed more willing to let Russia dominate east-central Europe then expend British lives and treasure in a strenuous effort to check such a development. Churchill was giving every indication during these latter years of the war that Britain was no longer capable of strenuous efforts. Perhaps he was right.

Having given up on a possible landing action in Europe anytime in 1942, the British and the Americans substituted a seemingly less risky and costly programme for themselves: an invasion of French North Africa, Morocco and Algeria, undertaken in November 1942. Even this enterprise, directed not against the Nazis but against Vichy French troops, who did not have much air support or armour, was viewed by the Allied military leadership with great trepidation.[7] Part of the Allied concern was with the possibility of German intervention by a possible strike through Spain and also hostile action against Gibraltar. Among the Allied military leadership, the nadir of confidence was represented by a naval commander who worried that the Nazis might employ one or more aircraft carriers against the Allied landing contingents. He did not realize that the Nazis did not have any aircraft carriers.[8]

In fact, the North African operation, Torch, proceeded fairly smoothly and with relatively low casualties; the Allied forces, principally American, edged toward Tunisia to engage the Axis retreating westward from Egypt and Libya. This relatively easy victory was a prelude to an Anglo-American summit at Casablanca in January 1943.[9]

The critical strategic direction for the Anglo-American alliance was reached at the Casablanca Conference between Churchill and Roosevelt.[10] Roosevelt did not abandon a European invasion but he endorsed a number of more immediate objectives desired by Churchill. These objectives included:

The invasion of Sicily, its conquest, and the securing of safe passage for Allied shipping in the Mediterranean; some effort to divert German pressure on the Eastern front of an unspecified and presumably distinctly minor character; attempt to enlist the participation of Turkey in the conflict; this was always a fascinating subject for the British although the real value of Turkey's participation had to be somewhat peripheral. (Assuming for example that Turkey gave the Allies access to its European enclave, the strategic foothold would have been less than impressive in location or topography; and given the condition of the Turkish armed forces then, not likely to be maintained for long against Nazi Germany.)

Another agreed-upon objective was to defeat the German submarine attacks in the Atlantic, certainly a laudable and necessary measure; and increase the bombing of Germany, an idea which fascinated Allied military and political leaders of the Second World War, although it was not nearly as effective in any respect, material or psychological, as its wartime proponents hoped and believed that it might be. Strategically most revealing was the agreement to "prepare for a re-entry on the Continent, if Germany weakened." This provision was crucial because it indicated a desire not to defeat Germany by invasion but rather, stripping down the phraseology used, to take advantage of an impending German defeat in order to land Allied forces in Europe. This was hardly aggressive strategy. Because of an alleged shortage of landing-craft, time constraints, and inadequate planning Roundup (invasion of Europe in 1943) was to be scrapped in favour of Husky (invasion of Sicily), that is, a minor operation substituted for a major one.[11]

The Churchillian strategy of 1942-1944, largely accepted by the Americans, was more concerned with engaging the Germans than with defeating them. It was all but explicitly oriented simply to keeping the Allies busy in all sorts of enterprises, none truly critical, while waiting for Germany to collapse or perhaps be defeated by the Russians, or perhaps a combination of the two. All the Mediterranean adventures in the Churchill version were meant to be fairly inexpensive and low-risk "shows", in part for the benefit of the public at home — British and American — and also for the benefit of Stalin and the Russians to make sure that they stayed in the fight and did not conclude a separate peace with Germany.[12]   Churchill's idea of occupying the island of Rhodes, which so provoked General Marshall, was a good example of this seemingly aimless strategy.[13]   In 1942 and 1943, contrary to legend, Churchill's Balkan designs had very little to do with meeting the Russians "as far to the east as possible". Their major implicit premise was to avoid and minimize British casualties, with the ghosts of the Dardanelles campaign of the First World War always in the back of Churchill's mind.

The irony of the situation, however, was that -- apart from political consequences such as allowing Stalin to occupy all of east-central Europe -- timidity in warfare is rarely, ultimately, the least expensive way of waging war. Nazi casualties were at their lowest and Allied casualties relative to them at their highest precisely when Hitler's warfare was at its most audacious, when Blitzkrieg ruled. Prolonging wars has its own risks and costs. One such cost was illustrated in the arduous Allied campaign up the boot of Italy. Relatively low casualties, if suffered in many places and over a long period of time, may eventually add up to a whole lot more than those resulting from one quick, audacious and successful blow.

Even when agreed upon "in principle" Anglo-American commitment to an invasion of Europe was always somewhat fragile. Note the following observation by General Dwight Eisenhower on 5 May 1942:

> Bolero is *supposed* to have the approval of the Pres and Prime Minister. But the struggle to get everyone behind it, and to keep the highest authority (!) from wrecking it by making additional commitments of airship-troops elsewhere is never-ending.

> The actual fact is that not 1 man in 20 in the Gov't (including the W[ar] and N[avy] Depts) realizes what a grisly, dirty, tough business we are in! They think we can buy victory.[14]

The process by which all Allied strategic decision-making was accomplished was characteristically democratic in its features. There were ample discussions, consultations, and meetings at various levels, even continuing dialogue between the parties, as well as all sorts of discussions conducted by politicians and military experts within the camp of each party. By some accounts, the time spent by Allied military and political leaders in multi-member conferences alone on issues of strategy between the end of 1941 and the beginning of 1944 was 90 days or three months. There was a familiar politics of interest groups -- by service, area, and nationality. There was also an unwritten and even unspoken rule in all of this, and that was the rule of consensus. Joint actions were seen as requiring joint approval. The strategy of both Britain and the United States could only be worked out subject to the ultimate satisfaction of both parties. Compromises might be necessary to achieve this, because mutual agreement was of the essence.

Looking at the respective positions of Britain and the United States in 1941, one could describe Britain as the more senior war partner with more past sacrifices and with more experience in fighting the Axis.[15] On the other hand, the bulk of resources and manpower was clearly on the side of the Americans in 1941 and from then on. Britain was very much in debt to the United States, both literally and figuratively, at the time of Pearl Harbor. Any hope of a future victory for Britain rested preponderantly with the Americans, if not the Russians, or perhaps both. Given the political traditions and institutions of both nations, and the sympathies between them, American "chivalry" toward the British, the willingness to treat Britain as virtually an equal partner in the process of making the big decisions of the war, is perhaps understandable. But that does not deny the consequences which flowed from this "two equal partners" or even "two nearly equal partners" formula.

Institutional habits, and political sympathies, or even the good personal relationship between Roosevelt and Churchill, at least in the early stages of the war, do not wholly explain the American willingness to treat the British as decisional co-equals. Even though General George Marshall personally might have chafed under the apparent British restraint, Roosevelt saw the British view as one that was not without some advantages to the United States. Easing up in Europe meant being able to devote more resources to the conflict in the Pacific. Certainly part of the President's military constituency, especially the Navy, was insistent on such a course and quite vocal about it. Secondly, if one could simplify the British military line to "making life easier" for themselves by holding down casualties, costs, and risks, there was some appeal in this sort of approach for the Americans, too. Clearly, invading Europe in order to *defeat* Nazi Germany, as Marshall would have preferred to do, was much tougher than invading Europe in order to take advantage of an on-going collapse of Nazi Germany as Churchill wanted to do. Democratic politicians, always with an eye on the pulse of public opinion and the prospects of the next election, are generally loath to promote great suffering at home.[16]

At the very outset of joint military planning, Churchill had succeeded in dissuading the Americans from contemplating any heroic adventures on the European continent. As General Eisenhower recorded in his Diaries:

22 July 1942

The last few days have been tense and wearing. We have had numerous conferences with General Marshall and Admiral King on the subject of the Sledgehammer attack. The British have placed themselves on record time and again as being definitely against this attack. First, because they believe it would have no beneficial effect on the Russian situation, and second, because the chances of tactical disaster are very great. The chances for tactical disaster arise out of the disparity between ourselves and the Germans in available military formations and out of the terrible weather conditions that prevail over the Channel during the fall.[17]

And within a few days of this observation, indicating that in his mind, at least, the British would rather accept Russian defeat than risk a cross-Channel operation any time soon, he wrote:

26 July 1942

On July 22, the British chiefs of staff and the prime minister definitely rejected our proposals that any offensive operation of this year should be directed against the French coast. We supported our recommendations with a brief outline of a plan for attacking Cherbourg, which we believe could be done rather effectively and with good chance of sustaining ourselves there.

Since both the British and Americans have been directed to conduct an offensive operation somewhere this year, the rejection by the British of our proposition forces the employment of additional United States troops in some theater other than this. Consequently, the British decision of July 22 may become one of the most far-reaching import on the future conduct of the war.

In effect, it rejects the thought that the allies can do anything to help the Russians remain in the war as an effective fighting force and compels action toward improving our own defensive situation in anticipation of a Russian collapse.

It is quite clear that Roundup may never come off, even with the most intensive and concentrated effort on our part, since the execution of Roundup must depend upon the existence of an effective Russian army, but the action of the British in rejecting Sledgehammer (offensive action against France this year) practically acknowledges that Roundup can never be executed, unless and until the whole German position experiences a very great deterioration. Our only effort to bring about that deterioration is a waiting one, rather than a positive one. [18]

What Allied policy, aimed at winning the war against Hitler, really was by the beginning of 1943 emerges from three top-level memoranda of American, British, and Combined Chiefs of Staff. These memoranda were drawn up for the benefit of the political leaders. The first of these was a Memorandum by the US Chiefs of Staff of 26 December 1942, which took note of the fact "... that Russia is exerting great pressure on Germany and is absorbing the major part of the war effort ... that Russia's continuance as a major factor in the war is of cardinal importance ... that timely and substantial support of Russia, directly by supplies and indirectly by offensive operations against Germany, must be a basic factor in our strategic policy".[19]

The second memorandum by the British Chiefs of Staff of 3 January 1943 declared that "the Russian war effort is also the greatest single drain on the power and hope of Germany and must be sustained and assisted at all costs".[20]

The third Memorandum of the Combined Chiefs of Staff, with Roosevelt and Churchill in attendance 18 January 1943, 5 p.m. at the President's Villa, in Casablanca, was summarized by General Sir Alan Brooke in the following item: "... we shall go on with preparing forces and assembling landing-craft in England for a thrust across the Channel in the event that the German strength in France decreases, either through withdrawal of her troops or because of an internal collapse".[21]

The British attitude toward the question of "how to win the war" was faithfully reflected in the following document contained in the Foreign Relations of the United States' series with the American response in the comments of Admiral WilliamLeahy.

MEETING OF THE COMBINED CHIEFS OF STAFF, 14 MAY 1943, 10.30 A.M., BOARD OF GOVERNORS ROOM, FEDERAL RESERVE BUILDING

PRESENT

UNITED STATES	UNITED KINGDOM
Admiral Leahy	General Brooke
General Marshall	Admiral of the Fleet Pound
Admiral King	Air Chief Marshal Portal
Lieutenant General McNarney	Lieutenant General Ismay
Lieutenant General Embick	Field Marshal Dill
Lieutenant General Stilwell	Field Marshal Wavell
Lieutenant General Somervell	Admiral Somerville
Vice Admiral Horne	Air Chief Marshall Peirse
Major General Street	Admiral Noble
Major General Chennault	Air Marshal Welsh
Rear Admiral Cooke	Lieutenant General Macready
Brigadier General Wedemeyer	Captain Lambe
Colonel Smart	Brigadier Porter
Commander Freseman	Air Commodore Elliot
Commander Long	Brigadier Macleod

Secretariat
Brigadier Redman
Brigadier General Deane
Commander Coleridge

JCS Files

Combined Chiefs of Staff Minutes

1. CONCLUSIONS OF THE PREVIOUS MEETING

Without discussion, the COMBINED CHIEFS OF STAFF accepted the record and conclusions of the 83rd Meeting of the Combined Chiefs of Staff.

2. GLOBAL STRATEGY

SIR ALAN BROOKE said that the British Chiefs of Staff had examined the views of the US Chiefs of Staff on the Global Strategy of the War. There were certain points in this paper with which they were not in entire agreement. They adhered to the views agreed to at Casablanca as set out in CCS 155/1.

The British Chiefs of Staff had two main points of difference which he would like to mention. Firstly, paragraph 2*b* of the US Chiefs of Staff paper referred to an extension of pressure against Japan. Such extension might well cause a vacuum into which forces would have to be poured and would thereby depart from the object set out in paragraph 2*a* of the same paper, i.e., to force an unconditional surrender of the Axis in Europe. Action in the Pacific must be co-ordinated with that in Europe and must not prejudice the defeat of Germany or the war would drag on indefinitely.

The second point of difference was in connection with paragraph 3 of the US Chiefs of Staff paper, i.e., ROUNDUP and its possibilities. *The British Chiefs of Staff believed that the possibilities of ROUNDUP were dependent on the success or failure of the Russians on the Eastern Front. Allied cross-Channel operations could only form a very small part of the whole continental land war, and our effort must be aimed therefore at supporting Russia and thereby creating a situation in which ROUNDUP was possible.*

The views of the British Chiefs of Staff with regard to ROUNDUP might be summed up as follows:

It was their firm intention to carry out ROUNDUP at the first moment when the conditions were such that the operations would contribute decisively to the defeat of Germany. These conditions might arise this year, but in any case, it was the firm belief of the British Chiefs of Staff that they would arise next year. They could be created only by the Russian Army. Our action, therefore, must consist of:

a. Continuing our increasing bombardment of Germany; and
b. Drawing off from the Russian Front as many forces as possible.

On the basis of this definition of ROUNDUP the British Chiefs of Staff had put forward their views on operations in the Mediterranean.

Paragraph 5 of the US paper pointed out how essential it was that Russia should be kept in the war. The British Chiefs of Staff looked on the matter differently and regarded it as essential not only that Russia should be kept in the war but that we should create a situation whereby Russian victories could be achieved.

ADMIRAL LEAHY said that he was unable to see that the US conception of global strategy differed materially from that set out at Casablanca. The intention was now and was then to prepare for and launch cross-Channel operations. The African venture was undertaken in order to do something this year while preparing for cross-Channel operations. Little preparation for the latter had, in fact, been made, since all available US resources had been sent to North Africa. The North African campaign was now completed. If we launched a new campaign in the Mediterranean, then we should continue to use our resources in that area. This would again postpone help to Russia since we should not be able to concentrate forces in the UK and thus cause a withdrawal of German troops from western Europe. If new operations in the Mediterranean were the best way to bring the European war to a conclusion, then they must be undertaken; but if these operations would have the effect of prolonging the war, he saw great difficulties in committing US resources to them.[22]

While Eisenhower was in London, General Marshall sent him on 13 July 1942 the following summary of his strategic views "for your information and for no other person":

The BOLERO plan was based on the conception of an American-British offensive in conjunction with Russian military action. Continued Russian operations are essential to either SLEDGEHAMMER or ROUNDUP. ROUNDUP in the event that the mass of the German ground and air forces are available for defence of the western coasts of Europe appears to be an impracticable operation.

The present action in the Don Basin indicates Russia's possible inability to halt the massed power of Germany and her allies. Considering the distribution of population in regard to density and race, the location of primary agricultural and industrial areas, and the railroad and road net of Russia, it is evident that unless this German offensive is soon halted Russian participation in the war will become negligible in magnitude, with the inevitable result of rendering all planning concerning ROUNDUP and all BOLERO movements (of ground troops at least) vain.[23]

Thus, the General linked all Allied offensive plans in Europe (Bolero, Sledgehammer and Roundup) to the continuing, critical leverage of Russian military effort. He also criticized the British for their "cold feet" attitude, and their diversionary proposals, ultimately accepted, however, by President Roosevelt over Marshall's objections:

It was our understanding that all plans, and every possible arrangement regarding collection of facilities would be pressed to the limit in a desperate endeavor to be prepared to carry out SLEDGEHAMMER with reasonable chances of success to prevent the collapse of the Russian Army. To slow down in arrangements for the purpose of raiding operations appears to be giving priority to minor harassing action over an operation upon which the fate of the British Empire may hang.

The geographical objective of the SLEDGEHAMMER operation, whether it is to be launched across the Pas de Calais or against Brittany, Normandy and/or the Channel Isles, is a subject for planning by the British Chiefs of Staff and you; the locality of its incidence must however be such that the great purpose of the operation can be achieved, namely, the diversion of German forces from the annihilation of Russia.

My view is that the execution of GYMNAST [invasion of North Africa], even if found practicable, means definitely no BOLERO-SLEDGEHAMMER in 1942 and that it would definitely curtail if not make impossible the execution of BOLERO-ROUNDUP in the spring of 1943. Furthermore, GYMNAST would be indecisive and a heavy drain on our resources and if we undertake it we would nowhere be acting decisively against any of our enemies. Naval forces required, particularly as to escort and carriers, would definitely jeopardize our naval position in the Pacific. Admiral King and I are in agreement on this matter and we have advised the President of our views. No operation on the continent of Europe can be successful without full and whole-hearted British support. If the United States is to engage in any other operation than forceful unswerving adherence to full BOLERO plans, we believe that we should turn to the Pacific and strike decisively against Japan with full strength and ample reserves, assuming a defensive attitude against Germany except for air operations. We have so recommended to the President.[24]

On 9 August 1943, the United States Chiefs of Staff drafted a memorandum to be discussed at the 108th, 109th, and 110th meetings of the Combined Chiefs of Staff on 15, 16 and 17 August 1943, declaring that:

It is assumed that Russia will continue to exert increasing and eventually crushing pressure against the German armies massed against her. In the unlikely event of either a separate Russo-German armistice or peace, the strategy of the United Nations will require reexamination. In that case, the defeat of Japan would probably take priority over the defeat of Germany.[25]

Secretary of War Henry L. Stimson travelled to Britain in the summer of 1943 and made a most revealing report to FDR following that trip on 10 August 1943. Stimson proposed that the United States take the leadership in a forthcoming invasion of Europe and recommended that General Marshall be named the commander of the Anglo-American forces because of his "towering eminence of reputation as a tried soldier and as a broad-minded and skilful administrator". His criticism of British unwillingness to engage the Nazis in any substantial way was devastating and clearly worth citing here at some length:

SECRET　　　　　　　　　　　WASHINGTON, 10 August 1943

DEAR MR. PRESIDENT: In my memorandum of last week, which was intended to be as factual as possible, I did not include certain conclusions to which I was driven by the experiences of my trip. For a year and half they have been looming more and more clearly through the fog of our successive conferences with the British. The personal contacts, talks, and observations of my visit made them very distinct.

First: We cannot now rationally hope to be able to cross the Channel and come to grips with our German enemy under a British commander. His Prime Minister and his Chief of the Imperial Staff are frankly at variance with such a proposal. The shadows of Passchendaele and Dunkerque still hang too heavily over the imaginations of these leaders of his government. Though they have rendered lip service to the operation, their hearts are not in it and it will require more independence, more faith, and more vigor than it is reasonable to expect we can find in any British commander to overcome the natural difficulties of such an operation carried on in such an atmosphere of his government. There are too many natural obstacles to be overcome, too many possible side avenues of diversion which are capable of stalling and thus thwarting such an operation.

Second: The difference between us is a vital difference of faith. The American staff believes that only by massing the immense vigor and power of the American and British nations under the overwhelming mastery of the air, which they already exercise far into the north of France and which can be made to cover our subsequent advance in France just as it has in Tunis and Sicily, can Germany be really defeated and the war brought to a real victory.

On the other side, the British theory (which cropped out again and again in unguarded sentences of the British leaders with whom I have just been talking) is that Germany can be beaten by a series of attritions in northern Italy, in the eastern Mediterranean, in Greece, in the Balkans, in Rumania and other satellite countries, and that the only fighting which needs to be done will be done by Russia.

To me, in the light of the postwar problems which we shall face, that attitude towards Russia seems terribly dangerous. We are pledged quite as clearly as Great Britain to the opening of a real second front. None of these methods of pinprick warfare can be counted on by us to fool Stalin into the belief that we have kept that pledge.

Third: I believe therefore that the time has come for you to decide that your government must assume the responsibility of leadership in this great final movement of the European war which is now confronting us. We cannot afford to confer again and close with a lip tribute to BOLERO which we have tried twice and failed to carry out. We cannot afford to begin the most dangerous operation of the war under half-hearted leadership which will invite failure or at least disappointing results. Nearly two years ago the British offered us this command. I think that now it should be accepted -- if necessary, insisted on.[26]

If Churchill could take comfort in the relative safety of his military initiatives, there was, however, no denying a great deal of political anxiety accompanying it. A message from Stalin sent to the British Prime Minister on 15 March 1943 is almost certainly one of the most significant warnings during the war about the likely political consequences of Allied procrastination.

PERSONAL AND SECRET MESSAGE
FROM PREMIER J. V. STALIN
TO THE PRIME MINISTER, Mr W. CHURCHILL[27]

I have received your reply to my message of February 16.

It appears from your communication that Anglo-American operations in North Africa are not being hastened, but are, in fact, being postponed till the end of April. Moreover, even this date is given in rather vague terms. In other words, at the height of fighting against the Hitler troops, in February and March, the Anglo-American offensive in North Africa, far from having been stepped up, has been called off, and the date fixed by yourself has been set back. Meanwhile, Germany has succeeded in moving from the West 36 divisions, including six armoured ones, to be used against Soviet troops. The difficulties that this has created for the Soviet Army and the extent to which it has eased the German position on the Soviet-German front will be readily appreciated.

For all its importance "Husky" can by no means replace a second front in France, but I fully welcome, of course, your intention to expedite the operation.

I still regard the opening of a second front in France as the important thing. You will recall that you thought it possible to open a second front as early as 1942 or this spring at the latest. The grounds for doing so were weighty enough. Hence it should be obvious why I stressed in my previous message the need for striking in the West not later than this spring or early summer.

The Soviet troops fought strenuously all winter and are continuing to do so, while Hitler is taking important measures to rehabilitate and reinforce his Army for the spring and summer operations against the USSR; it is therefore particularly essential for us that the blow from the West be no longer delayed, that it be delivered this spring or in early summer.

I have studied the arguments you set out in paragraphs 8, 9 and 10 as indicative of the difficulties of Anglo-American operations in Europe. I grant the difficulties. Nevertheless, I think I must give a most emphatic warning, in the interest of our common cause, of the grave danger with which further delay in opening a second front in France is fraught. For this reason the vagueness of your statements about the contemplated Anglo-American offensive across the Channel causes apprehension which I cannot conceal from you.

March 15, 1943

In fact, from June of 1941, with British participation only and from Pearl Harbor onwards with American participation, until September of 1943, i.e., the invasion of southern Italy, the Allies never engaged more than 6 Nazi divisions at one time. This was a period of 27 months. Actually, for most of it, that is from June of 1941 until virtually the end of 1942, the only Nazi land forces engaged by the Allies were the 3 German divisions of Rommel's Afrika Korps fighting the British in Libya and Egypt. In contrast, during the same period of time, the Russians fought against an average of perhaps 180 German divisions on the eastern front. As Trumbull Higgins explains:

> From early 1941, when advance elements of Hitler's Afrika Korps began landing in Libya, until the final overture of the cross-Channel invasion in June 1944, the entire strength of the British Empire and Commonwealth intermittently fought between two and eight divisions of the principal Axis power, Germany. On the other hand, during all but the first six months of this same period the Russians contained an average of about one hundred and eighty German divisions in more or less continuous action. Moreover, in the policy advocated by the British, the United States was also compelled to limit its effort against Germany during 1943 and the first five months of 1944 to an average of four or five divisions in actual combat most of the time.[28]

Until the latter part of 1942 the British did not show much promise in opposing the Nazis. Consider Rommel's capture of Tobruk, British stronghold in eastern Libya on 21 June 1942. This victory was effected by the Axis forces in a siege -- if it can be called that -- of only two days because the battle for the town itself did not begin until 20 June. Not only did the Germans and the Italians capture a large garrison army, 45,000 personnel, as prisoners of war but also a huge amount of supplies. These included 1,400 tons of gasoline, 2,000 trucks and 5,000 tons of food. This booty was not only obviously helpful to Rommel. It was also a sorry reflection on the Allied will to resist in a situation where the battle had been more nearly fought to the first shell rather than to the last shell. While Rommel did not get much support from Hitler, obsessed with the Eastern Front, the Desert Fox was neither delayed nor exhausted by Allied resistance, a most telling development.

James Lucas in his subsequent account says that:

> To British strategists, Tobruk had little real significance but politicians of both sides saw it in propaganda terms. Churchill considered its fall grievous, affecting the reputation of the British arms, Hitler made Rommel a field marshal for his victory and, not to be outdone, Mussolini promoted to the same rank his senior commanders, Cavallero and Bastico.[29]

It was quite natural, one would think, that Churchill was greatly dismayed by the events at Tobruk, regardless of the feelings of those anonymous British strategists who apparently saw no cause for concern in the easy collapse of their defences.[30]

The most publicized Allied victory against Nazi Germany until the invasion of Europe in 1944 was El Alamein in October-November 1942. While psychologically no doubt very important, and often paired with the Soviet victory at Stalingrad, it was, in fact, a relatively small-scale operation. Out of the 93,000 Axis troops facing Field Marshal Montgomery's 177,000, only about 40,000 were German and of these 10,000 were captured by the British. In Stalingrad, the Russians destroyed an army of 300,000 German soldiers and officers, and took 91,000 prisoners, among them 24 generals and a field marshal. This was a war on a much different scale.

On 12 May 1943 the Axis troops in Tunisia surrendered to the Allies; a total of 238,243 Axis German and Italian soldiers marched into Allied prisoner of war camps. Lack of shipping, air transport, and military aircraft to screen the evacuation of these troops was largely responsible for the Allies' rich booty of POWs. On 17 May, for the first time since Italy had entered the war on 10 June 1940, an Allied convoy sailed through the Strait of Gibraltar and continued all the way across to the Suez Canal without being attacked by anyone; no surface ships, no submarines, no airplanes, no shore batteries anywhere, challenged it.

In Italy the mood was one of despair. Public faith in an Axis victory, in Mussolini, and in Hitler, was at its lowest ebb. The defeats at El Alamein and at Stalingrad were now followed by the collapse in Africa. Most Italians, including many government and military officials, were eagerly looking to the possibilities of disengagement from Hitler's transparently failed, disastrous cause. No high-powered intelligence service was required for any reasonably attentive outside observer to notice these developments.[31]

The Allies were now presented with a unique opportunity of bringing the war to an end much earlier than might have been possible before the conclusion of the African campaign. In mid-May, the German position in the Mediterranean was very weak. The Nazis had no strong naval units to challenge the British. The Nazi air force was no longer a strong presence in the region.[32] The reliability, energy, and enthusiasm, of the Italian navy and armed forces were all very much in doubt. And two strategic prizes were within easy grasp of Allied military power -- Sardinia and Corsica. Because both of these islands could only be supplied by sea and air transport, their defence presented a particularly difficult task for the Nazis, one which it seemed even then they might be willing to forego altogether out of sheer, inexorable necessity, for lack of ships and planes. This was, from an Allied perspective, the optimum match-up between one side's strong suit and the other's weak suit.

In fact, within a few months of the Allied victory in Tunisia, the Germans did actually evacuate Corsica, and in the fall of 1943 it became the first part of European France to come under the authority of the French resistance movement. Sardinia was abandoned by the Germans in early September. The capture of Corsica, in particular, by roughly the middle of 1943, would have put the Allies in a highly advantageous strategic position, threatening to roll up the Nazis' whole European stronghold from the south-west.

Indeed, as Trumbull Higgins observes:

> From Sardinia, and its natural corollary, Corsica, it would have been infinitely simpler to have cut off the bulk of Italy by landings in Liguria or Tuscany without fighting all the way up the crenellated boot of the peninsula. Alternatively, and of far greater potential importance, as actually took place in 1944, the still-unfortified and

under-garrisoned coast of southern France might have been assaulted in 1943 from this Sardinian-Corsican *point d'appui.*

But there was a problem:

The trouble with Sardinia may have been that too obviously it did lead somewhere, and Mr. Churchill's careful and patient policy of winning American acquiescence in what is too often represented as a strategy of opportunism or expediency could not tolerate such an honest and logical anticipation of the future.[33]

Although Corsica is a largely mountainous, rocky island, it contains a substantial plain in its northern portion readily adaptable to the deployment of air power. And its location is all but synonymous with strategic opportunity. The island is only about 60 miles from the Italian mainland and it lies within less than 200 air miles of all the major industrial and population centres of northern Italy, including Genoa, Turin, Milan, Bologna, Verona and Padua. Its capture and use, analogous to the American transformation of Okinawa in the Pacific, could have put tremendous pressure on Italy to abandon its alliance with Nazi Germany. If, in consequence of the developing situation, the Italian armed forces were willing to assist the Allies, a penetration of only 100 miles in the Emilia Romagna region facing Corsica, from Livorno to Ravenna, would have cut off all of southern and central Italy from the north.

Even without any landings in north-central Italy, air bases in Corsica would have given the Allies an opportunity of severing Italy in two by massive bombing and strafing of the 100 mile corridor. This might have created a highly unwelcome problem for the Germans because it would have brought the war to the heart of Western Europe and bypassed the mountains of southern and central Italy which subsequently Field Marshal Kesselring was able to use as highly effective obstacles to Allied advance in 1943 and 1944. Corsica presented an even more exciting opportunity for the Allies in still another way. It lies less than 200 miles from the port of Marseilles in southern France, only 150 miles from the naval base of Toulon, and scarcely more than 100 miles from Nice. Although the Nazis occupied southern France on 11 November of 1942, they did not occupy the Mediterranean coast, and even more importantly, they had no opportunity of creating any sort of fortifications there, let alone anything analogous to the Atlantic Wall along the northern and western coasts of France. Hitler had stationed most of his troops charged with the task of repelling an Allied invasion of the continent in northern and north-western France. Hard pressed on the Eastern Front, the Nazis did not have huge, discretionary reserves to accommodate unforeseen emergencies. A massive blow from the south, anchored in Corsica, would have been difficult for them to parry.

If the Allies followed the scenario of invasion-through-southern-France, there would have been only one practical way to move north so as to trap Nazi armies in northern and north-western France and move toward the German borders. The road to central France lay through the Rhone River valley. Any concentration of Nazi land forces in this narrow corridor would have enabled the Allies to deploy their air superiority to maximum effect. Once again, here, too, the more dramatic opportunity -- an invasion of France from the south -- had its less grandiose but still very valuable back-up. Whatever the Allies chose to do once in possession of the island, Hitler would have been likely to divide his forces in France from north to south against the contingency of Allied attack in the Toulon-Marseilles area.

Of course, all military operations involve costs and risks. Neither seemed terribly high in the spring and summer of 1943. There was the possibility that Sicily in Axis hands would create difficulties for Allied shipping in the Mediterranean. But that scenario rested on the unlikely chance of a great Nazi-Axis revival in which Hitler -- or perhaps Hitler and Mussolini -- would plough huge new resources into Sicily in the form of ships, planes and submarines.

In the upshot, Allied decision-makers in full conformity with democratic, committee-style processes, acted -- very slowly -- to finally carry out in July the least imaginative and least useful operation possible, the invasion of Sicily. Sicily was but a prelude to a tedious advance up the Italian peninsula, with no particular effect on the outcome of the war as a whole but with significant Allied casualties.

Ironically, Sicily, although much nearer to the African coast than either Sardinia or Corsica, was more easily defensible for the Axis because the distance between it and the Italian mainland -- through the strait of Messina -- was so narrow as to be comparable with a major river or bay crossing as between, say, San Francisco and Oakland. No navy would be needed here, and shore batteries could easily cover the passage of troops from one coast to the other.

But perhaps this was the best decision that a multinational, multiservice committee could reach, especially when we keep in mind that, without powerful political compulsion applied from outside, such committees tend to register, above all, every participant's projected anxieties and difficulties. Avoiding the risk of failure (the MacClellan syndrome) is a more prevalent professional military attitude than is the willingness to take chances. The Allies invaded Sicily on 10 July, virtually two months after the victory in Tunisia.

General Eisenhower himself left us this appraisal:

> ... if the real purpose of the Allies was to invade Italy for major operations to defeat that country completely [and not just clear the Mediterranean for Allied shipping] then I thought our proper initial objectives were Sardinia and Corsica. Estimates of hostile strength indicated that these two islands could be taken by smaller forces than would be needed [for] ... Sicily, and therefore the operation could be mounted at an earlier date. Moreover ... this would force a much greater dispersion of enemy strength in Italy [because Sicily] lies just off the mountainous toe of the peninsula.[34]

General Omar Bradley in his autobiography left us this illuminating insight into Allied decision-making with respect to the Sicilian campaign:

> Seldom in war has a major operation been undertaken in such a fog of indecision, confusion and conflicting plans ... Much of the blame for the mistakes could be attributed to the unresolved conflicting views of the Combined Chiefs -- the inevitable compromises of coalition warfare.[35]

In his memoirs, Field Marshal Montgomery observed that:

> If the planning and conduct of the campaign in Sicily were bad, the preparation for the invasion of Italy, and the subsequent conduct of the campaign in that country, were worse still.[36]

> During the operations it was difficult to get things decided quickly. The responsible Cs-in-C had their headquarters widely dispersed; they did not live together. Eisenhower, the Supreme Commander, was in Algiers; Alexander, in command of the land forces, was in Sicily; Cunningham, the Naval C-in-C was in Malta; whereas Tedder, the Air C-in-C had his headquarters in Tunis. When things went wrong, all they could do was send telegrams to each other. It took time to gather them together for the purpose of making joint decisions.[37]

Judging by the Eisenhower comments, no one was really happy with the way the operations in Sicily and Italy were designed, not even the Supreme Commander. Much of the reason for this lay in the method of decision -- an ultra-democratic committee process in which power and responsibility were so diffused that ultimately no one mind and no one will could possibly prevail. The Supreme Commander was, in effect, a Chairman of the Board, convoking the participants for the purpose of reaching collective judgments from all sorts of disparate perspectives. This was a task probably analogous to writing a symphony by committee consensus. Theoretically empowered to make the "final decisions", Eisenhower was diplomatically and democratically loath to have people unhappy about his choices, and generally sought to bring everyone into one big tent.

The principles of the Allied decision-making system emphasized inclusion, participation, and, ultimately consensus in imitation of democratic legislative bodies. Since the command Eisenhower exercised involved leadership of two national armed forces -- British and American -- the position was, in some respects, a diplomatic one. It required the agreement of two sovereign nations to put into effect a common course of action. Ostensibly, democratic states in their domestic politics could avoid the hurdle of unanimity. They could enact policies and decisions by majorities or perhaps even pluralities; in fact, the tendency of democratic states has always been to look for widespread agreement on all things considered "important": thus the requirement of a qualified majority, two-thirds or three-fifths, typically, for constitutional amendments in many democracies. During Eisenhower's tenure as Supreme Commander, the United States Senate, while ostensibly operating under majority rule on all "ordinary" legislation, retained the privilege of filibuster for its individual members; the implication was that people might disagree and a majority might prevail, but it was prudent not to make anyone, especially any significant number of participants, very unhappy as opposed to, say, mildly disappointed.

The Allied system emphasized having the representatives of all services of both nations equally informed of all proposed actions; equally enabled to discuss them, and, it put a premium on general agreement, and, therefore, for practical purposes, compromise. Bold strokes are rarely produced by committee compromises.[38] In addition, Eisenhower was always subject to external interposition by the political leaders in Washington and London, by the Allied Combined Chiefs of Staff; and also, for practical purposes, by leading military personalities in each country, especially General

George C. Marshall in the United States, and General, and later Field Marshal, Sir Alan Brooke, in Great Britain.

Among some of Eisenhower's admirers, there has been a disposition to reject demeaning characterizations of the General's role, either in Africa or in London or in Western Europe. Conspicuous among these has been Stephen Ambrose. But even Ambrose presents evidence which suggests that the reality of Eisenhower's role was a good deal less glamorous than has often been claimed for him.

On the one hand, Ambrose says that:

> Eisenhower would never allow himself to be made into the chairman of the corporation, the man who maintained contact with the outside world while letting a board composed of Cunningham, Alexander, and Tedder run the show. The British wanted him to deal with the French and the US War Department, while turning operations over to a committee of British generals and admirals. It would have been easy enough for Eisenhower to accept that role, to spend the war pacifying Giraud and de Gaulle, entertaining visiting dignitaries, holding press conferences, and announcing victories. But he was convinced that the British system was inadequate to the demands of modern war, that whatever decisions had to be made the Supreme Commander should make, freely, 'under the principle of unified command'. He promised Marshall, 'I will be constantly on my guard to prevent any important military venture depending for its control and direction on the 'committee' system of command'.[39]

On the other hand, Ambrose emphasizes the "power of personality" allegedly making it possible for Eisenhower to exercise his role;[40] admits that Eisenhower on apparently more than one occasion referred to himself as "chairman of the board",[41] and, more importantly still, gives some background evidence of that role including the testimony of General Sir Alan Brooke. He says:[42]

> The CIGS [Chief of the Imperial General Staff] was especially worried about Eisenhower. 'The main impression I gathered was that Eisenhower was no real director of thought, plans, energy or direction'. Brooke feared that the Supreme Commander was 'just a co-ordinator, a good mixer, a champion of inter-Allied co-operation'. He wondered if those abilities were sufficient for the task at hand and doubted it. Years later, in looking over the diary entry, Brooke commented that he would repeat every word of it.

Eisenhower was 'a past-master in the handling of allies', he said, 'entirely impartial and consequently trusted by all. A charming personality and good co-ordinator. But no real commander'. Brooke thought it fortunate that Eisenhower had [Bedell] Smith to help him.

Eisenhower himself put the decision-making situation in this perspective:

In a war such as this, when high command invariably involves a president, a prime minister, six chiefs of staff, and a horde of lesser 'planners', there has got to be a lot of patience -- no one person can be a Napoleon or a Caesar ... It's a backbreaking job to get a simple battle order out, and then it can't be executed for from three to four months.[43]

Within a fortnight of the Allied invasion of Sicily, on 25 July 1943, another momentous event occurred. Mussolini was ousted from power in Italy. The Fascist Grand Council voted 19 to 7 to strip Mussolini of the command of the Italian armed forces and proposed that this power be exercised by King Victor Emmanuel III. At a meeting between the Duce and the King, held within a few hours of the Grand Council action, Mussolini was arrested on the King's orders and imprisoned on the island ofPonza.

That this event took place was in itself a strong testimonial to the widespread Italian unhappiness with the war and the Nazi alliance. That Mussolini could not retain even the support of the leaders of his own party was obviously the last straw. If the Grand Council did not back him, who in Italy would? The immediate reaction to this event in the Italian armed forces was widespread defection, and attempts to forge new links with the Allies and also with anti-Axis resistance movements in areas where Italian units were stationed such as Albania, Greece, and Yugoslavia.

Clearly, the on-going defection of Hitler's principal Axis partner -- Italy -- presented a major new opportunity to the Allies. If anything were to be done about it, it needed to be done quickly, for there was every reason to believe that Hitler would be less than tolerant of what he was bound to regard as Italian treachery. The Fuehrer was not known for a forgiving attitude, and it was clear that he would very likely undertake some drastic action not only to punish his former allies but also to safeguard the Nazi position in southern and south-western Europe.

On 26 July, a new Italian government was formed under the premiership of Marshal Pietro Badoglio. In addition to proclaiming martial law throughout the country, Badoglio issued a decree which instantly dissolved the Fascist party. No clearer sign of the new regime's direction could have been given, nor could it have been given more quickly, although, nominally at least, Italian troops in Sicily did continue to offer resistance to the Allies.

With German troops in Sicily, and in some numbers on the mainland, and with Hitler on his neck, Badoglio needed to be rather prudent. Peace negotiations between Italy and the Allies did not begin, however, until 2 August, and they were not concluded until 3 September; agreement was not made public until 8 September in an announcement by General Eisenhower, confirmed by a subsequent Badoglio radio broadcast. Alas, on 10 September, the Nazis, completing earlier incursions, swept upon the Italian mainland like vultures, occupying the northern cities and Rome, and disarming or taking control of 43 Italian divisions throughout the country as well as southern France and the Balkans. A large portion of the Italian navy, though not quite half, was seized by the Nazis, while the rest sailed to British ports in the Mediterranean. Ironically, on 11 September, the Nazis evacuated Sardinia because -- obviously -- they regarded its defence as no longer tenable.

The great democratic powers proved themselves in July and August and early September of 1943 to be the very opposite of what certain liberal theoreticians believe them to be. They were amazingly lacking in all those vaunted qualities of flexibility, responsiveness, and adaptability which, at a critical juncture in the Second World War, would have been so helpful and could have conferred enormous advantages upon them.

Apart from the particular question of how General Eisenhower operated within the Allied military command structure, is the more important issue of how that command as a whole performed its tasks.

According to [Harold] Macmillan [British political representative at Eisenhower's Headquarters] on 29 July 1943, "I spent from 9 to 12 going backwards and forwards between my own office and AFHQ [Allied Forces Headquarters] and conversation with General Eisenhower and Bedell Smith ... Poor Eisenhower is getting pretty harassed. Telegrams (private, personal and most immediate) pour in upon him from the following sources:

(i)   Combined Chiefs of Staff, his official masters.
(ii)   General Marshall, Chief of US Army, his immediate supervisor.
(iii)   The President.
(iv)   The Secretary of State.

(v)   Our Prime Minister (direct).
(vi)   Our Prime Minister (through me).
(vii)   The Foreign Secretary (through me).

All these instructions are naturally contradictory and conflicting. So Bedell and I have a sort of parlour game in sorting them out and then sending back replies saying what *we* think ought to happen. As this rarely, if ever, coincides with any of the courses proposed by (i), (ii), (iii), (iv), (v), (vi), or (vii), lots of fun ensues. But it gets a bit wearing, especially with this heat'.

... though the Germans disagreed among themselves, they were capable of acting. While the Allied governments and soldiers debated, the Germans started four more divisions on the road to Italy -- they even went to the extreme of withdrawing two SS Panzer divisions from the eastern front ...[44]

Had they moved much more quickly to strike a deal with the Italians after 25 July and taken advantage of it, the Allies would have been in position to occupy many critical locations in northern and central Italy.[45] They would have been able to add many Italian divisions to their own forces. The German military in Sicily and southern Italy could have been trapped, with blocked retreat routes and no realistic possibilities of logistical support. In northwestern Italy, in the region of Genoa and westward, an important beachhead for the invasion of southern France might have been established. Airborne allied troops could have been landed at major Italian airports north of Rome. Allied warships could have sailed into some Italian ports, especially Genoa. The Nazis might even have been forced into waging war in the tough Alpine mountain passes, on the very doorstep of the German Reich, especially if they sought, belatedly, to invade northern Italy.

In warfare, quite a bit could be accomplished in just a few weeks' time militarily -- if there is both willingness and ability to do it. Hitler's Nazis proved it in Poland, in Norway, and in Denmark, in France, and in the Balkans. In all those cases, they took much less time to consummate major acts of aggression than it took the Allies to produce no more than a publicly announced verbal formula, which is basically all that was achieved in Italy by the Allies between 25 July and 8 September 1943.

Any suggestion that Britain and the United States were presented with a totally surprising, unexpected situation in the ouster of Mussolini in July requires more than the proverbial grain of salt. It would be like saying that a man who was about to cross the Sahara in mid-summer could not anticipate that heat and lack of water might be obstacles in his way. Even a mediocre intelligence service could have told the Allies, months before the Duce's ouster, that Italy was a very unhappy Axis ally, teetering on the brink of collapse and defection. What was the Allied High Command doing with its time and resources?

Needless to say, great opportunities in war, as in life, are not everyday occurrences. There can be little doubt that the military-political mechanisms of the democratic Allies, through an inherent propensity to discord, stalemate, and delay, made a strongly negative contribution to the Allied war effort in the summer of 1943 on the Italian peninsula.[46]

During the Allies' "months of opportunity" in Italy, mid-May through August of 1943, the possibilities of great victory were simply given away through a combination of Anglo-American rigidity and timidity. The rigidity was reflected, in part, in the American position that any action in Italy or the Mediterranean as a whole, no matter the circumstances, was but a British diversion from the "true" objective -- the cross-Channel attack in northern France. There was, in effect, no such thing on the part of the Americans as adjusting to new, and, perhaps at least partly, unexpected opportunities.[47] By the latter part of 1943, Roosevelt and Marshall were impatient with British "trickery" and had their feet completely "in cement" with respect to "Overlord"; and so also, in response to their decisive attitude, did Eisenhower.

The other aspect of Western rigidity (and timidity) lay in the interpretation of the unconditional surrender formula. During the summer of 1943, there were increasing indications that units of the Italian armed forces -- not necessarily all of them, but certainly many, had had quite enough of their alliance with Germany. They would have been willing, and were demonstrably interested, in "switching sides" from the Nazis to the Allies. This was hardly a matter of mere sympathy or gallantry or even treacherous attempts to gain an advantage by going over to the winning side. There was *no* way for Italy to leave the war without incurring German reprisals, through the agency of Nazi occupation of the country, unless -- in collaboration with the Allies -- the Italian armed forces could prevent that from occurring. The Italian initiative was, therefore, all but inevitable, an attempt at self-preservation.

Admittedly, the Allies had committed themselves to the unconditional surrender formula. But what occurred in July of 1943 was an opportunity to pay some lip-service to this idea in more or less vague diplomatic declarations, while taking practical measures to help win the war against the principal Axis power. Helping Italy and being helped by Italy would have magnified Allied resources. It might have significantly shortened the war. It could have given the Allies great strategic opportunity in the south-west of Europe. The Russians would have been, no doubt, suspicious and unhappy. But they were always suspicious and unhappy. Stalin was not a man with a sunny, positive disposition. Would Allied collaboration with Italian navy, air force, or army, to gain an advantage on the Nazis, have been sufficient to cause Stalin to seek a separate peace with Hitler? Probably not. By 1943 a lot of blood separated Stalin and Hitler even though, admittedly, Stalin was not a sentimentalist.

What is of special interest here, is that Italian-Allied collaboration would almost certainly have enabled the Allies to conduct operations at a range, and in a manner, not otherwise possible. Airports, and harbours not ordinarily accessible to the Allies, could have been with Italian co-operation and assistance. Winston Churchill's favourite excuse for strategic passivity -- lack of landing-craft -- might have been obviated.[48]

When the Nazis seized Norway in 1940 and Crete in 1941, they did not even know what a landing-craft was. The use of ships and paratroopers was sufficient then to produce relatively quick Nazi victories. In Italy in 1943, it was not beyond the realm of possibility for the Allies to sail ships laden with troops and supplies into major Italian ports given a degree of co-operation from the local military authorities. Such measures could have trapped German forces in the southern part of the Italian peninsula and given the Allies air bases close to Germany's more vulnerable locations and transportation routes. Above all, they would have opened the way to an invasion of France from the south where, ultimately, it might have been more feasible without the obstacle of the Atlantic Wall.

But as so often on the Allied side in the Second World War, rigidity and timidity were the key strategic responses. An earlier invasion of Europe would have accomplished two valuable purposes. Many lives of European peoples would have been saved from Hitler's killing machine. (Ironically, even fewer Germans might have died if the war had been ended sooner.) Stalin's Soviet Union could have been held off from occupying most of East Central Europe, including parts of Germany and Austria, if the Allies had acted sooner. The history of the Cold War could have been profoundly altered by different results on the battlefield. If the objectives of fighting in the Second World War were to prevent any single power from dominating the continent of Europe, and to maintain self-determination for the nations of Europe, allowing the Soviets to advance as far as they did was contrary to both of them".[49]   It was a costly concession of weakness.

A completely safe, "guaranteed" war is not only unimaginative. It has its own costs. If the argument is made that the Western powers were faced with the unpalatable, if not unacceptable, choice of trading the lives of their own citizens for the lives of other countries' citizens, its hidden assumption needs to be confronted. Only a great lack of confidence in one's own ability would dictate the opinion that an invasion of Europe in 1943 would have -- necessarily -- led to greater casualties and less chance of success than it would or did a year later. The question of Allied losses would inevitably be decided by how skilful the Allied attack might be, how well and how quickly it might be executed.

The 90-division ceiling on the American Army established in 1943, a 90 division gamble, as US Army historian Maurice Matloff called it, was a clear indication that the United States, even together with Britain and all its other possible Western Allies could only defeat, and would only try to defeat, Nazi Germany in Europe with very substantial Soviet assistance. If, somehow, Stalin negotiated a separate peace with Hitler, even in the second half of 1944, or earlier, allowing close to two million Nazi troops to be sent westward, there were simply no adequate reserves of trained and equipped American and British manpower to compensate for this. Why was this "ceiling" decision taken by the United States in the first place? To maintain high levels of war production, industrial output more generally, and the over-all standard of living. The Roosevelt administration was eager not to push domestic austerity beyond generally acceptable, largely "civilized levels".[50]   So, the formula seemed to be "victory with Soviet help" or "no victory". The great, explicit reliance on the Soviet war effort for sustaining the Allied attack in the West was expressed by General Marshall shortly before D-Day, when he declared:

> We are about to invade the Continent and have staked our success
> on our air superiority, on Soviet preponderance, and on the high
> quality of our ground combat units.[51]

NOTES

[1]   Ernest J. King, *US Navy At War, 1941-1945, Official Reports to the Secretary of the Navy* (Washington, DC: United States Navy Department, 1946), p. 47.

[2]   Walter Lord, *Incredible Victory* (New York: Harper & Row, 1967), pp. IX-X. See also William Ward Smith, *Midway, Turning Point of the Pacific* (New York: Crowell, 1966). As he points out, after Midway, the Japanese "never again enjoyed the margin

of superiority they had held during the first six months of the war. By virtually destroying Japan's carrier air, the US Navy at Midway turned the tide in the Pacific": p. 2.

3   See Charles A. Willoughby and John Chamberlain, *MacArthur, 1941-1945* (New York: McGraw-Hill, 1954), p. 7. Note also William Manchester, *American Caesar, Douglas MacArthur, 1880-1964* (Boston: Little, Brown, 1978). No other military leader enjoyed the spotlight as much as MacArthur, but he was also an extraordinary intellect and a man whose knowledge and memory were legendary, and so was his ability to inspire confidence and loyalty in his subordinates, pp. 8-9. George Marshall considered him "our most brilliant general" although he personally disliked him, p. 4. Some of the work about MacArthur is so hostile to him, it is almost amusing. Note, e.g., Gavin Long, *MacArthur As Military Commander* (London: B. T. Batsford, 1969). This author does his best to diminish the General's military reputation and attributes his many successes to all sorts of factors, including the actions of others (e.g., Admiral William Halsey and the Joint Chiefs of Staff in Washington, DC), as well as to "luck", pp. 226-227. This is probably a little like attributing luck to the New York Yankees when Babe Ruth, Lou Gehrig, and Joe DiMaggio led the team.

4   See Frank O. Hough, *The Island War, The United States Marine Corps in the Pacific* (Philadelphia: J. B. Lippincott Company, 1947), pp. 80, 70.

5   "Months before Pearl Harbor, US military planners had suggested "that only land armies can finally win wars" and had proposed the building of a massive army of 8.75 million men to be used by 1943 in Central Europe, an area designated 'our principal theater of war'. Citing the probability of negative public reaction, President Roosevelt had disagreed at that time and even suggested decreasing army size. Even after Pearl Harbor, he had recoiled against the massive casualties that would be suffered in such a strategy and had found solace in Churchill's indirect approach, with its emphasis on a relatively easy invasion of French North Africa as well as the use of air and naval rather than massive land power." Maurice Matloff (ed.), The War Department, United States Army in World War II, *Strategic Planning for Coalition Warfare 1943-1944* (Office of the Chief of Military History, Department of the Army: Washington, DC, 1959), p. 9.

6   Note Correli Barnett, "Anglo-American Strategy in Europe", pp. 174-189; Ann Lane and Howard Temperley (eds.), *The Rise and Fall of the Grand Alliance, 1941-1945* (London: Macmillan Press, 1995), p. 179. In a 1942 memorandum Marshall's views for FDR were as follows: "[France] is the only place in which a powerful offensive can be prepared and executed by the United Powers in the near future. Moreover in other localities the enemy is protected against invasion by natural obstacles and poor communications leading towards the seat of hostile power or by elaborately organized and distant outposts. Time would be required to reduce these and to make the attack effective".

"It is the only place where the vital air superiority over the hostile land areas preliminary to a major attack can be staged by the United Powers. This is due to the existence of the network of landing fields in England and the fact that at no other place could massed British air power be employed for such an operation".

"It is the only place in which the bulk of the British ground forces can be committed to a general offensive in co-operation with United States forces. It is impossible, in view of the shipping situation, to transfer the bulk of the British forces to any distant region, and the protection of the British Isles would hold the bulk of the divisions in England".

"United States can concentrate and use larger forces in Western Europe than in any other place, due to sea distances and the existence in England of base facilities ...". See also Maurice Matloff, *Command Decisions: Crossroads of Strategy* (Center of Military History, US Army: Washington, DC: 1990): "The divergent approaches of the Allies toward the European war were at first most clearly reflected in the conflict between British and American strategy -- between the peripheral theory, espoused by Churchill and the British staff and the theory of mass and concentration advocated by General Marshall and his staff. The British wanted to hit the German Army at the edges of the Continent and launch a large-scale landing on the Continent only as the last blow against an enemy already in process of collapse; the Americans wanted to concentrate forces early at a selected time and place to meet the main body of the enemy head on and defeat it decisively": p. 385.

[7]   William B. Breuer, *Operation Torch: The Allied Gamble to Invade North Africa* (New York: St. Martin's Press, 1985), recalls that on 1 September 1939 the United States Army had fewer than 130,000 men under arms and not a single armoured division (p. X). The state of unpreparedness was well-nigh difficult to believe. By the summer of 1941 the Army rose to 1.5 million personnel "a majority of them reluctant draftees ... many men trained with broomsticks", (p. XII). On 1 April 1942 General Marshall and then Major General Eisenhower presented FDR with a plan for invasion of Europe in September 1942 (Sledgehammer). FDR approved it but the British, especially General Sir Alan Brooke, the Chief of Staff, saw it as "sheer madness" (p. XIII). All this did not keep FDR from making Molotov think, when he visited the White House in the summer of 1942, that the Allies would launch a "Second Front" in Europe in September.

"Brooke's grand design for victory over Nazi Germany was to bomb the Third Reich day and night, establish a naval blockade of German ports, keep the enemy off balance with commando raids and clever deceptions that would force Hitler to garrison some 2,000 miles of European coastline, strike at German morale with a propaganda blitz, encourage enemy rebellion from within, and conduct military operations on the fringes of the Fuehrer's empire. Brooke proposed launching this strategy with an invasion of Algeria and Morocco, two occupied French colonies in northwest Africa. When these combined pressures indicated a weakening of the

German strength and morale, then -- and *only* then -- should the allies launch a massive assault across the Channel and aim for the heart of Germany": pp. 6-7.

[8] *Ibid.*, p. 15.

[9] Allied losses amounted to 1700 killed, wounded, and missing out of the 65,000 landed and engaged, *ibid.*, p. 254. This compared with D-Day losses of 10,000 out of a force of 130,000 in Normandy in 1944. See Deer and Foot, *op. cit.*, p. 853.

[10] See Alan F. Wilt, "The Significance of the Casablanca Decisions, January 1943", *Journal of Military History*, Vol. 55, No. 4, October 1991, pp. 517-529.

Note the following observation by Walter Dunn, Jr., *Second Front Now, 1943* (University: University of Alabama Press, 1980), on the issue of applying a democratic free-for-all to military decisions, in this case the conference at Casablanca in January of 1943:

"Casablanca was a trade-off — the British wanted to stay in the Mediterranean, and several American leaders had vested interests elsewhere. Admiral King wanted to go on the offensive in the Pacific, and General Henry A. Arnold wanted a major air offensive against Germany. General Marshall alone was a proponent of the cross-Channel attack. Casablanca was a series of vague compromises, all of which diverted effort away from Germany toward British interests in the Mediterranean and American interests in the Pacific": p. 31.

[11] Steve Weiss, *Allies in Conflict, Anglo-American Strategic Negotiations 1938-44* (London: King's College, 1996), pp. 79-80. See also Keith Sainsbury, *Churchill and Roosevelt at War: The War They Fought and the Peace They Hoped to Make* (New York: New York University Press, 1994), on "second front" differences between the President and the Prime Minister, p. 67.

[12] Note Mark A. Stoler, *George C. Marshall, Soldier-Statesman of the American Century* (Boston: Twayne Publishers, 1989): "Contrary to popular opinion [Churchill's] plan did not call for a major invasion of the 'soft underbelly' of southern Europe and was not aimed at checking Soviet advances into the Balkans. Rather it was a strategy of attrition centreing on the use of Allied sea and air instead of land power to bring about a German collapse in the future at minimal cost in Western lives. Blockade, strategic bombing, commando raids, and support of resistance movements, were all emphasized in this strategy as means of weakening Germany but not suffering heavy losses, with Western land offensives limited to peripheral objectives in the Mediterranean".

"Roosevelt was strongly attracted to this British peripheral, or 'indirect', strategy, especially as expounded by the eloquent and overwhelming Churchill during their private sessions at the White House where the Prime Minister was staying as a special guest. Marshall's reaction was much more negative": p. 93. See also Forrest C. Pogue, *George C. Marshall: Organizer of Victory* (New York: Viking Press, 1973).

[13]   The Greek island of Rhodes was occupied by the Axis in 1941. It is located much nearer to the continent of Asia than to Europe, within about 50 miles of the coast of Turkey in the eastern Mediterranean. Its capture would have been probably as helpful to the ultimate defeat of Germany as an attack on Cuba or Bolivia.

[14]   A. D. Chandler, Jr. (ed.), *The Papers of Dwight David Eisenhower, The War Years: I* (Baltimore: The Johns Hopkins Press, 1970), p. 277. "Bolero" was the code name for the transfer of American troops to Britain for the purpose of a cross-Channel invasion of Europe.

[15]   See Alex Danchev, *Very Special Relationship, Field-Marshal Sir John Dill and the Anglo American Alliance* (London: Brassey's Defence Publishers, 1986), addresses the interesting psychological tensions of the Anglo-American alliance including British attitudes of condescension to American "novices" and "upstarts" and also on the debit side, as with Churchill and Dill, the sense of one's own increasing weakness *vis-à-vis* the US: see pp. 38-44.

[16]   See the excellent article by Tuvia Ben-Moshe, "Winston Churchill and the Second Front: A Reappraisal", *Journal of Modern History*, Vol. 62, No. 3, September 1990, pp. 503-537. The author presents this salient and well-supported conclusion: "The strategic conception behind the invasion of northern France proved itself. The invasion shortened the war and produced the largest Western contribution to the German defeat after the victories of the Red Army. If the invasion in the West had not been carried out in 1944, it is very doubtful that the Western democracies could have succeeded in defending their interests in Europe against the Soviet threat. After the event and without foundation, Churchill attributed to himself a clear, coherent strategic conception whose pivot and peak was the invasion of western Europe. If it had failed, he could have contended with the greatest of ease, on the strength of his quality as a writer and a correct presentation of his documents, that he had always opposed the invasion, had warned against it, and had finally been forced to agree to it": p. 537.

[17]   Robert H. Ferrell (ed.), *The Eisenhower Diaries* (New York: W. W. Norton, 1981), p. 72.

[18]   *Ibid.*, p. 73. Harry C. Butcher, *My Three Years with Eisenhower The Personal Diary of Captain Harry C. Butcher, USNR Naval Aide to General Eisenhower, 1942 to 1945* (New York: Simon & Schuster, 1946), on the mood of pessimism in the summer of 1942 surrounding early American "second front" considerations by Eisenhower and his staff in London: pp. 22-23, 27-28, 29, 33, 43. There were indications that in August 1942 the British military didn't think "invasion" was "do-able".

[19]   *Foreign Relations of the United States, The Conferences at Washington, 1941-1942, and Casablanca, 1943* (US Government Printing Office; Washington, DC, 1968), p. 736.

[20]   *Ibid.*, p. 741.

[21] *Ibid.*, p. 628.

[22] *Foreign Relations of the United States, The Conferences at Washington and Quebec 1943* (Washington, DC: Government Printing Office, 1970), pp. 52-54. A British Chiefs of Staff memorandum to the 108th meeting of the Combined Chiefs of Staff, dated 10 August 1943, declared that the invasion of Europe could not be attempted if the Nazis were able to switch as many as 15 divisions from the Eastern Front to the West: p. 484.

[23] Bland (ed.), The Papers of George Catlett Marshall, *op. cit.*, p. 273.

[24] *Ibid.*, p. 274. By early 1943, Marshall became convinced that the British would not co-operate with the United States in launching a cross-Channel attack on Germany "unless the Germans showed signs of weakening", p. 516.

[25] *Foreign Relations of the United States, The Conferences at Washington and Quebec 1943* (Washington DC: US Government Printing Office, 1970), p. 474.

[26] *Foreign Relation of the United States, The Conferences at Washington and Quebec 1943* (Washington, DC: US Government Printing Office 1970), pp. 496-497. Note also message from Presidential envoy Robert Murphy, and General Eisenhower to Secretary Hull and General Marshall of 30 August 1943 reporting Italian perceptions that a Soviet-German rapprochement was clearly in the offing. See A. D. Chandler, Jr. (ed.), *The Papers of Dwight David Eisenhower, The War Years: II* (Baltimore: The Johns Hopkins Press, 1970), p. 1371.

[27] See Ministry of Foreign Affairs, *Correspondence Between the Chairman of the Council of Ministers of the USSR and the President of the USA and the Prime Ministers of Great Britain During the Great Patriotic War of 1941-1945*, Vol. One, July 1941-November 1945 (Salisbury: NC: Documentary Publications, 1978), pp. 105-106. See also Matloff, Strategic Planning, *op. cit.*, p. 285.

[28] Trumbull Higgins, *Winston Churchill and the Second Front 1940-1943* (New York: Oxford University Press, 1957), p. 186.

[29] James Lucas, *War in the Desert: The Eighth Army at El Alamein* (New York: Beaufort Books, 1982), p. 25. See Len Deighton, *Blood, Tears, and Folly, Volume I, An Objective View of World War II* (New York: Harper Paperbacks, 1996): "Germany's titanic assault upon Soviet Russia had shown, to those who wanted to see it, how puny were the forces Britain had deployed. Until the end of 1942 Britain never faced more than four weak divisions out of Germany's total of 200": p. 397.

[30] Note Michael Carver, *Dilemmas of the Desert War, A New Look at the Libyan Campaign, 1940-1942* (London: B. T. Batsford, 1986), pp. 106-128, for a fairly detailed account of Allied confusion and incompetence in this episode.

[31] Allied conduct of the war is, and always will be, ironic in light of the intelligence and other more broadly technological capabilities developed by the British and the Americans, including such devices as Radar and the Ultra decoding system especially.

See Ronald Lewin, *Ultra Goes to War, The First Account of World War II's Greatest Secret Based on Official Documents* (New York: McGraw Hill, 1978), for an illustrative account. See also Arthur D. Larson, "The Secret Side of War: Anglo-American and German Intelligence in World War II", *Journal of Political and Military Sociology*, Vol. 8, No, 1, Spring 1980, pp. 121-124.

[32]   See Alfred D. Chandler, Jr. (ed.), *The Papers of Dwight David Eisenhower, The War Years: II* (Baltimore: The Johns Hopkins Press, 1970). In a 4 June 1943 message to General George Patton, Eisenhower wrote that "The enemy air forces had been swept out of the skies so completely that we could have a parade, if we chose, of all our North Africa forces in one field in Tunisia without any danger from enemy aircraft". p. 1174.

[33]   Trumbull Higgins, *op. cit.*, pp. 207-208.

[34]   Dwight D. Eisenhower, *Crusade in Europe* (New York: Doubleday, 1948), p. 159. Note also Marshal Pietro Badoglio, *Italy in the Second World War, Memoirs and Documents* (London: Oxford University Press, 1948). See pp. 98-99. "In my opinion the real and grave strategical blunder ... was the decision to seize Sicily. The occupation of that island, at the extreme south of Italy, involved the Allies, as they later found to their cost, in fighting their way up the whole length of the peninsula ... Their position would have been entirely different and they would have had a far larger zone of action had they chosen Sardinia. One glance at the map of Italy is enough to prove my contention. The occupation of Sardinia would not have presented greater naval and military difficulties to the Allies than that of Sicily, while their information services ought to have told them that there were fewer enemy forces in Sardinia than in Sicily. A landing between Civitavecchia and Leghorn would have seriously menaced the German lines of communication with southern Italy. And in Sardinia there were good aerodromes for use as bases for fighter aircraft". Badoglio gives credit to Italian troops for expelling the Germans from Sardinia and Corsica, p. 101.

[35]   Omar Bradley, *A General's Life* (New York: Simon & Schuster, 1983), pp. 167-168.

[36]   Field Marshal Bernard Montgomery, *Memoirs* (Cleveland: World Publishing Company, 1958), p. 171.

[37]   *Ibid.*, p. 169.

[38]   Writing of the Sicilian campaign, the noted British military historian, Colonel Seaton, observed that "if the Italian resistance is largely disregarded, then less than four scratch German divisions held between eight and twelve allied divisions for a period of more than four weeks. In the German war diaries the enemy was described almost daily, as 'timid' and 'cautious' ". Albert Seaton, *The Fall of Fortress Europe, 1943-1945* (London: B. T. Batsford, 1981), p. 77.

[39]   Stephen E. Ambrose, *The Supreme Commander: The War Years of General Dwight D. Eisenhower* (New York: Doubleday, 1970), pp. 162-163.

40   *Ibid.*, p. 163.

41   *Ibid.*, p. 337.

42   *Ibid.*, pp. 398-399.

43   Robert H. Ferrell (ed.), *The Eisenhower Diaries* (New York: W. W. Norton, 1981), p. 49. It should be pointed out that neither Napoleon nor Caesar was a democratic leader. See Norman Polmar and Thomas B. Allen, *World War II, America At War 1941-1945* (New York: Random House, 1991), who label Eisenhower as 'brilliant at least in the perceptions of American peers and superiors before Pearl Harbor" (p. 270). On the other hand, they may be credited with the following statement: "His lack of experience in command in the field (a career shortcoming he often lamented before the war), affected judgment of him, particularly in the debate over his conduct of the battlefield in Europe. Eisenhower's immediate subordinates, Gen. Omar N. Bradley and [George] Patton occasionally believed that Ike either was being swayed by the last person to talk to him or had become more British than the British. But more often than not Eisenhower's British commanders disparaged his military competence": p. 271. Compare Norman Gelb, *Ike and Monty* (London: Constable, 1994), p. 431: "there can be no doubt that he performed with great proficiency as managing director of the momentous Allied effort. Horrocks, who called him 'a superb co-ordinator', said, 'I do not believe that anyone else in the world could have succeeded in driving that [American-British] team to the end of the road'. From an uncertain and apprehensive start, he developed gradually, despite his occasional waverings, into a truly commanding, resolute figure": p. 431. Alex Danchev, *Establishing the Anglo-American Alliance: The Second World War Diaries of Brigadier Vivian Dykes* (London: Brassey's 1990), on generally warm feelings for Eisenhower. Note p. 160.

44   Harold Macmillan, *Blast of War* (New York: Harper & Row, 1968), pp. 242-243.

45   Note General Eisenhower's message to Winston Churchill of 29 July 1943, expressing some impatience with political impediments to the military's ability to take advantage of the unfolding Italian situation. "All I urge is that the governments decide quickly ... military opportunity may slip out of our fingers ...". A. D. Chandler, Jr. (ed.), *The Papers of D. D. Eisenhower, II, op. cit.*, p. 1300.

46   See Charles B. MacDonald, *The Mighty Endeavor, American Armed Forces in the European Theater in World War II* (New York: Oxford University Press, 1969): Marshall, King, Arnold and Leahy opposed British 1943 interest in concentrating forces in the Mediterranean to knock Italy out of the war. Cross-Channel attack was their interest and they threatened to transfer assets to the Pacific if the British persisted, p. 134. See Thomas M. Barker, "The Lubljana Gap Strategy: Alternative to Anvil/Dragoon or Fantasy", *The Journal of Military History*, Vol. 56, No. 1, January 1992, pp. 57-85, highly critical of Churchill ideas about pushing north-east from Italy rather than north-west. Note p. 84. Brian H. Reid, "The Italian Campaign, 1943-45:

A Reappraisal of Allied Generalship", *The Journal of Strategic Studies*, Vol. 13, No. 1, March 1990, pp. 1281-61, notes "the lack of clarity in operational aims during the campaign, and also failure to see the French and Italian theatres as part of one picture": p. 159.

[47] See Melton S. Davis, *Who Defends Rome? The Forty-five Days, July 25-September 8, 1943* (New York: The Dial Press, 1972), pp. 232-234, 243, 261, 254-255, 259-273, on contacts between Italy and the Allies in August and September. "On 10 August Roosevelt declared that he did not wish to advance into Italy beyond Rome, let alone into the Balkans. Accordingly, on 12 August Marshall had cabled Eisenhower that his orders remained unchanged despite events in Italy. Harry Butcher wrote in his diary that it was a pity that 'we didn't have the landing craft ready to move the Fifth Army on Naples(!) just as the battle of Sicily was ending'": p. 262.

The day President Roosevelt arrived in Quebec [17 August], along with the foreign ministers of Great Britain and the United States, to hear confirmation of the Italian peace feelers, "[it] was ... clear that [General Giuseppe] Castellano was asking for more than peace; he wanted to arrange for Italy to dump the Germans and replace them with the Allies. This posed quite a question for Roosevelt, who had stated his intention to 'have no truck with fascism in any way'. Of the King and Badoglio, Harry Hopkins, Roosevelt's adviser, said, 'I certainly don't like the idea of these two former enemies changing sides when they know they are about to be defeated and coming over to us in order to get help to maintain themselves in power'": p. 260.

As Melton Davis notes, "... there were those who said that if Badoglio could deliver all of Italy, giving the allies bases closer to central Europe, it would be foolish not to deal with him". [But] "Eden was against the idea, pointing out that all that would be gained would be unopposed landings and Italian co-operation in running railways, ports, etc.; the Allies could no doubt have this anyway, if unconditional surrender were insisted upon": pp. 260-261. Given the Nazi record of ruthless and lightning measures, this was probably one of the silliest opinions ever expressed by a British Foreign Secretary. Nazi planning for the occupation of all Italy began as early as May 1943. See Albert Seaton, *The Fall of Fortress Europe 1943-1945* (London: Batsford, 1981), p. 73. Davis' own conclusion was: "Although the end might have justified the means, the Allies, if they had known the true state of affairs in Italy, could have landed farther north, cut off the German divisions, and avoided bloody battles on the road to Rome. Better still would have been the Eisenhower-preferred plan, submitted at the Casablanca Conference, to invade Sardinia and Corsica rather than Sicily. This, as Eisenhower said, would' ... force a very much greater dispersion of enemy strength in Italy ...'. In the opinion of British commanders, Sardinia would have provided a better base for quick conquest of the peninsula even if it meant bypassing Rome".

"But Churchill, who was leading the Americans 'up the garden path in the Mediterranean', knew that if he expressed such an outright aim, the US Joint Chiefs would turn thumbs down on *any* Mediterranean effort and hopes of taking Rome would be relegated to limbo".

"The plan had also been discarded for fear of 'large-scale counteraction by the enemy', an estimate which was later seen to be inaccurate": *ibid.*, p. 258.

[48] See Robin Edmonds, *The Big Three, Churchill, Roosevelt and Stalin in Peace and War* (London: Hamish Hamilton, 1991), pp. 332-337, on how badly the Western Allies handled their Italian opportunity after the ouster of Mussolini in July 1943, and also how quickly Hitler reacted to it (especially p. 333). Too many cooks, on the Allied side, spoiled the broth, it seemed (see pp. 334-335).

[49] Note, among others, Walter S. Dunn, Jr., *Second Front NOW* (University: University of Alabama Press, 1980).

[50] See Maurice Matloff, *Command Decisions: The 90-Division Gamble* (Center for Military History, US Army, Washington, DC: 1990), pp. 365-381; p. 367 on why the US could not raise a larger army than 10.5 million according to official estimates as late as 1942 and early 1943.

[51] *Ibid.*, p. 411.

9 DEMOCRACIES AT WAR, 1944-1945

Granted human propensity for discordant perceptions, the Allied invasion of Europe in June 1944 was a costly, but wonderful event. At last, the people who represented the most humane values in the terrible conflict were not only back on the Continent, but they were in force, in striking distance of Germany's heartland, and they were victorious. The war seemed to be coming to a close, and for Europe's millions, liberation appeared to be just around the corner.

The Allied campaign in France in 1944 had some welcome parallels to the Nazi blitz of 1940, except that, at last, it was the Nazis themselves who were preponderantly on the receiving end of the bombs and the shells. Following some intense and difficult fighting on the beaches and in the hedgerows of Normandy in June, July, and early August, the Allies broke through the Caen-Falaise pocket and moved rapidly in virtually all directions throughout France. Air power, mobility, and armour, once the monopoly of Nazi armies, were now used by the likes of George Patton, Omar Bradley, and Bernard Montgomery to pursue the retreating Wehrmacht towards the German frontier. It was now the Nazis' turn to be strafed, day and night, all along highways and railroad tracks of France by enemy fighters and fighter-bombers. It was now their turn to find themselves outflanked and surrounded by mobile enemy columns deep inside their own territory.

There was much to celebrate in the Allied military victories in France in the summer of 1944. At last, Europe could see before it the prospect of true liberation from years of oppressive Nazi rule. It was in this respect that the Allied effort in the West differed most remarkably from the events taking place in the East. The liberation of Paris on 25 August 1944 by the Allied armies was truly a joyous event because it was, unlike the Red Army's capture of Warsaw, Riga, Bucharest, or Budapest, a genuine liberation.

No secret police followed in the footsteps of the Allied armies in France. No new mechanisms of subjection were about to be imposed upon the liberated populations. That France would be free in consequence of the victories of the American and British armies, no one in his or her right mind could doubt. But in Poland, Hungary, Romania, the Baltic states,

Czechoslovakia, Bulgaria and Yugoslavia, the situation was not nearly so promising. One yoke would replace another.

In the West, however long the waiting, liberation meant the restoration of the rights of political democracy to the people of Europe. In the most immediate, tangible, and gratifying sense, it meant that people could once again live their lives as they wanted to live them, protected by law in their persons and possessions, and free to think, speak, and act, publicly or privately, in whatever ways most pleased them. Liberty and the rule of law were restored along with suffrage, political associations, and an open, competitive political system. From Allied conquests, no innocent person needed to flee or seek refuge; a statement that could not be made with reference to the conquests of Stalin's armies.

However delayed, however flawed in any aspect of its execution, it was an enormous historical achievement, in virtually all its consequences one of the noblest deeds of human liberation in recorded time.[1] Coincidentally, Overlord not only hastened the day of final victory over Germany but kept a flood of Red Army troops and police contingents out of Western Europe.

When D-Day at last arrived on 6 June 1944, the Soviet armies were already on the pre-war territories of Poland, Romania, and Estonia, and within virtually shouting distance of Hungary and Czechoslovakia. Hitler refused to withdraw any significant forces from the Eastern front to deal with the Allied invasion in France -- until the Battle of the Bulge. The Russians, meantime, advanced to the heart of Poland, and the suburbs of Warsaw on the Wisla (Vistula) by early August. They also marched into Latvia and Lithuania. They had penetrated the borders of the Reich itself in East Prussia. In three months of their summer offensive, the Soviets had advanced over 400 miles westward. It was highly unlikely that the Nazis would be able to contain the next major Soviet thrust whenever it might resume. On 23 August Romania surrendered to the Soviets and on the 25th declared war on Germany. Bulgaria defected from the Nazi camp on 26 August. Soviet penetration of the Balkans was in full swing. Soviet troops entered the territory of pre-war Yugoslavia on 6 September. Finland quit the war two days earlier.

Had the Allied military command, especially and particularly General Eisenhower, acted with more political sensibility, it is quite possible that the capture of Berlin might have been denied to the Soviets, but the main outlines of the Soviet penetration of East-Central Europe were no longer capable of being significantly changed.[2] The Allies simply failed to move fast enough, far enough. A factor of great importance in these developments was the qualitative relationship between the Allied armies on the one hand and the Nazi German army on the other.

With all the "learning" of the previous 5 years, and all the material preparations for D-Day, the Allies were still unable to' match the degree of German superiority over Britain and France in 1940. Given the resource situation on both sides, the German resistance to the Allies in the weeks and months following D-Day was nothing short of remarkable. Unlike the Allies in 1940, the Nazis in 1944 were fighting a two-front war. Their chances of eventual victory were worse than slim.[3] Nevertheless, Hitler's totalitarian army still greatly outperformed the Allies of 1940. It put up a much better fight with considerably fewer resources *vis-à-vis* the enemy.

The most important difference was in air power. The Allies disposed of a huge air force on D-Day, including 5,409 fighters; 3,467 heavy bombers; 1,645 light and medium bombers, and 2,316 transport planes. The Nazis had only 319 aircraft of all types with only 100 fighters among them. This was an aggregate ratio of 40.5 to 1. In effect, the Nazis had no air defence or air capability worth mentioning. Allied airpower was not simply greater; it was overwhelming and devastating.[4] In May of 1940, the ratio of Nazi superiority to the Allies in aircraft numbers, without regard to quality, was a much more narrow 3,609 to 2,772 or, roughly, 4 to 3 ratio. The Allied total consisted of 1,660 British and 1,112 French aircraft. The British did not commit all of their planes to the defence of France, and even if only French aircraft were counted, the ratio between the Nazis and the Allies would have been 3.2 to 1 rather than the all but unreal disparity of 1944.

German troops in France on D-Day were virtually defenceless against Allied aircraft. Nevertheless, the Nazi army, consisting of less than their best military units, many understrength or undersized, achieved a number of objectives never realized by the Allies in the 1940 Battle of France.[5] They held up the enemy advance longer. The Allies did not reach the frontier of Germany until September. Even then, four and five months after D-Day, pockets of German resistance in France itself were still holding out. They inflicted much greater casualties on the enemy, certainly in the several hundred-thousand category. They staged a number of significant counter-attacks of which, of course, the Battle of the Bulge in December 1944 and January 1945, was the most famous, and these had no genuinely equivalent Allied counterparts in the 1940 campaign.

The superiority of the German armed forces (probably the best in the Second World War) under their totalitarian political system -- over the Allied armed forces, under their democratic political system -- could be defined by certain, rather obvious, factual relationships. During the Second World War the Nazis frequently defeated their Allied opponents under circumstances of their own numerical inferiority, or no better than parity, both with respect to manpower and equipment. The Allies (and for this purpose we can include the Russians) were never able to defeat the Nazis where they did not enjoy clear general superiority. The Nazis were almost always able to offer very strong resistance to their enemies even when numerically inferior and to exact a much higher price in casualties from them than was the case under equivalent circumstances on the Allied side.[6] It is especially noteworthy to keep in mind that some -- not to say many -- methods used in the German army to maintain fighting efficiency are an antithesis of all the alleged strengths of "democracy". Here we don't find emphasis on "participation in decision-making", dialogue, diffusion of information to those "affected", voluntarism, and doing things because we want to. Quite the contrary.

Gerhard Weinberg discusses the important role of Hitler's secret but substantial bribery of his generals and field marshals. He also reports, along with other sources, the very large number of death sentences imposed upon Nazi soldiers and officers whose performance, not to mention attempts at defection or desertion, was judged faulty by the political and military leadership of the Reich. It would seem that at least in this conflict, in accordance with Machiavelli's maxim, the power of fear was able to exceed that of spontaneous affection.[7]

To be sure, not even the German army maintained a perfect record of combat effectiveness in all theatres at all times.[8]

In a memorandum addressed to the Combined Chiefs of Staff of 20 November 1944, General Eisenhower declared:

> German morale on this front shows no sign of cracking at present. I am of the opinion that enemy's continued stolid resistance is a main factor postponing final victory which, in present circumstances, can only be achieved by prolonged and bitter fighting. Factors which are compelling the enemy to continue strong resistance appear to be:
> a. Overall iron discipline of the Wehrmacht and stranglehold by the Nazi party.
> b. Successful Nazi propaganda which is convincing every German that unconditional surrender means the complete devastation of Germany and her elimination as a nation, (Chandler, p. 2131).

In thinking about the experience of the Second World War, one needs to distinguish between certain moral and factual issues. The question why men fight, risk, and sacrifice their lives cannot be answered by a simple formula. There is no answer that would explain the behaviour of every soldier under all circumstances. Coercion and intimidation were far more important background factors in the Nazi and Soviet armies than they were in the American and British armies. Leadership from the top was more brutal and callous.

To the extent that anyone, voluntarily, would lay life and limb, all that matters in the here-and-now, to vindicate a noble ideal, to save the lives of others, to help one's friends, or even to demonstrate one's courage, whether to fellow soldiers or, ultimately, just to oneself, he performs an act worthy of admiration. It is especially noble and admirable when it occurs in a largely voluntary context and in a just cause.

The men (and a number of brave women nurses) who landed on Omaha Beach on 6 June 1944 did not have to do what they did in order to assure that their families at home would not be deprived of food rations or be otherwise subjected to government persecution. In the democracies, people could be conscientious objectors without facing the certainty of a firing squad. They also knew, by the practice of their armies, if not by the strict letter of the law, that various degrees of combat avoidance (as in the famous Patton slapping incident in 1943) were tolerated by their military establishments. In Sicily, General George S. Patton suffered more severe punishment for striking a soldier who would not fight -- because of "nerves" -- than did that very reluctant, battle-averse soldier.[9]

Every Allied grave marker on the continent of Europe and every veterans' hospital ward for many years after 1945, must be construed as an indelible testimonial to the heroism of those who risked all and gave all in a cause whose justice could never be in doubt. If ever there was honoured glory, Allied soldiers, airmen and sailors who fought against Hitler's Germany earned it.

Whether in conducting the war, democratic-politics-at-home assisted in obtaining victories at the front, however, is quite another matter. In "real" life, even though we may recognize right from wrong, and honour the right, most of us know that right is not always rewarded. Good does not always triumph over evil. "Good" is not always more effective. This, indeed, is a very old problem which people are historically reluctant to face.

As between West and East, Charles MacDonald, in a work devoted to the Allied invasion of Europe, makes an argument for the greater weight of Western contribution to the defeat of Hitler than is sometimes presented, especially by Soviet sources. He says, for example, that during the Battle of the Bulge "the Germans had only two-thirds as many tanks on the entire eastern front as they had in the Ardennes". Moreover, he points out that the Russians fought a one-front ground war, did not contribute anything to the strategic bombing of Germany, or to the war at sea in the Atlantic[10]

One problem with the argument is that the effectiveness of the Allied strategic bombing has always been difficult to demonstrate either in terms of German war production or the morale of the Nazi armies.

To be sure, bombing was not without some tangible and intangible effects. Richard Overy, in his recent interesting work on the subject, observes that Allied bombing forced the Germans to allocate more of their aircraft production to fighter planes, and, of course, keep more of them over Germany than would have been the case without Allied bombing. He says that "in 1942 over half the German combat aircraft produced were bombers; in 1944 the proportion was only 18 per cent. The German air threat at the battle of Kursk and in the long retreat that followed visibly melted". This diversion of resources weakened Nazi efforts on all fronts, he suggests.[11] Allied bombing undoubtedly induced great attrition of German air power both in planes and in trained pilots.

Overy is undoubtedly also right when he says that the bombing campaign "suited the preferences of the west, which did not want to place a much higher physical strain on their populations".[12]

The effects on overall German war production and on morale at the front were different matters. Overy concedes that between 1941 and 1944 "German military output trebled".[13] He resorts to somewhat acrobatic reasoning however when he says that "the effect of bombing on the German economy was not to prevent a sustained increase in output, but to place a strict ceiling (?!) on that expansion".[14]

(An important political effect of the Allied bombing of Germany, rarely mentioned, was in its seeming demonstration of Germany's increasing decline and powerlessness to the publics of neutral and occupied countries of Europe. The reduction of German cities to rubble was interpreted, understandably, as a portent of the impending defeat of Hitler's Reich, and also as a psychologically satisfying pay back for its predatory activities throughout the continent. It was also a tangible demonstration of the fact that the Allies were indeed "on the job" during periods of little overt land engagements between them and the Nazis.)

It should also be recalled that since the inception of *Barbarossa*, the war in Europe lasted for a total of 46.5 months. Hitler's Ardennes offensive lasted from 16 December 1944 to 16 January 1945. This amounted to little more than 2 per cent of war time, 1941-1945.

Those inclined to give excessive credit to the Western Allies in the Battle of the Bulge, and indeed in much of the fighting in the latter part of 1944 and early 1945, need a sobering reminder. When, under massive pressure from the Red Army, Romania's King Michael accepted Moscow's terms of surrender, and on the very day the Allies entered Paris, 25 August, Romania declared war on Nazi Germany, the most immediate consequence for Hitler was the loss of critically important oilfields.

Unlike the earlier Nazi offensives against the Russians at Moscow, Stalingrad, and even Kursk, German efforts against the British and the Americans in the latter part of 1944 not only lacked the support of appreciable air power; they even lacked sufficient gasoline to give the panzers, the mobile artillery, and all of the Wehrmacht's supporting vehicles, genuine flexibility of movement. Moreover, at the beginning of 1945, Nazi manpower losses for the war as a whole in killed, captured, and seriously wounded, probably exceeded 8 million irreplaceable young men. Approximately 85 per cent of those losses had been inflicted by the Russians. By the latter part of 1944, the flower of Hitler's once mighty army lay dead on the eastern front.

The truth about the Allied air war against Nazi Germany is that, apart from its marginal impacts, it was a mode of warfare which minimized the politically explosive human costs for the Western democracies. Its ultimate rationale was not really effectiveness; it was feasibility. The necessary "heavy lifting" for victory was being done by others, elsewhere.

With respect to the MacDonald arguments about the aggregate size of the respective, Western and Soviet, armed forces and the war against submarines, the question can really be turned against him as an efficacy problem. Large armies and ocean-going operations which do not translate into heavy blows against the enemy have to be, obviously and significantly, discounted.[15] Nazi casualties, east and west, did not support his argument.

The great eagerness of Churchill and Roosevelt for Stalin's help in the conquest of Germany and of Japan to follow, not only had unfortunate territorial consequences in postwar Europe. It also had unfortunate diplomatic-political results conferring an undeserved legitimacy on the Soviet's East

European conquests, especially at Yalta. In the later phases of the war, from 1942 onwards, wishful thinking about Russia produced a psychological effect on the leaders themselves, Roosevelt and Churchill, and their associates, which often occurs among lesser mortals. This effect was to confuse wish and reality and therefore to cause them to "interpret" Stalin and his regime in a far more benign and positive manner than was warranted by the harsh realities of the situation. All this had some "spillover" consequences with respect to Western public opinion in the closing period of the Second World War.[16]

Depending on Soviet co-operation in the conduct of the war -- and desiring to continue to enjoy it in the foreseeable future -- both Western leaders succumbed to illusions of major proportions.

One certainly could not anticipate the coming of the Cold War from this speech by FDR to an Advertising War Council Conference on 8 March 1944:

> ... We are now working, since the last meeting in Teheran, in really good co-operation with the Russians. And I think the Russians are perfectly friendly; they aren't trying to gobble up all the rest of Europe or the world. They didn't know us, that's the really fundamental difference ... They haven't got any crazy ideas of conquest ... And all these fears that have been expressed by a lot of people here -- with some reason -- that the Russians are going to try to dominate Europe, I personally don't think there's anything in it. They have got a large enough 'hunk of bread' right in Russia to keep them busy for a great many years to come without taking on any more headaches.[17]

Or from Winston Churchill's speech on 22 February 1944:

> There would be very few differences between the three great Powers if their chief representatives could meet once a month. At such meetings, both formal and informal, all difficulties could be brought out freely and frankly, and the most delicate matters could be approached without the risk of jars or misunderstandings, such as too often arise when written communications are the only channel.

> ... if the heads of the three Governments could meet once a month, there would be no problems between us which could not be swiftly and I trust sensibly solved.[18]

In a speech to the Dumbarton Oaks Conference in August 1944, Roosevelt, citing Alfred E. Smith, said:

> ... if you can get the parties into one room with a big table and make them take their coats off and put their feet upon the table, and give each one of them a good cigar, you can always make them agree. Well, there was something in the idea ...

> I think that often it comes down to personalities. When, back in 1941, at the time of the Atlantic Charter, just for example, I did not know Mr. Churchill at all well. I had met him once or twice very informally during the First World War. I did not know Mr. Eden. But up there in the North Atlantic -- three or four days together -- we got awfully fond of each other. I got to know him, and he got to know me. In other words, we met, and you cannot hate a man that you know well. Later on Mr. Molotov came here and we had a grand time together. Then during the following year, at Teheran, the Marshal and I got to know each other. We got on beautifully. We cracked the ice if there ever was any ice; and since then there has been no ice.[19]

An even more obtuse view of Stalin's European aspirations was offered by British Foreign Secretary Anthony Eden, in private talks in Washington, DC on 9 March 1943. In Eden's view, the Allies needed to keep Stalin from becoming a shy "wallflower":

> Eden ... thought Russia ... undoubtedly had two different plans up her sleeve -- one based on British-American co-operation with Russia and the other on the assumption that the United States would withdraw from all interest in European affairs after the war. Eden said he believed that Russia preferred and hoped for the former because Stalin was not prepared to face the implications of Russia's control over European affairs ...

> Eden said he believed that one of the reasons Stalin wanted a second front in Europe was political; that if Germany collapsed he had no desire, in Germany, to take the full responsibility for what would happen in Germany or the rest of Europe, and he believed it was a fixed matter of Russian policy to have both British and United States troops heavily in Europe when the collapse comes. Eden expressed this purely as his private opinion and said that he was

sure that in Russia a different view was held in some quarters (sic!) but, nevertheless, he thought he had stated Stalin's position.[20]

At Yalta the mood of the Western Allies, particularly toward the conclusion of the Conference, amidst banquets and toasts, approached exultation. Roosevelt declared in a toast on 10 February 1945, marking the final dinner meeting of the Conference, that "he felt the atmosphere at this dinner was as that of a family, and it was in those words that he liked to characterize the relation that existed between our three countries".[21] Churchill was hardly less effusive. Upon his return to Britain, the Prime Minister publicly defended his faith in the pledges of the Soviet government in these words:

> I feel that their word is their bond. I know of no government which stands to its obligations even in its own despite, more solidly than the Russian government. I decline absolutely to embark upon a discussion about Russian good faith. It is quite evident that these matters touch the whole future of the world.[22]

One of Churchill's biographers, Lewis Broad, described the Churchill-Stalin war relationship as follows:

> ... for all his knowledge of the Soviet past, Winston was prepared to give Stalin the benefit of the doubt and to trust to his intentions. It was difficult for him to do other than believe in the essential probity of those in high station with whom he did business. Great men in great places did not, in his conception, fall below the standards of greatness.[23]

Quite understandably, Churchill was not willing in 1938 to give this kind of benefit of the doubt to Chamberlain -- concerning Hitler!

Stalin's view of his relations with the two Western statesmen was harsh and cynical, even many months before Yalta.[24]

Looking through rose-coloured glasses, Churchill repeatedly took the position that the war, as it went on, was losing whatever ideological character it may have had. On 2 August 1944, he told the House of Commons: "I still hold to the view ... that as the war enters its final phase it is becoming, and will become, increasingly less ideological".[25] Apparently, the last virulent Russian Communist expired with Leon Trotsky. Stalin was perhaps a despot but one could understand him and deal with him in terms more characteristic of Catherine and Peter the Great than of Marx and Lenin.

In May of 1944 Churchill had taken the view that the British Government would not object to a Communist regime in Yugoslavia, provided it permitted free elections. He said: "In one place we support a King, in another a Communist -- there is no attempt by us to enforce particular ideologies. We only want to beat the enemy, and then, in a happy and serene peace, let the best expression be given to the will of the people in every way".[26] A strange misunderstanding or disregard of Leninist principles and abandonment of his own earlier prudence with respect to Communist guarantees![27]

If his position may be reconstructed here, Churchill apparently regarded the relationship of Soviet Russia to the world Communist movement as drastically changed by the elimination of Trotskyism and symbolized in the dissolution of the Comintern in 1943. Once Trotsky had been disposed of, two things remained: the solid, predictable nationalism of Stalin imposed upon a framework of institutions the Russians called "Communist", and beyond the Soviet frontiers bands of misguided zealots and malcontents who strove to emulate or aspire to some version of the Soviet model. These Communists could be troublesome (as they were in Greece), but Stalin's interest in them was, in this view, no greater than, say, Churchill's in the cause of American Anglophiles. Stalin could and would "use" foreign Communists, but only in furtherance of Russian national interests, for tangible purposes, not for the sake of any "revolution". Stalin's attitude in 1944 toward Greece seemed to confirm such a view.[28]

Thus, characteristically, Churchill believed that if the Polish Government in London had made the territorial concessions which Stalin desired more promptly, the Lublin Communist Government would never have been set up in the first place![29] The Prime Minister was so firmly convinced that Stalin was really indifferent to the forms of society outside Russia that he regarded the Moscow and Lublin Poles as a mere blackmailing device of the Soviet dictator, at least as late as October, 1944.[30] On the other hand, the Curzon Line seemed to Churchill a small price for a lasting European settlement, and indeed even for Poland's independence. Armed with such convictions Churchill found it not merely expedient but even morally justifiable to apply the strongest, well-nigh brutal, pressure on Prime Minister Stanisław Mikołajczyk and the Polish Government in London to come to terms with Stalin by acceding to his territorial demands.[31] In the Prime Minister's view, if the Poles gave him Wilno and Lwów, Stalin would hardly care what regime they had -- provided it wasn't pro-German. Similarly, Churchill's concessions on the western frontier of Poland, at the expense of Germany, were made on the assumption of a lasting settlement with the Soviets, in exchange for their "live-and-let-live" attitude toward Poland and the rest of East-Central Europe.[32]

In pressuring Mikołajczyk to accept not merely Soviet territorial claims but also a post in a bogus, Communist-dominated Government of National Unity, the Prime Minister went beyond the point of merely giving Stalin something which he already possessed or would soon possess anyway. The co-operation and consent of the London Poles and of the Western powers in Soviet designs were in effect easing the Communist conquest of Poland by conferring a measure of rightfulness and legitimacy upon it. In the absence of such recognition and aid, Soviet "liberation" would have been, to borrow a Soviet term, "unmasked".

It seems reasonable to conclude that both the relative weight of the Soviet war effort, its perception in the Allied war councils, as well as the anticipated Western need for Soviet assistance in defeating Japan, heavily influenced the political leaders' attitude toward Stalin. This is strongly suggested by a memorandum addressed to Harry Hopkins by military aide Major General J. H. Burns, as early as 10 August 1943:

The Executive of the President's Soviet Protocol
Committee (Burns) to the President's Special
Assistant (Hopkins)

SECRET   WASHINGTON, 10 August 1943

MEMORANDUM FOR MR. HOPKINS

Subject: Russia

Russia's Position, 2 August 1943.

Russia's position in War II is in marked contrast with that which she occupied in War I. She had collapsed before the termination of War I and had no effect whatsoever in the final defeat of Germany, which was accomplished by the allies without her assistance. In War II Russia occupies a dominant position and is the decisive factor looking toward the defeat of the Axis in Europe. While in

Sicily the forces of Great Britain and the United States are being opposed by 2 German divisions, the Russian front is receiving attention of approximately 200 German divisions. Whenever the Allies open a second front on the Continent, it will be decidedly a *secondary* front to that of Russia; theirs will continue to be the main effort. Without Russia in the war, the Axis cannot be defeated in Europe, and the position of the United Nations becomes precarious.

Similarly, Russia's post-war position in Europe will be a dominant one. With Germany crushed, there is no power in Europe to oppose her tremendous military forces. It is true that Great Britain is building up a position in the Mediterranean *vis-à-vis* Russia that she may find useful in balancing power in Europe: however, even here she may not be able to oppose Russia unless she is otherwise supported.

The conclusions from the foregoing are obvious. Since Russia is the decisive factor in the war, she must be given every assistance and every effort must be made to obtain her friendship. Likewise since without question she will dominate Europe on the defeat of the Axis, it is even more essential to develop and maintain the most friendly relations with Russia.

Finally, the most important factor the United States has to consider in relation to Russia is the prosecution of the war in the Pacific. With Russia as an ally in the war against Japan, the war can be terminated in less time and at less expense in life and resources than if the reverse were the case. Should the war in the Pacific have to be carried on with an unfriendly or a negative attitude on the part of Russia, the difficulties will be immeasurably increased and operations might become abortive.

The conclusion reached is that Russia is so necessary to victory and peace that we must give her maximum assistance and make every effort to develop and maintain the most friendly relations with her.[33]

The democratic Allies needed to maintain a certain balance in their relationship with Stalin. He was, and could be, useful to them, but at what price? According to the old saying, those who sup with the Devil need long spoons. Toward the end of the Second World War, such spoons seemed to be in short supply among the Anglo-American Allies.

Focusing upon the Yalta Conference in February of 1945, the question may be fairly asked whether the Second World War was not ending with another Munich for reasons that were analogous to those at the original Munich of 1938. At Yalta, the United States and Great Britain were making diplomatic concessions to Stalin which could not be justified by the terms of the Atlantic Charter and many other Allied pledges and declarations, including those made by Great Britain on behalf of Poland in 1939. In agreeing to the Soviet demands for half of pre-war Poland (which is what the so-called Curzon Line frontier implied) the United States and Britain were denying the right of self-determination to the people of an allied nation.[34]

The annexation of eastern Poland into the Soviet Union, or more specifically, into the territories of Soviet Ukraine and Byelorussia, was not made contingent on the choice of the people affected. While it is true that many of the inhabitants of eastern Poland, especially in rural areas, were ethnic Ukrainians and Byelorussians, this fact was not much of an excuse for Allied conduct at Yalta. Perhaps given a free choice between living in Stalin's Communist and totalitarian Soviet Union, or in a capitalist and relatively free Poland, many of these people might have chosen Poland over Russia. But, of course, they were never given that chance which is precisely what self-determination is all about. If even one out of every four Ukrainians and Byelorussians voted to remain in Poland, there would have been a very substantial overall majority throughout that region for union with Poland. The arguments sometimes made about the allegedly "reactionary", "anti-Soviet", and "unco-operative" attitudes of the Polish Government-in-Exile in London, however appealing to people who need to reassure their consciences, are fundamentally irrelevant to the issues of freedom and self-determination.

Another Yalta decision, based on the idea of two wrongs making a right, compensated Poland for her losses in the east by giving her, quite arbitrarily, substantial German territories in Silesia, Pomerania, and East Prussia. Ironically, this was a much greater violation of the principle of self-determination against Germany than anything that was agreed upon at the Versailles Conference of 1919! The territories ceded to Poland in 1945 had been German for centuries, and the share of indigenous Polish population in any of them was very small, not to say nil. Here, too, there was no question about allowing any voting to determine the future status of these territories. Implicitly, the Allies sanctioned substantial expulsion and expropriation of German civilians who had lived in these areas for many generations. In addition, of course, the Western Allies were also giving Stalin substantial territories and objectives in the possession of Japan and in the still earlier possession of China, also without any safeguards for the populations affected.[35]

The transfer of German territories, especially, to Poland and Russia was, in essence, a repudiation of the Anglo-Saxon principle of the rule of law. For while the swap of Polish territory in the east for German territory in the west implied at least some likelihood of compensation to the Poles who might be uprooted, no equivalent compensation was provided for the Germans. No international supervision was called for, let alone established, by the Allies at Yalta (or anywhere else) to oversee the process by which millions of perfectly innocent individuals, presumably, would be moved from their homes and properties into some veritable unknown. No one worried about some form of reimbursement for these people. This was not an issue of harshly punishing war criminals, people who clearly deserved to suffer for their misdeeds. In effect, the Allies were applying brutal and lawless measures to millions of innocents.[36]

The most tangible reasons why the Allies were willing to engage in these "give-aways", without any reference to self-determination, were two. First, there was implicit concern about continuing Soviet co-operation in the war against Nazi Germany. Given the size of the relevant forces, and Allied reluctance, not to say inability, to carry on the full brunt of a Continental war against Hitler, there was an Allied interest in keeping the Soviets engaged on the Eastern front. A last-minute, or let us say early-1945, Soviet-Nazi deal, would have likely deprived the Allies of any chance of a quick, clear-cut, and especially in human terms, relatively inexpensive, victory over Nazi Germany. The second reason, no less compelling, was the desire for Soviet help in bringing about a speedy and, once again, relatively inexpensive in lives, defeat of Japan.

This latter interest among the American and British political leaders was predicated on great uncertainty, not to say scepticism, about the potentialities of the as yet militarily untested atomic bomb. There was also a certain irony about it. The American military chiefs, King, Halsey, Nimitz, and MacArthur, could, by the end of 1944, all but guarantee the ultimate defeat of Japan. If the object of the struggle was to bring about this defeat, it was quite clear to the military at that time that, quite apart from any use of an atom bomb, Japan was on its way to an inevitable surrender. What was at issue, was how fast this could be done, and at what human cost to the Allies.

With its navy and air force in ruins, Japan, an island nation, could not long maintain the imports of raw materials and fuels that would be necessary for her bare survival, let alone a strong military posture. The combination of overwhelming American air and naval power surrounding Japan would bring her to an ultimate ruin. An invasion by the US forces would likely hasten this process, but it could involve hundreds of thousands of American casualties. Without Soviet participation, and discounting nuclear weapons as an unknown, the American choice was between patience in awaiting the results of blockade and bombing, that is a slower way to victory, or an invasion with many more casualties but also a quicker, favourable outcome of the war.

To Roosevelt and Churchill, Soviet participation in the war against Japan offered the attractive alternative of a victory which would be simultaneously quick and cheap in human terms at least as far as they were concerned.[37] In 1938, Chamberlain was willing to "finance" the peace of Europe on the sacrifice of Czechoslovakia. In 1945, Churchill and Roosevelt were willing to "finance" victory over Germany and Japan on the sacrifice of several populations and states. If this might have some adverse consequences in the more distant future, that did not seem nearly as important to the top allied leaders as the gratification of an enormous military-political victory in the here-and-now.[38]

Writing about the concessions which FDR made to the Russians at Yalta, including the "grant of the Kurile [Islands] and southern Sakhalin to a potential enemy of the United States", Forrest Pogue observes that among the American officials present at the Yalta Conference "no one doubted ... that the Japanese would be ultimately defeated, nor that the blockade might gradually starve the Japanese islands into submission. But Americans in the spring of 1945 had no desire to leave millions of soldiers, sailors, and airmen under arms, waiting for the ultimate surrender of the Japanese eighteen months or more into the future". Secretary Stimson believed that any US invasion of Japan would cost between 500,000 and 1 million casualties. On the other hand, the President's advisors were unsure, as yet, about the possible usefulness and impact of the atomic bomb which was being actively developed in the United States, with an anticipated readiness for deployment in August 1945.[39]

In the upshot, Pogue says:

> ... morality and reality were in conflict; reality won. Defenders of
> the Far Eastern concessions can only justify them in terms of (1) the
> need of Russian aid against Japan to shorten the war in the Far East

and save American lives, or/and (2) the need to prolong wartime co-operation with the USSR into the postwar era.[40]

In fact, Roosevelt's territorial concessions to Stalin were not so much a choice of reality over morality, as they were a characteristically democratic choice between the interests of the present and the interests of the future, generally favouring the former over the latter.[41]

NOTES

[1] In accord with Judaic, as well as Christian traditions, the author believes freedom to be an indispensable attribute of the human personality. To be truly human is to be able to make choices freely. This is not to say, however, that doing so makes the chooser necessarily "richer", "stronger", more "effective", more "successful", or morally correct. Perhaps sometimes just the opposite.

[2] As Richard Collier remarks, at Yalta in February 1945, "no matter how the talks had gone, Stalin held eastern Europe in the one way that counted". *The War That Stalin Won, Teheran-Berlin* (London: Hamish Hamilton, 1983), p. 237. That was certainly part of the picture, if not quite all of it.

[3] As late as 2 August 1944, Eisenhower tells General Marshall that "at this moment the enemy is bringing up such reinforcements as he can gather from *within France* to bolster his lines and to establish a defensive position that will prevent us breaking into the open". See A. D. Chandler, Jr. (ed.), *The Papers of Dwight David Eisenhower, The War Years: IV* (Baltimore: The Johns Hopkins Press, 1970), p. 2049. Italics mine.

[4] In a memorandum sent to General Henry Arnold of 3 September 1944, General Eisenhower declared that "the air has done everything we asked. It has practically destroyed the German Air Force". A. D. Chandler, Jr., (ed.), *op. cit.*, pp. 2112-2113.

[5] Gilles Perrault, *The Secret of D-Day* (Boston: Little, Brown 1965) believes that the key to Allied success in Normandy, despite the air power factor, was the Nazis' belief that the Allies would make their major landing in the Pas de Calais area where 19 German divisions kept vigil for them "until the end of July" by which time the Allies had already broken out in Normandy and the invasion could no longer be thrown back into the sea: pp. 238-239. His account is confirmed by General Bradley in *A Soldier's Story*. L. F. Ellis, *Victory in the West, Vol. II, The Defeat of Germany* (History of the Second World War, United Kingdom Military Series) (London: HM Stationery Office, 1968), p. 407. Gerhard Weinberg reports a German estimate of 250,000 total own casualties and 170,000 Allied casualties just for the period 6 June to 22 August 1944. See *infra*, p. 255. According to Matloff, *Strategic Planning, op. cit.*, Allied battle deaths from D-Day to end of the War were approximately 195,000; Nazi deaths

were 263,000. This was a much better performance by the Nazis against the Allies than the Allied performance against the Nazis in 1940, all with seemingly less favourable conditions for the Nazis in 1944-5.

[6] One may note here the conclusion of Max Hastings, *Overlord, D-Day and the Battle for Normandy* (New York: Simon & Schuster, 1984), pp. 315-316: "The Allies in Normandy faced the finest fighting army of the war, one of the greatest that the world has ever seen. This is simple truth that some soldiers and writers have been reluctant to acknowledge, partly for reasons of nationalistic pride, partly because it is a painful concession where the Wehrmacht and the SS were fighting for one of the most obnoxious regimes of all time. The quality of the Germans' weapons -- above all tanks -- was of immense importance. Their tactics were masterly: stubborn defence; concentrated local fire-power from mortars and machine-guns; quick counter-attacks to recover lost ground. Units often fought on even when cut off, which was not a mark of fanaticism, but of sound tactical discipline, when such resistance in the rear did tend to reduce the momentum of Allied advances ...". Hastings says that Montgomery and Bradley understood all this perfectly well. "They had not been sent to Normandy to demonstrate the superiority of their fighting men to those of Hitler, but to win the war at tolerable cost -- a subtly but importantly different objective": p. 317.

[7] Note Russell F. Weigley, *Eisenhower's Lieutenants, The Campaign of France and Germany 1944-1945* (Bloomington: Indiana University Press, 1981) who says that: "... the German army [even] in 1944 still could claim to be qualitatively the best army in the world": p. 28. "Its quality lay in fire-power enhanced by superior professional skill among the officers and superior combat savvy and unexcelled courage among the ranks", *ibid*. See Omer Bartov, "Indoctrination and Motivation in the Wehrmacht: The Importance of the Unquantifiable", *The Journal of Strategic Studies*, Vol. 9, No. 1, March 1986, pp. 16-34. Note especially pp. 32-33. See Roger A. Beaumont, "On the Wehrmacht Mystique", *Military Review*, Vol. LXVI, No. 7, July 1986, pp. 44-56. This author concedes a certain *reputation* to the German army of 1939-1945 but attempts to deflate it in some respects, e.g. "The Nazi victories in 1939-40 ... proved to be more image than substance(?!), While the numbers of forces overcome were great, the vanquished were not effectively allied(!)": p. 46. Another, almost humorous, example of denial! See Gerhard L. Weinberg, *Germany, Hitler, and World War II, Essays in Modern German and World History* (Cambridge: Cambridge University Press, 1995), pp. 308-309. The author speaks of bribery "on a colossal scale", p. 308. Also Manfred Messerschmidt and Fritz Wullner, *Die Wehrmachtjustiz im Dritten Reich: Zerstorung einer Legende* (Baden-Baden: Nomos, 1987) who speaks of 30,000 death sentences, most of them carried out, an amazing comparison with Allied armies. Note also Marlis G. Steinert, *Hitler's War and the Germans, Public Mood and Attitudes During the Second World War* (Athens, Ohio: Ohio University Press, 1977) generally on the German people's lack of enthusiasm about

the war, especially after *Barbarossa*, and general despondency after Stalingrad, but "calm and quiet attitude" among civilians generally held till the end of the war and "discipline among troops remained high" even in May 1945 in the northern part of Germany not yet occupied by the Allies: p. 313.

[8]   Note A. D. Chandler, Jr. (ed.), *op. cit.*, for the Eisenhower message of 4 September declaring that "enemy resistance on the entire front shows signs of collapse", p. 2115. Note also the editor's commentary on p. 2117 discussing "panic [which] infected rear areas", and "depressed enemy morale". But this condition did not last long.

[9]   For discussion of this incident and its comparative context, see Alexander J. Groth, "Totalitarians and Democrats: Aspects of Political-Military Relations 1939-1945", *Comparative Strategy*, Vol. 8, No. 1, Spring 1989, pp. 73-97.

[10]   Charles B. MacDonald, *The Mighty Endeavor: American Armed Forces in the European Theater* (New York: Oxford University Press, 1969), pp. 41-46, passim; see David MacIsaac (ed.), *The United States Strategic Bombing Survey, Volume I* (New York: Garland Publishing, Inc., 1976), pp. 181ff, on the disappointing effects of Allied strategic bombing on German war production until at least the latter part of 1944.   See also Kent Robert Greenfield, *American Strategy in World War II: A Reconsideration* (Baltimore: The Johns Hopkins University Press, 1963) who remarks that "what can fairly be said of the decisiveness of strategic bombing in Europe is that it hastened the internal collapse of Germany, though this had not had time to produce a decisive effect on the German ground combat forces when the Nazi Government surrendered": p. 120. Note Malcolm Smith, "The Allied Air Offensive", *The Journal of Strategic Studies*, Vol. 13, No. 1, March 1990, pp. 67-83; taking a wider perspective, which includes training of crews for bombing in support of the invasion forces in 1944, Smith believes that the contribution of the bombers "was quite basic to the victory in the West": p. 82.   Of course, Allied strategic bombing helped the Russians by tying up most of Germany's fighter aircraft in the West.   Paul Carell, *Invasion -- They're Coming! The German Account of the Allied Landings and the 80 Days' Battle for France* (New York: D. P. Dutton, 1963) says that "the war in the West was decided by Allied superiority in the air.   This was the second time that Rommel had been defeated by Allied airmen ... Allied superiority in the air grew into a complete air monopoly at the time of the invasion ... [it] cut off reinforcements ... rendered infantry helpless victims": p. 271.

[11]   Richard Overy, *Why the Allies Won* (New York: W. W. Norton, 1995), p. 129.

[12]   *Ibid.*, p. 128.

[13]   *Ibid.*, p. 130.

[14]   *Ibid.*

[15]   Charles B. MacDonald, *The Mighty Endeavor: American Armed Forces in the European Theater* (New York: Oxford University Press, 1969),   Loc. cit.

16 See P. M. H. Bell, *John Bull and the Bear, British Public Opinion, Foreign Policy and the Soviet Union 1941-1945* (London: E. Armond, 1990) who shows how "denial" worked with respect to British public opinion about Soviet murders at Katyn revealed by the Nazis in 1943. Media and popular denial were widespread; analogous response, though less favourable to the Soviets, occurred in the summer of 1944 with respect to the Warsaw Uprising, refusing to blame Moscow: pp. 107-172. See Warren F. Kimball, *The Juggler, Franklin Roosevelt as Wartime Statesman* (Princeton: Princeton University Press, 1991) who notes that FDR "never articulated a cohesive philosophy" (p. 185) but also that he "was a true twentieth-century American liberal ... [who] ... possessed a calm, quiet conviction that Americanism (a better word than liberalism) was so very sensible, logical, and practical, that societies would adopt those values and system if only given the chance". (p. 186). Lloyd C. Gardner, *Architects of Illusion, Men and Ideas in American Foreign Policy 1941-1949* (Chicago: Quadrangle Books, 1971) strongly implies that Roosevelt believed that somehow the end of the Second World War would usher in "the end of history". "His report to Congress [after Yalta] gave a dangerously over-optimistic assessment of the future ... [Yalta], he thought, spelled the end of "unilateral action and exclusive alliances": p. 52.

17 *The Public Papers and Addresses of Franklin D. Roosevelt*, 1944-45 Volume (New York: Harper & Bros., 1950), p. 99.

18 *The War Speeches of Winston S. Churchill*, compiled by Charles Eade, Volume III (London: Cassell & Co, 1952), p. 89.

19 *The Public Papers and Addresses of Franklin D. Roosevelt, op. cit.*, pp. 232-33. *Ibid.*, p. 198 (2 August 1944).

20 Robert E. Sherwood, *Roosevelt and Hopkins* (New York: Harper, 1948), pp. 708-709.

21 *Ibid.*, pp. 869-870.

22 Lewis Broad, *The War that Churchill Waged* (London: Hutchinson and Company, 1960), p. 356.

23 *Ibid.*, p. 358.

24 Cf. Milovan Djilas, *Conversations with Stalin* (New York: Harcourt, Brace & World, 1962), p. 73. Djilas quotes Stalin as saying in June of 1944: "perhaps you think that just because we are the allies of the English that we have forgotten who they are and who Churchill is. They find nothing sweeter than to trick their allies ... Churchill is the kind who, if you don't watch him, will slip a kopeck out of your pocket ... and Roosevelt? Roosevelt is not like that. He dips in his hand for bigger coins. But Churchill -- Churchill even for a kopeck". The Prime Minister, however, believed even in 1950 that Stalin sincerely held him in high regard. Cf. *Triumph and*

Tragedy, loc. cit., p. 238. Also see R. H. McNeal, "Roosevelt Through Stalin's Eyes", *International Journal*, Vol. XVIII, No. 2, Spring 1963, pp. 194-206.

[25] *The War Speeches, op. cit.*, p. 196.

[26] *Ibid.*, p. 147. See Fitzroy Maclean, *Eastern Approaches* (London: Cape, 1953), pp. 281, 402-403.

[27] See W. S. Churchill, *Triumph and Tragedy* (Boston: Houghton Mifflin, 1953), pp. 400-401, 420.

[28] Note his earlier work, Winston S. Churchill, *The Aftermath: The World Crisis -- 1918-1928* (New York: Scribner's, 1929), pp. 281-282.

[29] *The Dawn of Liberation: War Speeches by the Right Hon. Winston S. Churchill*, comp. Charles Eade (Boston: Little, Brown, 1945), p. 377.

[30] See Stanislaw Mikołajczyk, *The Rape of Poland* (New York: Whittlesey House, 1948), pp. 97, 99.   Jan Ciechanowski, *Defeat in Victory* (Garden City, NY: Doubleday, 1947), p. 333; Sir Llewellyn Woodward, *British Foreign Policy in the Second World War* (London: HM Stationery Office, 1962), p. 310.   Sir Llewellyn's work is based on the familiar implicit assumption that Churchill was aware of Soviet designs but Roosevelt was not. His account of Churchill's visit to Moscow in October, 1944 (pp. 306-313) blends facts with hindsight. ·

[31] See Edward J. Rozek, *Allied Wartime Diplomacy* (New York: Wiley, 1958), pp. 278-285; 306-313.

[32] See Z. M. Szaz, *Germany's Eastern Frontiers* (Chicago: Regnery, 1960), pp. 81-82, 89, 108.

[33] *Foreign Relations of the United States, The Conferences At Washington and Quebec* (Washington, DC: US Government Printing Office, 1970), pp. 624-625.

[34] The Curzon Line, of course, was first agreed upon by the Three Great Powers at the Teheran Conference of November 1943. It is noteworthy that, in a parallel with the Munich Agreement, the "victims", i.e., Czechoslovakia in 1938 and Poland in 1943 or 1945, were not allowed representation in the negotiations which decided their fate.

[35] See Edward R. Stettinius, Jr., *Roosevelt and the Russians, The Yalta Conference* (New York: Doubleday 1949), pp. 351-352, for the text of the territorial concessions in Asia made by the Anglo-American Allies to the Soviet Union on 11 February 1945. The agreement stipulated "that in two or three months after Germany has surrendered and the war in Europe terminated, the Soviet Union shall enter into the war against Japan on the side of the Allies on condition that, etc". The "condition that" included the acquisition of southern Sakhalin, the Kurile Islands, and the facilities of Port Arthur as a naval base for the Soviet Union.

It is of some interest to mention here the comment by Stettinius about the discussions held at Yalta among Stalin, Churchill, and Roosevelt. "I believe that the

... spirit of most of the Conference, furnishes a genuine example to the world that, where objective conditions exist, people with different backgrounds and training can find a basis of understanding": pp. 275-276. It seemed as if, after all was said and done, they had all returned to the time of Munich ...

[36] See Zoltan M. Szaz, *op. cit.*; see also G. Rhode and W. Wagner (eds.), *The Genesis of the Oder-Neisse Line* (Stuttgart: Brentario Verlag, 1959); note also Frederich von Wilpert, *The Oder-Neisse Problem, Towards Fair Play in Central Europe* (Bonn: Atlantic Forum, 1964) especially pages 79-80. Article XII of the Potsdam Agreement of 1945 declared that the leaders of the Big Three agreed that population transfers in Central Europe "should be effected in an orderly and humane way". Even then, however, it was left to the interested parties (i.e., Poland and Russia) to interpret "orderly and humane". Wilpert actually attempts to defend Churchill for agreeing to population transfers at the earlier Yalta Conference, in February 1945, on the preposterous ground that Churchill believed Stalin's assurance that there were no more Germans left in East Prussia, Silesia, and Pomerania: p. 80. If he could have believed that, he could probably also believe in the tooth fairy!

[37] See *Foreign Relations of the United States, Diplomatic Papers, The Conferences at Malta and Yalta 1945* (Washington, DC: US Government Printing Office, 1955) for a note from FDR to Stalin, conveyed through Ambassador Harriman, 4 October 1944, which declares "Our three countries are waging a successful war against Germany and we can surely join together with no less success in crushing a nation that I am sure in my heart is as great an enemy of Russia as she is of ours": p. 361. Note also memorandum by the Chief of the US Military Mission in the Soviet Union, General John R. Deane, of 15 October 1944, which included the following statement given earlier to Stalin: "I stated that from the military point of view our Chiefs of Staff were hopeful that the Soviet Union would enter the war against Japan as soon as possible after the defeat of Germany" and that "whatever preparatory measures were practicable should be started now": pp. 366-367. See pp. 368-374 for other top-level memoranda on the subject, all indicating a great interest on the part of the United States in enlisting Soviet participation in the war against Japan.

[38] Note Trumbull Higgins, *Soft Underbelly, The Anglo-American Controversy Over the Italian Campaign* (New York: Macmillan, 1968) on Churchill's belated interest, in the latter part of March 1945, in trying to keep the Russians, quietly, as far to the east as possible, pp. 204-205 and 210-211. Higgins also suggests that Winston Churchill was at that time less interested in using the Soviets to defeat Japan than were the Americans, *ibid.,* pp. 210-211. Of course, the prospective bloody invasion of Japan was shaping up as a principally American, not British, enterprise.

[39] See Forrest C. Pogue, "Yalta in Retrospect" in John L. Snell (ed.), *The Meaning of Yalta* (Baton Rouge: Louisiana University Press, 1956), pp. 188-208.

[40] *Ibid.,* p. 199.

[41]   See William Henry Chamberlain, "The Munich Called Yalta", pp. 48-55, in Richard Fenno, Jr. (ed.), *The Yalta Conference* (Boston: D. C. Heath, 1955). Chamberlain remarks that if the Japanese had been assured that they would be allowed to "keep the Emperor and ... that their commercial interests in Manchuria and Korea would not be entirely wiped out", they would have surrendered quite promptly. He also points out that the Yalta agreements "grossly violated the Atlantic Charter by assigning Polish territory to the Soviet Union and German territory to Poland without plebiscites", and that "the whole historic basis of American foreign policy in the Far East was upset by the virtual invitation to Stalin to take over Japan's former exclusive and dominant role in Manchuria": p. 55. Naturally, there is a considerable literature of "apologetics" about the Yalta agreement so far as British and American actions were concerned. See, e.g., Pierre de Senarclens, *Yalta* (New Brunswick: Transaction Books, 1988). This author's take on the problem is expressed in one sentence: "Had (FDR and Churchill) any other political choice in the Crimea than that of sincere co-operation with the USSR?", p. 87. Note also Diane Shaver Clements, *Yalta* (New York: Oxford University Press, 1970). She sees Stalin at Yalta giving up more than he was getting, p. 290. In her view, the problem was that the "spirit of Yalta" had not triumphed in the years following the Conference, p. 291. Some of the discussion here is based on the author's earlier, "On the Intelligence Aspects of Personal Diplomacy", *Orbis*, Vol. VII, Winter 1964, pp. 833-848; and "Churchill and Stalin's Russia", *Bucknell Review*, Vol. XIV, March 1966, pp. 74-94.

10 CONCLUSION AND PROLOGUE

The story of Adolf Hitler's struggle for power, his ascent and his downfall is not an indication of the efficacy of political democracy. Quite the contrary. It is more nearly an indictment of it. Even though much of the literature dealing with Hitler's rise to power dwells on the various behind-the-scenes conspiracies, such as Franz von Papen's role in persuading von Hindenburg to offer Hitler the Chancellorship, the reality is that Hitler rose to that position primarily because the German electorate, quite freely and openly, made him its substantial plurality choice.

It is true that President von Hindenburg, had he been tougher, of firmer mind, and more principled perhaps, might have refused to appoint Hitler in 1933. The world would have been much better off had he resisted that fatal appointment. But Hitler established a powerful claim for himself precisely because a plurality of the German people, repeatedly, in completely free and inclusive national elections made him their choice. The German electorate made its decisions in the light of more information available to more people than perhaps at any time anywhere previous to the Germany of the 1930s. And it was certainly a sophisticated electorate that was making the choices. This was a test which public opinion failed under the rules of a very impressive political democracy.

In fact, the openness of democracy's "information markets" was a great natural advantage for Hitler's demagogic abilities, and he played upon it to the hilt. The argument that people did not know what they were choosing when they voted for the author of *Mein Kampf* is one of those wonderful denials which is characteristic of what may be termed "liberal hypocrisy". (This is especially the case if we are willing to grant that there is a difference between not *knowing* and not *wanting* to know.)

The period from Hitler's accession to power in 1933 and the outbreak of the War in 1939 was one which illustrated all the less attractive features of democratic political behaviour outside Germany: confusion, weakness, self-indulgence, and myopia. It was an era which showed the inability of the world democracies to diagnose the menace of Hitlerism correctly and develop policies to thwart the danger of Nazi expansionism. These policies could have been, in some cases, as in France in 1936, substantially unilateral, and of course, they always could have been multilateral. Even between the two major democracies of Europe, Britain and France, however, no genuine cohesion of policy toward Nazi Germany ever really developed.

The positions of other world democratic states were even more "scattered" with many, like Sweden and Switzerland, looking toward "neutrality" as a way of saving themselves from Hitler's prospective predation. Only in light of recent disclosures perhaps, is it becoming clear that no small European nations could have hoped to stay out of Hitler's path by neutrality unless they were willing to engage in humiliating collaboration with a great modern embodiment of Evil.

With all the means at their disposal, much information, and the open media to "process" it, the world democracies proved unable to co-operate in stopping Hitler, or punish him for his piecemeal aggressions of the 1930s; nor did they demonstrate any real willingness to extend large-scale help to the first victims of Hitler's persecution, the Jews.

In 1939, they found themselves unprepared materially (although that only in a qualitative sense) and certainly intellectually to deal with Hitler's methods of waging war. They proved to be slow learners. France succumbed to Nazi onslaught with astonishing rapidity. Britain lost most of its military equipment on the Continent as it awaited Hitler's invasion in 1940. Fortuitously, Hitler chose not to persist in his assault on the British, though he had been doing much better at it than modern legend would have it. The world profited by a "lucky break" when Adolf Hitler turned away from Britain and launched his all-out attack on Soviet Russia. There, at last, he met a match in Joseph Stalin.

Meantime, the United States, with its democratic public opinion, continued on a course which was grossly insufficient to forestall a Nazi victory. Japan's attack on Pearl Harbor and Russia's resistance to the Nazis, created the circumstances in which the United States was eventually able to make genuinely significant contributions to the defeat of Hitler's Germany.

But before that defeat could be accomplished, Britain and America with all their universalistic humanitarian slogans, and once again, with all sorts of information available to them, acquiesced in the mass murder of the Jewish people of Europe, without so much as one serious effort to help in this great human, as well as Jewish, tragedy. And because both democracies were so eager (and for the most part successful) in off-loading the human costs of winning the war against Hitler on the Russians, they were also disposed to give Stalin not only material aid but diplomatic, political and territorial concessions both in East-Central Europe and in Asia.

Naturally, these events taken as a whole, from the 1920s to the 1940s, do not support the case for democratic efficacy, whatever the moral, normative considerations may be. They demonstrate rather that given political systems built largely on the idea of private gratifications, policies requiring great discipline and sacrifice are not easily obtained.

The "free markets of ideas" were just as likely to produce confusion and cacophony of conceptions as they were to distil consensus, let alone something called "truth". And the appeal of ideas, or of policies, appears to have been during that era more influenced by the "volume" and "packaging" of the messages than by their rational content. Since the "Hitler episode" was a prolonged experience, occurring in three decades, and involving not one or two but many world democracies in many different ways, it would seem that in this experience there is likely to be an important message for the future.

Some people, understandably, might question the lessons of the Hitler era based on post-1945 events. Did the democracies of the world actually learn something from their confrontation with Hitler? Did they learn enough to avoid the self-indulgent lethargy of the 1930s and the near defeat of the 1940s? There are indications -- which might yet prove to be less solid than they now appear -- that there has been some "learning": whether it is enough remains to be seen.

If indeed, the world has become more of a closely integrated "global village", there have also been indications that the democracies have acted in concert to deal with its various problems more effectively than they did in the 1930s. The post-1945 era has been an era of at least some vigorous international institutions in which different world democracies have played significant roles.

A certain amount of learning appears to have taken place both in the United States and among the democracies of Western Europe, a greater understanding that the domination of the whole European continent by one power, especially one with world-wide designs, was a genuine danger that required practical countermeasures. Seemingly many more people now realized that it was worth devoting considerable resources, and the taking of some serious risks, to repel this threat to the mutual security of the whole so-called Atlantic Community. But much of the impetus for this change seems to be attributable to a likely transient phenomenon, a Pax Americana, originally fueled by Yankee anti-Communism following the end of the Second World War.

In the instance of Stalin's take-over of East-Central Europe, there was a much more "reasonable" relationship between "information" and "response" especially in the United States, than was the case with respect to Hitler in the 1930s and early 1940s. Stalin proceeded to impose Communist regimes in Poland, Romania, Hungary, Czechoslovakia, and Bulgaria, using harsh and crude methods, without regard to the public opinion of the countries "liberated", and, of course, also controlled, by the Red Army.

With the participation of both local communists and the Soviet political and military authorities, people who were politically active but were neither Communists nor Communist-collaborators were subjected to persecution. Many were imprisoned, deported, or executed. The terms "anti-fascist" and "fascist" were being used by the Soviets to eliminate any opposition to the transformation of East European countries into Communist-controlled regimes. Freedoms of speech, assembly, and association were crudely violated throughout the new Soviet bloc -- which, for practical purposes, extended as far as the Red Army had reached. Elections were rigged. Oppositional press was soon eliminated. The Soviet secret police was busy supporting the establishment of new totalitarian regimes. Red terror was replacing Brown terror.

Within a few months of the end of the war, information about Soviet and Communist activities became not only well-known in Washington; it began to produce a series of countermeasures by the Truman administration, and a significant turn in the attitudes of the American public, which, after all, had just emerged from a five year period of seeing the USSR as a valuable war ally of the United States. It took roughly a year-and-a-half from the end of the War to realign US public opinion on its attitude *vis-à-vis* the USSR.

George Quester in his study of American foreign policy reports the results of 23 national polls taken between February 1942 and August 1945 asking American respondents: "Do you think Russia can be trusted to co-operate with us after the war is over?". In only five of the 23 polls was there a clear majority in favour of an affirmative answer to this question. The most "pro-Soviet" poll was taken in February 1945 with 55 per cent saying "yes", 31 per cent saying "no" and 14 per cent undecided or expressing no opinion. During the 1942-5 period, as a whole, an average of 47 per cent of American respondents thought Russia would be co-operative but 30 per cent did not think so.[1]

Apart from "facts" in Eastern Europe, the threat of Soviet-sponsored communist aggression in the 1940s struck a much more responsive chord with American public opinion than did the Nazi-Fascist challenge of the 1930s for what may be termed ideological reasons. The American people were more alarmed by the communist danger in large measure because "communism" assailed two very fundamental American values.

The first of these was capitalism, often styled in the United States "free enterprise". In the US, more than in any other country, a great entrepreneurial mystique attached to capitalism. It was generally perceived as everyone's birthright and opportunity, part of the idea of freedom and the open frontier, not merely geographic but economic and social. Few things were as admired in American culture as human ascent from "rags to riches", the poor men or women making good by rising to affluence through skill, hard work, and ingenuity. Yankee traders and merchants were not American villains but American heroes. And it was entirely appropriate in the light of such values for President Calvin Coolidge to have said that "the business of America is business". To be sure, the experience of the Great Depression tested the faith rather severely but it did not extinguish it. In America, capitalism was originally connected to the American Dream. It was part of a fundamental ethos. The Communists wanted to abolish capitalism and to substitute for it dictatorship, collectivism, and bureaucracy. They wanted to confiscate people's property and level everything out.

It should be noted that while Nazism and Fascism advocated, and introduced, a great deal of state regimentation of business, the attitude of these right-wing "isms" toward capitalism and "free enterprise" was not nearly so clear-cut or antagonistic. In fact, these ideologies and movements presented themselves as the saviours of capitalism and certainly as the sworn enemies of communism.

The second element mobilizing hostility toward communism in America was religion. The United States, in the 1940s and even since, has led the industrialized world in the proportion of the population regularly attending church services. The Communists were outright atheists, the deniers of God, the enemies of all churches and the persecutors of Christians in Russia and everywhere else to the extent that their presence and power enabled them to do what they wanted. Once again, if there was a contrast between Communism and Nazism, it was more unfavourable for the Communists. The German Nazis, like the Italian Fascists, may have had all sorts of bad ideas but they each negotiated a Concordat agreement with the Catholic Church, and in the case of Germany continued to tolerate a very large Protestant religious establishment. If Hitler was killing any priests or ministers it was only because (it seemed) they were politically against him, not because they were religious figures. Under communism, the situation was apparently clearer, and it was "all bad".

In consequence of such perceptions, there was strong support for anti-communist policies in the United States embracing, and uniting, not only the well-to-do elite elements of the American society but also the great mass public, Wall Street and Main Street, the corporate board rooms and the rural and small town enclaves of America. When in February of 1948 respondents in eight nations were asked if they thought Russia would start a war to get something she wanted, 73 per cent of American respondents thought that she would, while this opinion was shared by an average of only 48 per cent in the remaining seven countries (Canada, Holland, France, Italy, Brazil, Sweden, Norway).[2]

In the United States at the post-1945 juncture of history, motive and capability came together. Resolve was supported by great resources. This, in turn, has enabled Americans to bring about a situation rarely attained in history: the development of enormous military and foreign assistance programmes without any discernible sacrifice of domestic living standards and opportunities, especially for the most politically significant middle class. Quite the contrary. American post-1945 prosperity, granted all its peaks and valleys, has been so strong that most people in the United States could improve their personal prospects in life and never face situations of significant economic self-denial while at the same time spending hundreds of billions of dollars on managing America's international environment.

This has been an historically rare, prolonged "win-win" situation. American policy makers have never had to make economically excruciating either-or choices in domestic and foreign priorities, especially if the term "excruciating" is seen as the operative constraint. Between 1945 and 1977, the United States spent over 142 billion dollars on foreign aid, including loans as well as grants. Through a variety of treaty engagements, the US committed itself to the defence of more than 50 nations. It had sold over 70 billion dollars' worth of arms to 92 different countries. It also maintained in the mid-1970s nearly 700,000 military personnel in "222 major and 2,000 minor bases around the globe".[3]

Pax Americana influenced, and coincided with, a period of great prosperity and great security for most of the world's industrialized democracies. In 1947 the Marshall Plan represented a huge American material input into a revived European prosperity. The so-called Truman Doctrine was helpful, too. No less important than direct US aid was the nuclear, as well as conventional, military umbrella which the United States extended to various countries around the globe. This umbrella made it possible for modern democracies like Germany, Japan, and Italy to largely, if not entirely, escape the costs of their own security. It enabled them to devote more resources to the development of their own peacetime economies. Thus, the overall effect of the Pax Americana was to "lighten the load" among the other major democracies. It made possible a focus on dividing significantly increasing benefits rather than on sharing out ever greater burdens. The experience of the 1920s, 1930s, and 1940s suggests that the democracies are much less adept at the latter than they are at the former.

By way of illustration, we note that in 1994, the United States, which still deployed some 30,000 troops on the Korean peninsula and its Pacific Fleet at various locations between San Diego and Singapore, spent 4.2 per cent of its GDP on defence. Japan, without equivalent kinds of military forces, spent only about 1 per cent of its GDP on defence. Over the whole decade from 1984 to 1994, a single per cent of the Japanese GDP would have amounted to about 180 billion dollars. One can only imagine the magnitude of the burdens to its economy and society if Japan had been forced by an American withdrawal or collapse into spending 3 or 4 per cent more of its GDP on military purposes. Analogous considerations apply to Germany and to various other countries both in NATO and outside NATO.

The second factor in Pax Americana has been technological. The end of the Second World War was brought about by the American use of nuclear bombs over Japan in 1945. Since that time the United States enjoyed either a monopoly or at least strong preponderance in its nuclear arsenal and especially so in conjunction with appropriate delivery systems. The Soviet Union was the only power in the postwar world which seriously challenged -- or was at least thought to have seriously challenged -- the American preponderance in the field of nuclear weapons and delivery systems.

In the United States the technological advance was much more broadly based and general than it was in the Soviet Union, with its relatively archaic, primitive economy. (Granted that for a few years Stalin managed to get a lot out of it.) Moreover, the United States' great wealth, compared with the Soviets' general poverty and underdevelopment, gave the Americans a decisive advantage in the arms race driving the Russians toward bankruptcy in their futile attempt to keep pace. The arms race became increasingly too expensive and too sophisticated for the Soviets. American persistence over five decades paid a huge dividend.

In the postwar period, the apogee of American might was reached just as the Cold War had ended, during the 1990-1991 Gulf War against Iraq. The sophistication of the American military establishment was such that the United

States was able to defeat Iraq, a nation state with one of the largest land armies in the world, in a land battle of only 4 days. Electronically-guided missiles and other "science fiction" military devices came into their own. The United States was able to defeat Iraq at an unbelievably low cost of about 380 total casualties to its own forces, while inflicting perhaps 100,000 casualties on the enemy. With the collapse of the Soviet Union in 1991, if not even earlier, it became entirely clear that the United States technological-military power was in a class of its own, surpassing all other world military establishments by a large qualitative margin.

This situation still prevails as the world approaches the third millennium. And, once again, the United States maintains this greatly preponderant world power without inflicting any very painful costs and choices upon its own citizens. Substantial costs, yes, very painful choices, not yet. The unique combination of technological and material supremacy has allowed the United States to exercise an unprecedented global role not only militarily but also politically, economically, and even culturally. There is no question as to who the leader is and this leader, directly as well as indirectly, sets the standards of legitimacy in the world community of nations. There are great incentives for all its members to "fit into" the American set of rules, values, and expectations, ranging from the more tangible things such as loans, grants, trade privileges and investment opportunities to less tangible ones, including the need to please those who themselves need, for one reason or many reasons, to "fit in" with the Americans.

Under American leadership, the democracies of Europe, which in the 1930s refused to adopt a common front of resistance to Hitler, behaved with far greater solidarity toward the danger posed by Stalin's Russia. Even Norway and Denmark, although still not Sweden, or Switzerland, joined the North Atlantic Treaty Organization, pledging themselves to joint military action in case of a Soviet (or any other) attack upon any of their members. Beyond simply "alliance on paper", NATO was, from the outset, a formidable organization conducting joint military exercises, sharing facilities, bases, weapons, and technologies, and providing an organizational framework for the deployment of joint forces in the event of war.

In addition to confronting military danger from the Soviet Union, the world democracies have also engaged in various other measures of enlightened intervention, much beyond anything achieved in the 1930s. One of these has been economic assistance begun on a large scale by the United States with the Marshall Plan in 1947. Since that time, foreign aid, and aid to less-developed countries, has become a feature of the foreign and economic policies of several world democracies, including, notably, Japan and Germany. Both economic and political co-operation -- and democratic influence -- have been promoted by new multilateral organizations and institutions, ranging, in effect, from the United Nations to the World Bank.

In virtually all acts of international intervention of the post-Second World War period -- those concerned with "stopping the spread of communism" as in Korea and Vietnam; those concerned with "stopping aggression" as in the Gulf War or in Bosnia; those concerned with bringing humanitarian relief to war-torn lands as in Somalia; those concerned with restoring, or establishing, political democracy as in the case of Haiti, there has always been some form of international and multilateral legitimation by the consent and participation of several members of the international community, especially, of course, the United Nations.[4] But in virtually all such cases, the principal burden of the enterprise was always carried by the United States, and in many cases, the participation of other Allies has been little more than a token.

During the height of the Cold War, western intervention in domestic affairs of countries around the globe was based on the principle of anti-Communism, a criterion not necessarily always compatible with that of democracy itself, or with popular self-determination. Here, too, the United States was generally in the vanguard, with interventions ranging from activities that, in some cases, at least, fell under the umbrella of the Monroe Doctrine, and many that did not. In addition to places like Guatemala, Nicaragua, Honduras, and Cuba, there was Chile (perhaps a more doubtful case in terms of past patterns of US Latin American interventions). There have also been cases like those involving the replacement of pro-Communist Patrice Lumumba by the more anti-Communist but also authoritarian and corrupt, Joseph Mobutu in the Congo, or the support of the military and authoritarian rule in places like Taiwan, Indonesia, Greece, South Korea, Pakistan, Spain or Thailand, and Saudi Arabia.

In all these cases, people often talked about the role of the CIA and other US agencies, but rarely, if ever, about British, French, Italian or German agencies.[5] Many other illustrations come to mind, beginning with US aid to Greece under the Truman Doctrine, and especially in the Korean and Vietnam wars. In the Korean War, direct US expenditures amounted to some 50 billion dollars and the casualties added up to over 33,000 Americans killed and 103,000 wounded.[6] In the Vietnam War, the direct costs were about 140 billion and 58,000 killed with 153,000 wounded.

Outside of Koreans and Vietnamese, no one in the international community, or all others put together, paid anything resembling these American costs.[7] The trend has continued in the more recent nominally "international" interventions.

While in economic terms the United States has been able to exercise its role of world leadership rather easily, it has demonstrated much greater vulnerability in the area of *human* costs of international intervention. The Korean War during the early 1950s and the Vietnam War in the 1960s and 1970s were, in many respects, difficult times in the United States. There was great political unrest, especially, or more so, in the case of the Vietnam conflict. Even though the level of casualties in both wars was not nearly as great -- given the size of the US population -- as in most previous American wars, the political system experienced a great deal of turbulence. Many credit the Republican victory of 1952, after 20 years of Democratic rule, to the discontents induced by the Korean War. Not only the casualties but conscription, personal hardships, and uncertainty associated with the conflict produced unquestionable dissatisfaction within the American electorate. In the 1960s and 1970s, as the Vietnam War and the American role in it escalated, the unhappiness at home was even greater. There was not only protest at the polls but a great deal of anomic opposition in the form of demonstrations, marches, sit-ins, and sundry manifestations of civic unrest and discontent. Lyndon Johnson found himself a president-non-grata with the majority of his Party and the American electorate. In 1968, he clearly viewed himself as politically "untenable". The Vietnam War, even more than the Korean, rendered democratic public life in the United States strident, harsh, acrimonious, and unruly.

The Persian Gulf War was a marked contrast to the previous conflicts largely because it was short, successful, involved few casualties and was fought by a professional army without resort to conscription. Therein one finds not only an explanation of the differences among these conflicts but implicitly also a prescription of American vulnerability in the future. Avoidance of prolonged human costs may well constitute a requirement for continuing American world leadership, and given the nature of rapid economic, social and cultural changes in the world, that requirement may not be indefinitely met.

The balance of American leadership since the 1940s could be put forward as follows: the Soviet challenge to the rest of the world has been defeated. No world war had been fought between 1945 and the late 1990s.

Many nations, especially the affluent democracies of the pre-Second World War era, have managed to improve their standards of living. Many nations which were not free before 1939 have gained their independence. Only one superpower has remained in the world: the United States. Because of advances in science, technology, medicine, and communications, a significant portion of the world's population (though not all) lives better, richer, and longer lives than was the case thirty, forty, or fifty years ago, i.e., in the era preceding the Second World War.

But there has been a significant downside to all of this. Many regional wars and domestic conflicts have been fought since the 1940s with millions of people murdered and maimed. And millions have been forced to flee their homes and live the lives of exiles and beggars. According to the account compiled by Patrick Brogan in 1990, the number of people killed in assorted wars, rebellions, coups, revolutions, and all kinds of massacres of the post-Second World War period, was between 15. and 20 million, or roughly between one-third and one-half of all the deaths in Second World War.[8]

Confining himself only to successful revolutions, coups, and conquests, all leading to changes of governments, Brogan reported 102 such events around the world between 1945 and 1989. These were reported from 88 different country locations during the period, all of them outside the Communist bloc except for Hungary in 1956.

In 1996, according to information compiled by the *Encyclopedia Americana Annual* of 1997, 60 nations around the globe reported significant instances of domestic violence, such as guerrilla warfare, assassinations of public officials, and repeated acts of terrorism directed against the public or the government. This represented almost one-third (32 per cent) of the total (185) membership of the United Nations at the beginning of 1996. (Obviously, there is no reason to think that *only* societies which manifested overt forms of violence in 1996 have serious problems of conflict resolution and internal stability.)

If the assumptions of liberal democracy were correct, the conjunction of the greatest self-determination or national freedom ever experienced on earth, combined with maximal human exposures to education and information yet seen, and supported in most places by an unparalleled escape from the evils of famines and epidemics, would have been a gateway to an era of inspiring, peaceful co-operation and reconciliation among the nations. World peace and the general progress of human civilization should be henceforth secure. But, as the century comes to a close, a new paradox is shaping up in the international environment.   Thanks largely to American efforts, political democracy has received a great deal of support in the international system and formally, at least, it has become the regime-of-choice on the threshold of the twenty-first century.   The United States has generally insisted (especially after the fall of communism) on the principle of governments conducting multi-party elections and submitting to the dictates of popular will.   It has also demanded legal and political guarantees of rights for individuals and minorities roughly subsumed under a commitment to human rights, along with political democracy.

Yet, US-supported democratization has been occurring simultaneously with a very high level of world conflict, violence, and instability.   If the threat posed first by Hitler and then by Stalin was hegemony, the threat apparent in the 1990s was chaos within and among world political systems.   And if the experience of the democracies' prolonged and multiple confrontation with the evils of Hitlerism should be our guide, it is clear that the current problem is not structural-institutional.   It is not a question of organizing more free elections, or improving the organization and management of the World Bank.   It is not an issue of a more effective World Trade Organization.   Even a better UN and a larger NATO won't solve the world's disorders.[9]

The challenge is one which involves the nature of human beings.   In view of the Hitler experiences, it seems that people are intrinsically not nearly as rational, co-operative, benign, and willing to sacrifice for the common good, as liberal democracy has traditionally assumed.   No amount of institutional tinkering is likely to overcome that.   There may never be a singular structural answer to the problem of human development, "democracy" included.   Nor is the future ever likely to evolve into some version of "they lived happily forever after" or even "they had some problems but they were all manageable".

In a world in which the emergent problem seems to be the clash of insatiable, and mutually contradictory claims from all sorts of quarters, it remains to be seen whether the prescriptions of liberal democracy may not actually help fuel the fires and sustain the conflicts.   At least in many places. After all, the democratizing experiences in the former Soviet Union and the former Yugoslavia have left hundreds of thousands of people killed in civil wars, and produced masses of refugees estimated in the several millions.   The effect of removing the lid from a pot has a lot to do with what is in it.   In all likelihood, the liberal faith will be severely tested in the twenty-first century.

NOTES

[1] See George H. Quester, *American Foreign Policy, The Lost Consensus* (New York: Praeger, 1982), p. 155.

[2] *Ibid.*, p. 156.

[3] See Benjamin I. Page and Mark P. Petracca, *The American Presidency* (New York: McGraw Hill, 1983), p. 368.

[4] See Leland M. Goodrich, *Korea, A Study of US Policy in the United Nations* (New York: Council on Foreign Relations, 1956), "... pursuing its objectives in Korea through the United Nations ... placed United States resistance to the North Korean attacks on a higher plane than the defence of a purely national interest": pp. 210-211. It also brought "substantial support from other countries", p. 211.

[5] Even if US Allies were co-operative, they also generally tended to be more interested in proceeding cautiously. See, for example, Trumbull Higgins, *Korea and the Fall of MacArthur* (New York: Oxford University Press, 1960), pp. 116-177, on the pressure applied by the British in Washington to keep the Korean War from escalating as MacArthur seemed to be advocating. Note also analogous Canada concerns, p. 87.

[6] See Ronald J. Caridi, *The Korean War and American Politics: The Republican Party as a Case Study* (Philadelphia: University of Pennsylvania Press, 1968) on the great domestic unhappiness generated by this relatively prolonged, costly and inconclusive war. The Republican opposition pursued somewhat contradictory objectives of cutting down US efforts, especially financial, in creating a large war machine, but it also wanted a "victory" in Asia; and an interesting way out of this dilemma was discovered, it would seem. "One of the most popular Republican remedies to relieve the financial and military burden of the Korean War was to permit the Chinese Nationalists to participate in the war effort in Asia, a remedy long advocated by the GOP", p. 186. Caridi inclines to the view that Korea was the principal issue which lost the 1952 election for the Democrats.

[7] Jeffrey Grey, *The Commonwealth Armies and the Korean War, An Alliance Study* (Manchester: Manchester University Press, 1988) reports that as of June 1951, the total strength of all UN forces in Korea, other than United States or South Korea troops, amounted to 24,128 persons: p. 44. See Dennis Stairs, *The Diplomacy of Constraint: Canada, the Korean War, and the United States* (Toronto: University of Toronto Press, 1974). Canada contributed, at various periods, 22,000 army and 3,600 naval personnel to the Korean War, with losses of 11 army officers and 298 other ranks killed. Direct costs of the war to Canada were estimated at 200 million dollars, p. 279. See Larry Berman, *Lyndon Johnson's War, The Road to Stalemate in Vietnam* (New York: W. W. Norton, 1989). Berman records that in the aftermath of the North Vietnamese Tet Offensive of 1968, President Johnson asked General Earle Wheeler during a National Security Council meeting (7 February 1968) about any possible

Allied help. The General replied: "The Australians are incapable of providing more troops. The problems in Korea are such that it will be hard to get the South Koreans to even send the light division they had promised. The Thai troops are in training and to move them in now would be more detrimental than helpful". The President replied: "So it would be only Americans?", p. 157.

[8] See Patrick Brogan, *The Fighting Never Stopped, A Comprehensive Guide to World Conflict Since 1945* (New York: Vintage Books, 1990), p. 568.

[9] As Robert Jervis remarks, "One clear lesson of the 1990s is that very little concerted international action is possible without American leadership ... Despite some decline in American power and perhaps a greater decline in American will, the United States still dwarfs others in resources of almost every kind ...". D. J. Caraley and B. H. Hartman (eds.), *American leadership, Ethnic Conflict and the New World Politics* (New York: The Academy of Political Science, 1997), p. VI: "... getting agreement among even the fairly small number of leading states in Europe is extremely difficult ...": *ibid.*

INDEX

References from Notes indicated by 'n' after page reference